SITES OF WRITING: ESSAYS IN HONOR OF ANNE RUGGLES GERE

PERSPECTIVES ON WRITING

Series Editors: Rich Rice and J. Michael Rifenburg
Consulting Editor: Susan H. McLeod
Associate Editors: Johanna Phelps, Jonathan M. Marine, and Qingyang Sun

The Perspectives on Writing series addresses writing studies in a broad sense. Consistent with the wide ranging approaches characteristic of teaching and scholarship in writing across the curriculum, the series presents works that take divergent perspectives on working as a writer, teaching writing, administering writing programs, and studying writing in its various forms.

The WAC Clearinghouse and University Press of Colorado are collaborating so that these books will be widely available through free digital distribution and low-cost print editions. The publishers and the series editors are committed to the principle that knowledge should freely circulate and have embraced the use of technology to support open access to scholarly work.

Recent Books in the Series

Jaclyn Wells, Lars Söderlund, and Christine Tulley (Eds.), *Faculty Writing Support: Emerging Research from Rhetoric and Composition Studies* (2025)

Jenn Fishman, Romeo García, and Lauren Rosenberg (Eds.), *Community Listening: Stories, Hauntings, Possibilities* (2025)

Steven J. Corbett (Ed.), *If at First You Don't Succeed? Writing, Rhetoric, and the Question of Failure* (2024)

Ryan J. Dippre and Talinn Phillips (Eds.), *Improvisations: Methods and Methodologies in Lifespan Writing Research* (2024)

Ashley J. Holmes and Elise Verzosa Hurley (Eds.), *Learning from the Mess: Method/ological Praxis in Rhetoric and Writing Studies* (2024)

Diane Kelly-Riley, Ti Macklin, and Carl Whithaus (Eds.), *Considering Students, Teachers, and Writing Assessment: Volumes 1 and 2* (2024)

Amy Cicchino and Troy Hicks (Eds.), *Better Practices: Exploring the Teaching of Writing in Online and Hybrid Spaces* (2024)

Genesea M. Carter and Aurora Matzke (Eds.), *Systems Shift: Creating and Navigating Change in Rhetoric and Composition Administration* (2023)

Michael J. Michaud, *A Writer Reforms (the Teaching of) Writing: Donald Murray and the Writing Process Movement, 1963–1987* (2023)

Michelle LaFrance and Melissa Nicolas (Eds.), *Institutional Ethnography as Writing Studies Practice* (2023)

Phoebe Jackson and Christopher Weaver (Eds.), *Rethinking Peer Review: Critical Reflections on a Pedagogical Practice* (2023)

SITES OF WRITING: ESSAYS IN HONOR OF ANNE RUGGLES GERE

Edited by James Edward Beitler and Sarah Ruffing Robbins

The WAC Clearinghouse
wac.colostate.edu
Fort Collins, Colorado

University Press of Colorado
upcolorado.com
Denver, Colorado

The WAC Clearinghouse, Fort Collins, Colorado 80524

University Press of Colorado, Denver, Colorado 80203

© 2025 by James Edward Beitler and Sarah Ruffing Robbins. This work is licensed under a Creative Commons Attribution-NonCommercial-NoDerivatives 4.0 International license.

ISBN 978-1-64215-245-6 (PDF) 978-1-64215-246-3 (ePub) 978-1-64642-728-4 (pbk.)

DOI 10.37514/PER-B.2025.2456

Produced in the United States of America

Library of Congress Cataloging-in-Publication Data

Names: Gere, Anne Ruggles, 1944– honoree | Beitler, James Edward, III editor | Robbins, Sarah editor
Title: Sites of writing : essays in honor of Anne Ruggles Gere / edited by James Edward Beitler and Sarah Ruffing Robbins.
Description: Fort Collins, Colorado : The WAC Clearinghouse, 2025. | Series: Perspectives on writing | Includes bibliographical references.
Identifiers: LCCN 2025022971 (print) | LCCN 2025022972 (ebook) | ISBN 9781646427284 paperback | ISBN 9781642152456 adobe pdf | ISBN 9781642152463 epub
Subjects: LCSH: English language—Rhetoric—Study and teaching | English language—Composition and exercises—Study and teaching | LCGFT: Festschriften
Classification: LCC PE1404 .S565 2025 (print) | LCC PE1404 (ebook)
LC record available at https://lccn.loc.gov/2025022971
LC ebook record available at https://lccn.loc.gov/2025022972

Copyeditor: Karen Peirce
Designer: Mike Palmquist
Cover Photo: Photo by Shannon Schultz, Michigan Photography, University of Michigan
Series Editors: Rich Rice and J. Michael Rifenburg
Consulting Editor: Susan H. McLeod
Associate Editors: Johanna Phelps, Jonathan M. Marine, and Qingyang Sun

The WAC Clearinghouse supports teachers of writing across the disciplines. Hosted by Colorado State University, it brings together scholarly journals and book series as well as resources for teachers who use writing in their courses. This book is available in digital formats for free download at wac.colostate.edu.

Founded in 1965, the University Press of Colorado is a nonprofit cooperative publishing enterprise supported, in part, by Adams State University, Colorado School of Mines, Colorado State University, Fort Lewis College, Metropolitan State University of Denver, University of Alaska Fairbanks, University of Colorado, University of Denver, University of Northern Colorado, University of Wyoming, Utah State University, and Western Colorado University. For more information, visit upcolorado.com.

Citation Information: Beitler, James Edward & Sarah Ruffing Robbins (Eds.). (2025). *Sites of Writing: Essays in Honor of Anne Ruggles Gere*. The WAC Clearinghouse; University Press of Colorado. https://doi.org/1010.37514/PER-B.2025.2456

Land Acknowledgment. The Colorado State University Land Acknowledgment can be found at landacknowledgment.colostate.edu.

CONTENTS

Acknowledgments ix

Introduction. Learning, Justice, and Collaboration in Our Writing Sites 3
    James Edward Beitler and Sarah Ruffing Robbins

PART 1. FRAMING OUR FIELDWORK

Chapter 1. Anne Ruggles Gere: An English Studies Scholar Par Excellence . . 27
    Ellen Cushman

Chapter 2. Thirty Years After *Into the Field* 35
    Douglas Hesse

Chapter 3. Rescuing Reading: Centering Real Readers 45
    Lizzie Hutton

Chapter 4. Language, Literacy, and the Intersections of Identity 57
    Morris Young

PART 2. LEARNING FROM LANGUAGE AND LINGUISTICS

Chapter 5. Dakota Language, Rhetorical Sovereignty, and the Ineffable Influence of Anne Ruggles Gere on English Studies 71
    Kel Sassi

Chapter 6. Language Knowledge and Linguistic Justice 81
    Laura Aull

Chapter 7. Re-visioning the Role of "Grammar" in Writing Studies 95
    Anne Curzan

PART 3. DISCIPLINARY-CROSSING DYNAMICS

Chapter 8. Writing to Learn and Think Critically in STEM: Engaging Students in Disciplinary Knowledge and Practices 107
    Mike Palmquist

Chapter 9. STEM Courses as Sites of Writing: Students' Disciplinary Experiences with Writing-to-Learn Assignments 121
    Ginger Shultz, Amber J. Dood, and
    Solaire A. Finkenstaedt-Quinn

Chapter 10. Sites of Digital Writing and Community: Anne Gere and the Sweetland Digital Rhetoric Collaborative 137
Naomi Silver

Part 4. Engaging the Extracurriculum

Chapter 11. Phenomenal Women Gettin' It Right in the Extracurriculum . 151
Beverly J. Moss

Chapter 12. Laying the Matter on the Table: Composing Kitchen Judaism. 163
Rona Kaufman

Chapter 13. "Now I Think with My Own Mind": Malcolm X, Epistemic Disobedience, and the Extracurriculum 175
Elizabeth Vander Lei

Part 5. Advancing Assessment

Chapter 14. The Extracurriculum of Writing Assessment 187
J. W. Hammond

Chapter 15. Toward a More Human Approach to Assessment. 201
Jathan Day, Naitnaphit Limlamai, and Emily Wilson

Chapter 16. The Intellectual Work of Writing Program Review 217
*Shirley K Rose, Deborah H. Holdstein, Chris Anson,
Chris Thaiss, and Kathleen Blake Yancey*

Part 6. Enriching English Education

Chapter 17. The Readiness is *Not* All: Strengthening the Bridge from High School to College Reading and Writing. 231
Christine Farris

Chapter 18. Writing Through the Complexities of Culturally Responsive Teacher Education 241
Jennifer Buehler

Chapter 19. "Changing with the Times": Ebony Elizabeth Thomas and Anne Ruggles Gere in Conversation. 253
Ebony Elizabeth Thomas and Anne Ruggles Gere

Part 7. Rhetorics of Renewal

Chapter 20. Making the Case for Reading and Writing and Teaching and Research 263
    Paula M. Krebs

Chapter 21. Listening, When the Listening Is Hard 271
    Cheryl Glenn and Heather Brook Adams

Chapter 22. Intimate Practices for Neoliberal and Pandemic Times 285
    Margaret K. Willard-Traub and Deborah Minter

Chapter 23. For Sites Both Sacred and Secular: Composing a Language to Bridge Spiritual Identity and Rhetorical Practice 299
    Heather Thomson-Bunn

Part 8. Reflections and Recollections

Chapter 24. The Space between Butter and Salt 313
    Jennifer Sinor

Chapter 25. Memories 325
    Victor Villanueva

Coda 331
    Anne Ruggles Gere

Contributors 333

ACKNOWLEDGMENTS

If every book has many people who make it possible, an essay collection like this certainly has far too many to name comprehensively. That said, we of course must acknowledge Anne Ruggles Gere here, as we do through the making of this Festschrift. We thank our series editors (Rich Rice, J. Michael Rifenburg, Jonathan M. Marine, Johanna Phelps, Qingyang Sun, and Susan McLeod) and all at the WAC Clearinghouse (especially Mike Palmquist, Heather Falconer, and Karen Peirce), who have been so supportive of this project from the start. Thanks as well to our talented and hard-working contributors, our anonymous reviewers, the Joint Program in English and Education community at the University of Michigan, all the many student writers and researchers in the field whose thinking and work are reflected here, and the many colleagues at our home institutions, friends, and family members in our respective networks who have supported our work (especially Tim Larsen, Richard Hughes Gibson, and Brita Beitler).

SITES OF WRITING: ESSAYS IN HONOR OF ANNE RUGGLES GERE

INTRODUCTION.
LEARNING, JUSTICE, AND COLLABORATION IN OUR WRITING SITES

James Edward Beitler
Wheaton College

Sarah Ruffing Robbins
TCU

I believe that we can use our [field's] entanglements to achieve several goals: to develop courses that better prepare all our students for the actual lives that await them; to undertake scholarship and research that explore the similarities between the readerly and the writerly; to make the holistic nature of our work more visible to the public; and to affirm that we are all, as authors and readers, engaged in what Rosenblatt calls transactional relationships with texts. We can embrace our entanglements to re-vision our language, texts, and theories in order to "see—and therefore live—afresh."

– Anne Ruggles Gere, "Presidential Address 2019–
Re-visioning Language, Texts, and Theories"

When Anne Ruggles Gere became president of the Modern Language Association in 2018, 111 years had passed since the organization had entrusted the position to a scholar of what we now refer to as writing studies, a consequence of longstanding divisions in the MLA (Gere, "Presidential Address" 454 and "My Kairotic" 56). Referencing Ann E. Berthoff's notion of "killer dichotomies," Gere spoke against these divisions in her presidential address, calling on the organization's members to imagine the field more inclusively. "It is time," she declared, "to move beyond the divisions in English studies and recognize that literary scholars' underconceptualization of writing and composition scholars' underconceptualization of reading have led our profession to destructive collisions" ("Presidential Address" 452, 457). She has been putting this message into practice throughout her career. Gere's scholarship has repeatedly broken new ground, inviting us to conceptualize our fields and sub-fields more expansively and interactively. *Sites of Writing* builds upon the manifold contributions of Anne Ruggles Gere and, in that spirit, invites readers to embrace more capacious imaginings of our disciplinary spaces.

Comprised of essays by leading scholars, including some of Gere's former students, this collection includes pieces on disciplinary history, language and literacy, writing across the curriculum, digital rhetoric, writing's extracurriculum, assessment, English education, and more. By connecting these multiple fields of activity, *Sites of Writing* aims to answer Anne's call to move beyond English studies' divisions. To borrow a phrase from her introduction to *Writing Groups: History, Theory, and Implications*, we hope this collection "helps transform dichotomy into dialogue" (6). We also hope our project exemplifies several of her own values as a scholar. As we see it, Anne's field leadership has not been about defending existing disciplinary structures (as if, for example, the field of writing studies was a fortress under siege). Rather, her vision has been about holding firm to a particular view of writing (as a powerful social and cultural activity) and to a series of interrelated professional commitments: to teaching and learning, to justice, and to collaboration. With these commitments at the center of her work, Gere and her collaborators have capitalized on the potential of literacy, broadly conceived, to enable cultural transformations, transforming writing studies (and other fields) in the process.

Accordingly, while the model of Anne's career was a major impetus bringing together the diverse voices of this collection, our aim for readers goes beyond seeing this text as honoring a single field leader. We urge readers to consider how the accounts assembled exemplify collaborative conversation about the history of writing studies as a field, about the importance of its impact across multiple academic and social divides today, and about the many ways continued thoughtful leadership in research and teaching will expand existing sites of writing and launch new ones. Collectively, we can continue building the inclusive sites of writing Gere's work models.

In the introductory remarks that follow, we elaborate on the three professional commitments we've just highlighted—to teaching and learning, justice, and collaboration. We conclude with an overview of the book's sections and chapters. First, however, we address this book's affiliation with the Festschrift, since one way we aim to honor Anne Gere's legacy is through our engagement with the genre's conventions.

A WRITING FESTIVAL FOR ANNE AND THE FIELD

A Festschrift is an edited volume that celebrates the special achievements of a field's honored scholar by other leading scholars, including some of the honoree's former students. Among classical scholars, the first significant Festschrift to honor an individual was published in the 1860s (Whitaker 352). Since then, the Festschrift has become an established academic genre, serving not only to recognize a field's leading figures but also to reflect on the field's development and forecast new directions inspired by the honoree's work (Horowitz 234). Our book shares such aims. Given Anne Gere's remarkable career, we joyfully embrace the name of the genre: the word Festschrift is a combination of the German words for "festival" and "writing," and we along with all our contributors enthusiastically present this festival of writing in Anne's honor. But like exemplary works in the Festschrift genre, this prose party has other purposes, both "retrospective" and "prospective" (Horowitz 237). Some of the pieces gathered here reflect on Gere's work to enrich our understanding of the development of writing studies and related fields; others extend her concepts and methods to new sites or apply them in novel ways. But whether their chapters help us better understand who we have been or who we might be, all of the contributors attempt to embody Anne's commitment to collaboration as a path to knowledge-making. We balance our salute to her work with a reaffirmation of her view of scholarship as a communal and ongoing process. This Festschrift, then, offers a tribute not only to Anne but also to her many collaborators along the way, including those not directly contributing chapters here, as well as to future pathways she has helped define.

Though some academic presses shy away from the genre, we believe that the Festschrift will claim a vital space in writing studies in the coming decades. An emerging discipline throughout much of the 20th century, writing studies has reached a point in which acts of field definition often proceed by reviewing where we've been. As we're "naming what we know" to one another and teaching "writing about writing" in our classrooms, we expect Festschriften—which, as one scholar has noted, are "decisive to the development of a discipline"—to proliferate (Horowitz 237). In fact, a Festschrift was recently published for Charles Bazerman in the same series as the present book, and another, *The Hitchhiker's Guide to Writing Research*, honored Steve Graham's contributions to research and teaching as related to writing studies (Rogers et al.; Liu et al.). Thus, as writing studies scholars, we should reflect on what we want Festschriften to look like in our field.

In our own exploration of the genre, we've found that Festschriften are often judged on their "coherence," even as their "variety of subjects and approaches" is often (though certainly not always) celebrated (Colăcel 38; Klingbeil; Nwahunanya 122–23; Richetti 237–38, 241; Whitaker 353). Though not without its challenges, this tension between coherence and variety has turned out to be an exciting space for us to work in as editors. We think that such genre expectations are particularly well suited for recognizing scholars like Gere, whose vision of literacy as "a capacious space where reading and writing . . . support and nurture each other" has offered so many focused explorations of its social power in individual writing sites ("Presidential Address" 451). Indeed, the enriching experience of assembling this collection has highlighted—for us as editors—ways that writing studies, as a field, increasingly blends an emphasis on studying diverse individual sites of literacy in action with possibilities for formulating larger conceptual frameworks, or navigating between individual case studies (such as of a classroom or of a particular extracurricular space) and broader-scale histories and theories. We anticipate that readers coming to this multi-faceted essay collection will take away questions about, and ideas for, seeking this balance in their own work.

Moreover, the nature of Anne's work mitigates against some of the genre's more problematic aspects, such as its history with respect to gender. Irving Louis Horowitz has observed that "the *Festschrift* honored the fathers of science and culture, but no less, served to identify the sons and grandsons as well" (235). The quotation is unfortunately, cringeworthily *accurate*: far too few women have received a Festschrift in their honor, especially during the genre's first hundred years. Writing about Festschrifts in classical scholarship, Graham Whitaker notes, "Women honorands are few before the 1960s and, even afterwards, there are only one or two each year until the 1980s" (365). Celebrating scholars like Anne Gere, whose groundbreaking work on the writing practices of turn-of-the-century clubwomen helped to transform our field, has transformative potential for the genre as well (Gere, "Constructing Devout Feminists," "Kitchen Tables," *Intimate Practices*, and "My Kairotic"). A related critique of the genre is its capacity to reinforce "academic conventions and dominant forms of knowledge," creating a "culture of conformity" that can "diffuse dissent" (Nagasawa et al. 1; Colăcel 39–40). A focus on Gere's scholarship tempers these genre troubles as well; her emphasis on neglected sites and figures, along with her many boundary-crossing efforts, are important aspects of her field leadership.

Overall, we envision readers of this book taking note of ways that Anne Gere's career often embraced outlier positions that pushed the field forward—and then asking themselves how they might extend such pioneering work even further. Given Gere's repeated calls to focus on women's under-studied literacy cultures, for example, what still-under-researched writing communities might claim a spotlight now, in research and teaching? What methodological approaches that Anne has used so creatively in her own scholarship could be adapted to such new inquiry?

ANNE GERE'S FIELD LEADERSHIP

One way to illustrate Anne Gere's field leadership is to consider her prominent roles in our national organizations, institutional service at the University of

Michigan, directorship of the Joint Program in English and Education (JPEE), work for the WPA Consultant-Evaluator Service, and editorial responsibilities. Several chapters here bring these aspects of Anne's career into relief.

We also see Gere's leadership reflected through her mentoring of undergraduates, graduate students, preservice teachers, primary and secondary school teachers, college instructors, and educational administrators. Many, many people can claim Anne as one of their teachers, and her influence on these many lives—her legacy as a teacher—is immeasurable. In testimonies woven throughout the collection, we celebrate Anne the teacher (of teachers) as well.

Then, of course, there is Anne Gere the writer and scholar—the author or co-author of a dozen books and over one hundred essay publications.[1] Though we don't pretend that we can do justice to the depth and breadth of this remarkable legacy, we've highlighted several significant nodes of her scholarly activity. In each of eight sections, our contributors reflect on, apply, and extend the concepts, methods, and theories central to Gere's scholarship. Following, we provide an overview of sections and chapters. Here, however, we offer another way of understanding Anne's leadership as scholar.

Anne has certainly made many methodological and theoretical contributions to writing studies—most notably, those related to her historiographies of writing groups and clubs outside of the university. However, her leadership as a scholar has not primarily been about the development of a particular approach or theory. Gere has led our field, in large part, by holding firm to professional commitments and by utilizing many different methodologies and theories in order to re-vision (or, to use another of her metaphors, restructure) the field along those lines (*Into the Field* 1). Three commitments we highlight throughout this collection—to learning, to justice, and to collaboration—accordingly underscore a coherence in her work consistent with a Festschrift's aim of providing a focused portrait of a scholar's legacies. Thanks to Anne's own integrity as a scholar, these notably feminist professional commitments radiate from every section and chapter of the book.

ENACTING A COMMITMENT TO STUDENT LEARNING—
AND LEARNING ALONG WITH STUDENTS

Anne Gere pursued her Ph.D. for pedagogical purposes. Having studied British and American literature for her bachelor's and master's degrees, Anne discovered that, as a young high school English teacher, she knew little about how to teach writing to her students (Gere, "Presidential Address" 451 and "My Kairotic" 49). She was, in other words, motivated to learn for the sake of her students, and

---

[1]   For a comprehensive listing of Gere's extensive publications, see her CV at https://sites .google.com/umich.edu/anne-ruggles-gere/curriculum-vitae.

this motivation and approach to the craft of teaching—i.e., improving student learning through her own learning—has continued throughout her professional life, giving shape to her various academic projects and extracurricular pursuits.

Shortly after completing her Ph.D., for example, Gere was asked to teach a course called "Theories of Writing Instruction" at the University of Washington. But her Ph.D. program hadn't offered the guidance about teaching writing that she had been hoping for, and, despite learning about rhetoric and literacy studies from scholars outside of her program, she still (in her own words) "felt almost fraudulent offering advice about how to teach writing" ("My Kairotic" 51). The solution to this problem was once again to keep learning, this time by developing the Puget Sound Writing Project, a local site of the National Writing Project. Reflecting on her connections with the NWP, Anne writes,

> The NWP model, with its emphasis on teacher expertise and one's own writing, helped me understand writing instruction in an entirely new way. Watching an excellent teacher of first graders show how she had her students create narratives, seeing a middle school teacher's demonstration of strategies for drafting and being captivated by a high school teacher's display of seventeen versions of one of his poems to emphasize the importance of revision—these and many other presentations by highly effective teachers stimulated my thinking about writing. This, combined with joining a writing group and embarking on a program of self-study to read authors like Janet Emig, Ed Corbett, and Donald Murray along with a host of writers in the journals *College Composition and Communication* and *College English* who had not been part of my graduate education helped me feel more confident about writing instruction. (51)

And in addition to making her a more effective teacher, what she learned from teachers and writers in the Puget Sound Writing Project prompted her to want to learn more about writing groups (52). The result was *Writing Groups: History, Theory, and Implications*, published in 1987. The book itself represents a significant scholarly achievement, but it also serves as a testament to a version of the scholarly life that recognizes teaching and research as mutually enriching practices.

A noteworthy aspect of Gere's ongoing learning as a teacher has been her ability to find her own teachers *everywhere*. Throughout her career, Anne has cultivated opportunities to learn from anyone and everyone, even when—perhaps *especially* when—they're not card-carrying members of her own disciplinary circles. In graduate school, this meant a foray into literacy studies, prompted by the work of British anthropologist Ruth Finnegan (52; "Presidential Address" 451). In her work with the NWP, it meant learning from an exemplary first grade teacher (and many other teachers as well). And in subsequent years, it meant learning from voices *outside* of our academic walls. In developing her article "Kitchen Tables and Rented Rooms: The Extracurriculum of Composition" and her subsequent book *Intimate Practices: Literacy and Cultural Work in U.S. Women's Clubs, 1880–1920*, Gere found more writers she could learn from. In doing so, her scholarship has helped our field understand its activity and membership more expansively, while contributing to theories of multiple literacies in action (Gere and Robbins, "Gendered Literacy"). Distinguishing "pedagogy from the traditional pedagogue" (80) in her "Kitchen Tables and Rented Rooms" article, Anne writes that "composition's extracurriculum shows the importance of learning from amateurs. After all, as the Latin root *amatus* reminds us, members of the Tenderloin Women's Writing Workshop or the Lansing, Iowa Writers Workshop write for *love*" (88).

Which brings us back to Gere's students. Anne has always held a high view of her students, seeking not just to teach them but also to learn from them. In that vein, one of the central theoretical ideas that Anne put forward in her MLA presidential address for overcoming the divisions in English studies was the subject of a dissertation by her then-recent graduate student Elizabeth Hutton, whom Anne publicly acknowledged ("Presidential Address" 454).

This posture towards her students, along with her eagerness to find teachers everywhere, also shaped the ethos of the University of Michigan's Joint Program in English and Education, which, beginning in 1988, Gere chaired or co-chaired through the remainder of her tenure at Michigan. Anne's graduate students always found a teacher and fellow learner who, to borrow her own language from "Kitchen Tables and Rented Rooms," "see[s] them as individuals who seek to write, not be written about, who seek to publish, not be published about, who seek to theorize, not be theorized about" (89). And Anne's students have also found that the doors leading to other disciplines, and beyond the walls of the academy, are wide open. In her chapter in an edited collection on *The Doctoral Degree in English Education*, Gere asserts that the "interdisciplinary nature of our field ought to foster the wider vision and freer exploration of our students" ("Establishing the Field" 162). Her own teaching and learning have helped to make this claim a reality.

Championing a Commitment to Justice

In the *College Composition and Communication* article "Communal Justicing: Writing Assessment, Disciplinary Infrastructure, and the Case for Critical Language Awareness," Gere et al. remind us that social injustice is a *structural* problem and, therefore, that justice work in writing studies must address the field's *infrastructure*. They write,

> For justicing in Writing Studies to be sustainable and scalable, its target must extend to . . . the disciplinary codes, conditions, and conventions that guide, practice, and shape how knowledge in the field is created, curated, and circulated. This disciplinary infrastructure includes (but is not limited to) the *pasts* that provide the field its historical memory, the *policies* that structure disciplinary norms and imperatives, and the *publications* that provide the field a way to publicize innovations and organize intellectual commitments. (386–87)

The statement is one that Gere's leadership has repeatedly embodied. Throughout her career, Anne has helped our field re-vision its past, policies, and publications to be more inclusive and equitable, and her historiography is at the heart of this work.

Consider again her scholarship on the writing and literacy practices of the extracurriculum. In *Intimate Practices,* Anne critiques the ways that "public perceptions . . . have stereotyped women's clubs as white middle-class groups, thereby erasing the varying class, racial, and ethnic/religious backgrounds represented in the club movement" (3). She continues, "This book counters such stereotypes by considering clubs formed by women from Mormon, Jewish, working-class, African American and white Protestant backgrounds. Women representing a rich variety of social positions formed clubs in cities and towns across the country" (3). The significance of Gere's scholarship goes beyond a critique of public perceptions, however. By focusing on vital yet neglected figures such as Josephine Ruffin and Angel DeCora, Anne has challenged and helped to re-vision our field's historical memory (*Intimate Practices* 162, 165–66, "Kitchen Tables" 84, and "A Rhetoric").

Gere engages in this sort of justice work in her MLA presidential address as well, going beyond the "re-visioning" of "language, texts, and theories" suggested by the talk's title. Even as she addresses the divisions between literary scholars and writing scholars in English studies, she makes an implicit but powerful parallel argument born of her career-long commitment to feminism. Reread the speech again, and you'll find that the stars of the speech are women: Anne recognizes executive directors Phyllis Franklin, Rosemary Feal, and Paula Krebs (450); quotes past president Florence Howe, herself quoting Adrienne Rich (451–52); highlights Rich's "When We Dead Awaken: Writing as Re-vision," written for the MLA Commission on the Status of Women in the Profession (452); applies Berthoff's notion of "killer dichotomies" (452); builds on the work of former graduate student Elizabeth Hutton by presenting Louise Rosenblatt's "transactional theory of language" as a way forward for the field (452, 454–55); and spotlights the scholarship of Gertrude Buck, whose name Anne chose for her collegiate chair at the University of Michigan because she was "the first woman in the United States to earn a PhD in rhetoric and composition" (454 and "My Kairotic" 56). The address is a masterclass in constitutive rhetoric, not only calling *for* a particular vision of the field but also calling us *into* one.

We could go on and on, discussing, for example, Gere's resistance to our field's "implacable secularism," which has sometimes hampered students and faculty members who are interested in writing about religious topics and beliefs (Brandt et al. 47; Gere, Foreword ix and "Constructing Devout Feminists"). Or we could point to her team's refusal in their longitudinal study on developing writers to adopt, as she put it in the introduction to *Developing Writers*, "a single definition of writing development, because such a definition could lead instructors to expect students to follow a single path in their development as writers" and "would not value the diversity of available methods and of students themselves" (2). Our contributors explore such aspects of Anne's vision in more detail. Within individual essays, we anticipate that readers will see a shared commitment to justice work, along with a related value guiding Anne's career—approaching learning and seeking justice as communal activities. Along those lines, in the "Communal Justicing" article, Anne and her colleagues write, "To change the disciplinary infrastructure that shapes assessment, justicing must be *communal*: we all need to participate in the revision of the pasts, policies, and publications on which writing assessment depends" (386). Throughout Anne's career, the second word of the article's title has indeed gone hand-in-hand with the first.

Embracing a Commitment to Collaboration

Anne's approach to scholarship is deeply collaborative, embracing the "social view of writing and knowledge" embodied by the writing groups and women's clubs that she has studied (*Writing Groups* 5). And as with the call to communal work in the "Communal Justicing" article as well as her rejection of disciplinary divisions in her MLA presidential address, she has emphasized the importance of collaboration in her own writing. In her introduction to *Roots in the Sawdust*, for example, Anne asserts that "the Puget Sound Writing Program . . . demonstrated the power of collaborative work" (3). Relatedly, she and Kel Sassi conclude their textbook *Writing on Demand for the Common Core State Standards Assessments* on the following note:

> One thing is for certain: we need to collaborate. We can't do it alone. We have to work with our colleagues—be they down

> the hall, at the next building, in higher education, across the country, or in one of our professional organizations. There is support available in consulting each other, strength in consensus-building around new curricula, and power in collective action. It is a time to tap into those rhetorical skills we teach our students each day and use them to shape the future for our students. (203)

Given her calls for and commitment to collaboration, it is unsurprising that Gere has found an academic home in interdisciplinary and transdisciplinary institutional spaces at the University of Michigan, including the Joint Program in English and Education and the Sweetland Center for Writing. Whether it is helping Ph.D. students navigate the overlapping domains of writing studies and English education or investigating writing-to-learn pedagogies with STEM colleagues, Anne thrives on the collaborative "interactions" that take place between academic disciplines (Gere, "Establishing the Field" 159–62, "My Kairotic" 55–56, and *Into the Field* 4).

The focus on "interactions" in the previous sentence is Anne's. Indeed, when discussing the relationships between our various fields of activity, Anne has supplied us with a number of refined images for re-visioning our work together. In her introduction to *Into the Field,* Gere critiques the use of the "bridge-building metaphor" to portray the relationship between composition and other disciplines because it "assumes an unproblematic and unidirectional borrowing by composition" (1). In its place, she proposes we conceptualize interdisciplinary efforts as "restructuring" activities; she notes, "Restructuring connotes radical realignments and a critique of the disciplines being restructured, and it suggests that change, disruption, and even challenges to prevailing knowledge emerge from interdisciplinary relations" (1). Borrowing from physics, she invites us to think of our "field" as "a kind of charged space in which multiple 'sites' of interaction appear" (4). Twenty-five years later, in her MLA presidential address, she elaborated on the idea. After lamenting that "divisions between literary scholars and writing scholars have led to 'destructive collisions,'" she returns to physics to reframe the situation:

> However, collisions have a bright side because, as quantum mechanics teaches us, they lead to entanglement. Entanglement happens when collisions between particles create pairs in which particles behave in tandem, so that affecting one particle affects the other no matter how far apart they are. When two particles are entangled, information about one improves knowledge of the other. (456–57)

By highlighting the knowledge that comes with entanglement, Anne teaches us, once again, that our teachers are to be found everywhere. Without glossing over the divisions in our field, she suggests that we can address them by re-visioning our collisions as sites of connection and communication.

The idea that we might learn to see points of contact and possible collaborations in our divisions applies to our relationships with those beyond the academy as well. Drawing on remarks by French philosopher Simone Weil, Gere notes in "Kitchen Tables and Rented Rooms" that "walls can be a means of communication as well as a barrier," and she recommends that "we listen to the signals that come through the walls of our classrooms from the world outside" (76). The last line of the article leaves readers with a challenge along these lines. "The question remains," writes Anne, "whether we will use classroom walls as instruments of separation or communication" (91).

But perhaps the most potent image from this article is the kitchen table itself. Tables are ubiquitous. Like the one found in the home of Richard and Dorothy Sandry in Lansing, Iowa, where a group would "meet on Monday evenings during the lull between fall harvest and spring planting" to "spend two hours reading and responding to one another's writing"—they serve as a sign for and site of collaborative activity (75). Anne's career has been spent at such tables. Ask graduates of the Joint Program in English and Education to discuss the program's strengths, and they're likely to tell you about the support and mentorship they received through "Chalk and Cheese," the mid-week table gathering of JPEE faculty and students in the program's office. And students who conducted research with Anne will have a similar story. In the introduction of *Developing Writers in Higher Education: A Longitudinal Study,* Gere et al. write, "Given the large amount of data collected across five years, this was a highly collaborative project requiring many hands, and various configurations of us sat around the oak table in Anne Gere's office week after week and year after year to plan and analyze" (13). Moreover, Anne and her team have also ensured that such collaborations can continue: they've made the data from the study publicly available in order that, in their own words in the conclusion of the collection, "others can join us in investigatings that can lead all of us to do even better at preparing students for the life-long journey that is writing development" (325). You, too, in reading this Festschrift honoring Gere's commitments and associated ways of doing work in writing studies, are invited to the table.

OVERVIEW OF CHAPTERS

The many voices included here are a testament to Gere's influence, in and beyond writing studies, at national and local levels, within JPEE and across departments at the University of Michigan, and inside and outside of the classroom. We have organized this collection's core content in clusters highlighting major themes in Anne Gere's expansive oeuvre. Meanwhile, in the spirit of Anne's work, we've sought to make the writing processes for this collection as collaborative as possible. A notable number of the chapters are co-authored. We encouraged contributors to read drafts of others' work while composing their own, and to make connections between their essays and others in the collection, publications by Anne herself, and major points about the field identified in this introduction and throughout the text. In all these ways, we hoped to provide readers with threads connecting the individual essays to the book's larger themes while also signaling opportunities for continued field growth through diverse sites of writing where Anne Gere brought leadership.

Part 1, "Framing Our Fieldwork," presents four essays demonstrating ways that Anne—through her professional affiliations, interpersonal networking, and research itself—has shaped multiple subfields of writing studies and related humanities enterprises. Readers coming to this section will find a compatible array of approaches for joining in the ongoing endeavor of field formation. Ellen Cushman, in "Anne Ruggles Gere: An English Studies Scholar Par Excellence," outlines the intellectual, methodological, and leadership vision embodied in Anne's career. Beginning with a survey of major publications, Cushman then reflects on Gere's program leadership at the University of Michigan for the Joint Program in English and Education. The essay salutes Anne's notable shepherding of students and scholars as shaping English studies itself along the way.

Doug Hesse's contribution, "Thirty Years after *Into the Field*," revisits in detail one of Gere's most influential publications, 1993's *Into the Field: Sites of Composition Studies*. Hesse reflects back on his original response to reading that groundbreaking text. To illustrate that book's move to highlight the generative energy of composition as a field of study, he revisits its table of contents, where Anne had assembled a group of key scholars to help make the case for the field as a site of interactive theory-making. Hesse spotlights a number of specific ways in which that volume achieved impact, setting and anticipating agendas still relevant today. In "Rescuing Reading: Centering Real Readers," Lizzie Hutton taps into what she sees as Gere's "longstanding commitment to surfacing the agentive power of literacy practices and perspectives traditionally overlooked by the academy" to show that such a commitment can help "rescue reading from the deficit narratives that keep it so stubbornly consigned to the margins of our field."

Extending Hesse's and Hutton's reflections on Gere's scholarship as consistently pushing writing-linked fields forward, Morris Young highlights Anne's support of still-underrepresented scholars and their contributions. Thus, "Language, Literacy, and the Intersections of Identity" appreciates Anne's robust theoretical framework for analyzing ways people have used their literacies to enact identity-oriented agency. One especially revealing element in Young's analysis takes the form of his revisiting Gere's University of Michigan dissertation, titled "West African Oratory and the Fiction of Chinua Achebe and T. M. Aluko." As a former student who produced his own dissertation under Anne's guidance, Young explains that, from graduate school onward, his scholarship content and ways of writing have been shaped by her intellectual mentoring. She has, he affirms, guided his efforts, as he puts it, "to compose a professional life, to weave together a personal and cultural history of literacy, a critical awareness of the intersections of language, literacy, and identity, and a developing sense of [him]self as a writer."

Part Two, "Learning from Language and Linguistics," focuses on a key dimension of Gere's scholarship and teaching. These essays speak to one another in their affirmation of linguistic diversity, in their commitment to socially contextualized study of language, and in their attention to how writers, readers, and speakers make culturally significant decisions in all their language choices. Readers of this section will take away concrete ideas for putting language study in dialogue with writing studies. They will also find big-picture inquiry possibilities for future research linking these areas of scholarship to classroom teaching and research on writing praxis as a language-building enterprise. Kel Sassi's essay, "Dakota Language, Rhetorical Sovereignty, and the Ineffable Influence of Anne Ruggles Gere on English Studies" honors Anne's role in promoting understandings of Native sovereignty rooted in a critique of ways that the English language served as a tool of assimilation pedagogy. Sassi affirms Anne's influential modeling of listening across cultures, respecting rhetorical sovereignty, honoring Native American writers, and generating resources to support teachers of Native students. To exemplify this vital legacy of Gere's leadership, Sassi describes her own collaborative contributions to a Dakota Studies initiative at North Dakota State University, as well as programs at Sitting Bull College on the Standing Rock Reservation. Linking her learning about how, as she observes, "[l]anguage holds . . . cultural values" to teachings from Anne—as well as from Anne's daughter Cindy and granddaughter, Denali—Sassi urges readers to confront our complicity in "settler colonizer history."

Laura Aull's "Language Knowledge and Linguistic Justice" provides another compelling example of Gere's impact on language studies. Aull explicates a still-evolving project that is extending work by Gere and several of her students, who have argued that attention to language itself enriches what we can know about genres, assessment, and language-related ideologies. Adapting methods from Gere et al.'s 2019 *Developing Writers in Higher Education*, Aull shows how student interview data, when interpreted via analysis of rhetorical moves, can expand our linguistic knowledge, thereby promoting appreciation of social justice issues related to language variations. Anne Curzan's "Re-visioning the Role of 'Grammar' in Writing Studies" rounds out this section by revisiting definitions of "grammar" and what she notes have been debates "about the role of grammar in writing classrooms" as a productive way to address the sometimes-assumed dichotomy between grammar and critical or creative engagement in texts and text-making. This chapter echoes a theme of Anne's 2019 MLA presidential address, wherein she resisted the "killer dichotomy" between reading and writing. Curzan therefore joins Sassi and Aull in reminding readers that Gere's career-long emphasis on language study has persistently promoted communal goals for social justice.

Part 3 addresses the "Disciplinary-Crossing Dynamics" of Gere's legacies. These essays model for readers an array of approaches for interdisciplinary inquiry and pedagogical practices affirming the centrality of teaching itself in writing studies. In "Writing to Learn and Think Critically in STEM," Mike Palmquist celebrates the writing-across-the-curriculum (WAC) dimensions of Anne's career while stressing the benefits of, as he puts it, "[d]istinguishing between writing to learn and writing to engage." His chapter extends his own previous work on that topic "by exploring how complex writing-to-engage tasks in the STEM disciplines can move beyond writing-to-learn activities into assignments that begin to engage students in writing in the disciplines." In calling for such an agenda, Palmquist credits Gere for pedagogy and research on "how to use writing . . . to engage students in course content in a way that goes far beyond working to remember and understand" major concepts, instead cultivating a practice that "deepens" students' critical thinking. Ginger Shultz, Amber J. Dood, and Solaire A. Finkenstaedt-Quinn present a related argument in "STEM Courses as Sites of Writing." Illustrating Palmquist's point about WAC, writing-to-learn (WTL), and writing-in-the-disciplines (WID) as building disciplinary understandings as well as conceptual learning and critical thinking across disciplines, they revisit the work of MWrite at the University of Michigan. Revisiting student interviews situated in the specific context of undergraduate chemistry courses, they examine how students perceive their experiences of writing and WTL in STEM courses.

Like her fostering of WAC and WID, traceable back to early-career texts such as *Roots in the Sawdust* (1985; republished in 2012 by the WAC Clearinghouse), Gere's linkage of pedagogy-based research to her directorship of the Sweetland Center for Writing has enabled new digital literacies in the classroom and beyond. Naomi Silver's "Sites of Digital Writing and Community: Anne Gere and the Sweetland Digital Rhetoric Collaborative" salutes a more recent path of Anne's scholarship. Drawing on her interviews of several program collaborators, Silver offers a narrative history of the Digital Rhetoric Collaborative that highlights its field-wide impact and, in so doing, emphasizes "the work and influence of Anne Ruggles Gere."

At the center of our volume, Part 4, "Engaging the Extracurriculum," foregrounds one of Anne Gere's most influential publications, "Kitchen Tables and Rented Rooms: The Extracurriculum of Composition" and her associated *Intimate Practices* monograph on literacy practices in the women's club movement. Essays in this section share scholarly commitments to building on that pioneering work. As such, they also invite readers to revisit Anne's original publications in this groundbreaking area and to take note of how she framed her then-new concepts and inquiry methods, thereby generating expanded scholarly possibilities for others. Readers will be able to note similarly generous moves by the authors of these contributions to the Festschrift.

Beverly J. Moss opens this cluster with "Phenomenal Women Gettin' It Right in the Extracurriculum." Moss's case study addresses how literacy practices in a contemporary Black women's club, Phenomenal Women Incorporated (PWInc), promote community-building. For Moss, studying this club takes up Gere's mandate to "consider the various sites in which the extracurriculum has been enacted, the local circumstances that supported its development, the material artifacts employed by its practitioners, and the cultural work it accomplished" ("Kitchen Tables" 90). Rona Kaufman, like Moss, builds upon Gere's study of clubwomen's literacy agency. For Kaufman, doing so produces an analysis of cookbooks published by Reform Jewish women in Seattle across many years of the 20th century. Accordingly, Kaufman's "Laying the Matter on the Table" considers how, as her subtitle "Composing Kitchen Judaism" signals, this group's collaborative cookbooks also represent collective authorship in a genre enacting public negotiation of women's multiple identities as individuals and as members of a Jewish sisterhood. Elizabeth Vander Lei's "'Now I Think with My Own Mind'" essay then presents a reminder that Gere's focus on women's literacies in her "Kitchen Tables and Rented Rooms" text and her associated book on clubwomen, *Intimate Practices*, also supports interpretations of the ongoing literacy practices of Black Americans in the civil rights movement. Seeking to promote critical histories of activist literacies, Vander Lei advocates for a close study of Malcolm X's linguistic metaphors. Positioning Malcolm X as "one of America's most famous beneficiaries of an extracurricular education," Vander Lei (consistent with her subtitle's "Epistemic Disobedience" concept) emphasizes that this "homemade education enabled him to think decolonially."

One important site of Anne Gere's field-shaping leadership has been in her advocacy for principled assessments of writing. Part 5, "Advancing Assessment," celebrates this commitment. We expect readers of this cluster to find not only concrete ideas for enhancing assessment in their classrooms but also useful frameworks for theorizing this vital topic. J. W. Hammond's "The Extracurriculum of Writing Assessment" connects concepts from Gere's scholarship on the extracurriculum to a vision for assessing writing that embraces its extracurricular sites. These include, Hammond demonstrates, such contexts as office culture, the algorithmic tools and platforms ubiquitous in writing today, and both self-sponsored and social-media-based exercises of "expert" determinations of "fitness." Taking Gere's scholarship as a point of departure, his chapter draws on present-day and historical examples to illustrate the ways that, as he notes,

> (i) the extracurriculum of composition is always already subtended by writing assessment; (ii) public life is policed by extracurricular testing regimes; (iii) everyday linguistic judgments are encoded into and enforced through digital programs and platforms; and (iv) the specter of extracurricular assessment haunts and possesses academic assessment, conditioning curricular practices and priorities.

A collaborative essay by Jathan Day, Naitnaphit Limlamai, and Emily Wilson joins Hammond's call to build on Gere's sustained interest in assessment practices. These co-authors advocate for connecting assessment to students' lived experiences in and beyond the classroom. Their "Toward a More Human Approach to Assessment" paints verbal portraits of classrooms ranging from a small private university in Saudi Arabia (Wilson) to a teacher education program in the U.S. Southwest (Limlamai) to online courses (Day). Together, they aim to enact Gere's advocacy of making assessment a tool preparing students "for the actual lives that await them" (Gere, "Presidential Address" 457). While this topic has claimed much of Anne's attention as a classroom teacher and a leader of enterprises like National Writing Project sites and the Sweetland Center for Writing, assessing has also been a role she has regularly taken on through the WPA Consultant-Evaluator Service. A collaborative essay by Shirley K Rose, Deborah H. Holdstein, Chris Anson, Chris Thaiss, and Kathleen Blake Yancey, "The Intellectual Work of Writing Program Review," honors this combination of professional service and scholarship-in-action in Gere's career. Their remembrances highlight, too, Gere's blending of professional service with scholarly vision. In revisiting approaches to program assessment gleaned from collaborating with Gere, they simultaneously extend the profession-shaping reach of their past communal program-building.

Consistent with her role as director of Michigan's Joint Program in English and Education, Anne has maintained an active agenda in teacher education, both in preparation of preservice educators and in their ongoing professional development. Publications like her coauthored methods textbook, *Language and Reflection*; her co-edited *Making American Literatures* based in a multi-year NEH-funded project; and her collaborative *Writing on Demand: Best Practices and Strategies for Success* all speak to this commitment. The essays in Part 6 also affirm this influential element in her career. This section may have special value for other teacher educators. But we urge all readers, additionally, to mine these essays for their affirming vision of writing studies as a path to connectivity: between secondary school and university, between classroom practice and research, and between graduate program leadership and multiple landscapes of writing and learning. In this sense, readers can see teacher preparation (and growth) as ongoing, and as enriched by many sites of learning within and beyond classrooms.

First, Christine Farris, in "The Readiness is *Not* All," makes the case for a goal named in her chapter's subtitle: "Strengthening the Bridge from High School to College Reading and Writing." Farris focuses on the professional development of high school English instructors who so often shape the writing habits and expectations students bring to college. Describing a series of summer institutes fostering cross-level collaboration, she advocates for increased opportunities for college-level writing specialists and secondary educators to connect their learning and teaching. Jennifer Buehler, in "Writing Through the Complexities of Culturally Responsive Teacher Education," then offers discussion of a specific program initiative embodying the bridging Farris hopes for; Buehler explains how this multi-year project generated multiple sites of collaborative writing for the research team. She describes innovative pedagogical approaches Gere and three coresearchers designed for the Teachers for Tomorrow initiative (a curriculum for prospective secondary educators seeking careers in urban and under-resourced schools). Buehler also analyzes how the team wrote multiple journal articles for different audiences to report on their initiative. She explains how this collaborative composing—across several years—exemplifies Gere's commitment to teaching junior teacher-scholars how to produce meaningful academic writing. In the final chapter of Part 6, "Changing with the Times," Ebony Elizabeth Thomas, who succeeded Gere as chair of the Joint Program in English and Education at the University of Michigan, interviews Anne. Together, they explore questions about the development of the field of writing studies, about Gere's research, and about the interdisciplinarity of JPEE. Anyone interested in building an academic program guided by principled envisioning will find much to savor in this exchange.

How does writing studies—now and in the future—best interact with broader humanities sites in academe and beyond? How can writing studies shape our efforts to do all our work ethically, while coping with the many pressures we face as citizens today? Readers drawn to such questions will find powerful experiential accounts and calls to action in Part 7, which is grounded in Gere's sense of writing as always a potential site for ethical action. This section honors her contributions to studies of rhetoric as a pathway to cultural influence, productive social interaction, thoughtful engagement with institutional challenges, and spiritual renewal.

An essay by MLA Executive Director Paula Krebs situates Gere's career in the vital context of public humanities leadership during a time when the liberal arts require inspired leadership. In her chapter, Krebs is therefore "Making the Case for Reading and Writing and Teaching and Research" as invaluable enterprises while honoring the example Anne's career provides of that very work. Krebs posits that writing like Gere's, which continually addresses gaps between specialist humanities expertise and public needs such as the promotion of listening-oriented civil discourse, models how to make the knowledge of humanities fields accessible and useful beyond the academy. Such cultural stewardship, Gere has always known and shown, requires a sustained commitment to learning from others as well as teaching with expertise. In that vein, in their coauthored essay, "Listening, When the Listening Is Hard," Cheryl Glenn and Heather Brook Adams celebrate Gere's longstanding commitment to a practice she articulated in 1987's *Writing Groups: History, Theory, and Implications*, anticipating by more than fifteen years Krista Ratcliffe's *Rhetorical Listening*. They explore possibilities for making difficult listening productive by rethinking the dynamics between rhetor and non/listener, especially when that non/listener might be ourselves.

As the essays by both Krebs and Glenn and Adams acknowledge, carrying out our responsibilities in today's university settings is increasingly challenging. With this often-stressful context in mind, Margaret Willard-Traub and Debbie Minter proffer "Intimate Practices for Neoliberal and Pandemic Times." Resisting a tendency in writing studies to perform a particular brand of scholarly rigor and to devalue reflection as an individual and inward-looking activity, they revisit Anne's focus in *Intimate Practice* on clubwomen's literacies. They assert, with Gere, that the affective and social ties these women fostered among themselves did in fact result in increased abilities to shape public culture. A similar fostering of shared critical reflection and purposeful collaborative rhetoric, they argue, can gird today's scholar-teachers for facing many challenges to agency arising from today's neoliberal society.

In the final essay in this cluster, "For Sites Both Sacred and Secular: Composing a Language to Bridge Spiritual Identity and Rhetorical Practice," Heather Thomson-Bunn invokes Gere's call to recognize the place of religion and spirituality in academic discourse. Thomson-Bunn recalls how, in 2001, Anne wrote in *College English*, within her "Articles of Faith" contribution to a multi-vocal symposium-like essay, that "[t]hose who wish to write about religion not only lack the highly complex and compelling language of, say, queer theory, but they face an implacable secularism" (qtd. in Brandt et al. 47). In a rhetorical space she credits Gere with helping to create, Thomson-Bunn traces signs of an enabling vision for spirituality in works over the past two decades that have answered Anne's plea.

Our closing essay cluster, Part 8's "Reflections and Recollections," reaffirms Anne's own self-reflexive praxis, her encouragement of creative reflection, and her ever-sensitive commitment to individual relationships as touchstones of feminist work conjoining the personal and the professional, the relational and the broadly social. Jennifer Sinor's "The Space between Butter and Salt" can be read both as a salute to Anne Gere's valuing of personal writing and an embodiment of its social power. In her braided essay Sinor represents a writer whose creative voice—eschewing any need to perform disciplinary specialist expertise—nonetheless draws on deep intellectual-academic roots to make a story-based case for writing as a healing force. Thus, implicitly, and through the nuance of storytelling, Sinor affirms that subtle writing like Anne Gere's own can enrich daily life through nonlinear narrative channels. Similarly, the second essay in this closing cluster presents a personal story from Victor Villanueva. In his chapter, "Memories," he shares the history of being the first graduate student to claim Anne Gere as a mentor. In recalling her patient but demanding guidance, continually reiterating unshakeable confidence in his abilities, Villanueva—writing now from a position of revered leadership in academe himself—urges readers of this volume to join both of them in affirming literacy histories and personal storytelling as powerful agents of knowledge-making, but also of interpersonal care. Even readers who have not had the benefit of personal learning connections with Anne Gere will be able to tap into this section's illustration of the personal as a vital site of writing, since the memory pieces from Sinor and Villanueva memorably exemplify the attention to writerly craft so evident, too, in their many other well-known texts. Simultaneously, of course, these pieces that make up our closing section reaffirm the Festschrift genre itself by reminding readers of personal writing's rhetorical power and significance.

Blending the personal and professional, Anne Gere's "Coda" rightly claims the last word. In an expression of gratitude for this collection's essays and authors, she also indirectly celebrates, we propose, this book's bringing together of diverse sites of writing, unified by the intellectual, ethical, and community-oriented commitments also embodied in her career.

WORKS CITED

Brandt, Deborah, et al. "The Politics of the Personal: Storying Our Lives against the Grain." *College English*, vol. 64, no. 1, 2001, pp. 41–62, https://doi.org/10.58680/ce20011239.

Colăcel, Onoriu. "The Festschrift: Typicalities of the Genre." *Messages, Sages and Ages,* vol. 6, no. 2, 2019, pp. 38–40, msa.usv.ro/2019/11/28/festschrift-typicalities-genre/.

Gere, Anne Ruggles. "Constructing Devout Feminists: A Mormon Case." *Renovating Rhetoric in Christian Tradition,* edited by Elizabeth Vander Lei et al., U of Pittsburgh P, 2014, pp. 3–16.

———, editor. *Developing Writers in Higher Education: A Longitudinal Study.* U of Michigan P, 2019. *University of Michigan Press Ebook Collection,* https://doi.org/10.3998/mpub.10079890.

———. "Establishing the Field: Recognition, Interdisciplinarity, and Freedom in English Education Doctoral Studies." *The Doctoral Degree in English Education,* edited by Allen Webb, Kennesaw State P, 2009, pp. 157–65.

———. Foreword. *Charitable Writing: Cultivating Virtue Through Our Words,* by Richard Hughes Gibson and James Edward Beitler III, IVP Academic, 2020, pp. xi–xiii.

———. *Intimate Practices: Literacy and Cultural Work in U.S. Women's Clubs, 1880–1920.* U of Illinois P, 1997.

———, editor. *Into the Field: Sites of Composition Studies.* Modern Language Association, 1993.

———. "Kitchen Tables and Rented Rooms: The Extracurriculum of Composition." *College Composition and Communication,* vol. 45, no. 1, 1994, pp. 75–92, https://doi.org/10.58680/ccc19948799.

———. "My Kairotic Career." *Women's Professional Lives in Rhetoric and Composition: Choice, Chance, and Serendipity,* edited by Elizabeth Flynn and Tiffany Bourelle, Ohio State UP, 2018, pp. 49–57.

———. "Presidential Address 2019–Re-visioning Language, Texts, and Theories." *PMLA,* vol. 134, no. 3, 2019, pp. 450–58. *Cambridge Core,* https://doi.org/10.1632/pmla.2019.134.3.450.

———. "A Rhetoric of Pen and Brush." *Lost Texts in Rhetoric and Composition,* edited by Deborah H. Holdstein, Modern Language Association of America, 2023, pp. 33–42.

———, editor. *Roots in the Sawdust: Writing to Learn Across the Disciplines.* The WAC Clearinghouse, 2012, https://wac.colostate.edu/books/landmarks/sawdust/. Originally published by National Council of Teachers of English, 1985.

———. *Writing Groups: History, Theory, and Implications.* Southern Illinois UP, 1987.

Gere, Anne Ruggles, et al. "Communal Justicing: Writing Assessment, Disciplinary Infrastructure, and the Case for Critical Language Awareness." *College Composition and Communication,* vol. 72, no. 3, 2021, pp. 384–412, https://doi.org/10.58680/ccc202131160.

Gere, Anne Ruggles, et al. *Language and Reflection: An Integrated Approach to Teaching English.* Pearson, 1991.

Gere, Anne Ruggles, et al. *Writing on Demand: Best Practices and Strategies for Success.* Heinemann, 2005.

Gere, Anne Ruggles, and Sarah R. Robbins. "Gendered Literacy in Black and White: Turn-of-the-Century African-American and European-American Club Women's Printed Texts." *Signs,* vol. 21, no. 3, 1996, pp. 643–78, https://doi.org/10.1086/495101.

Gere, Anne Ruggles, and Peter Shaheen, editors. *Making American Literatures in High School and College.* National Council of Teachers of English, 2001. Classroom Practices in Teaching English, vol. 31.

Horowitz, Irving Louis. *Communicating Ideas: The Politics of Scholarly Publishing.* 2nd ed., Routledge, 1991. *Taylor and Francis eBooks,* https://doi.org/10.4324/9781351313247.

Klingbeil, Gerald A. "'Inside and Outside the Circle': What Does the Festschrift Genre Tell About Our Discipline?" *Society of Biblical Literature Forum,* vol. 8, no. 5, 2010, www.sbl-site.org/publications/article.aspx?ArticleId=861.

Liu, Xinghua, et al., editors. *The Hitchhiker's Guide to Writing Research: A Festschrift for Steve Graham,* Springer, 2023. *Springer Nature Link,* https://doi.org/10.1007/978-3-031-36472-3.

Nagasawa, Mark K., et al. "Introduction to the Special Issue on the Scholarship of Generosity: A Festschrift in Honor of Beth Blue Swadener." *The International Critical Childhood Policy Studies Journal,* vol. 9, no. 1, 2022, pp. 1–9, journals.sfu.ca/iccps/index.php/childhoods/article/view/165.

Nwahunanya, Chinyere. "The Festschrift Tradition in African Literature: Its Implications for the Future of African Literary Criticism." *Tydskrif vir Letterkunde,* vol. 50, no. 1, 2013, pp. 112–25, https://doi.org/10.4314/tvl.v50i1.9.

Ratcliffe, Krista. *Rhetorical Listening: Identification, Gender, Whiteness.* Southern Illinois UP, 2005.

Richetti, John. "The Value of the *Festschrift*: A Dying Genre?" *The Eighteenth Century,* vol. 53, no. 2, 2012, pp. 237–42. *Project Muse,* https://doi.org/10.1353/ecy.2012.0021.

Rogers, Paul M., et al., editors. *Writing as a Human Activity: Implications and Applications of the Work of Charles Bazerman,* The WAC Clearinghouse / UP of Colorado, 2023, https://doi.org/10.37514/PER-B.2023.1800.

Sassi, Kelly, and Anne Ruggles Gere. *Writing on Demand for the Common Core State Standards Assessments.* Heinemann, 2014.

Whitaker, Graham. "Congratulations and Celebrations: Unwrapping the Classical Festschrift." *Classical Scholarship and Its History: From the Renaissance to the Present. Essays in Honour of Christopher Stray,* edited by Stephen Harrison and Christopher Pelling, De Gruyter, 2021, pp. 351–76, https://doi.org/10.1515/9783110719215-015.

PART 1. FRAMING OUR FIELDWORK

CHAPTER 1.
ANNE RUGGLES GERE: AN ENGLISH STUDIES SCHOLAR PAR EXCELLENCE

Ellen Cushman

Northeastern University

Few scholars in English studies have the intellectual, methodological, and leadership vision of Anne Ruggles Gere. During her career, she fearlessly crossed disciplinary boundaries to fashion a legacy of research unparalleled in English studies. Gere created ecologies of thought that invited multiple forms of inquiry and teaching, always with methodological acumen and her signature graciousness.

I first met Gere in 1994. I was a second-year Ph.D. student at Rensselaer Polytechnic Institute. I had been studying literacy in urban community settings, trying to understand how adult women came to learn and teach each other the reading and writing they needed to create and endure change. "Kitchen Tables and Rented Rooms: The Extracurriculum of Composition," based on her Conference on College Composition and Communication (CCCC) chair's address in 1993, was published in the February 1994 issue of *College Composition and Communication*. Her article sparked in me the sense that literacy studies outside of writing classrooms could be undertaken and needed to be advanced. It provided me the intellectual grounds and methodological foundation from which to advance research on community literacy with attention to inequity and power. Later that spring, I asked Gere if she would be willing to present on a panel at the CCCC together with myself, Arnetha Ball and Lee Odell. I was over the moon when they all agreed, and I submitted a panel proposal that was eventually accepted.

"Kitchen Tables and Rented Rooms: The Extracurriculum of Composition" presented a novel observation: "writing development occurs outside of formal education" (76) around kitchen tables and in rented rooms. The extracurriculum of composition presented a paradigmatic shift away from a focus on writing development as a solely individual enterprise unfolding in the cognitive and rhetorical moves of writers in classrooms. Based on a nascent area of emerging qualitative research in literacy studies (Heller) and historical accounts of women's clubs between 1880 and 1990, Gere suggested that writing development, teaching, and learning had long been practiced outside of classrooms and that these practices merited further investigation, particularly because they provided insight into power, inclusion, belonging, and social change. Central to the argument was the understanding that much disciplinary knowledge making at the time in rhetoric and writing "focused inside classroom walls" (78). With this article, Gere invited the field to consider literacy development as a social and collaborative activity taking place outside of school-based learning and teaching settings. She presented a paradigmatic shift, a university-community-boundary-bridging shift, for the field of rhetoric and writing and English studies generally.

Beyond creating a gravitation force that effectively helped to move the field of writing and literacy studies away from the individual, the essay, and the writing classroom as the primary loci to study writing development, "Kitchen Tables and Rented Rooms" offered the profession of writing and rhetoric a means to question its own professionalization practices. Importantly, Gere points out that the culture of professionalization "abhors amateurism, but composition's extracurriculum shows the importance of learning from amateurs" (88). She argued to broaden what counts as a literacy practice worthy of study. She urged the field to expand its focus to include expert writers in specialized areas as well as writers in communities who otherwise might have been dismissed as amateurs—"as the Latin root *amatus* reminds us" community-based writers teach each other to "write for *love*" (88).

Methodologically, the article prompted early-career scholars in the 1990s, myself included, to take up the call for qualitative research in communities and archives to better understand the ways in which writing develops outside of writing classrooms. Where the field of writing and rhetoric had focused on establishing itself as a legitimate area of disciplinary work within English studies, Anne Gere's scholarship and her 1993 leadership of the Conference on College Composition and Communication presented a viable path to pursue a broader understanding of writing development. For when we study and earnestly value the reading and writing practices of community members, we must necessarily understand what writing means to them, how it works for them, how they share and publish their work, and how they create knowledge together. The methodological shift here has had a lasting impact on the field and on pedagogical practice. Students could now be understood as "individuals who seek to write, not be written about, who seek to publish, not be published about, who seek to theorize, not be theorized about" (89). In other words, Gere's research provided leadership to rhetoric and writing as a field, encouraging it to move beyond the classroom into communities and even more into archives to establish for itself a basis for professionalization that focuses squarely on understanding the close connections between literacy practice, power, and creating and enduring change with literacy practices.

Let me stay with the idea of moving beyond classrooms to study writing as a key moment of Gere's leadership in the field to highlight two ways in which this unfolded, the first through curriculum, the second through archival research. Published in 1998, Schutz and Gere's article "Service Learning and English Studies: Rethinking 'Public' Service" navigated the relationships between universities and communities to underscore the nuanced ways in which student projects outside of the classroom might be framed. In the article, Schutz and Gere question the strict distinctions being drawn at the time between public and private spaces for writing. They argue that the writing classroom could be constituted as a "'public space' in which students could begin to articulate and address" community issues that they identified (136). They detail outcomes of a student-led writing project responding to the practices of the University of Michigan student union, which had adopted practices that treated African American students differently, e.g. asking for IDs of all African American students, but not all students. Schutz and Gere argue that writing about the community within the university constituted a type of public writing precisely because it offered one way for students to experience "multiple public and private spaces, operating at multiple levels" with the effect of allowing "myriad kinds of difference to emerge into dialogue" (146). Service learning and public writing projects for students, they contend, allow "us to see the work of English studies, in all its different configurations, as always precariously poised between myriad locations, activities, and discourses—each with its possibilities and limitations" (146). Such reflections shed light on the ways in which English studies as a discipline could begin to carefully take up the call for service learning by inviting students to write about communities they encounter.

During this stage of her career, Gere had been undertaking serious historical study of U.S. women's clubs between 1880 and 1920 through archival research. Her 1997 book *Intimate Practices: Literacy and Cultural Work in U.S. Women's Clubs, 1880–1920* details the diversity of these clubs, pointing out the ways in which the women's club movement included Mormon, Jewish, working-class African American, and white Protestant women. She notes, "Women representing a rich variety of social positions formed clubs in cities and towns across the country" (3). She chronicles through rich archival textual analysis the ways in which women's clubs enacted cultural work crucial to civic life during these decades. The book's publication fell in line with Gere's earlier arguments on the feminist's alternative to rhetoric and writing, an alternative that chose to understand and create space for collaboration, women's writing, and the importance of personal writing. Gere had an eye on creating a space to value these writings in scholarship, the field, and in classrooms.

This scholarship during the early stages of her career illustrates the ways in which she worked at interdisciplinary intersections in the field of rhetoric and writing and English studies. It's small wonder that Gere herself was field-forming and interdisciplinary given her own intellectual history. She was among the earliest cohorts of Ph.D. students to graduate from the Joint Ph.D. Program in English and Education, a program she would later lead at the University of Michigan. Patti Stock would later gather essayists, including Gere, who traced the intertwined historical legacy of close connections between English education and composition. While working on her dissertation that explored West African oratory and fiction, her experience teaching high school English would prompt her to better understand writing instruction. She sought out Richard Enos, who was a rhetoric professor in the department of communication at the University of Michigan during the time she was working on her Ph.D. She wanted to "understand more about how rhetoric could help" her appreciate writing curriculum and instruction (50). Her dissertation research, on West African fiction and oratory, primed her to study texts closely to present their rhetorical force. But as a graduate student who was also a high school English teacher, she understood that English studies had to be broad and embracing of multiple dimensions of humanistic study of textual practice.

As chair and co-chair of the Joint Program in English and Education at the University of Michigan, Gere helped to launch the careers of several authors in the present collection and many others recognizable in literacy studies and education.[1] Graduates from the program she led or co-led have benefited from her interdisciplinary blend of English and education—the study of literature and literacy, the teaching of reading and writing, the practices of literacy outside of classrooms and across disciplines—and the power of these disciplinary perspectives to shape a broad use and understanding of text and textual practice. With Jay Robinson's legacy of work to build upon (Stock), Gere trained key figures in rhetoric, writing, literacy studies, and English education. Her trajectory as a knowledge maker and doer melded inquiry into writing, teacher training, and the history of women teachers and writers.

She asked the field of English studies and education to identify a broader conception of valued texts and textual practices that moved beyond the transactional and generic. She has modeled leadership in these endeavors, seamlessly weaving her own scholarly innovations and interventions into her professional

---

1   Students of Anne's in this collection include Aull, Beitler, Buehler, Day, Farris, Hammond, Hutton, Kaufman, Limlamai, Minter, Robbins, Sassi, Sinor, Thomas, Thomson-Bunn; Villanueva, Willard-Traub, Wilson, and Young.

style and philosophies, and with a steadfast commitment to equity, inclusion, and creating a space for belonging in scholarship, teaching, and knowledge making with communities. She provided innovative methodologies for bringing students and scholars to the place she helped to envision. In a staggeringly brilliant career spanning nearly fifty years, Gere has always anticipated where English studies needed to be. And she always modeled for scholars and teachers ways in which we could enact these possibilities in our own professional lives.

Gere's personal life is the background against which her inquiry figures. In 2001, Gesa Kirsch and Min-Zhan Lu collaborated on a symposium with Gere, Deborah Brandt, yours truly, Anne Herrington, Richard E. Miller, and Victor Villanueva. Together, we began a conversation among rhetoric and writing scholars about the ways in which "uncritical celebration of personal narrative" had created "expectations to story our lives within the personal narrative" even when a person might have multiple ways of narrating what has prompted their scholarly and professional lives (Brandt et al. 42). In Gere's contribution to the symposium titled "Articles of Faith," she describes how she and her daughter, Cindy, had begun to co-author a double-voiced memoir about their spiritual journeys and family's lives. She soon realized that their writing "required some attention to religion" (46), yet, as she had learned early on in her career, she ought not to mention being Christian and being married to a Presbyterian minister in academic contexts. But, her understanding of religion broadened as she followed her daughter Cindy, an Athabaskan from the Yukon, into "talking circles, autumn moon ceremonies, women's sweats, and other sacred rites" that Cindy experienced "as she moved into womanhood" (46). As they wrote, Gere saw two tensions emerging between the desire to understand her daughter's ceremonies and the desire to write about her growing understanding of religious beliefs: "the available language for talking about religious faith is impoverished; expressions of spirituality that fall outside traditional norms risk being exotic" (46). In literacy narratives of personal becoming, she observes, "It is much more acceptable to detail the trauma of rape or abuse than to recount a moment of religious inspiration" (47). Anyone wishing to write about religion "not only lack the highly complex and compelling language of, say, queer theory, but they confront an implacable secularism" (47). Her words resonate in interesting and profound ways today in the age of tell- and show-all social media feeds and public rhetoric where evidentiary basis for claims, if it exists, is routinely stretched beyond credibility and too often trucks in the sensational or panders to the cultivation of outrage.

Gere's provocative insight about the study of religion and its intersection with literacy, civics, and learning provides a steppingstone to a nascent body of scholarly literature on the connection of religion and education (Juzwik et al.;

Weyand and Juzwik). She also takes up the still-relevant insight concerning why and how the personal comes to be constructed, valued, and circulated, or overlooked, devalued, and silenced. Gere's work has everything to do with who is constructing the other and what values are placed on the literate practices of the other.

Throughout her studies of literate and teacherly lives, she has threaded an emphasis on populations who have been excluded or marginalized, e.g. with a focus on women's literacy in communities and through personal stories, on students of color and more just standards of assessment, and on Native people's teaching and learning ("An Art of Survivance" and "Indian Heart / White Man's Head"). One of the most admirable aspects of Gere's legacy of research rests in her understanding of teaching and teacher training from historical examples of teachers. Gere has always illustrated the subtle and lasting ways power circulates in the literate lives of individuals beyond and within the academy's walls.

I'll never forget seeing Anne at a mid-Michigan conference celebrating Native writers around 2007 or 2008.[2] At the time, she had pulled up a chair at the table of Indigenous scholars and writers where I was sitting. I greeted her with surprise and took the liberty of introducing her as the leader of both the National Council of Teachers of English (NCTE) and the CCCC. I went on about her work with teacher preparation, English education, and community literacy. Folks at the table looked at me, then at her, politely nodding, and waiting for me to get to the punchline—what was this woman's connection to the assembled Indigenous literary scholars and creative writers? My enthusiastic introduction trailed off. I was reluctant to mention her familial and personal connection to the work of the conference. That was her personal story to tell about her family and her story of learning and moments of growth with her daughter Cindy that was close to her heart. With a warm smile, Anne Ruggles Gere stepped into the opening left by my overly exuberant if superficially professional introduction of her. She generously added a fuller and personal description of her work. Folks smiled and visited with her. Looking back, I see now that I proved the points she had made in "Articles of Faith." Hers was a personal a story that had brought us together around the conference table that day, and I only felt comfortable to gush on about her professional accomplishments in English studies. Yet her story was precisely what everyone there wanted to hear and needed to hear. As is her way, Anne was forgiving and kind about my awkwardness. To the table assembled, she offered her intellectual origin story, but for me, she modeled again another way to weave artfully and seamlessly the personal with the professional, to bring heart and integrity to inquiry, and to make everyone feel at ease.

---

2   About this time, we were on a first name basis.

The next time I saw Anne Ruggles Gere in person was in 2017 at the CCCC in Portland, Oregon. I was making my way through the cavernous convention center, and she was quickly walking toward my direction. I stepped in front of her with a smile and congratulated her on becoming first vice president of the Modern Language Association. As I tend to do when Anne Gere's around, I gushed on about her being chair and president of three major organizations at the intersection of teacher education, writing studies, and English studies: CCCC, NCTE, and MLA! Was her hat trick a first for English studies? Well, maybe. She smiled.

We agreed to stay in touch, and we have. She's kindly supported me with letters of recommendation and shared a book project description with me she's been working on about Indigenous women teachers. She and I have been in a parallel headspace for some time, reading and writing about similar topics: teaching and learning, sustaining literacy practices, and writing with and for the Indigenous peoples and learners in our lives. When our paths do meet, however briefly, I'm left feeling stronger, gleaning light from her presence, insight from her wisdom, and inspiration from her model. In the times between, though, I read her work and aspire to do better. She's been that kind of professional role model. Able to talk across disciplines, research with rigor, support and mentor so many, run programs and lead organizations, and somehow through it all, she writes books and articles about the topics that have always mattered most to her and to the many fields of English studies.

WORKS CITED

Brandt, Deborah, et al. "The Politics of the Personal: Storying Our Lives against the Grain. Symposium Collective." *College English*, vol. 64, no. 1, Sept. 2001, pp. 41–62, https://doi.org/10.58680/ce20011239.

Gere, Anne Ruggles. "An Art of Survivance: Angel DeCora at Carlisle." *The American Indian Quarterly*, vol. 28, no. 3/4, 2004, pp. 649–84.

———. "Indian Heart / White Man's Head: Native-American Teachers in Indian Schools, 1880–1930." *History of Education Quarterly*, vol. 45, no. 1, 2005, pp. 38–65, https://doi.org/10.1111/j.1748-5959.2005.tb00026.x.

———. "Kitchen Tables and Rented Rooms: The Extracurriculum of Composition." *College Composition and Communication*, vol. 45, no. 1, 1994, pp. 75–92, https://doi.org/10.58680/ccc19948799.

Heller, Caroline E. *Until We Are Strong Together: Women Writers in the Tenderloin*. Teachers College P, 1997.

Juzwik, Mary M., et al., editors. *Legacies of Christian Languaging and Literacies in American Education: Perspectives on English Language Arts Curriculum, Teaching, and Learning*. Routledge, 2020.

Schutz, Aaron, and Anne Ruggles Gere. "Service Learning and English Studies: Rethinking 'Public' Service." *College English*, vol. 60, no. 2, 1998, pp. 129–49, https://doi.org/10.58680/ce19983675.

Stock, Patricia L., editor. *Composition's Roots in English Education*. Heinemann, 2012.

Weyand, Larkin, and Mary M. Juzwik. "Schooling Activist Evangelical Literacy: Speaking, Writing, and Storying Christian Faith in Dialogue with Public Secondary Literacy Curriculum." *Linguistics and Education*, vol. 55, Feb. 2020, pp. 1–16. https://doi.org/10.1016/j.linged.2019.100789.

CHAPTER 2.
THIRTY YEARS AFTER *INTO THE FIELD*

Douglas Hesse
University of Denver

In 1987, I was flying home from the Conference on College Composition and Communication (the Cs) meeting in Atlanta and happened to sit next to Winifred Horner. I knew her son, David. We'd been undergrads together at the University of Iowa, both of us in the marching band and, later, both performing in the Old Gold Singers, a small show choir for which he played drums, and I sang and danced. We talked mostly about Dave and the sessions we'd seen in Atlanta, but I've lost any details to the residue of time.

In fact, I'd forgotten that encounter altogether until I was re-reading *Into the Field: Sites of Composition Studies*, which Anne Gere edited in 1993. In the third sentence of her introduction, Anne situates her volume in philosophical contrast to Horner's book of a decade earlier, *Composition and Literature: Bridging the Gap*. Rather than "bridging," in which composition borrows from other disciplines (literary studies, of course, but also psychology, linguistics, and rhetoric), Anne suggests the better metaphor is "restructuring," in which "composition shapes as much as it is shaped by other fields because questions about the nature of discourse, writing, and subjectivity emerge from mutually defining stances" (4). Curious about what Win Horner had been doing at the Atlanta Cs, I learned that she was chairing a session on "The State of the Discipline," with speakers David Chapman, Gary Tate, and Nan Johnson. One of many striking things about Anne's introduction for *Into the Field* is her confident stance that "questions about the status of composition—whether it possesses the features of a discipline, whether it merits a place in the disciplined academy—give way, in these essays, to new ways of talking about composition," rejecting a "totalizing disciplinary narrative" (3).

Concerns about the status of composition have occupied our field for the past 40 years. At one level, the motivations have been political, with desires for respect and fair material resources. Composition has been largely defined through much of its history as the activity of required first-year courses, staffed especially at larger schools by teaching assistants or adjuncts on their way to "something better." Faculty with scholarly commitments to the field resented how composition was dismissed as a site of scholarship deserving the staffing, status, funding, and autonomy that literary studies enjoyed. (My, how literature's times have changed.) The stakes were trenchantly and brilliantly outlined in the Composition Blues Band song, "Scorned by the MLA," set to the Springsteen tune, "Born in the USA": "In my profession now I'm just a slob / Cause I teach composition to the human mob / Scorned by the MLA / Scorned by the MLA" (Diogenes).

At another level, though, concerns about status have been motivated less by defensive positioning for academic turf than by intellectual curiosity. Given a baggy collection of epistemologies, objects of inquiry, and pedagogical practices, is composition studies actually a discipline? Or does it rather have the status of Wittgenstein's games? Just as chess, baseball, bridge, catch, and pin-the-tale-on-the-donkey have a family resemblance to one another as games, not a limited shared quality, so might composition be a federation of activities rather than a discipline, an assemblage united by family resemblance of its members. I appreciate the philosophical puzzle of disciplinary definition, smartly enacted in books like *Composition, Rhetoric, and Disciplinarity* (Malenczyk et al.). And I appreciate the strategic value of being able to articulate our identity in the higher education firmament, even though recognition as a discipline has relatively less value than it once might have had. These are days of program closures even at flagship universities, from political science to languages, from English even to mathematics. I worried a few years ago that people were unrealistic about disciplinary strength in current conditions (Hesse). My worries have accelerated.

It's both nostalgic and refreshing, then, to peer thirty years back, at the world invoked by *Into the Field*. I remember two reactions to getting my copy of the book, published the year I was tenured. The first and most immediate was that it had been published by the Modern Language Association (MLA), for some in the profession the avatar of inequality for rhetoric and composition. I understood the rancor, but by then I'd already been an MLA member nine years and will soon retire as a lifetime MLA member, so I've generally been charitable. Still, serious books in rhetoric and composition (rhet/comp) then came from publishers like the National Council of Teachers of English, Southern Illinois University Press, or Boynton/Cook, not MLA. It was a few years before composition-friendly scholar Bob Scholes would become president of MLA, and it was twenty-five years before Anne herself would be the first modern composition studies scholar elected to that role. I still remember Rosemary Feal, then MLA Executive Director, confiding in excitement to me during a hotel breakfast, that the upcoming ballot would feature Anne and Michael Bernard-Donals. Back in 1993, I figured it would do rhet/comp good to have a book with such exemplary scholars in the MLA catalog. Many of its chapters originated in convention sessions organized by the MLA Division on Teaching Writing. The field benefitted from MLA as another publishing option; 1994 would bring another MLA book, *Writing Theory and Critical Theory* (Clifford and Schilb).

My second reaction was to the tenor of *Into the Field*. Rather than defensively wanting turf, its dozen authors were confidently doing intellectual work in a field they assumed needed no justification or borrowed status (an implication of Horner's earlier book). Unlike a fine volume roughly its contemporary, *The Politics of Writing Instruction: Postsecondary*, edited by Richard Bullock and John Trimbur (in which Anne has a chapter), *Into the Field* more directly engages theory-building, in approaches alternatively philosophical and essayistic. The orientation is clear from Anne's distinction between the common usage of "field" as connoting "a bounded territory, one that can be distinguished and set apart" and her preferred less common usage, out of physics, of field as "a kind of charged space in which multiple 'sites' of interaction appear" (4). The book's work, then, was not to demand attention but to articulate ideas in the intellectually energetic space of composition.

To accomplish this work, Anne gathered a dozen prominent scholars. Here's her table of contents:

> Anne Ruggles Gere, "Introduction"
>
> Part One: The Philosophical Turn
>
> Kurt Spellmeyer, "Being Philosophical about Composition: Hermeneutics and the Teaching of Writing"
>
> Brenda Deen Schildgen, "Reconnecting Rhetoric and Philosophy in the Composition Classroom"
>
> Judith Halden-Sullivan, "The Phenomenology of Process"
>
> Barbara Gleason, "Self-Reflection as a Way of Knowing: Phenomenological Investigations in Composition"
>
> Richard J. Murphy, Jr. "Polanyi and Composition: A Personal Note on a Human Science"
>
> George Dillon, "Argumentation and Critique: College Composition and Enlightenment Ideals"
>
> Part Two: Postmodern Subjectivities
>
> James A. Berlin, "Composition Studies and Cultural Studies: Collapsing Boundaries"
>
> John Trimbur, "Composition Studies: Postmodern or Popular"
>
> Irene Papoulis, "Subjectivity and Its Role in 'Constructed' Knowledge: Composition, Feminist Theory, and Psychoanalysis"

- Rosemary Gates, "Creativity and Insight: Toward a Poetics of Composition"
- Derek Owens, "Composition as the Voicing of Multiple Fictions"
- David Bleich, "Ethnography and the Study of Literacy: Prospects for Socially Generous Research"
- "Not a Conclusion: A Conversation"

The section headings, "The Philosophical Turn" and "Postmodern Subjectivities," reflect a certain historical moment. English studies in the 1980s and early 1990s were characterized by what got shorthanded as "the theory wars." Continental theorists disrupted traditional ways of reading and writing by foregrounding the economic, ideological, and political nature of texts. Textual meanings of value were constructed (and thus, amenable to deconstruction) rather than immanent or natural. In literary studies, syllabus real estate occupied by fiction and poetry gave some way to works by Lyotard, Althusser, Derrida, Jameson, Eagleton, Foucault, Kristeva, Spivak, Deleuze and Guattari, and so on. Theory wars were fought over this displacement; many people were appalled by reduced attention to the kinds of creative works that were central to English. They believed most theory dealt with interests outside or peripheral to literary studies. Most—but not all—of the fights were public and led by conservatives like Allan Bloom, whose book *The Closing of the American Mind* protested that theory disparaged Western civilization, with detriments not only for individual development but also for the larger social good.

While most English professors rejected those critiques, some others agreed with them, including a few notable compositionists who thought teaching writing was plenty complicated, important, and interesting without the larger social and political freight of theory. Maxine Hairston controversially articulated this position in her 1992 article, "Diversity, Ideology, and Teaching Writing," which warned against indoctrinating students at the expense of teaching them writing. Just as some worried that literature-based writing courses focused less on teaching writing than on teaching about literature, so others shared Hairston's view that theory-forward writing instruction eclipsed teaching writing itself.

Other compositionists at the time welcomed theory both as a point of engagement with colleagues in literature but also as an extension of rhetorical theory in, say, the tradition of Kenneth Burke. This was the atmosphere in which Anne published *Into the Field*. New theory challenged Aristotelian and formalist ideas about naturally desirable features of texts by arguing that what seemed inevitable was, in fact, a function of convention. Conventions derived from social and political power and tradition rather than from universals of language and thought. Some writing teachers did, of course, embrace postmodernism's critique of metanarratives, often for political purposes, as happens in James Berlin and John Trimbur's *Into the Field* chapters. Less controversially, postmodern theories helped advance the idea of discourse communities, accounting for epistemological and rhetorical differences among academic disciplines.

In a wise 2018 chapter defining composition's disciplinary status, Kathi Yancey reviews several turns in composition studies over the past several decades: the social, the public, the queer, the archival, and the global, for example (15). To these, we might add the political, the multimodal, the technological, and, from *Into the Field*, the philosophical. Yancey locates these turns against a larger backdrop of five "episodes" in the discipline, starting in the 1940s and 1950s, contemporaneous with the founding of the Conference on College Composition and Communication (17). The first applied linguistics to teaching writing to new types of students; the second embraced the rise of process pedagogies and research; the third turned to cultural theory that "displaced research while underscoring the field's commitment to students and making the field look more like its literary cousins"; the fourth returned to teaching as the *field's* subject matter, informed by the three previous episodes while emphasizing students; the fifth episode celebrated disciplinarity (17–21).

In Yancey's terms, *Into the Field* exemplifies composition's theoretical episode. Many of its ideas and artifacts have morphed into a later emphasis on teaching as a subject matter, just as a glacier (or an avalanche) uses gathered rock and ice to shape new terrain. We don't much see a heavy deposit of theory per se in composition scholarship these days. The high theory of thirty years past has rather composted into the loam of contemporary composition. No serious teacher or scholar accepts that there are universally natural features of writing. None would see "good" writing as innocent of historical forces: ungendered, unclassed, unraced, in ways unproblematically achievable by all students through standard pedagogy. We assume the critique of old assumptions and focus more on applications—particularly in course design and practices like grading and assessment. We analyze specific writers or writerly identities, often to the ends of social justice. In composition studies' current phase, high theorizing has given way to more applied or empirical approaches, including to studying itself. More on that later. So it is, for example, that David Bleich's *Into the Field* chapter on ethnography seems nearly quaint, though I'm reminded how fresh these ideas were thirty years ago. Yes, Steve North had defined the qualitative tradition a few years previously, so while Bleich was hardly tilling unbroken ground, he wrote while the social turn was still being theorized.

Another residual of *Into the Field's* theory is how writing courses currently get defined. A version of cultural studies (or at least a soft version) has largely triumphed in first-year composition (FYC), where course descriptions often foreground topics and themes. While writing about writing has strong advocates, other practices demonstrate the appeal/value/advantage of writing courses being about cultural phenomena, ostensibly through a critical lens, sometimes warranted by a prefixed "rhetoric of." So, for example, current offerings in a FYC program I know well include "Food and Culture," "Tattoos," "Horror," "Student Life and Campus Space," "Craft, DIY, and Maker Movements," and so on. These cultural studies-inflected FYC courses may not use the overtly economic lenses shaped by Berlin and Trimbur in their *Into the Field* chapters, and they may have traces without knowing it of the hermeneutical or phenomenological interests of Spellmeyer and Schildgen in theirs. But their justification for being about something can mostly stay tacit, for better or worse, because of that earlier theory. Perhaps the field might explore, in light of its attraction to thematic courses, whether FYC might cede more fully to writing-across-the-curriculum (WAC) and writing-in-the-disciplines (WID).

THIRTY YEARS FORWARD

I wonder what a 2023 *Into the Field* volume might contain, imagining it had an editor as masterful as Anne Gere. I'm thinking here not of a Dick Fulkerson-like axiological analysis, nor of Gary Tate, Amy Rupiper, and Kurt Schick's catalog of pedagogies, nor of Linda Adler-Kassner and Liz Wardle's distillation of threshold concepts. I'm imagining, rather, an exploration of how composition practices and needs interact with and shape other research traditions. Such a book would look vastly different from *Into the Field*, not only in topics but also in gaze. Among other things, it would have to look extensively beyond the field, at seismic changes in higher education's status and in technology's relentless ubiquity.

In February 2023, I was flying to Amsterdam, on my way to the Writing Without Borders conference in Trondheim, Norway. Sitting next to me, alas, was no one of the stature of Anne Gere, and of course Win Horner had passed a decade earlier. The window seat held the CEO of a company called Causal Design, a consulting firm for NGOs, staffed by economists and data scientists, "with a vision of making evidence-based programming affordable for NGOs, practical to field workers, and digestible to policy makers and the general public" ("Causal"). The company might analyze how, say, food distribution in Yemen or small-business stimulators in Madagascar achieve their goals. The CEO was on his way to the Middle East. When he learned I was a writing professor, he asked my opinion on generative AI, and I asked his, which was highly enthusiastic. He said that reports to clients inevitably require sections analyzing broad social, political, and economic conditions surrounding specific projects. In his experience, generative AI drafted those sections not only more quickly but also more effectively than did recent hires from graduate programs in international studies. Drafts require editing, but they are solid enough starts. Plus, there are no egos. He also saw promise for the "tedious" work of "writing up" statistical findings into prose. I was interested to learn the evolution of a practice I'd started following in 2011, when a Chicago company called Narrative Science started offering to turn data into stories.

Clearly, any new site of composition, in the spirit of Anne's book, might involve considering how GenAI informs (or should inform) the process and status of writing, whether as invention or revision. That discussion might draw from ideas raised in the Postmodern Subjectivities section of *Into the Field*. Among several intriguing issues has been the concern that GenAI will flatten style, producing unleavened prose lacking traces of writers' lived experiences, scrubbed of their identities. In the spirit of Anne's 1993 characterization of composition studies not only as absorbing ideas from other disciplines but also as shaping them, a new chapter would insistently explore how composition studies should inflect understandings of GenAI. Certainly, our field could do so far beyond the meager lenses of plagiarism. Recently I had an undergraduate composition theory class look at a GenAI product called Sudowrite, targeted for fiction writers. Its home page promised in fall 2024 to "write a novel from start to finish. In a week" by generating "1,000s of words, **in your style**." My students could understand why people might want to have an AI do mundane, obligatory writing, but they had a harder time imagining why people wouldn't want to write their own novels. Why not have an AI just write their personal journals, while they're at it? (Actually, this is not far-fetched; some people are having ChatGPT write wedding vows.) We figured there was something about the appeal of having written or, better, "having writing attributed to me" over the act of writing itself. We connected this desire to the influencer imperative, the desire to be noted (and paid) as a content producer, the source and nature of that content being immaterial.

In any case, GenAI re-complicates subjectivity and identity in ways that would benefit from theorizing through a philosophical lens polished through composition studies, beyond the practical, educational, or economic analyses now rampant. I'd love to see a set of thinkers equal to the bunch that wrote thirty years ago address the fundamental question of how writing stands in relation to self and identity—its constitution and comportment—in the 2020s versus in the 1990s.

A second chapter might be about how composition has broadly shaped general university pedagogy. Writing classrooms were flipped decades before folks in teaching centers "discovered" the idea, Columbus-like. In fact, many teaching centers were themselves significantly shaped by WAC workshops and initiatives that started in the 1970s and accelerated through the 2000s. I speculate that a disproportionate number of people directing university centers for teaching and learning have come from composition. (I held such a position myself at Illinois State, years back.) The concepts of teaching being student-centered and learning-centered; of active engagement; of learning as a knowledge-making activity, not simply as a knowledge-receiving one; of teachers as coaches and collaborators; of peer interaction; of teaching assistant (TA) training; of the very spirit of "across the curriculum": all these and more had roots in composition studies before being taken up in centralized teaching centers. A chapter examining composition's relationship with the pedagogical turn in higher education would trace our field's historical pedagogical lineage. Such a chapter would also theorize the implications of teaching centers taking up composition studies, as well as composition's long commitment to pedagogy being reframed by this recent enterprise. At one institution I know well, the writing program nearly twenty years ago began offering intensive professional development activities in WAC. Workshops, seminars, and research projects reached hundreds of faculty across campus. Those efforts have now been largely re-housed under the university teaching center. Writing's disciplinary expertise is incrementally effaced.

That raises a third potential area for theorizing. I'll call it composition's Status Turn or, perhaps, its Inward Turn. I mean something other than articulating recognition as a discipline. I'm pointing to how much our field has made itself, its practices and practitioners, the object of study, over students and writing. We increasingly describe issues of labor (including faculty status, teaching loads, and course sizes). We survey faculty and writing program administrator (WPA) experiences, attitudes, and practices. Requests for interviews and program/course documents or policies are pervasive. Perhaps research *about* the field is simply more visible than is research *in* the field. Perhaps this turn is magnified by current crises as higher education sinks under tuition costs and public skepticism about its value and values. To be fair, the ninety composition studies books published in 2023 (Lockridge) reflect more projects about writing and writers than about status and institutional formations. But the general trend is toward the empirical, whether quantitative or qualitative, rather than the theoretical or historical. Perhaps the latter epistemologies were more attractive to an earlier generation of scholars formed substantially out of literary study, the generation of *Into the Field*. A chapter in an imagined new volume would theorize how the educations and circumstances of current scholars versus their ancestors have shaped attention and practices.

NEGLECTED, NOT LOST

In 2023, Deborah Holdstein edited an anthology published by the MLA, *Lost Texts in Rhetoric and Composition*, in which several authors discuss articles or books in the field that have fairly disappeared from current interest but merit renewed attention. Anne Gere wrote a chapter as did, from the 1993 collection, Kurt Spellmeyer. (I'll disclose that I did, too.)

Every discipline continually sorts and resifts its history. There's a strong imperative to focus on the recent, to keep the cutting edge sharp. Earlier publications and ideas get namechecked or summarized in a few sentences that perhaps send readers back to earlier sources but more likely have them quickly nod in recognition. Composition studies is not yet to the point of the sciences and social sciences, where a summative single sentence often spawns a parenthetical list of a dozen or more citations, gestured by author and date. Our field still values paraphrase and summary, but with 90 books published a year, plus hundreds of articles, decisions are made.

Steve North's dictum may still be true: nothing disappears from the house of lore (27). But that doesn't mean everyone knows how it got there or how to find it. *Into the Field: Sites of Composition Studies* remains important as a reminder of where foundational theories in our field came from and, importantly, of the contexts in which they were generated, a time of high theory and of high confidence, as composition studies could assume its status and get on with exploring heady ideas. Individually and collectively, we may feel the subconscious tug to Marie Kondo-ize our professional bookshelves and memories. The task is made easier by not re-reading a book when you pull it off the shelf to ask, "Does it give you pleasure?" The question for *Into the Field* gets answered yes, as does the question, "Does it make you think?" The lucky thing about books is that you needn't rely on a chance airplane seat assignment to encounter Anne Gere's profound ideas and generous contributions, still decades after.

WORKS CITED

Adler-Kassner, Linda, and Elizabeth Wardle, eds. *Naming What We Know: Threshold Concepts of Writing Studies*. Utah State UP, 2015.

Bloom, Allan. *The Closing of the American Mind: How Higher Education Has Failed Democracy and Impoverished the Souls of Today's Students*. Simon and Schuster, 1987.

Bullock, Richard H., and John Trimbur, editors. *The Politics of Writing Instruction: Postsecondary*, Charles Schuster, general editor. Boynton/Cook, 1991.

"Causal Design." *Causal Design*, 2024, causaldesign.com.

Clifford, John, and John Schilb, editors. *Writing Theory and Critical Theory*. Modern Language Association of America, 1994.

Diogenes, Marvin. "Scorned by the MLA." *Composition Blues Band Complete Song List*, web.stanford.edu/~marvind/Song_lyrics.htm#mla.

Fulkerson, Richard. "Summary and Critique: Composition at the Turn of the Twentieth Century." *College Composition and Communication*, vol. 56, no. 4, 2005, pp. 654–87, https://doi.org/10.58680/ccc20054826.

Gere, Anne Ruggles, editor. *Into the Field: Sites of Composition Studies*. Modern Language Association of America, 1993.

Hairston, Maxine. "Diversity, Ideology, and Teaching Writing." *College Composition and Communication*, vol. 43, no. 2, 1992, pp. 179–93, https://doi.org/10.58680/ccc19928882.

Hesse, Doug. "Redefining Disciplinarity in the Current Context of Higher Education." Malenczyk, et al., pp. 287–302.

Holdstein, Deborah H., editor. *Lost Texts in Rhetoric and Composition*. Modern Language Association of America, 2023.

Horner, Winifred Bryan, editor. *Composition and Literature: Bridging the Gap*. U of Chicago P, 1983.

Horner, Winifred Bryan. "The State of the Discipline." 19–21 Mar. 1987, Conference on Composition and Communication, Atlanta, GA. Conference Session Chair Commentary.

Kondo, Marie. *The Life-Changing Magic of Tidying Up*. Ten Speed P, 2014.

Lockridge, Tim. "Home." *Rhetorlist*, rhetorlist.net/. Accessed 24 February 2025.

Malenczyk, Rita, et al., editors. *Composition, Rhetoric, and Disciplinarity*. Utah State UP, 2018.

North, Stephen M. *The Making of Knowledge in Composition: Portrait of an Emerging Field*. Boynton/Cook, 1987.

"Sudowrite." *Sudowrite*, sudowrite.com. Accessed 22 November 2024.

Tate, Gary, et al., editors. *A Guide to Composition Pedagogies*. Oxford UP, 2001.

Yancey, Kathleen Blake. "Mapping the Turn to Disciplinarity: A Historical Analysis of Composition's Trajectory and Its Current Moment." Malenczyk et al., pp. 15–35.

CHAPTER 3.

RESCUING READING: CENTERING REAL READERS

Lizzie Hutton
Miami University, Ohio

In 2012, Mariolina Rizzi Salvatori and Patricia Donahue published a much-cited analysis of the dramatic "disappearance" of the topic of reading from the composition-rhetoric scholarship of the previous two decades ("What is College English"). Reading, to be sure, has always been central to college writing instruction. What struck these researchers was the waning of reading as a subject of study—especially notable for a field increasingly devoted to inclusively ecological views of student literacy development.

In this chapter, I reconsider the intellectual-institutional habits that, over the last thirty years, have kept the study of reading relegated to this marginal status. Since 2012, scholars have made important strides in starting to better "secure," in Ellen Carillo's terms, "a place for reading" in both the composition classroom and writing support more generally (*Securing a Place*). Yet for all this renewed attention, much of this college reading scholarship continues to hew to a narrowly corrective agenda, one prescriptive rather than descriptive, set only on fixing students' purported reading ills, rather than investigating and revealing more capaciously all that reading is. Writing research assiduously attends to the varied and often still emergent aims, technologies, and social forces that shape the messy work of students' (and, indeed, all writers') textual productions. The reading scholarship, by contrast, remains bound to an essentially remedial framework, upheld by a persistent scholarly neglect of the diverse complexities of the real student reader. Drawing on Anne Ruggles Gere's longstanding commitment to surfacing the agentive power of literacy practices and perspectives traditionally overlooked by the academy, I ask how attention to these real readers—and the more inclusive conceptions of reading this can engender—might rescue reading from the deficit narratives that keep it so stubbornly consigned to the margins of our field.

DOES THE STUDY OF READING BELONG IN WRITING STUDIES?

A number of cases can be made for increased attention to reading in the context of higher education. Reading, like writing, is undeniably central to most academic and professional pursuits, not to mention our personal lives. Whether through phones, laptops, Kindles, books, intake forms, menus, or highway billboards, to maintain communication with others in most contemporary spaces is to be awash in running tickertapes of written language.

Reading research, moreover, has long shown that the ability to read effectively does not constitute a one-and-done skill. Especially in the case of the specialized reading tasks of academia, most professions, and civic life, one's ability to make sense of one or another given text in ways that are useful and/or context-appropriate will require of the reader a wide range of processes, knowledge sets, and presuppositions. As Sam Wineburg illustrates in his 1991 study of professional historians' reading of historical artifacts, different forms of reading each entail a "distinctive epistemological stance" (495); for the historians he studies, this includes not only attention to a text's possible "subtexts," but an even more fundamental "belie[f] that [such subtexts] exist" (510). Comparing this historical mode to other forms of reading pushes these distinctions even more into relief. Making sense of an instructional manual requires a very different approach—different knowledge, different kinds of attention, and different beliefs about what texts can tell—than the mode Wineburg describes; as does skimming one's personal newsfeed for updates to some unfolding event; as does critically evaluating an op-ed's nested set of claims. Navigating such tasks and texts, as one needs to in new communities of practice, thus entails what David Jolliffe calls a "continuing education" in new reading processes, presumptions, and attentional resources ("Review Essay").

Yet research also shows that neither college students nor faculty tend to understand the act of reading in these complex ways. Daniel Keller's ethnography of U.S. high school readers demonstrates that, while these students' everyday reading practices were quite rich, school had provided them few metacognitive frameworks with which they might recognize, much less describe and develop, these varied kinds of reading. These students, instead, conceived of reading as a single endeavor, whose demands were intensely felt if little understood: for them, per Keller's description, "Reading was simply reading, and [they] were asked to do a lot of it" (77). Many higher education contexts only further reinscribe such thin conceptions. As Howard Tinberg argues, most college instructors eschew explicit reading instruction, considering it "someone else's business" (247), thus, a number of writing scholars' persistent complaints about the field's striking absence of reading research and pedagogies (e.g. Jolliffe, "Review Essay" and "'Learning to Read'"; Adler-Kassner and Estrem; Horning et al.; Carillo, *Securing a Place*; Del Principe and Ihara; Ihara and Del Principe).

It is hardly surprising, then, that two decades of empirical research also confirm the extent to which students' reading practices little align with higher education's curricular expectations. Studies show that students' reading of course materials is, contrary to many instructors' injunctions, often cursory (e.g. Hoeft); and that few undergraduates recognize the cursory nature of their engagements (e.g. Howard et al.). Few students display much metacognitive knowledge about learning or themselves as learners (Keller; Pintrich) or acknowledge many connections between their engagement with assigned readings and course success (Gorzycki et al.; Del Principe and Ihara).

In many ways, the field has begun to attend more rigorously to these needs. The same year (2012) Salvatori and Donahue published their analysis ("What is College English"), the Conference on College Composition and Communication (CCCC) launched a special interest group devoted to the role of reading in composition, and in 2021 the organization published an official position statement ("CCCC Position Statement"). In 2014, Carillo made her influential case for a "mindful reading" paradigm (*Securing a Place*) and in 2017 released a textbook on the topic (*A Writer's Guide*). A 2016 special issue of *Pedagogy* edited by Salvatori and Donahue and several edited collections (e.g. Sullivan et al.; Horning et al.) confirm a rising interest in improving college-level reading-writing theory and instruction. In other ways, however, reading remains a footnote to the field's overall project. Adler-Kassner and Estrem note the absence of reading theory and pedagogy in doctoral-level courses on composition theory and teaching preparation (36). The CCCC's 2021 position statement puts it even more pointedly: that "outside of community colleges," there persists a lack of "sustained attention to reading as the counterpart of writing in the construction and negotiation of meaning." Yet perhaps the clearest sign of this continued neglect is the fact that the field's touchstones of reading research and theory—say, Christina Haas and Linda Flower's "Rhetorical Reading Strategies and the Construction of Meaning," or Charles Bazerman's "Physicists Reading Physics" and "A Relationship between Reading and Writing"—were produced over thirty years ago. That the conditions of reading have since changed so radically—especially regarding the digital platforms on which many of us now read—only makes this time gap all the more glaring.

RECONSIDERING "NEGLECT" AND ITS REMEDIES

For many historians of the field, this neglect results from a thirty-year bias against the topic itself, now baked into the field's disciplinary identity. By Carillo's account, the field's marginalization of reading can be traced to its increased dissociation from literary-cultural studies, that subfield of English studies where the explicit study of reading has long been presumed to live (*Securing a Place*).¹ During the 1970s and 1980s, to be sure, literary/composition/rhetoric/critical theory scholars ushered into the composition-rhetoric scholarship (as it was then known) a brief flowering of reading-writing theory and pedagogies (think the previously cited Haas and Flower and Bazerman, as well as Louise Wetherbee Phelps, Ann Berthoff, and David Bartholomae and Anthony Petrosky). At the same time, however, the field was working to establish itself as an independent discipline, with its own doctoral programs and tenure-track positions, prompting comp-rhet scholars to more stringently distinguish their own methods and goals from those espoused by literary studies, the field to which, in many English departments, comp-rhet had long been considered subordinate because merely preparatory. What Salvatori and Donahue call composition-rhetoric's "separatist project" ("What is College English" 201)—the understandable effort to disaggregate investigations of literacy from investigations of the literary—thus also enabled a disaggregation of reading and writing, with the implication that these activities could in fact be dissociated as each belonging to entirely separable programs of study.

For most writing scholars, then, reading quickly lost its status as viable topic of disciplinary inquiry (and even, to many, became disciplinarily suspect—a seemingly retrograde attempt to smuggle back into writing studies the very literary critical concerns from which comp-rhet was so keen to distance itself). By this "great divorce" narrative (Carillo, *Securing a Place* 76), the field's neglect of reading can be understood as a form of collateral damage—damage that, moreover, can be remedied by a mere return of attention to the topic. Indeed, it is the quantity of attention that writing scholars granted to reading that Salvatori and Donahue's analysis uses as its metric for measuring the topic's "neglect" and "revival": specifically, the changing number of reading-related "program categories" offered in CCC's annual calls for papers (which, for much of the 2000s, dropped to zero) ("What is College English" 213, 210).

Yet to focus on this metric alone risks simplifying both the problem and its potential solution. Attending only to changing quantities of reading scholarship—as the C's position statement also does—is to overlook another important feature at play: this scholarship's qualitative nature, including its prevailing aims, methods, presumptions, and blind spots. This observation is not to devalue the reading scholarship as it currently stands; nor to suggest there are no exceptions (e.g. Keller) to the broader trends I here identify. It is, instead, to prompt a recalibration of how we understand the field's widespread "neglect" of reading

---

1   U.S.-U.K. literary studies arguably took its contemporary form when scholars of the early twentieth century expanded their investigations of literary artifacts to include the forms of reading purportedly required for critical engagement with such artifacts (e.g. Richards; Ransom; Brooks and Warren).

and to ask whether this neglect can indeed be rectified by a current influx of scholarship that mainly functions as a collection of handbook-like injunctions, each applicable only to its own pedagogical context. I thus propose that this scholarship, while in some cases necessary, is still not sufficient for the kind of comprehensive, research-based theory building that would truly "secure" the study of reading, and the reading-writing connection, as fundamental to the study of writing.

Like usage handbooks, of course, the field's current reading injunctions offer crucial support to students working towards specific, predetermined expectations and learning outcomes. Whether aimed at improving readers' open-minded engagement with long-form prose (Sullivan et al.'s "deep reading"), developing rhetorical awareness (e.g. Bean), learning from models (e.g. Bunn) or confirming claims' credibility (e.g. Wineburg and McGrew), current work on college reading-writing provides students with a valuable array of situation-specific strategies. Newer work on digital literacies further taxonomizes the varied approaches beneficial for careful engagement with texts on screens and online (e.g. Cohn; Baron). Yet also like usage handbooks, this reading research—to borrow Jolliffe's astute observation—has "tended more toward the applied and pedagogical than toward the conceptual and theoretical" ("'Learning to Read'" 13). I would go even further. As pure applied pedagogy, such scholarship is also limited by its pervasively corrective aims.

Here the lens of linguistic or grammatical prescriptivism proves useful. As Sidney Greenbaum explains, "[P]rescriptive grammar evaluates and advises" (22), providing guidelines for what one or another grammar expert—say, Bryan Garner, or Diana Hacker and Nancy Sommers—considers proper and improper uses of language. I argue the current reading scholarship functions in much the same way. Its aims are directive: to advise how students should read. Methodologically, it tends to draw only from anecdotal or hypothetical-aspirational examples. Because primarily prescriptive, it also frequently leaves its own biases unchecked, presuming its one way of reading ("slow," "deep," "rhetorical," et cetera) to function as the best and only standard. Of course, as linguist Deborah Cameron has argued, a prescriptive agenda can be considered an understandable, even inevitable, form of "hygiene" among members of a community. As Cameron argues, this "urge to improve or 'clean up'" (1) is "part of what language-using is all about" (2).

Yet—as with studies of language use—to reduce our study of reading *only* to the prescriptive is to default to a purely remedial model for how reading is best learned, studied, and reflectively understood. After all, a purely prescriptivist framework tends to position varietal preferences as universal truths and to view those unschooled in these varietal preferences not through the lens of difference, but deficit.

Here, too, the institutional-intellectual history of writing studies offers guidance. College writing research and pedagogy have long been saddled with the institutional mandate of remediating literacy skills that, it is widely presumed, students should already have in hand when they arrive in college. Such a deficit paradigm orients pedagogies around backward-looking correction and resolutely not around forward-looking introduction to, and education in, sets of field-specific knowledge that students could not possibly arrive in college having already learned. As Downs and Wardle have argued, this remedial strain in writing instruction thus rests on a fundamental "misconception" of what college-level literacy knowledge and learning entail, reducing literacy to portable skills, and upholding the presumption—now well debunked (e.g. Anson and Moore)—that such skills, once learned, will transfer wholesale to new contexts. By encouraging this acontextual universalism, this misconception further masks the situation-specific values and behaviors that actually shape all literacy practices and expectations. As Brian Street famously argued, such an "autonomous" view of literacy—as one monolithic skillset learners can apply successfully across all contexts—is a view blinkered by a failure to cop to its own "ideologies," and by an illusory conviction that its particular ways of reading and writing are the only ways to properly communicate (19–38).

For writing studies, it was only by breaking free—or, at the least, by looking more critically upon—these institutional-intellectual habits that the field was able to come fully into its own. Crucial to this evolution was a new refusal to leave unquestioned the very crisis narratives and subsequently universalized fix-it prescriptions that justified the institutionally superimposed mandates by which the field had long been reductively defined. To be sure, alternate theorizations of what it means to study and teach writing and rhetoric can be glimpsed as far back as the turn of the last century, in the work, say, of Fred Newton Scott or Gertrude Buck (as examined by Bordelon); the history of composition instruction is more complex than some disciplinary histories have claimed (see also Gere, "Presidential Address"; Carter and Durst).

Nonetheless, a more comprehensive paradigm shift did not arrive until scholars were able to name and turn explicitly against the mechanistic, acontextual constructs of literacy that long defined "first year comp." Thanks to this social turn, composition-rhetoric expanded from a merely preparatory teaching subject, so-called, to a broadly inclusive, critically informed, research-based "human science," to use Phelps' crucial term (76–77). This evolution entailed a reformation of what writing might mean in and for higher education. No longer only an "activity" requiring the remediations of first-year composition, writing became newly positioned as a complex and far-reaching "subject of study," as Adler-Kassner and Wardle have put it (4).

Also important is how this recalibration was substantiated and enabled by the new methodologies the field came to embrace. As writing scholars grew skeptical of literacy constructs and pedagogies based purely on anecdote and aspiration, research became more empirical, examining not only the diverse expectations writers face, but the real practices, processes, sponsors, and forces that enable and constrain writing. Researchers took up new units of analysis, by which they could challenge longstanding presumptions about the purportedly universal textual and rhetorical features once considered the sole source of writerly efficacy and by which they could attend instead to the diverse human behaviors, contexts, and values whereby texts are produced, circulated, and granted culturally sanctioned meanings and approval. In short, these new methods—ethnographic, qualitative, situation-sensitive—allowed writing scholarship to adopt a newly descriptive approach to the study and teaching of writing. And a newly ecological view of writing emerged, one rejecting prior idealizations of writing and focused instead on a methodologically rigorous research agenda: delineating what real writers, in real communities of practice, actually make when they write, and how.

The field's approach to reading would do well to heed the lessons of this field-history, and especially to its self-scrutinizing revising of its own goals, methods, and disciplinary identity. Compared to writing, reading is, of course, famously difficult to study—it is by definition an act whose traces are elusive and subjective, as much felt as they are thought, so interior are they to an individual's situated, embodied experience. This should not suggest, however, that empirical investigations are impossible. In the early throes of the field's ambitious reinvention of the study of writing, the study of reading seemed poised to keep pace, especially through methodologically innovative inquiries into varied readers' acts of meaning making for specific contexts. Yet this promise faded fast, as much, I argue, due to anxiety over disciplinary boundaries as to a growing skepticism about the very methods (soon maligned as a crude "cognitivism") that make empirical study of reading possible in the first place.

Indeed, one great irony of the reading scholarship is that the more the field embraced its current context-sensitive, ecological paradigm, the less reading itself appeared a disciplinarily appropriate subject of study. Or, put another way, the more reading was confined to its current auxiliary position, as a subject relevant only for classroom-specific remediation. What resulted—albeit tacitly—was that reading was rebranded as a purely pedagogical issue. The "neglect" of reading does not constitute, then, a general failure of interest or attention. It constitutes instead a specific failure to apply to reading the same descriptivist research agenda that has so successfully reshaped the study of writing.

CENTERING REAL READERS IN EXPANDED SITES OF READING

The remediational agenda driving most of the reading-focused writing scholarship has in some ways become so naturalized to writing studies that it can be difficult to imagine alternatives. The US is—and has long been—saturated with literacy crisis narratives, never more so than in our current age, whose practices are so dramatically shaped by the ever-changing digital systems that mediate so many of our textual engagements. But alternatives to remediation and prescriptivism exist. Moreover, these alternatives must—pedagogically and empirically—be embraced in writing studies' reading and reading-writing scholarship.

Salvatori and Donahue rightly observe that some of the most insightful reading-writing scholarship of earlier decades emerged from a then-new focus on the real student reader ("What is College English"). But that research was also enabled by a devotion to empirical study, resisting the field's longstanding mandate to put the pedagogical cart before the horse. The aim of this then-new reading scholarship was not merely to "fix" reading by prescribing better ways of reading, a goal requiring scholars only to delineate idealized guidelines for what they'd like readers to do. The aim of such research instead was to explore, in real scenarios, how the meaning making that reading enables actually gets accomplished—this through a focus on what real readers do, regardless of a scholar's own personal preference about how reading ought to be carried out.

Yet writing studies provides another lesson, showing how understandings of literacy are also limited by overly narrow conceptions of the very sites in which literacy takes place and from which our study of literacy can continue to learn. Reading scholarship, I thus argue, should return its focus not just to real student readers but also to the many diverse contexts in which these readers read and make meanings that matter—and not only to us, but to them. In her crucial "Kitchen Tables and Rented Rooms: The Extracurriculum of Composition," Anne Ruggles Gere exhorted her field to reconsider its habitually exclusive focus on writing that takes place "inside classroom walls," and to attend more inclusively, more empirically, and, indeed, more empathetically, to writing taking place at many other value-laden sites of meaning construction (78). Only through such investigation, Gere argues, can scholars begin to dismantle the field's longstanding "gatekeeping function" (89). The same "extracurricular" investigations would substantially deepen our own—and our students'—understanding of reading and the reading-writing connection.

Of course, examining what real student readers do outside the classroom forces uncomfortable questions. Such study would prod us to reconsider whether certain reading practices and aims are really as universally applicable as we might assume and whether our expressed reading values are driven more by wishful thinking or nostalgia than by the realities of most readers' experiences and goals (including our own). Pointing to one such unchecked piety, Doug Downs notes the field's continuing "resistance to screen literacies" (206), despite the reality that digital reading is now most readers' "default" rather than the exception. I would build on Downs' observation to argue that such resistance is only enabled by a body of reading scholarship focused almost exclusively on the controlled context of the college classroom, where such realities can be blithely recommended against, if not outright ignored, and where students are often positioned only as learners whose reading behaviors and conceptions require nothing more than our well-intentioned realignments.

For reading-writing scholars, a central question then remains about what exactly it means in the context of writing studies to teach and study reading. If by teaching and studying reading we mean teaching and theorizing only how readers ought to read, in order to more effectively reach one or another predetermined outcome, our scholarship has made some important strides. If, however—and following the example of writing scholarship—by teaching and studying reading we mean teaching, exploring, and theorizing what reading more fundamentally *is,* across contexts and conditions, the field falls short. The former is most properly understood as a prescriptive project, delineating one or another form of "good reading" that scholars have found useful for meeting specific ends. The latter, by contrast, is an empirical, descriptivist project—exploring and teaching an ontology of reading, and asking, essentially, how reading works, both in and across contexts, and what this study can teach us, as scholars (as much as it can teach our students), about our own ideological and pedagogical presuppositions.

WORKS CITED

Adler-Kassner, Linda, and Heidi Estrem. "Reading Practices in the Writing Classroom." *Writing Program Administration*, vol. 31, no. 1–2, 2007, pp. 35–47, association database.co/archives/31n1-2/31n1-2adler-kassner-estrem.pdf.

Adler-Kassner, Linda, and Elizabeth Wardle. *Naming What We Know: Threshold Concepts of Writing Studies*. Utah State UP, 2015.

Anson, Chris, and Jessie Moore. *Critical Transitions: Writing and the Question of Transfer*. The WAC Clearinghouse / UP of Colorado, 2017, https://doi.org/10.37514/PER-B.2016.0797.

Baron, Naomi. *How We Read Now: Strategic Choices for Print, Screen, and Audio*. Oxford UP, 2021. *Oxford Academic*, https://doi.org/10.1093/oso/9780190084097.001.0001.

Bartholomae, David, and Anthony R. Petrosky. *Facts, Artifacts and Counterfacts: Theory and Method for a Reading and Writing Course*. Boynton/Cook, 1986.

Bazerman, Charles. "Physicists Reading Physics: Schema-laden Purposes and Purpose-laden Schema." *Written Communication,* vol. 2, no. 1, 1985, pp. 3–23, https://doi.org/10.1177/0741088385002001001.

———. "A Relationship between Reading and Writing: The Conversational Model." *College English,* vol. 41, no. 6, 1980, pp. 656–61, https://doi.org/10.58680/ce198013907.

Bean, John C., et al. *Reading Rhetorically.* 4th ed., Pearson Longman, 2014.

Berthoff, Ann E. *Forming, Thinking, Writing: The Composing Imagination.* Heinemann Educational Books, 1982.

Bordelon, Suzanne. *A Feminist Legacy: The Rhetoric and Pedagogy of Gertrude Buck.* Southern Illinois UP, 2009.

Brooks, Cleanth, and Robert Penn Warren. *Understanding Poetry: An Anthology for College Students.* H. Holt and Company, 1939.

Bunn, Michael. "Motivation and Connection: Teaching Reading (and Writing) in the Composition Classroom." *College Composition and Communication,* vol. 64, no. 3, 2013, pp. 496–516, https://doi.org/10.58680/ccc201322720.

Cameron, Deborah. *Verbal Hygiene.* Routledge, 2012. *Taylor and Francis eBooks,* https://doi.org/10.4324/9780203123898.

Carillo, Ellen C. *Securing a Place for Reading in Composition: The Importance of Teaching for Transfer.* Utah State UP, 2014.

———. *A Writer's Guide to Mindful Reading.* The WAC Clearinghouse / UP of Colorado, 2017, https://doi.org/10.37514/PRA-B.2017.0278.

Carter, Christopher, and Russel K. Durst. *Composing Legacies: Testimonial Rhetoric in Nineteenth-Century Composition.* Peter Lang Verlag, 2021.

"CCCC Position Statement on the Role of Reading in College Writing Classrooms." *Conference on College Composition and Communication,* National Council of Teachers of English, Mar. 2021, cccc.ncte.org/cccc/the-role-of-reading.

Cohn, Jenae. *Skim, Dive, Surface: Teaching Digital Reading.* West Virginia UP, 2021.

Del Principe, Annie, and Rachel Ihara. "A Long Look at Reading in the Community College: A Longitudinal Analysis of Student Reading Experiences." *Teaching English in the Two-Year College,* vol. 45, no1. 2, 2017, pp. 183–206, https://doi.org/10.58680/tetyc201729430.

Downs, Doug. "Critical Reading in a Screen Paradigm: from Deficit to Default." *Pedagogy,* vol. 21, no. 2, 2021, pp. 205–24, https://doi.org/10.1215/15314200-8811398.

Downs, Douglas, and Elizabeth Wardle. "Teaching about Writing, Righting Misconceptions: (Re)Envisioning 'First-Year Composition' as 'Introduction to Writing Studies.'" *College Composition and Communication,* vol. 58, no. 4, 2007, pp. 552–84, https://doi.org/10.58680/ccc20075923.

Garner, Bryan A. *Garner's Modern English Usage.* 5th ed., Oxford UP, 2022.

Gere, Anne Ruggles. "Kitchen Tables and Rented Rooms: The Extracurriculum of Composition." *College Composition and Communication,* vol. 45, no. 1, 1994, pp. 75–92, https://doi.org/10.58680/ccc19948799.

———. "Presidential Address 2019–Re-Visioning Language, Texts, and Theories." *PMLA,* vol. 134, no. 3, 2019, pp. 450–58. *Cambridge Core,* https://doi.org/10.1632/pmla.2019.134.3.450.

Gorzycki, Meg, et al. "'Reading Is Important,' but 'I Don't Read': Undergraduates' Experiences with Academic Reading." *Journal of Adolescent and Adult Literacy*, vol. 63, no. 5, 2020, pp. 499–508, https://doi.org/10.1002/jaal.1020.

Greenbaum, Sidney. *The Oxford English Grammar*. Oxford UP, 1996.

Haas, Christina, and Linda Flower. "Rhetorical Reading Strategies and the Construction of Meaning." *College Composition and Communication*, vol. 39, no. 2, 1988, pp. 167–83, https://doi.org/10.58680/ccc198811161.

Hacker, Diana, and Nancy Sommers. *A Pocket Style Manual: With Exercises*. 9th ed., Bedford/St. Martin's, 2021.

Hoeft, Mary E. "Why University Students Don't Read: What Professors Can Do To Increase Compliance." *International Journal for the Scholarship of Teaching and Learning*, vol. 6, no. 2, 2012, https://doi.org/10.20429/ijsotl.2012.060212.

Horning, Alice S., et al., editors. *What Is College Reading?* The WAC Clearinghouse / UP of Colorado, 2017, https://doi.org/10.37514/ATD-B.2017.0001.

Howard, Pamela J., et al. "Academic Reading: Comparing Students' and Faculty Perceptions of Its Value, Practice, and Pedagogy," *Journal of College Reading and Learning*, vol. 48, no. 3, 2018, pp. 189–209, https://doi.org/10.1080/10790195.2018.1472942.

Ihara, Rachel, and Ann Del Principe. "What We Mean When We Talk about Reading: Rethinking the Purposes and Contexts of College Reading." *Across the Disciplines*, vol. 15, no. 2, 2018, pp. 1–14, https://doi.org/10.37514/ATD-J.2018.15.2.06.

Jolliffe, David A. "'Learning to Read as Continuing Education' Revisited: An Active Decade, but Much Remains to be Done." Sullivan et al., pp. 3–22.

———. "Review Essay: Learning to Read as Continuing Education." *College Composition and Communication*, vol. 58, no. 3, 2007, pp. 470–84, https://doi.org/10.58680/ccc20075915.

Keller, Daniel. *Chasing Literacy: Reading and Writing in an Age of Acceleration*. Utah State UP, 2013.

Phelps, Louise Wetherbee. *Composition as a Human Science: Contributions to the Self-Understanding of a Discipline*. 1991. Oxford UP, 2023. *Oxford Academic*, https://doi.org/10.1093/oso/9780195067828.001.0001.

Pintrich, Paul. "The Role of Metacognitive Knowledge in Learning, Teaching, and Assessing." *Theory Into Practice*, vol. 41, no. 4, 2002, pp. 219–25, https://doi.org/10.1207/s15430421tip4104_3.

Ransom, John Crowe. "Criticism, Inc." *The Virginia Quarterly Review*, vol. 13, no. 4, 1937, pp. 586–602.

Richards, I. A. *Practical Criticism: A Study of Literary Judgment*. Harcourt, Brace and Company, 1929.

Salvatori, Mariolina Rizzi, and Patricia Donahue, editors. Special issue on reading, *Pedagogy*, vol. 16, no. 1, 2016. *Project Muse*, muse.jhu.edu/issue/32683.

———. "What is College English? Stories about Reading: Appearance, Disappearance, Morphing, and Revival." *College English*, vol. 75, no. 2, 2012, pp. 199–217, https://doi.org/10.58680/ce201221643.

Scott, Fred Newton. "The Genesis of Speech." *PMLA*, vol. 22, appendix, 1907, pp. xxvi–liv.

Street, Brian V. *Literacy in Theory and Practice*. Cambridge UP, 1984.

Sullivan, Patrick, et al., editors. *Deep Reading: Teaching Reading in the Writing Classroom*. National Council of Teachers of English, 2017.

Tinberg, Howard. "When Writers Encounter Reading in a Community College First-Year Composition Course." Sullivan et al., pp. 244–64.

Wineburg, Sam. "On the Reading of Historical Texts: Notes on the Breach between School and Academy." *American Educational Research Journal,* vol. 28, no. 3, 1991, pp. 495–519, https://doi.org/10.3102/00028312028003495.

Wineburg, Sam, and Sarah McGrew. "Lateral Reading and the Nature of Expertise: Reading Less and Learning More When Evaluating Digital Information." *Teachers College Record,* vol. 121, no. 11, 2019, pp. 1–40, https://doi.org/10.1177/016146811912101102.

CHAPTER 4.
LANGUAGE, LITERACY, AND THE INTERSECTIONS OF IDENTITY

Morris Young
University of Wisconsin, Madison

Throughout the disciplinary history of writing studies, from the establishment of composition courses at Harvard and other elite colleges in the late 19th century to the opening of higher education institutions through the G.I. Bill and open admissions in the mid–20th century to current scholarly examinations of language ideologies, linguistic justice, and communication technologies, we have seen the linking of language, literacy, and identity—whether implicit or explicit—inform discussions about ways of composing, the teaching and learning of writing, and the meanings of literacy, whether in the contexts of school, work, or the daily routines of life. In many of these early conversations, descriptions, complaints, or laments about the quality of writing, status of literacy, or decline in language proficiency were often proxies for the identities of writers, to imply without directly naming social class, race, ethnicity, gender, or other categories of identity as deficits, denying a sense of belonging, full citizenship, and dignity.

However, we have seen an explosion of scholarship in writing studies in the early 21st century that has reimagined the necessary and productive relationship between language, literacy, and identity. Archival work by scholars like Ellen Cushman and Romeo Garcia and Damian Baca has examined the writing traditions of Indigenous communities in the Americas, while qualitative studies by Kate Vieira and Rebecca Lorimer Leonard have looked closely at the relationship between migration and literacy in transnational contexts. Jacqueline Jones Royster, Beverly Moss, and Shirley Wilson Logan have considered the literacy and rhetorical work of African American people across time, while Victor Villanueva, Juan Guerra, and Aja Martinez have helped us to understand the language and literacy practices of Latinx communities. And in the work of Jessica Enoch, David Gold, and Laura Gonzales and Michelle Hall Kells we see language and literacy educators of color made visible, often working under conditions that challenged both them and their students but that also provided opportunities for the intentional and meaningful use of writing, rhetoric, and literacy.

In my own work, I have explored the histories of literacy in Hawai'i,[1] especially the experiences of immigrant workers from Asia and their families as they settled in a place where they had to negotiate among a white American elite, an Indigenous Native Hawaiian community displaced by settlers, and a range of people from different homelands from across the world. This created a complex social order, often marked by race, indigeneity, language, and social class. The emergence of Hawai'i Creole English, colloquially known as Pidgin, provided a means of communication across communities but was also often used to enforce distinctions of identity. Those who spoke Standard English had privilege and power; those who spoke Pidgin or even English with an accent—not to mention 'Ōlelo Hawai'i (the Indigenous language of Native Hawaiians) or a language from an Asian or Pacific nation—were at a disadvantage. However, as attitudes about language have changed and Pidgin, other forms of English, or multilingual or translingual writing have become more present, we have seen the positive assertion of language, literacy, and identity that does not conform to Standard English ideology. My work has also taken up the rhetorical activity of Asian/Americans,[2] from petitions and claims for belonging and citizenship in the 19th century to the present as Asian/Americans respond to the rise in anti-Asian discourse in the wake of the COVID-19 pandemic. What I have tried to do in my own scholarship and also in my teaching is to explore the relationship between language, literacy, and identity, whether in the narratives created by writers who foreground identity or use innovative forms, or in the communities that provide contexts for understanding why and how language, literacy, and writing matter.

---

1 In writing about Hawai'i and its peoples and cultures I use and present terms and concepts as they are used in Hawai'i. I have used Stephen Sumida's note "About Spelling and Capitalization" from his book *And the View from the Shore: Literary Traditions of Hawai'i* and the *University of Hawai'i Style Guide* for university publications for guidance in the use of Hawaiian words. Necessary to the spelling of Hawaiian words are the 'okina, or glottal stop, which appears thus as a single open quotation ('), and the kahakō or macron (-) to indicate elongated vowel duration. When I have quoted words that have appeared in published texts, they appear as printed. In my own text I spell Hawaiian names and words with the diacritical marks. When Hawaiian words are Anglicized, these marks generally are not used: for instance, the 'okina is not used in the word "Hawaiian," which is considered an English word. However, the *University of Hawai'i Style Guide* advises that the use of an apostrophe and an "s" is acceptable in forming English possessives of Hawaiian singular nouns (Hawai'i's people).

2 Drawing from David Palumbo-Liu, I use Asian/American in order to distinguish between Asian and American and to acknowledge "the nature and national identity at once less stable and more dynamic" (3). As Monberg and Young have described, use of the *solidus* or slash "acts as both border and bridge and perhaps provides both a textual and graphic representation of movement, relationships and a reaching across and beyond–beyond the nation-state [and] beyond the mere representation of Asian American rhetorical legacies in the discipline" (N.P.).

For me, identity has been key to shaping my research: my identity as an Asian/American; my history of growing up in Hawai'i and the child of parents who themselves were raised in the two-tier public education system of English Standard Schools; and now as a scholar who has worked with a range of graduate students exploring the purposes of writing informed by their own literacy histories. However, my work as a scholar and teacher is built on a foundation provided by Anne Ruggles Gere, for her model of intellectual daring in examining the language and literacy practices of people and communities often marginalized, for her example as a committed teacher of writing and teacher educator, and in her generosity as scholar, colleague, and mentor.

From her earliest scholarship in examining the oral tradition in West African literature to exploring writing groups as a site for interaction to the theorizing of literacy as an intimate and constitutive practice in the lives of women, Anne Ruggles Gere has developed a robust theoretical framework to analyze the ways people have used language, literacy, and writing and their relationship to identity as shaped by historical, social, political, and cultural contexts. This framework has had implications for understanding the curricular work of writing in classroom settings as well as making visible writing and literacy in extracurricular spaces that have often served women, people of color, and others whose identities have limited their access to educational institutions. In this chapter, I consider how Gere's scholarship has provided a way to examine the intersections of identity through the range of language and literacy practices in diverse communities of writers. The capaciousness of her theoretical framework allows for a productive engagement in moving from examinations of the relationship between gender and literacy to a consideration of the sociomaterial implications of literacy in communities of color. In the case of my own research and teaching, Gere's scholarship has allowed me to think deeply about how language and literacy have shaped the experiences of people of Asian descent in the US, especially in the way their identities have been constructed through acts of writing to navigate the exigencies of racism and trauma or to express moments of belonging and joy.

ATTENDING TO LANGUAGE

In her 1974 dissertation, *West African Oratory and the Fiction of Chinua Achebe and* T. M. *Aluko*, completed at the University of Michigan, Anne Ruggles Gere focuses on two West African writers to examine the rhetorical uses of oratory. Such a consideration had its risks for sure since a range of scholarly traditions at the time would have read African literature and the African experience through Western critical lenses and expectations. The Western Gaze might read the literature of African writers as anthropological descriptions of life or to identify exotic elements to attach to African identity and culture. For Gere, scholars reading West African literature through the Western Gaze reduced rich, complex, and highly culture-specific *literatures* to folklore and myths that allow them to make meaning *about* Africans without actually understanding the historical, social, political, and cultural contexts of African communities that inform the literary and rhetorical work of African writers.

While Gere does begin her own theoretical framing of oratory in Western rhetorical theory, beginning with Aristotle's *Rhetoric* and then moving to Kenneth Burke's concept of identification, she does the critical work of situating the use of oratory in specific communities—Igbo for Achebe and Yoruba for Aluko—to examine the use of literary forms such as poetry or song and to disrupt beliefs about a primitive or preliterate culture prior to and under British colonialism. What Gere also argues is that Achebe and Aluko use oratory as a form to express alienation, performing a specific kind of rhetorical work that illustrates the relationship between language and identity. What I find especially important in this first fully articulated argument about language and identity by Gere is her attention to the work that needs to be done. Throughout *West African Oratory and the Fiction of Chinua Achebe and* T. M. *Aluko*, she does not concede that the lack of scholarship about West African oratory suggests that it has little value; rather she makes the case for why this work must be done and why West African oratory, and especially in specific historical, social, cultural, political, and linguistic contexts, must be theorized on its own terms rather than interpellated through Western critical lenses that will misread these practices in order to make them legible to Western readers.

Gere's attention to language continued in her co-authored study, *Attitudes, Language, and Change*, with Eugene Smith, published five years after the 1974 Conference on College Composition and Communication statement on "Students' Right to their Own Language." Here Gere and Smith focus their attention on the teaching of English and how attitudes about language inform how and what teachers do in the classroom and how and what students learn. Turning away from the impulse to fault students for their uses of language, Gere and Smith instead look to understand broader attitudes about language and how these attitudes shape beliefs and practices in the classroom: "We believe the examination of attitudes is part of our urgent business as English teachers, that the route to better language teaching lies in serious attention to attitude. What do we and our colleagues believe about language? How can we scrutinize these attitudes? Should we change any of our attitudes about language?" (ix). Using these last three questions to frame their project, Gere and Smith provide a useful survey and discussion about the language myths that are often the source of attitudes that make value judgments about people based on the quality and features of their spoken and written English. While these attitudes exist in our broader culture and society, they are often most strongly felt in classroom settings where students are subject not only to the curriculum but also to the beliefs of their teachers, which may conflate language, identity, and student performance.

What is fascinating about *Attitudes, Language, and Change* is that Gere and Smith take up as their charge the transformation of teacher attitudes, providing a framework for teachers to have conversations about language, to become researchers about language in their own classrooms, and to invite students to engage in this research as a way for them to develop their own understanding about how language works, how language and writing are related, and how language may provide students with the tools for communication in a variety of rhetorical situations. Even more importantly, Gere and Smith argue for structural change by creating opportunities for conversations about language in professional contexts, from in-service training in schools and districts to the development and distribution of research by professional scholarly organizations. They also recognize the need for change in community attitudes, which seems even more pressing today as we see rising violence against communities marked by race, ethnicity, culture, and language driven by discourses of white supremacy and authoritarianism.

In attending to language, Gere has demonstrated an ethical and compassionate approach to understanding how language as an activity is used by people across communities in intentional and purposeful ways. For Gere, the contexts that shape the use of language, writing, and literacy are part of a rich and complex story that may include struggle, trauma, and sadness as well as joy, excitement, and anger. Language is embodied and is expressive of the feelings and experiences of people no matter what their background. To engage language in this way is to engage a community and its history and culture. And in my own work, this attention to language and care for community has allowed me to understand what value exists in researching the literacy and rhetorical practices of Asian/Americans and to understand that the knowledge created here is knowledge that can apply more broadly and should not be reduced to the ethnic enclaves, borderlands, sub-disciplines, or area studies that often function intentionally or unintentionally to contain difference.

WRITING COMMUNITY

Gere's attention to community has been central to her scholarship. In her 1987 *Writing Groups: History, Theory, and Implications*, she presents an important introduction to the history of writing groups that provided a useful context for the collaborative learning and peer workshops that became central in composition instruction. Building on this work, her 1993 chair's address to the Conference on College Composition and Communication at its annual convention offered an innovative and complex theory for the work of composition both within and beyond academic settings. Based on this address, in "Kitchen Tables and Rented Rooms: The Extracurriculum of Composition," Gere acknowledges both a long history of writing in communities often ignored and the extracurricular sites where writing instruction and practice occurred because the communities were often denied or had limited access to formal education, or were engaged in writing to address exigencies that were often viewed as inappropriate subjects to take up, especially if addressing social or political issues. What Gere theorizes is a way to understand how writing is developed, whether in formal or informal settings, and driven by a need to write. As she describes:

> In contrast, my version of the extracurriculum includes the present as well as the past; it extends beyond the academy to encompass the multiple contexts in which persons seek to improve their own writing; it includes more diversity in gender, race, and class among writers; and it avoids, as much as possible, a reenactment of professionalization in its narrative. (80)

I find Gere's resistance to a "reenactment of professionalization," in particular, to be insightful and powerful since the professionalization narrative is often invoked to delegitimize writing that is not produced in formal settings under the instruction of experts. This is reminiscent of her work to change attitudes about language and to contextualize writing in order to acknowledge its purpose and presence. For Gere, the extracurricular "is constructed by desire, by the aspirations and imaginations of its participants" (80).

While this address to our primary scholarly organization of researchers and teachers of composition served as a call to the profession to broaden its understanding of what writing instruction looked like, where it took place, and who engaged in creating the curriculum and extracurriculum, I experienced her invocation in a different, perhaps more personal way. When Gere delivered this address, I was in my second year of graduate school at the University of Michigan where I was a doctoral student in the Joint Ph.D. Program in English and Education. I applied to the program on the recommendation of my advisor at the University of Hawai'i, Jeffrey Carroll, who had been Gere's student at the University of Washington. To be honest, I didn't know much about Gere's work. However, as an undergraduate writing tutor, steeped in Kenneth Bruffee's ideas about collaborative learning, and with an identified interest in rhetoric and writing already, I saw Michigan and Anne Ruggles Gere as an opportunity that I might only dream of. When I got to Michigan I took every class I could with Gere and became immersed in her thinking and research, including a seminar on gender and literacy and an interdisciplinary seminar on literacy co-taught by Gere, Deborah Keller-Cohen, and Walter Mignolo.

"Kitchen Tables and Rented Rooms" was an early articulation about the power of the extracurriculum and the places of writers and writing beyond academic institutions. Her 1997 book, *Intimate Practices: Literacy and Cultural Work in U.S. Women's Clubs, 1880–1920*, was a fuller argument for the relationship between gender and literacy as demonstrated in the range of women's groups who used their writing to make arguments in the public sphere. During this time, I started to see how the fragments of ideas I brought with me about people doing writing in Hawaiʻi might come together to make an argument for the intention and purpose of their writing in expressing identity, claiming belonging, and addressing injury.

Gere's theoretical framework for understanding the relationship between gender and literacy helped me to develop a framework to understand the history of literacy in Hawaiʻi and its enduring legacy in attitudes about language, the development of literary culture in Hawaiʻi, and a complex multilingual landscape. In *Intimate Practices*, Gere's historical work also provided a way for me to understand how literacy work was also cultural work and how this evolved under conditions of the late 19th century and early 20th century, when the US was undergoing enormous transformation through global expansion and rising immigration. This period also coincided with the rise of restrictive immigration policies that excluded immigration from Asia and barred naturalization of people who had lawfully immigrated from Asia before these restrictions were put in place.

What began as a very vague idea about language in Hawaiʻi became the basis for my dissertation, *Literacy, Legitimacy, and the Composing of Asian American Citizenship*, which examined literacy narratives as forms that do cultural work to create a sense of identity and belonging through acts of language, literacy, and writing. This dissertation became my monograph, *Minor Re/Visions: Asian American Literacy Narratives as a Rhetoric of Citizenship*, which expanded on the history of literacy in Hawaiʻi through the consideration of my own personal literacy history growing up under conditions that structured social relations through language, race, social class, a sense of place, and the dispossession experienced by the Indigenous people of Hawaiʻi by American settlers who then transformed the islands through immigration, capitalism, and U.S. nationalism.

While my own experience of literacy growing up did not include the trauma of earlier generations, the legacy of these policies still shaped attitudes about language and literacy. As I moved through school there were subtle messages in the curriculum to signal that we students were still being marked by language: a specially designed curriculum to address students' use of Hawai'i Creole English or the constant reminders to remediate our accented speech. But a high school English teacher chose to include a short story by a local writer that relied on dialogue in Hawai'i Creole English, or Pidgin as we all called it. Here the language of the community was made literary, and I saw for the first time that we could be writers in our own voices, we could tell stories that reflected our lives, and we could believe that our language did not limit what we could do or who we could become. This was a response to Hawai'i poet Eric Chock's impassioned question, "If there is no such thing as a Hawaii writer, how can you teach a Hawaii kid to write?" (8).

I also considered the literacy narratives of Asian/American writers who transformed commonplace references to physical difference (bodies), unintelligible gibberish or silence (language), alien status (citizenship), and unassimilability (identity) invoked to do damage upon Asian/Americans, into productive sites of rhetorical activity for Asian/Americans to make claims on their own terms. These narratives often created complex discussions about the relationship between literacy and identity, whether in *The Woman Warrior* by Maxine Hong Kingston, whose innovative memoir used story to unpack questions about gender, race, and generational trauma, or in *America Is in the Heart* by Carlos Bulosan, whose working-class narrative challenged the promises of the American Dream by revealing the difficult lives of migrant laborers.

While the influence of "Kitchen Tables and Rented Rooms" and *Intimate Practices* on my own work is undeniable, for providing theoretical frameworks to use in examining literacy and identity, I have begun to realize the broader influence of Gere's entire body of work even if much of it was unknown to me at the time. In remembering my training as a graduate student and reflecting on my scholarship, I can see more clearly how Gere's attention to language and its complexity, theorization of the social contexts for writing, and embrace in understanding the literacy and language practices of diverse communities on their own terms have created the contexts for my own education.

INTERSECTING IDENTITIES, COMPOSING A LIFE

I have recalled here the impact that Gere's scholarship has had on my own scholarly career, from the direct influence of taking graduate seminars at Michigan to reading the work that she created from the conversations and ideas that were shared in those classrooms to the direct mentorship and advising she provided whether in small gestures such as a birthday card or in the hard conversations about a difficult job market. But in all of these experiences, I perhaps best remember her as a writing teacher, as someone who demystified scholarly writing, saw potential and value in the turn toward narrative that often allowed me to express the ideas I was still trying to develop, and treated me as a peer.

While I had been fortunate enough to get a couple of pieces published early in my graduate career, I would hesitate to call them significant: an Instructor's Manual to a textbook, *The Active Reader: Composing in Reading and Writing*, written by Anne Ruggles Gere and Jeffrey Carroll (which was my first introduction to Gere), and an essay in a conference proceedings. When Gere offered to co-author an essay with any interested student for a collection of essays she was invited to contribute to, I jumped at the opportunity. The collection, *Critical Theory and the Teaching of Literature: Politics, Curriculum, Pedagogy*, was edited by James F. Slevin and Art Young and sought to reimagine what the teaching of literature might look like during a time when the nature of reading and the contexts for writing were undergoing a dramatic shift away from the text itself to the contexts under which texts were created. At the time, I was taking a seminar with her titled, "The Teaching of Literature, The Literature of Teaching," in which we read a variety of work including *Ceremony* by Leslie Marmon Silko and *Their Eyes Were Watching God* by Zora Neale Hurston. When we sat down to discuss ideas for the essay, I suggested we consider Silko's *Ceremony* and Hurston's *Their Eyes Were Watching God* along with *The Woman Warrior* by Maxine Hong Kingston. We soon settled on examining how these writers had been institutionalized through critical scholarship and became cultural institutions because of their positions as women of color writing during a time when representation of women of color in the literary canon was sparse.

These three writers provided an important opportunity to consider how identities intersect—in this case identities involving gender and race/indigeneity—and how these intersecting identities informed innovative narrative strategies. The work was exciting and gave us an opportunity to also consider the relationship between literature and composition, between texts and the composing of those texts. But what was most profound to me in this experience was writing alongside Gere. We were collaborating in a time before Google Docs or other platforms that would allow easy collaboration. We were literally sitting side by side reading drafts together and making decisions about the form of an argument, style, and other matters for revision. It was in this moment that I experienced what Gere had been researching, theorizing, and arguing in her work: that writing was a social experience, that writing is collaborative, and that writing is a dialogue that allows for the development and revision of ideas and arguments. It was also a moment of demystification, to understand that a revision might be as simple as making a different choice of word, or a rephrase of a sentence, or simply cutting something if it doesn't work. While these are practices that we all share with our students, such practices are easier said than done when the stakes feel high. In this case, I felt the pressure to produce, to not disappoint, and perhaps to not allow the anxiety of imposter syndrome to create paralysis. But this experience revealed to me that the stakes are not so high when we understand our purpose for writing, trust the process and our collaborator, and believe that what we have to say is important. Gere helped me to see all of these things in her generosity to write with me, to write alongside of me, and to share in a conversation that we both felt was necessary and important.

In this way, I was able to compose a professional life, to weave together a personal and cultural history of literacy, a critical awareness of the intersections of language, literacy, and identity, and a developing sense of myself as a writer. When I work with my own graduate students, I often ask them, "What is the story you want to tell through your research?" The research they pursue is often informed by stories that they have either heard or experienced in their own lives and that they begin to see in the lives of their communities and students. They have told stories about the use of rhetoric by people with disabilities, the creation of community writing groups for adult learners, the development of linguistic justice awareness by instructors, and the imagining of Nigerian national identity, among the many others that bring visibility to vulnerable people who have often felt that language, literacy, and writing were gatekeeping tools used against them but who then found that they could use language, literacy, and writing on their own terms to meet their own needs. This is what I have learned from the work of Anne Ruggles Gere and that I hope I have been able to do in my own work as a scholar, teacher, and writer.

WORKS CITED

Bulosan, Carlos. *America Is in the Heart: A Personal History.* 2nd ed., U of Washington P, 2014.

Chock, Eric. "On Local Literature." *The Best of Bamboo Ridge: The Hawaii Writers' Quarterly*, special issue of *The Hawaii Writers' Quarterly*, edited by Eric Chock and Darrell H. Y. Lum, no. 31–32, 1986, pp. 6–9. *University of Hawai'i System Repository*, hdl.handle.net/10790/6704.

Cushman, Ellen. *The Cherokee Syllabary: Writing the People's Perseverance.* U of Oklahoma P, 2011.

Enoch, Jessica. *Refiguring Rhetorical Education: Women Teaching African American, Native American, and Chicano/a Students, 1865–1911.* Southern Illinois UP, 2008.

Garcia, Romeo, and Damian Baca, editors. *Rhetorics Elsewhere and Otherwise: Contested Modernities, Decolonial Visions.* National Council of Teachers of English, 2019.

Gere, Anne Ruggles. *Intimate Practices: Literacy and Cultural Work in U.S. Women's Clubs, 1880–1920*. U of Illinois P, 1997.

———. "Kitchen Tables and Rented Rooms: The Extracurriculum of Composition." *College Composition and Communication*, vol. 45, no. 1, 1994, pp. 75–92, https://doi.org/10.58680/ccc19948799.

———. *West African Oratory and the Fiction of Chinua Achebe and T. M. Aluko*. 1974. University of Michigan, PhD dissertation. *Deep Blue Documents*, https://doi.org/10.7302/21103.

———. *Writing Groups: History, Theory, and Implications*. Southern Illinois UP, 1987.

Gere, Anne Ruggles, and Jeffrey Carroll. *The Active Reader: Composing in Reading and Writing*. Holt, Rinehart, and Wilson, 1990.

Gere, Anne Ruggles, and Eugene Smith. *Attitudes, Language, and Change*. National Council of Teachers of English, 1979. *ERIC*, eric.ed.gov/?id=ED176309.

Gere, Anne Ruggles, and Morris Young. "Cultural Institutions: Reading(s) (of) Zora Neale Hurston, Leslie Marmon Silko, and Maxine Hong Kingston." *Critical Theory and the Teaching of Literature: Politics, Curriculum, Pedagogy*, edited by James F. Slevin and Art Young, National Council of Teachers of English, 1996, pp. 153–71.

Gold, David. *Rhetoric at the Margins: Revising the History of Writing Instruction in American Colleges, 1873–1947*. Southern Illinois UP, 2008.

Gonzales, Laura, and Michelle Hall Kells, editors. *Latina Leadership: Language and Literacy Education across Communities*. Syracuse UP, 2022.

Guerra, Juan C. *Close to Home: Oral and Literate Practices in a Transnational Mexicano Community*. Teachers College P, 1998.

Hurston, Zora Neale. *Their Eyes Were Watching God: A Novel*. Perennial Library, 1990.

Kingston, Maxine Hong. *The Woman Warrior: Memoirs of a Girlhood among Ghosts*. Vintage Books, 1977.

Leonard, Rebecca Lorimer. *Writing on the Move: Migrant Women and the Value of Literacy*. U of Pittsburgh P, 2017.

Logan, Shirley Wilson. *We Are Coming: The Persuasive Discourse of Nineteenth-Century Black Women*. Southern Illinois UP, 1999.

Martinez, Aja Y. *Counterstory: The Rhetoric and Writing of Critical Race Theory*. National Council of Teachers of English, 2020.

Monberg, Terese Guinsatao, and Morris Young. "Beyond Representation: Spatial, Temporal and Embodied Trans/Formations of Asian/Asian American Rhetoric." *enculturation: a journal of rhetoric, writing, and culture*, no. 27, 2018, www.enculturation.net/beyond_representation.

Moss, Beverly J. *A Community Text Arises: A Literate Text and a Literacy Tradition in African-American Churches*. The WAC Clearinghouse, 2024, wac.colostate.edu/books/landmarks/arises/. Originally published by Hampton P, 2003.

Palumbo-Liu, David. *Asian/American: Historical Crossings of a Racial Frontier*. Stanford UP, 1999.

Royster, Jacqueline Jones. *Traces of a Stream: Literacy and Social Change among African American Women*. U of Pittsburgh P, 2000.

Silko, Leslie Marmon. *Ceremony*. Penguin Books, 1986.

"Students' Right to Their Own Language (with Bibliography)." *Conference on College Composition and Communication*, National Council of Teachers of English, 2024, cccc.ncte.org/cccc/resources/positions/srtolsummary. Originally published in *College Composition and Communication*, vol. 25, no. 3, 1974, pp. 1–18, https://doi.org/10.58680/ccc197417210.

Sumida, Stephen H. *And the View from the Shore: Literary Traditions of Hawai'i*. U of Washington P, 1991.

University of Hawai'i Style Guide. Office of the Vice President for External Affairs and University Relations, 2013, https://www.hawaii.edu/offices/eaur/styleguide-2013.pdf.

Vieira, Kate. *American By Paper: How Documents Matter in Immigrant Literacy*. U of Minnesota P, 2017. *Minnesota Scholarship Online*, https://doi.org/10.5749/minnesota/9780816697519.001.0001.

Villanueva, Victor. *Bootstraps: From an American Academic of Color*. National Council of Teachers of English, 1993. *ERIC*, eric.ed.gov/?id=ED362865.

Young, Morris. "Conflicting Communities, Collaborative Communities: Negotiating Authority in a Tutorial Group." *Academic Literacies in Multicultural Higher Education: Selected Essays*, edited by Thomas Hilgers, Marie Wunsch, and Virgie Chattergy, Center for the Studies of Multicultural Higher Education, University of Hawai'i at Mānoa, 1992, pp. 182–89.

———. Instructor's Guide to *The Active Reader: Composing in Reading and Writing*, by Anne Ruggles Gere and Jeffrey Carroll. Holt, 1990.

———. *Literacy, Legitimacy, and the Composing of Asian American Citizenship*. 1997. University of Michigan, PhD dissertation. *Deep Blue Documents*, hdl.handle.net/2027.42/130617.

———. *Minor Re/Visions: Asian American Literacy Narratives as a Rhetoric of Citizenship*. Southern Illinois UP, 2004.

PART 2. LEARNING FROM LANGUAGE AND LINGUISTICS

CHAPTER 5.

DAKOTA LANGUAGE, RHETORICAL SOVEREIGNTY, AND THE INEFFABLE INFLUENCE OF ANNE RUGGLES GERE ON ENGLISH STUDIES

Kel Sassi
Northern Michigan University

I first met Dr. Anne Ruggles Gere (hereafter referred to simply as "Anne") when she was reviewing the English program (a part of her career discussed in Chapter 16) at Eastern Washington University, where I was working as a consultant in the writing center. As she interviewed us about the work of the center, I mentioned that I was returning to Alaska to enroll in Teachers for Alaska (TFA). Anne said that her daughter, Cindy, would also be in TFA. This program, much like the Teachers for Tomorrow program described by Buehler in Chapter 18, was designed to foster culturally responsive pedagogy, specifically responsive to Alaska Native cultures. One of the program requirements was to complete a practicum in an Alaska Native village school. I didn't know it at the time, but this experience set me on a path that eventually led to studying pedagogical approaches to Native American literatures under Anne's direction in the Joint Program of English and Education (JPEE) at the University of Michigan (UM).

For the practicum, I was assigned to Tanacross Village with Cindy Gere, Anne's adopted Kaska Athabaskan daughter. I thought that we would drive to Tanacross, a village about two hundred miles from Fairbanks, and report to the principal at the school. Cindy had different ideas. She said we first needed to drive to a trading post to buy large spools of moose gut, work gloves, and other gifts for the people in the village. I remember Cindy was especially concerned with finding the right moose gut. She also had bundles of sage that she had picked and prepared herself. Once we arrived at the turnoff from the highway to get to the village, I pulled the car up to the school, thinking that now we would check in. Cindy said, "No, let's go for a walk." So, we started walking through the village, which consisted of some houses in the forest—no lawns, no landscaping. I could see moose meat drying on wooden structures behind the houses. This was not the suburban neighborhood of my own upbringing in Fairbanks.

Soon, children ran out to meet us and walk with us. They were curious about who we were, asking us questions. We talked with them and walked. Then one child steered us toward his house, and we met his mom. After a brief conversation, we continued on our way. Then more people invited us in. At that point, Cindy and I split up. I was invited to go for a walk with a woman a little older than myself.

On the walk, I got the sense of how different this village was from any small town I had ever visited. It was in the middle of the wilderness. There were no paved roads, sidewalks, or curbs. There was a forest of black spruce surrounding the village. It was fall, and I still recall the pungent smell of ripe, high bush cranberries under the stands of birch trees that were turning bright yellow in the brief period between the short growing season under the midnight sun and a long subarctic winter. As we walked farther away from the houses, I began to worry about bears, as I often did in Alaska, having come across so many unexpectedly in my hikes and mountain bike rides. I asked my companion if it was common to see bears here. She said, "We don't say the name of that animal when we are out like this," an important teaching, though I didn't fully realize it at the time.

When we got back to the village, we again saw Cindy, who had met some elders. They had invited us to the community center that evening. Only then would Cindy allow us to "check in" at the school, which we then did. Villages like Tanacross don't have hotels, so visitors sleep at the school. We stowed our sleeping bags in the principal's office and then went to the community center.

At this point, Cindy brought out the gifts and gave them to the elders. They then began to tell us stories. Maybe one of the elders had heard that I had asked about bears because I remember him telling us that in "story time" (which means back when people and animals could change natures), Bear and woman were married. So, he advised, if you ever encounter a bear, just rip open your shirt (he pantomimed ripping open his shirt) and show Bear that you are woman. He will remember that you were married, and he will leave you alone. I thought maybe he was joking with me, but I had read those Athabaskan stories about woman and Bear.

When I reflect back on that practicum, I remember vividly being a stranger, a white woman in a Native village, and not really knowing what to do. I imagine the reception I received would have been very different if I had not been traveling with Cindy. I trusted her advice on how to enter this place, and it made a difference. I think this story is a pivotal one in my life because it was the first time I set aside institutional requirements in favor of Indigenous imperatives. When later I would read Krista Ratcliffe's *Rhetorical Listening* about "standing under" (28) discourses for true understanding (and "hard listening," as Glenn and Adams describe in Chapter 21), I would have the Tanacross experience as a touchstone.

After the practicum in Tanacross and after six years of teaching English at the high school I had attended in Fairbanks, Alaska, a high school with about 14 percent Alaska Native students, I joined the 2003 JPEE cohort at the University of Michigan. I was surprised when the course Anne taught on literacy included reading *Wynema* by S. Alice Callahan, the first published novel (1891) by a woman of Native American descent. I would have expected a book like that to be offered only in a Native American literature course, but at that time, I did not know about Gere's interdisciplinary expertise. I did, however, know that Cindy had had a daughter, Denali, because Denali was born at a hospital in Fairbanks in between the time my two sons were born there. And I knew that Anne was adept at blending the personal and the professional, having published about her journey with Cindy in a book edited by my Alaska Native high school classmate Dr. Siobhan Wescott and University of Alaska professor Dr. Judith Kleinfeld. These attributes of Anne's work—interdisciplinarity and the blurring of boundaries—influenced my approach to becoming a researcher and scholar.

NATIVE LANGUAGE LEARNING

In addition to studying with Anne at UM, I had the opportunity to take an American Indian rhetorics course with Dr. Malea Powell (Miami, Shawnee) at Michigan State. Dr. Powell was a member of the Modern Language Association's committee on the literatures of people of color in the United States and Canada (CLPCUSC) when they prepared a "Statement on Native American Languages in the College and University Curriculum," which was approved in May of 2005 by the MLA executive council, of which Anne Gere was a member. As cited in the statement, the Committee drew on "the Native American Languages Act (Public Law 101–477, Title I), dated October 30, 1990" in making its recommendations (226). The statement calls for the following:

> Whenever possible, institutions of higher education should work with Native American language communities and with Native American educational and governing bodies to implement these recommendations.
>
> 1. To grant credit for the study of Native American languages when undertaken to fulfill undergraduate and graduate requirements in foreign languages.
> 2. To include, where appropriate, Native American languages in the curriculum in the same manner as foreign languages and to grant proficiency in Native American languages the same full academic credit as proficiency in

foreign languages. Institutions of higher education are particularly encouraged to teach the languages of Native American nations in their regions, whenever possible.

3. To encourage research to create and update dictionaries, grammars, orthographies, curricula, and other materials to support the teaching of Native American languages. The preparation of these materials is especially important for languages for which they have never been developed. (227)

In 2006 the CLPCUSC endorsed the "Statement on Indigenous Languages of the World" by the MLA ad hoc committee on Native American Languages, which reads:

> Throughout the world, many Indigenous languages have been so depleted that their survival is now in a critical state. . . . Preserving and revitalizing Indigenous languages must be central. . . . [I]nstitutions should, whenever possible, support the study of and research in Indigenous languages and literatures worldwide and devise means for native speakers of Indigenous languages to fulfill foreign language requirements with their Indigenous languages. (Modern Language Association, "Statement on Indigenous Languages")

The MLA statements were useful to me as a new assistant professor at North Dakota State University (NDSU) when I collaborated with others in the College of Arts, Humanities, and Social Sciences on a Dakota Initiative, which brought Dr. Clifford Canku, a Native speaker of Dakota, to our department starting in the fall of 2009 for the purpose of teaching Dakota literature, history, and culture and also to serve as a role model and mentor to Native students on our campus. Dr. Canku said there were only three hundred speakers of Dakota on his reservation—the Lake Traverse reservation of the Sisseton Wahpeton Oyate.

We created a faculty position for Dr. Canku to teach the Dakota language with commitments of support from various departments—history, sociology, and anthropology; modern languages; and English. The NDSU press release led with the precarity of the language as the main impetus for the position:

> Linguists worldwide are trying to save languages, and nowhere are they dying more quickly than in North America. With 25,000 speakers on 15 U.S. and Canadian reservations, Dakota is considered an "unsafe" language in terms of

longevity. "[Languages] are dying here," said Bruce Maylath, professor of English. "That's what we are trying to avoid happening to Dakota." ("Dakota Studies Courses")

Although the courses taught by the Dakota professor would have course numbers from history and modern languages, we hosted his office in our department—a physical reminder, in addition to the statements by our professional organizations, to make space in English studies for Indigenous languages.

As someone married to an Italian citizen, with whom I have been a partner in raising bilingual children, I felt an obligation to learn the Italian language, and to use it. I thought about our family's move to North Dakota, the land where Dakota people have lived for millennia. Shouldn't I—out of respect for this land and its people—learn Dakota as well?

I decided to enroll in Dr. Canku's beginning course in the Dakota language. One of the more senior faculty members in my department warned me that members of the promotion and tenure committee might look askance at my taking a class when I should be doing my research, so I thought about my reasons for doing so. For one, if I were working at a university in another country, I most certainly would have learned, or be actively working to learn, the language spoken by the people of that place. Here I was, at North **Dakota** State University, and for the first time the language for which the university was named was being taught. To me, it seemed like a matter of basic respect to the Indigenous people to learn something of the language spoken on their land. Sometimes exhibiting respect is more important than institutional expectations, to go back to my experience with Cindy Gere in Tanacross Village.

Another reason had to do with my research interests in studying how Native American literatures are taught. With so much damage caused by non-Native researchers who have worked with Native people in the past, we non-Native people cannot just barge in and start researching. As Devon Abbott Mihesuah (Choctaw) writes, "For decades anthropologists and other writers have treated Natives as second-class citizens" (76–77). When Dr. Mihesuah was at Northern Arizona University, she chaired a committee of scholars charged with "researching the problems of knowledge appropriation and ethical transgressions when researching and writing about Indians" (75). Her book, *So You Want to Write about American Indians?*, provides a lot of important information, including ethical guidelines in Chapter 6.

In addition to guidelines, I believe, as a non-Native person, that it is best to wait and see if we are invited to work with a Native community. If invited, it is important to behave as a respectful guest, listening and taking care to learn what questions the community wants to ask and collaborating with the community to design research that answers their questions. Furthermore, the results of the research should reside with the people studied. Reciprocity and respect should be at the core of whatever project emerges. Something that makes this work easier today is the presence of tribally controlled Institutional Research Boards (IRB) that spell out additional requirements for how research is to be conducted and also review research proposals themselves. Many of Dr. Mihesuah's guidelines have been incorporated into tribal research protocols.

While waiting for an invitation that might or might not come, I attended Dakota class, reflecting on my previous experiences with studying language. I had studied Spanish from middle school through a minor in college, and Spanish was the language exam I took for entering my doctoral program. From past experiences with studying Spanish, French, and Italian, I expected to work on vocabulary acquisition, learn verb conjugations, actively repeat what the teacher has said or speak with classmates, and learn grammar.

Dakota class started out very differently.

First, the class was mainly in English. It soon became clear why—Dr. Canku wanted us to first understand some essential information about Dakota culture along with learning the language, teachings that continued throughout the course. This made sense; after all, culture is transmitted through language.

In the textbook used for the course, Nicolette Knudson et al. write in the foreword, "We'd like to stress, that the culture of the Dakota people is not captured in this workbook" (ix), which could be another reason why Dr. Canku emphasized culture in class. Even though the foreword makes this statement, the very first chapter of the book doesn't start with basic greetings and vocabulary, like the first chapter of my Spanish textbook. Instead, it covers "The Great Sioux Nation," "Early European Contact," "Treaties and Government Policy," "Modern Accomplishments," and "Resources." Some advice given in this last section: "Remember! There are many myths and untruths about the Dakota and Native Americans in general. Always question the source, use your own judgement, and, if possible, verify the information with an elder" (6).

Dr. Canku told us about the Oceti Sakowin (Seven Council Fires) of the Dakota, the names of each group, and where their lands are. He also shared his land values in class: "We have a sacred relation with the land, Mother Earth; it is a living entity that we have to take care of." This value was shared multiple times throughout the class, whether through stories or advice given. For example, Dr. Canku told us that when you die, your relatives call out to you by your tribal name and your spirit flies away to be with them. He said when you come to the Milky Way, an old woman asks, "What did you do down there?" He told us the answer is you learned that everything is your relative, a belief encapsulated in the phrase Mitakuye Owasin—we are all related. He clarified that the Dakota have a relationship with everything—including Wakan Tanka, the Great Spirit—but don't worship anything. This word, "wakan," meaning sacred or divine, came up again and again. The land is sacred, and it has a healing power, Dr. Canku told us, saying that when he has a headache, he doesn't take an aspirin; he takes a walk in nature. The land and everything around us are also a source of knowledge, he emphasized during a class lecture: "We humans—we were created last, so we are supposed to learn from everything that came before us."

Dr. Canku also talked about how language means something different to him than it does to most others. He explained how when Dakota warriors came back to the village after fighting, the community would bring them into the inipi, the sweat lodge. It was where they got to talk to Wakan Tanka and get anything off their chests that they needed to so they wouldn't suffer in the future. Whatever is said in the inipi is not repeated outside because it belongs to God. Dr. Canku emphasized that "language is alive" and also that "we look at language as a creative force." He also said, "Every language has its own spirit, and you have to respect that." He said when you go to a wacipi (pow-wow), don't pay attention to what people look like, the way their hair is done; instead, pay attention to the language you hear because, "To us, language is a living entity that is very, very sacred."

My point here, in talking about the experience of studying the Dakota language, is that there was much more being taught than just vocabulary and grammar. The stories and teachings from Dr. Canku were communicating to me a different epistemological view of the world. This view is reflected even in the syntax of a Dakota sentence. The sentence, "I have a dog" is said this way in Dakota:

Sunka wan bduhe.

Sunka means dog; wan is the article, and bduhe means I have. Dr. Canku explained that the reason the sentence starts with dog is that Dakota people value life first, *all* forms of life. Possession is not as important for Dakota people as it is for white people, so the sentence doesn't start with "I have." He likened the Dakota sentence to a flight of stairs going down, with the most important things at the beginning of the sentence and the least important at the end.

Other early lessons had to do with how the language is different for men and women. For example, a simple thank you for a man is Pidamayaye-do and for a woman it is Pidamayaye-ye. The different endings—do and ye—mean the same thing: "it is said" or "it is so." Dr. Canku stated that men and women are equal in Dakota culture, but they have different roles in society. The importance of this was emphasized when Dr. Canku gave me a handout, "The Five Stages of Becoming a Dakota Man or Woman." Diane Wilson, who is a Dakota descendant, writes about this lesson in her book (86–87). In the chapter about Dr. Canku, Wilson shares how teaching about these roles helps Dakota people heal from the trauma they have experienced. Mona Susan Power, in *A Council of Dolls*, also emphasizes the healing power of her Dakota language.

When I reflect on the Dakota class, I realize that—in addition to learning some language—I was learning about the importance of being an ally. Everything—our country's violent history of settler colonization, the genocidal practice of assimilation carried out in over 500 boarding schools around the country, as well as resilience and survival, even healing, and more—is carried in the language. I took another Dakota language class, and this time a non-Native professor from the history department joined in. In later years, he and I would advise and serve on committees for many Native graduate students. I believe Dakota language class helped us to support these students.

SUPPORTING RHETORICAL SOVEREIGNTY IN WRITING ASSESSMENT

The value of studying Dakota also helped me when I was invited by Karen Comeau to work with teachers at Sitting Bull College on the Standing Rock Reservation and at the reservation middle school and high school on writing assessment. The Lakota language is dominant at Standing Rock, but the languages—some say dialects—are similar.

As I was working with the teachers, most of whom were non-Native, one of the principal concerns they had was that students did poorly on writing assessments, like the COMPASS test. I noticed this focus on standardized assessments had led to some deficit thinking about the writing abilities of the Native students, so I was trying to shift the discussion to assets. One day I had an opportunity to use the structure of a Dakota sentence to make this shift. Once teachers could see that what they assumed was an entrenched "error" in student writing was actually a marker of Dakota language structure, they were able to focus on teaching strategies for code-switching instead of "fixing the errors" in the student writing.

Out of respect for Sitting Bull College, we first published the results of our writing assessment in *Tribal College Journal* because that is where they wanted the work to be seen (Sassi et al.). Unfortunately for me as an untenured professor, this was not a peer-reviewed publication at the time. Later, I was able to publish a book chapter about the work with Mya Poe, Asao Inoue, and Norbert Elliott as editors and mentors for my work. This allowed me the space to explore the data in more detail and in relation to the concept of rhetorical sovereignty. Scott Richard Lyons (Leech Lake Ojibwe) conceptualizes rhetorical sovereignty as "the inherent right and ability of peoples to determine their own communicative needs and desires in this pursuit, to decide for themselves the goals, modes, styles, and languages of public discourse" (449–50). Rhetorical sovereignty, I argue, also extends to the right to determine how writing is assessed (Sassi, "Bending"). Shortly after we did this study, Sitting Bull College stopped using the COMPASS test as a measure of student writing and later the test itself was discontinued.

LANGUAGES AND LITERATURE

Another reason to learn Native languages is that Indigenous authors are using more and more of their Native languages in their books. For example, in Louise Erdrich's *The Night Watchman*, based on her grandfather's work to prevent termination of the Turtle Mountain Band of Chippewa, the final scene is of Zhanaat tapping birch trees as Patrice returns home. They drink the tonic of birch sap together, and the last line is "Ambe be-izhaan omaa akiing miinawa" (439). There is no translation of this line (or others in the book) and there is no glossary of Ojibwe words, so the expectation is that the reader knows some Ojibwe and/or is willing to learn. When Erdrich won the Aspen Award for this book, she said, "So, this particular award will also go to assist in the revitalization of the Ojibwe language" (Travers).

We non-Native people, especially those of us teaching English language arts, which is a *second* language on this continent, are starting with an understanding gap (Sassi, *Rhetorics*) due to our history of (and continued complicity in) settler colonization. We have to bridge that gap by learning about our settler colonizer history, and that begins with understanding differences in world views (Cull et al.). Language holds these views and cultural values. What if doctoral programs required an exam on the language traditionally spoken on the land the institution occupies? What if all scholars could freely move across boundaries and connect the personal and the professional, as Anne Gere has so courageously done? The forces of colonization—often invisible and seemingly benign (my urge to report to the principal's office in the village of Tanacross, for example) have trapped us in a scholarly world that has yet to reach the potential of rigor, wholeness, and vitality that we need. Anne Gere, her daughter, Cindy, and her granddaughter, Denali, have ineffably influenced my scholarly journey and pursuit of these questions.

WORKS CITED

Callahan S. Alice. *Wynema: A Child of the Forest*. Edited and with an introduction by A. LaVonne Brown Ruoff, U of Nebraska P, 1997. Originally published by H. J. Smith and Company, 1891.

Cull, Ian, et al. *Pulling Together: A Guide for Front-Line Staff, Student Services, and Advisors*. BCcampus, 2018, opentextbc.ca/indigenizationfrontlineworkers/.

"Dakota Studies Courses Offered." *North Dakota State University*, 28 Aug. 2009, www.ndsu.edu/news/view/detail/4502.

Erdrich, Louise. *The Night Watchman*. Harper Collins, 2020.

Gere, Anne Ruggles. "Cindy's Story." *Fantastic Antone Succeeds!: Experiences in Educating Children with Fetal Alcohol Syndrome*, edited by Judith Kleinfeld and Siobhan Wescott. U of Alaska P, 1993, pp. 55–68.

Knudson, Nicolette, et al. *Tokaheya Dakota Iapi Kin: Beginning Dakota*. Minnesota Historical Society P, 2010.

Lyons, Scott R. "Rhetorical Sovereignty: What Do American Indians Want from Writing?" *College Composition and Communication*, vol. 51, no. 3, 2000, pp. 447–68, https://doi.org/10.58680/ccc20001387.

Mihesuah, Devon Abbott. *So You Want to Write about American Indians?: A Guide for Writers, Students, and Scholars*. U of Nebraska P, 2005.

Modern Language Association Committee on the Literatures of People of Color in the United States and Canada. "Statement on Indigenous Languages of the World." *Modern Language Association*, 23–24 Feb. 2007, https://tinyurl.com/v7u745db.

———. "Statement on Native American Languages in the College and University Curriculum." *Profession*, 2005, pp. 226–27, https://tinyurl.com/mz6u9283.

Power, Mona Susan. *A Council of Dolls*. Mariner Books, 2023.

Ratcliffe, Krista. *Rhetorical Listening: Identification, Gender, Whiteness*. Southern Illinois UP, 2005.

Sassi, Kelly J. "Bending the Arc of Writing Assessment Toward Social Justice: Enacting Culturally Responsive Professional Development at Standing Rock." *Writing Assessment, Social Justice, and the Advancement of Opportunity*, edited by Mya Poe et al. The WAC Clearinghouse / UP of Colorado, 2018, pp. 319–54, https://doi.org/10.37514/PER-B.2018.0155.2.10.

———. *Rhetorics of Authority, Space, Friendship, and Race: A Qualitative Study of the Culturally Responsive Teaching of Native American Literatures*. 2008. University of Michigan, PhD dissertation. *Deep Blue Documents*, hdl.handle.net/2027.42/60712.

Sassi, Kelly, et al. "Improving Student Assessment." *Tribal College Journal*, vol. 24, no. 3, 2013, pp. 24–25, tribalcollegejournal.org/improving-student-assessment/.

Travers, Andrew. "Louise Erdrich's 'The Night Watchman' Wins Aspen Words Literary Award." *Aspen Times*, 22 Apr. 2021, https://tinyurl.com/5n8dpep4.

Wilson, Diane. *Beloved Child: A Dakota Way of Life*. Minnesota Historical Society P, 2011.

CHAPTER 6.

LANGUAGE KNOWLEDGE AND LINGUISTIC JUSTICE

Laura Aull
University of Michigan

Here's the good news: U.S. writing studies has long held commitments to inclusion and justice. Composition courses have been described as "institutional and professional responses to challenged standards . . . by writers who were said to be unprepared" (Bartholomae 11). A specific focus on linguistic justice has been visible at least since the Conference on College Composition and Communication 1974 adoption of "Students' Right to Their Own Language" (SRTOL). Subsequent efforts, including "This Ain't Another Statement! This is a DEMAND for Black Linguistic Justice!"[1] and writing research on language ideologies (Davila; Milu; Pattanayak 82–83), translingual writing (Horner et al.), communal justicing (Gere et al., "Communal Justicing"), and Critical Language Awareness (CLA) (Alim; Shapiro), raise awareness about linguistic injustice and illustrate alternatives.

There's bad news, too. We are far from linguistic justice in writing classrooms. Linguistic miseducation continues, focused on prescriptive rules instead of how language works (Smitherman, "Raciolinguistics"). Standardized English is still often treated as inherently correct or singularly necessary (Richardson). Nonstandardized usage is often treated as error, even as research suggests student success doesn't depend on standardized mechanical correctness as much as instructors think (Crossley et al.; Freedman; Matsuda). And many instructors who believe in linguistic diversity still end up perpetuating language hierarchies because they fear not doing so will be a disservice to students (Weaver 14).

We are still, in other words, living in a language regulation paradigm, characterized by a lot of language discrimination but very little language knowledge.

The decades-long divide between linguistic theory and writing pedagogy hasn't helped. The SRTOL statement was "solidly grounded" in linguistics but ultimately "fell short in terms of linking language theory to teaching practice" (Smitherman, "Raciolinguistics" 10). Since then, writing studies has suffered

---

1   The statement can be accessed at https://cccc.ncte.org/cccc/demand-for-black-linguistic-justice.

"the dismissal of various insights from language studies" (Matsuda 150) and decades of the "erasure of language" (Connors; MacDonald). Historically, writing studies has attended to language itself *or* to language ideologies, but not both together (Aull, "Attention to Language"). In turn, writing studies scholarship suggests that linguistic training is necessary to disrupt "the inertia of the discipline's discriminatory pasts" (Gere et al., "Communal Justicing" 391; Shapiro).

Put another way: we need language knowledge to advance linguistic justice. We need awareness of how language works in systematic (rule-governed) ways at the level of lexis, grammar, and paragraphs to advance linguistic justice, a mission for writing education in which language variation is valued and viewed with equity and language users are empowered with rhetorical agency, or the ability to understand and make informed language choices in diverse situations. We need the former to achieve the latter; otherwise, widespread linguistic miseducation and erasure of language and language knowledge will continue to work against even our most well-intentioned efforts.

We already have clear illustrations of how language knowledge supports linguistic justice. For example, Geneva Smitherman outlines Black English discourse and syntax patterns on the 1988–1989 NAEP exams to debunk the notion that that Black English features were rhetorically ineffective ("'The Blacker the Berry'"). Anne Curzan traces usage change and the rule-governed nature of nonstandardized usage to make a case for questioning the rules of grammar and who makes them. Staci Perryman-Clark shows how knowledge of phonological and syntactical features of African American English helps students analyze genres and achieve rhetorical goals. April Baker-Bell discusses syntax, semantics, and phonology of Black Language with students as part of challenging anti-Black racism in the classroom. Gere et al. briefly note four facts about language variation in support of communal justicing ("Communal Justicing").

In a similar vein, this study makes a case for analyzing language patterns as part of demonstrating linguistic equality and supporting rhetorical agency, and it draws from open access data in Gere's *Developing Writers in Higher Education* to do so. First, I show evidence of common misconceptions about written English. Then, I analyze move patterns in published and student writing to illustrate how we can counter misconceptions with language knowledge.

In this way, the study builds on and extends work done by Anne Ruggles Gere in order to show how language knowledge helps us learn more, and judge less, in encounters with written English. The study illustrates how students' and instructors' knowledge of linguistic patterns can expand our conscious understanding of written genres (Gere et al., "Local Assessment" 624–25) and support more just approaches to language variation (Gere et al., "Communal Justicing").

THE MOTIVATION, PART 1: MISCONCEPTIONS ABOUT WRITING

Many instructors have "impressionistic," rather than concrete or systematic, ideas about writing and grammar (Duncan and Vanguri xiii), such as "know[ing] a good essay when [they] see it" (Lea and Street 40). Impressionistic ideas coexist with more precisely false ideas about writing, which circulate in public understandings held by teachers, students, parents, administrators, and lawmakers (Ball and Loewe). Unfortunately, vague and discriminatory ideas about English usage and writing have a long history in policies, tests, and college admissions, which refer to *writing* as prescriptively correct or not, rather than according to what is grammatically possible and meaningful in English (Aull, *You Can't Write That*).

In their *Developing Writers in Higher Education* study, Gere and her colleagues show that undergraduate students internalize these misconceptions. The study includes interviews with over 150 University of Michigan undergraduates about their writing, and the interview transcripts are freely accessible.[2] I was thus able to download all interview transcripts and identify and read every reference to the word "grammar," all of which showed one or both of the following themes:

1. Grammar is something students do not feel they know, but they want to know; and/or
2. Grammar is simple—referring only to conventions, or to prescriptive rules.

In other words, many references to grammar showed that students were eager for more language knowledge. Many also pointed to what Smitherman calls "linguistic miseducation," or when "teachers be obsessed wit teaching 'correct' grammar, spelling and pronunciation rather than teaching students what language is and allows human beings to do" ("Raciolinguistics" 6).

Theme 1: Grammar Is Something Students Don't Know, but Want to Know

Most students who referred to *grammar* described lacking explicit language knowledge, even if they felt they were proficient writers. Tellingly, one student described that learning English grammar would occur through self-study—not something they would be taught in English or writing class. The student therefore said they wouldn't study English grammar, despite that they would "love" it:

---

2 The interview transcripts are available under the "Resources" heading at https://doi.org/10.3998/mpub.10079890.

"I don't know if it's so much important for me to know exactly how everything is written and the grammar to it . . . —if I had enough time, I would love to do so. I don't have enough motivation to self-teach myself or go through and independently study English."[3]

Another student described an experience in the business school that highlighted their lack of conscious language knowledge: "I remember there was a checklist that asked, 'Oh, are you bad with pronouns or adjectives or syntax?' I was like, 'Uh, I'm not even sure what half of this really means, exactly.'"[4]

This theme, grammar as something students did not know but wanted to know, also came up in answer to the following interview question: *If you could tell your teachers one thing about writing or how to teach writing better, what would you tell them?* One student replied that "grammar usage" was "really important," especially for introductory courses.[5] Another noted that even seemingly "repetitive" grammar instruction "can sometimes be really helpful."[6]

THEME 2: GRAMMAR IS SIMPLIFIED OR NARROWLY UNDERSTOOD

Several interviews reflected limited conceptions of grammar, as: (a) conventions, such as punctuation; (b) "simple" or "little"; and/or (c) narrowly correct or incorrect. For example, the following interview response illustrated (a) and (b): "We also did, I remember with each class, we had some sort of grammar lesson. I think one of the one's we spent the most time on was the colon and the semicolon. Yeah, I think just little things of tweaking writing."[7]

Describing English language learning in their family, another student suggested their own grammar learning focused on (c). The student noted, "One of my [relatives], he's learning English right now. I was teaching him. I was like, 'I can only tell you what's right or wrong. I can't actually describe it to you.' He was like, 'The adjective goes here, then it's the pronoun.' He was listing all these—I was like, 'That's not how I learned my language.'"[8] In this case, we can see both themes: a lack of explicit grammar knowledge, and an understanding of English writing as narrowly right or wrong, regardless of context or use. Another student described a similar experience: "They didn't really teach writing . . . but they taught you how—when writing was incorrect, I guess."[9]

---

3   *Developing Writers* Interview 06W13C2ExitEdited.
4   Interview 11W13C3ExitEdited.
5   Interview 01F11C2EntryEdited.
6   Interview 01F11C2ExitEdited.
7   Interview 01F11C2EntryEdited.
8   Interview 11W13C3ExitEdited.
9   Interview 06W13C2ExitEdited.

In answer to the question *If you could tell your teachers one thing about writing or how to teach writing better, what would you tell them?*, another student evoked misconceptions (a) and (c): "I'm big on grammar, so make sure you use the proper grammar, word choices, stuff like that."[10] In answer to the same question, another student emphasized misconception (b), noting, "I know some students do struggle with grammar and simple things like that."[11] A related misconception separates grammar from structure and ideas, as though grammar has only to do with more superficial choices. A representative interview statement was: "I found that the best classes that I had were where they said, 'We want none of your comments to be about grammar. We want them all to be about structure and the flow of ideas.'"[12]

But what if the structure and flow of ideas were clearly connected to grammar, and this kind of language knowledge could help us understand more and discriminate less? In the remainder of this essay, I want to show how rhetorical introductory moves and associated linguistic cues can be analyzed in diverse writing—and how analyzing them can help us demonstrate linguistic equality and support rhetorical agency.

THE MOTIVATION, PART 2: EXPLAINING MOVES AND WHY THEY MATTER

Explaining Introductory Moves

John Swales investigated introductory rhetorical moves in academic research articles, and Gere and colleagues analyzed them in early college student writing ("Local Assessment"). As described in *Genre Analysis*, the first move focuses on "establishing a territory," or introducing a topic, whether that be a phenomenon, an existing view, or an area of research (141). For instance, at the start of this essay, I opened with the "good news"—the commitment to inclusion and justice in U.S. writing studies—and cited examples of this research territory.

Swales' second move focuses on establishing a gap or "niche" in the territory noted in the first move, by noting a lingering question, an absence, or a further explanation (141). For example, in this piece, my second opening move introduces the "bad news": the relative lack of attention to language itself in calls for linguistic justice in writing studies.

Swales' third move focuses on "occupying the niche," by, e.g., offering a new proposal or otherwise clarifying what the unfolding piece of writing will offer as

---

10 Interview 01F11MEntryEdited.
11 Interview 01F11MExitEdited.
12 Interview 36F12MExitEdited.

a response to the niche noted in the second move (141). In my own essay here, I indicated what this piece of writing aims to do: offer an example of language knowledge in support of linguistic justice. Gere et al.'s analysis of first-year writing found similar introductory moves tailored to the constructed response task in a student placement process (Gere et al., "Local Assessment").

WHY MOVES MATTER

By moving from more general, known territory to a more specific, unknown niche and contribution, introductory moves display writer knowledge and ease readers' cognitive burden. The linguistic cues associated with each move further support writer and reader knowledge, in that they display how sentences relate to one another.

This clarifying value of move patterns helps explain why readers respond positively to them. Research on published academic writing shows that moves are regularly used by writers regardless of discipline (Knight et al.; Suntara and Usaha; Tankó). Studies of student writing show that rhetorical moves correlate to highly-evaluated writing (Aull, *How Students Write*; Gere et al., "Local Assessment"; Swales; Tedick and Mathison). In their "Local Assessment" study, Gere et al. describe introductory moves and cues as meso- and micro-level ways to "define what 'college writing' means in a specific context" (613). In turn, this same knowledge can help us question why these patterns are prevalent, as part of communal justicing that questions conventional writing practices (Gere et al., "Communal Justicing" 395).

In this short chapter, I show how even in a few texts, identifying language patterns can advance linguistic justice in two overlapping ways. One way is that it refuses impressionistic talk about writing by noting what writers actually do with grammar and lexis, not just what people *think* writers do. A second way is that it offers counter training to linguistic miseducation by supporting the practice of descriptive analysis of similarities and differences across diverse writing.

ANALYZING MOVES IN SUPPORT OF LINGUISTIC JUSTICE

As I do in first-year writing courses, I'll start by analyzing Vershawn Ashanti Young's "Should Writers Use They Own English?" This piece does double-duty in my classes—we read it like readers and like writers. As readers, we can learn about linguistic miseducation and its ideological manifestation, the shaming of language variation. As writers, we can analyze Young's cohesive introductory moves and rule-governed lexico-grammatical patterns. Below, I've excerpted parts of the piece for the sake of brevity, and I've labeled the moves where they begin and bolded phrase-level features that help signal the moves.

Move Analysis 1: Young, "Should Writers Use They Own English?"

[Move 1: The territory] Cultural critic Stanley Fish (2009d) **come talkin bout**—in his three-piece *New York Times* **"What Should Colleges Teach?"** suit—there only one way to speak and write to get ahead in the world, that writin teachers should "clear [they] mind of the orthodoxies that have taken hold in the composition world." **He say** don't no student have a right to they own language if that language make them "vulnerable to prejudice"; that "it may be true that the standard language is a device for protecting the status quo, but that very truth is a reason for teaching it to students." (61; alteration in source)

[Move 2: The niche] Lord, lord, lord! **Where do I begin**, cuz this man sho tryin **to take the nation back** to a time when we were less tolerant of linguistic and racial differences. Yeah, I said racial difference, tho my man Stan try to dismiss race when he speak on language differences. **But** the two be sho nuff intertwined . . . And Fish himself acquiesce to this linguistic prejudice when he come sayin that people make theyselves targets for racism if and when they don't write and speak like he do. **But don't nobody's** language, dialect, or style make them 'vulnerable to prejudice.' . . . (61–62)

[Move 3: Occupying the niche] **To me**, what make these "markings," i.e., "standard" and "dialect," problematic, even though I use the designations myself, is that what we call standard English is part of a common language system that include Black English and any other so-called variety of English. **I'm sho not trying to say here** that Black English don't have some rhetorical and grammatical features that differ from what is termed standard English. **What I'm sayin is** that the difference between the two ain't as big as some like to imagine. . . . (62–63)

In his first move, Young introduces his territory: Stanley Fish's "What Should Colleges Teach?" As part of this first move, Young summarizes Fish's argument—that "don't no student have a right to they own language if that language make them 'vulnerable to prejudice (61).'" Using the linguistic cues "come talkin bout" and "he say" along with the name of Fish's article (61), Young orients the reader to an existing view, which they might have read before.

Young's second paragraph introduces his second move, identifying the gap in Fish's view, which is that it supports linguistic prejudice. Young uses linguistic cues to highlight that there is a problem, including "Where do I begin"; "take the nation back"; "But" and "But don't nobody's" (61–62). With these countering and negation signals and his explanation, Young uses his second move to lay out the problem in the view identified in the first move, before continuing on to the third move.

I see Young most explicitly begin his third move on the second page of the piece. There, his linguistic cue "To me . . ." shows a departure between Fish's view and his own (62). He further clarifies his stance with the help of not-this/but-this micro moves: "I'm sho not tryin to say here" and "What I'm sayin is" (63).

With these introductory moves, Young provides a good example of how writers can go from introducing an existing view, to noting a problem with it, to addressing the problem, in that order. To do so, the writer has to identify a general entry point, a specific lingering or concerning idea within that topic, and a particular contribution the writer will make. This writing knowledge, in turn, leads the reader step-wise from what might be more familiar information to newer information.

Along with these common informational writing moves, Young's piece illustrates other systematic patterns in English: grammatical patterns common across varieties of written English, including subject-verb-object order—e.g., "He say don't no student . . ." (61), sentences made of one or more independent clause and one or more dependent clause, and morphemes like the -s to make nouns plural—e.g., "teachers" (61). And he uses lexico-grammatical patterns common in the dialect referred to as Black English, like double negation—e.g., "don't no student have" (61), the contraction "ain't" (63), third person singular zero—e.g., "he say" (61), and g-dropping—e.g., "talkin" (61).

Move Analysis 2: Fish, "What Should Colleges Teach?"

Fish's own piece, to which Young responds, is similarly patterned; it too includes the three introductory moves, linguistic cues to signal the moves, and rule-governed lexico-grammatical choices.

> [Move 1: The territory] **A few years ago,** when I was grading papers for a graduate literature course, **I became alarmed** at the inability of my students to write a clean English sentence. They could manage for about six words and then, almost invariably, the syntax (and everything else) fell apart.

I became even more alarmed when I remembered that these same students were instructors in the college's composition program.

[Move 2: The gap] What, I wondered, could possibly be going on in their courses?

I decided to find out, and asked to see the lesson plans of the 104 sections. I read them and found **that only four** emphasized training in the craft of writing. . . .

[Move 3: Occupying the niche] As I learned more about the world of composition studies, **I came to the conclusion** that unless writing courses focus exclusively on writing they are **a sham**, and I advised administrators **to insist** that all courses listed as courses in composition teach grammar and rhetoric and **nothing else**.

Fish uses his first move to introduce the territory—"the inability of my students to write a clean English sentence"—with linguistic cues to signal the move—e.g., "a few years ago," "I became alarmed," and "even more alarmed." His second move notes a problem—that students aren't being taught "the craft of writing" in composition courses—with cues that signal a perplexing problem—e.g., "What . . . could possibly be going on," and "only." Finally, in his third move, Fish notes what he will contribute, his "insist[ence] that all courses listed as courses in composition teach grammar and rhetoric and nothing else."

Also like Young, Fish uses grammatical patterns common across varieties of written English, including subject-verb-object order—e.g., "I became alarmed . . .," sentences made of one or more clauses with subjects and verbs, and morphemes like the -s to make nouns plural—e.g., "teachers." Fish likewise uses systematic lexico-grammatical features of English, from a dialect referred to as standardized English, including single negation—e.g., "was not their focus," the contraction "aren't," third person singular -s—e.g., "one argument says," and undropped -g—e.g., "training."

Finally, to apply this same attention to student and STEM writing, we'll look to Gere's *Developing Writers* to analyze a student introduction from an upper-division mathematics course.

MOVE ANALYSIS 3: CELESTE, WRITING SAMPLE 4, "LONG-TERM CARE INSURANCE FOR ALL ACTIVE EMPLOYEES"

[Move 1: Establishing the territory] Long-term care (LTC) insurance provides protection against the inability to finance costs for long-term care which, according to the Society of Actuaries (2012), is "the overall term for care provided to an incapacitated person over a prolonged period." Such care **encompasses** care provided to individuals who cannot perform activities of daily living (ADLs) **such as** dressing, bathing, and eating. It **also includes** care provided to individuals who need help with instrumental activities of daily living (IADLs) **including** preparing meals and shopping. (2)

[Move 2: Establishing the niche] **These types** of care **are covered** by long-term care insurance **if they are provided** in places such as private homes and assisted-living facilities among others (Society of Actuaries, 2012). (2)

[Move 3: Occupying the niche] **This paper will discuss** both **the merits and drawbacks of** purchasing long-term care (LTC) insurance by highlighting the common issues of contention in discussions of LTC insurance. **Ultimately, the paper will** compare and contrast two opposing positions in the LTC insurance debate regarding whether all active employees should purchase the insurance. **To do so, the paper will present** the perspectives of both proponents and opponents of LTC insurance on three main issues, particularly, LTC insurance cost, plan design, and market conditions. (2)

In this brief student introduction, Celeste includes the three moves, just as do Young and Fish. Celeste's opening move names the topic of long-term care, defining this "overall term" and signaling explanatory illustrations—e.g., "encompasses," "such as," and "also includes" (2). Her second move identifies an area for further explanation within this topic—coverage and what it depends on—e.g., "are covered" and "if they are provided" (2). Finally, her third move occupies the niche, addressing how the paper will further explain the "merits and drawbacks" of insurance coverage (2). Celeste also includes a map of the paper in her third move, using the linguistic cues "this paper will discuss" and "ultimately, the paper will present" (2). In addition to these informational move patterns, Celeste uses lexico-grammatical patterns common in what is called standardized English, including single negation and third person singular verbs—e.g., "encompasses" (2).

CLOSING REMARKS

Different though they are, these three introductions offer a clear if brief illustration of the patterned nature of writing. They illustrate Young's claim—the difference between language varieties "ain't as big as some like to imagine" (63)—and they also showcase systematic differences. In analyzing such similarities and differences, we build our language knowledge, concretely identifying and describing what language is doing. We resist abstract ideas about language, since even sufficiently critical abstract ideas about language will not overturn a language regulation paradigm in which we find language discrimination and little language knowledge.

To upend language discrimination, we need to replace language ignorance and hierarchy with critical attention to language beliefs and language knowledge. Then, we compile systematic evidence of the equally rule-governed and responsive nature of all shared language varieties. Then, we value (the study of) language variation, support language beliefs that advance fairness and equity, and empower language users with rhetorical agency. In other words, then we use language knowledge in support of linguistic justice. This is my hope for how we carry on Gere's ideas, data, and legacy into the future of writing studies.

WORKS CITED

Alim, H. Samy. "Critical Language Awareness in the United States: Revisiting Issues and Revising Pedagogies in a Resegregated Society." *Educational Researcher*, vol. 34, no. 7, 2005, pp. 24–31, https://doi.org/10.3102/0013189X034007024.

Aull, Laura Louise. "Attention to Language in Composition." *Composition Forum*, vol. 51, 2023, compositionforum.com/issue/51/attention.php.

———. *How Students Write: A Linguistic Analysis.* Modern Language Association, 2020.

———. *You Can't Write That: 8 Myths about Correct English.* Cambridge UP, 2023. *Cambridge Core*, https://doi.org/10.1017/9781009231299.

Baker-Bell, April. *Linguistic Justice: Black Language, Literacy, Identity, and Pedagogy.* Routledge, 2020. *Taylor and Francis eBooks*, https://doi.org/10.4324/9781315147383.

Ball, Cheryl E., and Drew M. Loewe, editors. *Bad Ideas About Writing.* West Virginia University Libraries Digital Publishing Institute, 2017. *Open Access Textbooks*, textbooks.lib.wvu.edu/badideas/badideasaboutwriting-book.pdf.

Bartholomae, David. "What Is Composition and (If You Know What That Is) Why Do We Teach It?" *Composition in the Twenty-First Century: Crisis and Change*, edited by Lynn Z. Bloom et al., Southern Illinois UP, 1996, pp. 11–28.

Celeste. "Writing Sample 4 from Celeste: Long-Term Care Insurance for All Active Employees." Gere, *Developing Writers in Higher Education: A Longitudinal Study*, https://doi.org/10.3998/mpub.10079890.cmp.153.

Connors, Robert J. "The Erasure of the Sentence." *College Composition and Communication*, vol. 52, no. 1, 2000, pp. 96–128, https://doi.org/10.58680/ccc20001409.

Crossley, Scott, et al. "What Is Successful Writing? An Investigation into the Multiple Ways Writers Can Write Successful Essays." *Written Communication*, vol. 31, no. 2, 2014, pp. 184–214, https://doi.org/10.1177/0741088314526354.

Curzan, Anne. "Says Who? Teaching and Questioning the Rules of Grammar." *PMLA*, vol. 124, no. 3, 2009, pp. 870–79. *Cambridge Core*, https://doi.org/10.1632/pmla.2009.124.3.870.

Davila, Bethany. "The Inevitability of 'Standard' English: Discursive Constructions of Standard Language Ideologies." *Written Communication*, vol. 33, no. 2, 2016, pp. 127–48, https://doi.org/10.1177/0741088316632186.

Duncan, Mike, and Star Medzerian Vanguri. Introduction. *The Centrality of Style*, edited by Mike Duncan and Star Medzerian, The WAC Clearinghouse / Parlor Press, 2013, pp. xi–xiv, https://doi.org/10.37514/PER-B.2013.0476.1.3.

Fish, Stanley. "What Should Colleges Teach." *The New York Times Opinionator*, 24 Aug. 2009, archive.nytimes.com/opinionator.blogs.nytimes.com/2009/08/24/what-should-colleges-teach/.

Freedman, Joel M. "Echoes of Silence: Empathy and Making Connections through Writing Process." *English Journal*, vol. 98, no. 4, 2009, pp. 92–95, https://doi.org/10.58680/ej20087032.

Gere, Anne Ruggles, editor. *Developing Writers in Higher Education: A Longitudinal Study*. U of Michigan P, 2019. *University of Michigan Press Ebook Collection*, https://doi.org/10.3998/mpub.10079890.

Gere, Anne Ruggles, et al. "Communal Justicing: Writing Assessment, Disciplinary Infrastructure, and the Case for Critical Language Awareness." *College Composition and Communication*, vol. 72, no. 3, 2021, pp. 384–412, https://doi.org/10.58680/ccc202131160.

Gere, Anne Ruggles, et al. "Local Assessment: Using Genre Analysis to Validate Directed Self-Placement." *College Composition and Communication*, vol. 64, no. 4, 2013, pp. 605–33, https://doi.org/10.58680/ccc201323661.

Horner, Bruce, et al. "Language Difference in Writing: Toward a Translingual Approach." *College English*, vol. 73, no. 3, 2011, pp. 303–21, https://doi.org/10.58680/ce201113403.

Knight, Simon, et al. "AcaWriter: A Learning Analytics Tool for Formative Feedback on Academic Writing." *Journal of Writing Research*, vol. 12, no. 1, 2020, pp. 141–86, https://doi.org/10.17239/jowr-2020.12.01.06.

Lea, Mary R., and Brian V. Street. "Student Writing and Staff Feedback in Higher Education: An Academic Literacies Approach." *Student Writing in Higher Education: New Contexts*, edited by Mary R. Lea and Barry Stierer, Open UP / Society for Research into Higher Education, 2000, pp. 32–46.

MacDonald, Susan Peck. "The Erasure of Language." *College Composition and Communication*, vol. 58, no. 4, 2007, pp. 585–625, https://doi.org/10.58680/ccc20075924.

Matsuda, Paul Kei. "Let's Face It: Language Issues and the Writing Program Administrator." *Writing Program Administration*, vol. 36, no. 1, 2012, pp. 141–63, associationdatabase.co/archives/36n1/36n1matsuda.pdf.

Milu, Esther. "Diversity of Raciolinguistic Experiences in the Writing Classroom: An Argument for a Transnational Black Language Pedagogy." *College English*, vol. 83, no. 6, 2021, pp. 415–41, https://doi.org/10.58680/ce202131357.

Pattanayak, Anjali. "There Is One Correct Way of Writing and Speaking." *Bad Ideas About Writing*, edited by Cheryl E. Ball and Drew M. Loewe, West Virginia University Libraries Digital Publishing Institute, 2017, pp. 82–87.

Perryman-Clark, Staci M. "African American Language, Rhetoric, and Students' Writing: New Directions for SRTOL." *College Composition and Communication*, vol. 64, no. 3, 2013, pp. 469–95, https://doi.org/10.58680/ccc201322719.

Richardson, Elaine. "Race, Class(es), Gender, and Age: The Making of Knowledge about Language Diversity." *Language Diversity in the Classroom: From Intention to Practice*, edited by Geneva Smitherman and Victor Villanueva, Southern Illinois UP, 2003, pp. 40–66.

Shapiro, Shawna. *Cultivating Critical Language Awareness in the Writing Classroom*. Routledge, 2022. *Taylor and Francis eBooks*, https://doi.org/10.4324/9781003171751.

Smitherman, Geneva. "'The Blacker the Berry, the Sweeter the Juice': African American Student Writers and the National Assessment of Educational Progress." Annual Meeting of the National Council of Teachers of English, November 17–22, 1993. *ERIC*, files.eric.ed.gov/fulltext/ED366944.pdf.

———. "Raciolinguistics, 'Mis-Education,' and Language Arts Teaching in the 21st Century." *Language Arts Journal of Michigan*, vol. 32, no. 2, 2017, pp. 4–12, https://doi.org/10.9707/2168-149X.2164.

"Students' Right to Their Own Language (with Bibliography)." *Conference on College Composition and Communication*, National Council of Teachers of English, 2024, cccc.ncte.org/cccc/resources/positions/srtolsummary. Originally published in *College Composition and Communication*, vol. 25, no. 3, 1974, pp. 1–18, https://doi.org/10.58680/ccc197417210.

Suntara, Watinee, and Siriluck Usaha. "Research Article Abstracts in Two Related Disciplines: Rhetorical Variation between Linguistics and Applied Linguistics." *English Language Teaching*, vol. 6, no. 2, 2013, pp. 84–99, https://doi.org/10.5539/elt.v6n2p84.

Swales, John. *Genre Analysis: English in Academic and Research Settings*. Cambridge UP, 1990.

Tankó, Gyula. "Literary Research Article Abstracts: An Analysis of Rhetorical Moves and Their Linguistic Realizations." *Journal of English for Academic Purposes*, vol. 27, 2017, pp. 42–55, https://doi.org/10.1016/j.jeap.2017.04.003.

Tedick, Diane J., and Maureen A. Mathison. "Holistic Scoring in ESL Writing Assessment: What Does an Analysis of Rhetorical Features Reveal?" *Academic Writing in a Second Language: Essays on Research and Pedagogy*, edited by Diane Belcher and George Braine, Ablex Publishing, 1995, pp. 205–30.

"This Ain't Another Statement! This is a DEMAND for Black Linguistic Justice!" *Conference on College Composition and Communication*, National Council of Teachers of English, July 2020, cccc.ncte.org/cccc/demand-for-black-linguistic-justice.

Weaver, Megan Michelle. *Critical Language Awareness Pedagogy in First-Year Composition: A Design-Based Research Study*. 2020. Old Dominion U, PhD Dissertation. *ODU Digital Commons*, https://doi.org/10.25777/ghyt-v912.

Young, Vershawn Ashanti. "Should Writers Use They Own English?" *Writing Centers and the New Racism: A Call for Sustainable Dialogue and Change*, edited by Laura Greenfield and Karen Rowan, Utah State UP, 2011, pp. 61–72.

CHAPTER 7.

RE-VISIONING THE ROLE OF "GRAMMAR" IN WRITING STUDIES

Anne Curzan
University of Michigan

When I teach writing courses, I sometimes use an introductory assignment called "What Grammar Means to Me" so that I can learn about the grammatical baggage students may be bringing with them. One of my colleagues started using the assignment too, and over a decade ago he shared with me a memorable and telling response from a student:

> The student reported that the word "grammar" immediately caused flashbacks to their sixth grade English teacher. The teacher could see her students were struggling to understand prepositions. Her solution: She brought in a Mickey Mouse doll and a Barbie playhouse. She then moved Mickey around the house, saying things like "Mickey is *in* the house," "Mickey is *by* the house." The student remembered vividly the teacher then warning the class that if they ever put a preposition at the end of a sentence, Mickey would die. The student ended the story by saying that grammar has terrified them ever since.

This passage describes a potentially engaging lesson in descriptive grammar that took a deadly prescriptive turn: deadly for Mickey and, arguably, deadly for this young student's interest in the workings of language.

My previous sentence works from the premise that young people bring to classrooms an interest in language—because they are human. Humans like to play with language: we pun and experiment with rhyme and alliteration; we make up new slang; we create beautiful linguistic metaphors; we construct derivative languages like pig Latin; and we play games like Scrabble, Wordle, Bananagrams, hangman, Spelling Bee, and the list goes on. What breaks my heart about the way that "grammar" is often taught in school—from K–12 through college—is that it can drill our pleasure in language out of educational and academic spaces. And I've put scare quotes around the word *grammar* because "grammar" in school often refers solely to prescriptive usage rules (such as the

DOI: https://doi.org/10.37514/PER-B.2025.2456.2.07

rule not to end a sentence with a preposition), as opposed to the descriptive grammar and other linguistic knowledge that help explain how a language—and all the dialects that make up a language—actually work (e.g., Aull, Chapter 6, this collection; Orzulak).

In this piece, I am offering a straightforward argument: Grammar or usage, in the descriptive sense of the terms, can be (a) a site to engage students' curiosity and creativity as speakers and writers, and (b) a powerful, approachable vehicle for opening up and grappling with fundamental questions about diversity, inclusion, justice, and access.

This piece honors the career of my long-time colleague and friend Anne Ruggles Gere in a couple of ways. First, Anne's generous intellectual partnership over the past 20-plus years has helped me hone my linguistic scholarship, both my academic publications and my public intellectual work. Anne has spent her career pursuing academic work that matters for students and teachers in real time, and she supported my interest in public intellectual work and advancing linguistic justice even before I had tenure, when I wasn't hearing that message from other senior faculty. Second, the title of this piece picks up a theme from Anne's presidential address at the 2019 MLA Annual Meeting, focused on re-visioning, and specifically the "killer dichotomy" between reading and writing (452). Theories of language are woven throughout her address, from Fred Newton Scott's presidential address in 1907 to Louise Rosenblatt's "Transactional Theory of Reading and Writing" (454, 455–56). This chapter re-visions definitions of "grammar" and "the teaching of grammar" within writing studies to address the implicit dichotomy between the teaching of grammar and critical or creative engagement.

DEFINITIONS OF GRAMMAR

I've been playing a little fast and loose with the word *grammar* up to this point, and sometimes referring more generally to *language* (e.g., my comment in the first paragraph of this chapter about a student's "interest in the workings of language"), so let me pause on terminology. In the writing classroom, the term *grammar* is sometimes used to cover everything from punctuation to word choice to syntax to style. This whole range of sentence- and paragraph-level language issues is relevant in a writing classroom, and as a linguist, I would suggest that when we're referring generally to these issues, we employ the term *usage* instead. In linguistics, the word *grammar* typically is used more narrowly to cover morphology (the structure and form of words, including inflectional endings) and syntax (how words combine into sentences). *Usage* broadly encompasses how words and phrases are used in speech and writing; as such, usage can include pronunciation, word meaning and word choice, morphology, syntax, and punctuation. All the choices we make about usage can and do have rhetorical effects (Kolln and Gray). Both terms *grammar* and *usage* can be used descriptively to refer to what speakers and writers actually do with the language and more prescriptively to refer to what they should do to demonstrate "good usage" or "correct grammar."

Debates about the role of grammar in writing classrooms go back decades (e.g., Hartwell), with many studies concluding that the teaching of grammar—sometimes specified as "formal grammar" and sometimes not—does not serve any "practical purpose" for most students (e.g., Weaver 15). The practical purpose referred to is often understood to be the consistent adoption of prescriptive rules in students' own writing. But the teaching of usage in its broadest sense—including descriptive approaches and awareness of the imposition of the prescriptive rules—can serve the practical purpose of engaging students in understanding the most fundamental of human characteristics and our expressive capabilities. It can also engage students in raising the most fundamental questions about power and justice.

LANGUAGE, CURIOSITY, AND WRITING

Language is a fundamental part of who we are and the families and communities that have shaped us. As Geneva Smitherman has been reminding us for years, in terms of why un- or misinformed language "correction" can be so devastating, "the student's mother tongue is the language of his/her mother. Dissin a student's mother tongue can thus be perceived as talkin bout they momma" (8). Language is a key resource for performing our identities and interpreting the identities of others as we navigate the social landscape. Language is one of our most powerful tools to hurt and heal, inform and misinform, reveal and hide, include and exclude.

For all these reasons and more, we should study language with as much seriousness and descriptive rigor as we use when we study other components of the human experience and natural world. Over 20 years ago, Kirk Hazen noted, "No biology teacher would ever say to a class, 'Okay, kids, today we learn how to breathe,' but all too often in English classes, students believe they are 'learning' language" (271–72). This belief manifests itself in a student comment such as "I don't know grammar"—which, of course, every speaker of a human language knows in order to be able to communicate with a language. What that student likely means is "I don't feel like I control the terminology to describe grammar" and maybe "I don't feel like I effectively control the standardized variety of English, especially in writing." We should teach students about language and grammar such that they can articulate what they want to know and what they are worried they don't know—and then help them gain that knowledge.

The combination "what [students] want to know and what they are worried they don't know" captures the juxtaposition of curiosity and judgment about language that, I would argue, lives in each of us. I have most recently framed this as the inner wordie and the inner grammando that dialogue inside our heads (Curzan, *Says Who?*).[1] The inner wordie enjoys language; the inner grammando has absorbed notions of "right" and "wrong" and judges language along those lines. Both the inner wordie and the inner grammando notice things in language—be that a new development in the language (e.g., "based off" rather than "based on") or a usage that differs from what we learned (e.g., "she walks" if we grew up saying "she walk"). The question is what we learn to do with that noticing. Have we been taught to be curious about linguistic diversity and language change as a natural part of language? Or have we been taught that there is only one correct way to use the language, and that is the formal, standardized variety? The latter is linguistically misinformed, and it forecloses the kind of engaged, rigorous exploration that should characterize teaching and learning.

Students' inner wordies should be educationally engaged in the writing classroom because effective writing comes from, among other things, a deep caring about—and ideally pleasure in—language and how it is used to convey ideas and images and arguments in written genres. A dictionary can become a treasure trove of cultural information and human decisions rather than a generic resource with "the answers" about what words mean (Curzan, "Lexicography")—and once that happens, students often engage in different ways with defining words they are using for their arguments.

I recognize that teaching usage issues doesn't have a great reputation, but it can be engaging. For example, with punctuation, we can start by asking students to record the rules of texting punctuation (e.g., the period suggests seriousness if not anger; the semicolon is only for winky faces). Once we have established the nuance and systematicity of texting punctuation and affirmed students' deep knowledge of this usage, we can compare this system with academic punctuation—another punctuation "game" to master to write in different settings, as opposed to the only "correct" way to use punctuation. As a second example, students can discuss how many educated speakers need to use the phrase *between you and I* before it can be recategorized as "educated usage" rather than a mistake propagated by all these educated speakers. Or students can debate the pros and cons of using *literally* to mean "figuratively" in formal writing or of employing singular *they* even though not all style guides yet endorse it.

---

1   *Wordie* is a relatively new word: it was added to the Merriam-Webster Dictionary in 2018 and defined as "a lover of words." *Grammando* appeared in Lizzie Skurnick's "That Should Be a Word" feature in 2012, in *The New York Times Magazine*, and is defined as "One who constantly corrects other people's linguistic mistakes."

As these last two examples suggest, it's important to acknowledge the grammandos that lurk, both in our heads and in our audiences as writers and speakers. Deborah Cameron has made the powerful argument that "verbal hygiene," or the desire to clean up or improve other people's language, is a natural part of speech communities (1–3). We as humans notice differences in other humans, including the way they use language, and we can be both curious and judgmental. We police each other's language as part of creating and preserving communities and their boundaries. We hear new bits of language and may at first resist language change or linguistic diversity.

I'll share a personal example: my initial reaction to the jargon *double-click* as a verb to mean "dive deep into." One of my colleagues consistently uses this to transition between slides in a slide deck, and the first dozen times I heard it, I rolled my eyes. "Business school jargon!" my inner grammando complained. And then over dinner one evening, my partner countered that it actually is a clever metaphorical extension of the computer-based terminology, and suddenly my inner wordie could enjoy it.

I'm about as descriptively minded as they come, and yet I am still managing reactions to changes in the language I grew up with. The point is that I am managing those reactions with a lot of linguistic information (which empowers my very vocal inner wordie). Too often teachers, with their list of peeves that students may not use in their writing, are unwilling to rethink these peeves or quiet their pen as they read student essays.

The policing of language happens at the institutional level and at the individual level, and the power of standardized English permeates classrooms at all levels. Notions of correctness are so powerful that we regularly talk about our responses to grammar in physical terms such as "makes my skin crawl" (Curzan et al., "Language Standardization"). And notions of correctness can be deeply biased, discriminatory, ill-informed, and silencing. This gets us to the power of talking about grammar or usage to address issues of diversity, inclusion, access, and justice.

GRAMMAR, AUTHORITY, AND JUSTICE

When students are empowered to ask probing, critical questions about the prescriptive usage rules that have been imposed on them as writers and speakers throughout much of their schooling, they will find themselves examining issues at the intersection of language, power, and identity—issues at the heart of the diversity, equity, inclusion, access, and justice work that we have been pursuing across higher education. Who said there's something wrong with the word *ain't*? Where did the rule about ending a sentence with a preposition come from? Why is African American English often described as broken or unacceptable? Why can't people use their home languages or dialects at school?

This is not a new argument, but it is clearly one that we need to keep repeating. For example, linguist James Sledd has pointed for decades, back into the 1960s, to the necessity of recognizing, for students, the racial politics of grammar instruction; here is a version of his argument from 1996: "If [students] are ready for abstractions like subjects and predicates, they are ready for the abstractions of race and class" (62). But as April Baker-Bell points out in *Linguistic Justice*, too often approaches such as code-switching to teaching grammar and usage have allowed the educational system to maintain the status quo, centering "White Mainstream English as the be-all and end-all for Black speakers" (7), without interrogation. In the Foreword to Baker-Bell's book, Smitherman summarizes the need as follows: "We need a language pedagogy which teaches us to explore why things are the way they are. A language pedagogy which forces us to confront the questions: How did the present social order come into being? What do we need to do to take it out of being?" (xv).

As imagined by scholars such as H. Samy Alim, these questions live at the heart of Critical Language Awareness (CLA): "How can language be used to maintain, reinforce, and perpetuate existing power relations?" And, as its counterpoint: "How can language be used to resist, redefine and possibly reverse these relations?" (28).

The answers to these questions allow us to talk about standard language ideologies (Lippi-Green) and how they shape our view of which varieties of English are "correct" or "acceptable" and which are not. They provide the critical distance to see dictionaries and usage guides as the products of human hands—attached to human brains with beliefs and preferences and biases, situated within specific cultural moments—that can be critiqued and revised. Suddenly dictionaries and usage guides are not dusty relics or ultimate authorities. The Framework for Success in Postsecondary Writing, a central resource for writing program administrators, can be revised to account for linguistic diversity and language change—and encourage teachers to foster in students the meta-awareness to explore and question prescriptivism and its social power (Gere et al., "Communal Justicing").

It has been exciting to see CLA, as a coherent approach, gaining prominence in the United States, both in writing studies scholarship and in classroom practice (Shapiro). This work has been out there for decades, in linguistics and in composition, without always enough scholarly dialogue between the two. It foregrounds how language—from descriptive approaches to linguistic diversity and grammar to interrogation of prescriptive usage rules—can foster the kind of inclusive, transformative pedagogy that is core to the diversity, equity, inclusion, access, and justice work that universities have been pursuing more generally.

CLA invites all students in, with all the language varieties they bring with them, and it empowers them to challenge discourses that may have devalued their linguistic identities and potentially created barriers to access.

We can think about this pedagogical shift within the frame of Jamila Lyiscott's redefinition of the word *articulate* in her brilliant TED talk, "3 Ways to Speak English." For decades, *articulate* has been a loaded term (to say the least) for people of color, often implying a kind of exceptionalism (i.e., that speakers from some literacy communities are not expected to be skilled speakers and writers and it is noteworthy that they are) as well as often referring specifically to control of standardized English (Alim and Smitherman). Lyiscott describes being articulate as treating all three of her languages as equal, as being able to switch among her languages with rhetorical intent and for rhetorical effectiveness, and, crucially, to be able to ask the probing, powerful questions she poses to her professors, to her family members, and to her audience in the talk itself.

CONCLUSION

Far from being cut-and-dried or drill-and-kill (or terrifying, to return to the words of the student who opened this essay), "grammar"—and all that can and often is encompassed by that term in the writing classroom—is one of our most powerful tools and resources to engage students in fundamental questions about identity, power, and justice. As Anne Gere reminds us in her scholarship and through her own career trajectory, we should eschew constricting dichotomies and disciplinary boundaries in the interest of more inclusive, evidence-informed pedagogies and writing classrooms. With the study of grammar and language more broadly, if we can start by tapping into students' genuine curiosity about linguistic diversity and language change, we can foster the kind of care with and knowledge about language that characterizes effective writers (e.g., Aull, *First-Year*; Lancaster). It is then imperative that students also have the opportunity to surface the power dynamics at play and ask equally genuine questions about who makes the rules and how they can be changed to create more equity and access for linguistically diverse speakers and writers.

WORKS CITED

Alim, H. Samy. "Critical Language Awareness in the United States: Revisiting Issues and Revising Pedagogies in a Resegregated Society." *Educational Researcher*, vol. 34, no. 7, 2005, pp. 24–31, https://doi.org/10.3102/0013189X034007024.

Alim, H. Samy, and Geneva Smitherman. *Articulate While Black: Barack Obama, Language, and Race in the U.S.* Oxford UP, 2012.

Aull, Laura. *First-Year University Writing: A Corpus-Based Study with Implications for Pedagogy.* Palgrave Macmillan, 2015. *Springer Nature Link,* https://doi.org/10.1057/9781137350466.

Baker-Bell, April. *Linguistic Justice: Black Language, Literacy, Identity, and Pedagogy.* Routledge, 2020. *Taylor and Francis eBooks,* https://doi.org/10.4324/9781315147383.

Cameron, Deborah. *Verbal Hygiene.* Routledge, 2012. *Taylor and Francis eBooks,* https://doi.org/10.4324/9780203123898.

Curzan, Anne. "Lexicography and Questions of Authority in the College Classroom: Students 'Deconstructing the Dictionary.'" *Dictionaries: Journal of the Dictionary Society of North America,* vol. 21, 2000, pp. 90–99. *Project Muse,* https://doi.org/10.1353/dic.2000.0005.

———. *Says Who? A Kinder, Funner Usage Guide for Everyone Who Cares about Words.* Crown, 2024.

Curzan, Anne, et al. "Language Standardization and Linguistic Subordination." *Dædalus,* vol. 152, no. 3, 2023, pp. 18–35, https://doi.org/10.1162/daed_a_02015.

Gere, Anne Ruggles. "Presidential Address 2019–Re-visioning Language, Texts, and Theories." *PMLA,* vol. 134, no. 3, 2019, pp. 450–58. *Cambridge Core,* https://doi.org/10.1632/pmla.2019.134.3.450.

Gere, Anne Ruggles, et al. "Communal Justicing: Writing Assessment, Disciplinary Infrastructure, and the Case for Critical Language Awareness." *College Composition and Communication,* vol. 72, no. 3, 2021, pp. 384–412, https://doi.org/10.58680/ccc202131160.

Hartwell, Patrick. "Grammar, Grammars, and the Teaching of Grammar." *College English,* vol. 47, no. 2, 1985, pp. 105–27, https://doi.org/10.58680/ce198513293.

Hazen, Kirk. "Better Science ~ Better Science Education." *American Speech,* vol. 75, no. 3, 2000, pp. 270–73, https://doi.org/10.1215/00031283-75-3-270.

Kolln, Martha, and Loretta Gray. *Rhetorical Grammar: Grammatical Choices, Rhetorical Effect.* 8th ed., Pearson, 2016.

Lancaster, Zak. "Do Academics Really Write This Way? A Corpus Investigation of Moves and Templates in '*They Say / I Say.*'" *College Composition and Communication,* vol. 67, no. 3, 2016, pp. 437–64, https://doi.org/10.58680/ccc201628067.

Lippi-Green, Rosina. *English with an Accent: Language, Ideology, and Discrimination in the United States.* 2nd ed., Routledge, 2012. *Taylor and Francis eBooks,* https://doi.org/10.4324/9780203348802.

Lyiscott, Jamila. "3 Ways to Speak English." *TED: Ideas Change Everything,* Feb. 2014, www.ted.com/talks/jamila_lyiscott_3_ways_to_speak_english.

Orzulak, Melinda J. McBee. "Beyond What 'Sounds Right': Reframing Grammar Instruction." *Language Arts Journal of Michigan,* vol. 27, no. 2, 2012, pp. 21–24, https://doi.org/10.9707/2168-149X.1901.

Shapiro, Shawna. "A Kairotic Moment for CLA? Response to Anne Ruggles Gere et al.'s 'Communal Justicing: Writing Assessment, Disciplinary Infrastructure, and the Case for Critical Language Awareness.'" *College Composition and Communication,* vol. 74, no. 2, 2022, pp. 373–79, https://doi.org/10.58680/ccc202232280.

Skurnick, Lizzie. "Grammando." That Should Be a Word. *The New York Times Magazine*, 4 Mar. 2012, https://tinyurl.com/ms9nunfe.

Sledd, James. "Grammar for Social Awareness in Time of Class Warfare." *English Journal*, vol. 85, no. 7, 1996, pp. 59–63, https://doi.org/10.58680/ej19964841.

Smitherman, Geneva. "Raciolinguistics, 'Mis-Education,' and Language Arts Teaching in the 21st Century." *Language Arts Journal of Michigan*, vol. 32, no. 2, 2017, pp. 4–12, https://doi.org/10.9707/2168-149X.2164.

Weaver, Constance. "Teaching Grammar in the Context of Writing." *English Journal*, vol. 85, no. 7, 1996, pp. 15–24, https://doi.org/10.58680/ej19964835.

"Wordie." *Merriam-Webster Dictionary*, 2024, www.merriam-webster.com/dictionary/wordie.

PART 3. DISCIPLINARY-CROSSING DYNAMICS

CHAPTER 8.

WRITING TO LEARN AND THINK CRITICALLY IN STEM: ENGAGING STUDENTS IN DISCIPLINARY KNOWLEDGE AND PRACTICES

Mike Palmquist
Colorado State University

> Many claims have been made in the past four decades about the efficacy of writing as a means of fostering student learning in a variety of disciplines. Yet, reviews and meta-analyses of publications about the implementation of writing-to-learn (WTL) pedagogies show mixed results.
>
> – Anne Ruggles Gere et al. ("A Tale of Two Prompts")

The use of writing as an aid to learning has long been recognized as an effective educational practice (see, for example, Kuh's 2008 discussion of writing in the disciplines as a high-impact practice). I'm tempted to think that it was among the earliest uses of writing, following only its uses in record keeping, naming, law, and religion (Clayton). It supports remembering knowledge, developing and demonstrating understanding, reflecting on what has been learned, and engaging in analysis, synthesis, and evaluation. Writing activities and assignments, as a result, have served as an enduring aspect of education in general and of higher education in particular.

Yet we seem to find it difficult to talk with precision about the roles writing serves and the forms it takes in higher education. We treat it in much the same way we treat concepts such as creativity, critical thinking, and engagement—as something that is widely understood even when it is abundantly clear that we mean quite different things when we talk about it. Consider the wealth of terms we use to describe writing in higher education: *writing across the curriculum (WAC)*, *writing in the disciplines (WID)*, *writing to learn*, *learning to write*, and *writing to communicate* come immediately to mind. And there are others, such as *writing to demonstrate learning*, a term used widely in secondary education, and the evocative *writing to think*.

There are advantages to this wealth of terminology—this "big tent," so to speak. That said, a lack of precise terminology—and, perhaps more important, divergent understandings of how we might use writing to support our work as educators—can lead to misunderstandings about our curricular goals and a consequent lack of effectiveness in our instructional practices.

For several years, I've focused on what I see as an overly broad definition of a key concept within the WAC movement: writing to learn (see "A Middle Way," "WAC and Critical Thinking"). In common practice, it includes such diverse activities as

- listing key ideas in a reading assignment or class discussion,
- summarizing and responding to readings,
- reflecting on personal and professional connections to course concepts,
- applying disciplinary interpretive frameworks to a text or video,
- analyzing texts and other forms of media, and
- evaluating the strengths and weaknesses of competing claims or approaches.

These are all important and productive assignments. They help students learn. And they hold significant advantages over activities such as cramming for a quiz or an exam.

Yet they exhibit marked differences from one another. Consider the critical thinking skills, for example, required to jot down three questions about an assigned reading at the beginning of an economics class meeting and those required to apply a Keynesian analysis of claims made in a presidential debate. Consider as well where they fall along a spectrum from low-stakes to high-stakes writing tasks (Elbow) and from writer-based to reader-based prose (Flower). Finally, consider how they might vary in their meaningfulness for the students who work on them (see work by Eodice et al.).

Unfortunately, in disciplines outside writing studies the concept of writing to learn is understood broadly as anything that is not geared toward helping students prepare for communication in their disciplines or professions. In other words, it's everything except writing in the disciplines. In this sense, expressing a desire to use writing-to-learn tasks in a course is much like saying you want students to develop critical thinking skills. It's a laudable goal, but it lacks the specificity that is an essential characteristic of assignments that are well-aligned with course goals.

I've argued elsewhere about the value of distinguishing between writing-to-learn activities that focus largely on remembering, understanding, and reflecting and writing-to-engage activities that involve applying, analyzing, and evaluating ("Middle Way"). This focus on critical thinking supports alignment between the curricular goals of a course and instructor expectations about the kinds of work they assign. It also calls instructor attention to the development of the general and disciplinary critical thinking skills students encounter as they progress from lower-division to upper-division courses. Distinguishing between writing to learn and writing to engage can contribute in useful ways to student learning and to their preparation for further work in their disciplines. In this chapter, I extend that argument by exploring how complex writing-to-engage tasks in the STEM disciplines can move beyond writing-to-learn activities into assignments that begin to engage students in writing in the disciplines.

WRITING TO LEARN AND WRITING TO ENGAGE AS CONTIGUOUS AND OVERLAPPING ACTIVITIES

Within the STEM disciplines, educators have made extensive use of writing to support student learning. Two major research projects led respectively by Anne Ruggles Gere and Meena Balgopal that have resulted in several publications, for example, have advanced our understanding of the use of writing tasks in STEM courses. In this volume, for example, Ginger Shultz and her collaborators Amber J. Dood and Solaire A. Finkenstaedt-Quinn—who have worked closely with Gere—report on a study of students' perceptions of how writing shaped their learning in chemistry courses at the University of Michigan (see Chapter 9). And while these projects are noteworthy, they are far from alone. Searches of databases for the phrase *writing to learn* in the STEM disciplines produce hundreds of results (e.g., Graham et al.).

Certainly, the writing activities and assignments described in these studies vary widely in the stakes and meaningfulness they hold for students as well as in their cognitive complexity. But they also, as a group, show learning gains associated with the use of writing. By considering the characteristics of successful writing activities and assignments in light of the course in which they are assigned, the students in the course, and the goals of the course, we can make progress on identifying writing activities and assignments that are well aligned with curricular goals. Developing a classification scheme based on this information would support decisions regarding when to assign writing in a given course, what type of writing activity to assign, and how to support students as they work on their writing.

My attempts to create such a scheme have involved aligning typical writing assignments with the taxonomy of educational objectives in the cognitive domain developed by Benjamin Bloom and his colleagues in the 1950s and later modified by Loren W. Anderson and David R. Krathwohl in the early 2000s. I've modified it further to include a key critical thinking activity that is treated implicitly in Bloom's taxonomy: reflecting.

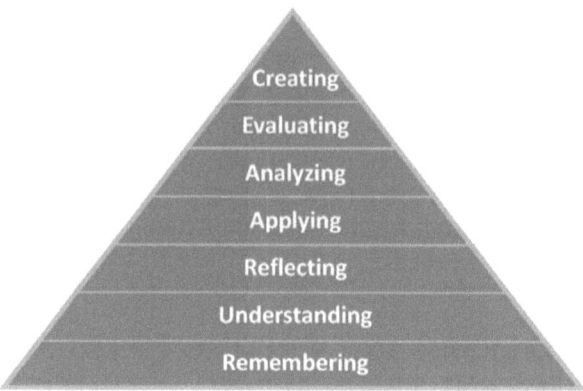

Figure 8.1. Bloom's taxonomy as modified by Anderson and Krathwohl and modified further to add reflecting as a distinct cognitive skill.

Using this modified version of Bloom's taxonomy, I've proposed a spectrum of writing activities and assignments ranging from low-stakes, writer-based writing-to-learn activities to highly rhetorical, high-stakes, genre-informed, and reader-based writing-in-the-disciplines activities. Between the ends of the spectrum, I've placed a new category of writing-to-engage activities which align with Bloom's higher-order thinking skills but do not necessarily share the characteristics of genres that commonly circulate within publication venues in a disciplinary or professional community.

This spectrum is not offered as an argument that we've been getting the "writing to learn" discussion wrong all along but rather to suggest that we can benefit from greater precision in discussing the impact of assignments that have quite distinct characteristics. Much of this thinking emerged from my experiences working as the director of a teaching and learning center. My efforts to introduce writing tasks as a key part of a large, five-year course-redesign initiative helped me recognize the need for more nuanced distinctions among the various writing activities that could be used to accomplish course goals. It was also shaped by conversations with colleagues including Terry Zawacki, Marty Townsend, Susan McLeod, Linda Adler-Kassner, Justin Rademaekers, and Chris Anson, as well as numerous publications that address the relationship between writing and critical thinking (see, for example, McLeod and Elaine Maimon's work in this area). Over time, I began to differentiate activities that focused primarily on gaining an understanding of course concepts and processes and those that engaged students in using those course concepts and processes to accomplish particular goals.

With this in mind, I have attempted to tease out the distinctions among writing to learn, writing to engage, and writing in the disciplines (see Table 8.1).

Figure 8.2. WAC activities and assignments are aligned along a spectrum of critical thinking skills.

Table 8.1. Approaches to WAC

Writing to Learn (WTL)	Writing to Engage (WTE)	Writing in the Disciplines (WID)
Using writing to help students remember, understand, and reflect on course concepts, conceptual frameworks, skills, and processes.	Using writing to help students assess and work with course concepts, conceptual frameworks, skills, and processes.	Using writing to help students learn how to contribute to discourse within a discipline or profession.
Best characterized as "low-stakes" writing: • The focus is on content; recognizing that students often struggle with new ideas, little or no attention is given to form. • Limited feedback, if any, is provided by the instructor.	Can be characterized as either "low-stakes" or "high-stakes" writing, or it might fall somewhere between the two. Writing to engage assignments can: • Build on WTL activities and assignments. • Support a higher level of engagement with disciplinary concepts and processes than WTL activities and assignments. • Focus on reflecting, applying, and analyzing and might include some attention to evaluating.	Best characterized as "high-stakes" writing: • A greater investment of instructor time is required for designing and responding to student writing. • There is greater potential for student academic misconduct, especially among students who lack confidence in producing original work.
Typical activities include: • In-class responses to prompts • Reflections • Summary/response • Forum discussions • Definitions and descriptions	Typical activities include: • Application of frameworks to texts, media, and cases • Evaluations of alternative approaches and methods • Reflections, critiques, and comparisons • Topic proposals, progress reports, and other brief reports	Typical activities include: • Articles and essays • Presentations • Longer reports • Poster sessions

WRITING TO LEARN AND WRITING TO ENGAGE IN THE STEM DISCIPLINES

While other disciplines have explored the use of writing tasks that align well with the concept of writing to engage, STEM educators have made significant progress in this area. For example, a series of studies conducted by Gere and her colleagues across several STEM disciplines employed a promising assignment-design framework that

- provides a well-defined purpose and audience,
- directs students to work within common and reasonably well-understood genres,
- provides clear indications of the kind of critical thinking required to complete the work,
- requires students to carry out peer review of classmates' work in progress, and
- allows time for reflection on the feedback provided through peer review.

These assignments are described in detail in articles published by teams of scholars led variously by Gere, Finkenstaedt-Quinn, Trisha Gupte, Audrey Halim, Alena Moon, Michael Petterson, Shultz, Robert J. Thompson, Jr., and Field M. Watts.

While these assignments vary from summaries and essays to memos, email messages, and articles, they share a focus on working in substantive ways to understand, reflect upon, and engage critically with the information, ideas, and processes typical of specific STEM disciplines. Their assignment designs range from fairly straightforward directions to write "a summary of how Lewis proposed to simplify the depiction of electron sharing and valence in covalent bonds" (Shultz and Gere 1326)[1] to more complex tasks such as taking on the role of "a volunteer in a social service program who needed to explain the implications of recycling on polymer structure to their supervisor, who hopes to convince donors that recycled plastic can be used to make backpacks for impoverished school children" (Finkenstaedt-Quinn et al., "Investigating" 1611).

These assignments, according to the teams of researchers led variously by Gere, Finkenstaedt-Quinn, Gupte, Halim, Moon, Petterson, Shultz, Thompson, and Watts, draw on three key assignment features derived from a meta-analysis conducted by Paul Anderson and his colleagues of effective writing-to-learn activities and assignments: interactive writing processes, clear expectations, and

---

[1] Shultz and Gere note that "Lewis dot structures form the basis of the symbolic language that is used for communication among chemists" (1325). The task they ask students to complete is based on Gilbert Lewis' 1916 article "The Atom and the Molecule," available at https://pubs.acs.org/doi/10.1021/ja02261a002.

meaning-making activities. A 2019 review of several of these published reports (Thompson et al.) found that these features, in combination with the metacognitive reflection identified in a 2004 meta-analysis by Robert Bangert-Drowns and his colleagues, produced evidence of conceptual learning. For the studies addressed by the Gere, Finkenstaedt-Quinn, Gupte, Halim, Moon, Petterson, Shultz, Thompson, and Watts teams, metacognitive reflection is typically fostered through the use of peer review of initial drafts using tools such as MWrite in combination with subsequent revision (see a description of MWrite in Finkenstaedt-Quinn et al., "Praxis," and its relationship to work conducted by Shultz and Gere in "Writing-to-Learn").

Some of the writing assignments discussed in the studies reported by the Gere, Finkenstaedt-Quinn, Gupte, Halim, Moon, Petterson, Shultz, Thompson, and Watts research teams might fall into the overlap between writing to learn and writing to engage. This is particularly true of assignments that focus primarily on summarizing. The addition of the reflection associated with peer review as well as the higher stakes associated with grading suggests, however, that most of the assignments reported on in these studies require cognitive skills that are more commonly associated with writing to engage, such as application, analysis, and evaluation. Requirements such as the following certainly suggest a high level of engagement with course content and processes:

> Write a memo to the trainer explaining what the statistics show and make an argument for or against inclusion of dark chocolate in the athletes' diet. Your memo should include a discussion of how crossover design affects the data analysis, statistical significance, and what the p values indicate about the results, and explain the difference between the meaning of a confidence interval versus confidence level. (Finkenstaedt-Quinn et al., "Utilizing" 370)

This assignment begins with summary, but it also requires application of skills and knowledge gained through the course, analysis of evidence, and the development of an argument for a specific audience. This kind of assignment goes well beyond those that would fit comfortably within the definition of writing to learn found in Table 8.1.

An analysis of the assignments reported in the work by the Gere, Finkenstaedt-Quinn, Gupte, Halim, Moon, Petterson, Shultz, Thompson, and Watts research groups suggests that most of the assignments are consistent with the concept of writing to engage. Each requires students to carry out reflection, application, analysis, and/or evaluation. They often rely on providing a set of recommendations or conclusions. And they sometimes explicitly ask writers to develop an argument. The annotated assignments found in Figures 8.3 and 8.4 illustrate the ways in which these activities are integrated into the assignments. They also show how purpose, audience, role, and genre play central roles in the assignments.

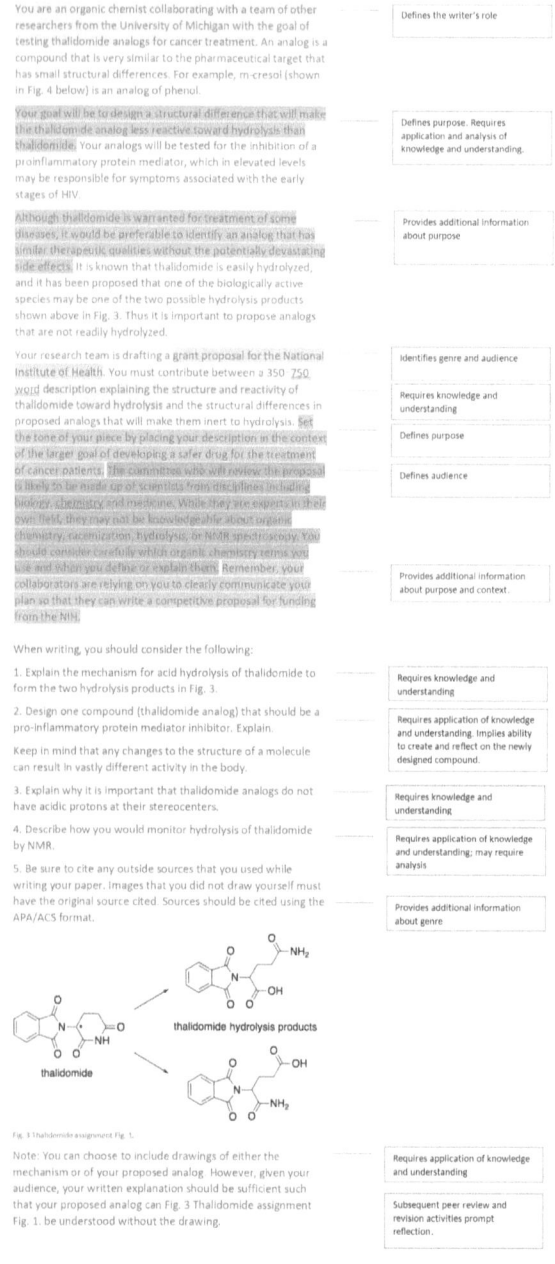

Figure 8.3. Annotated assignment for an organic chemistry course.
Source: Gupte et al. 409.

Figure 8.3 shows how the assignment provides guidance in three areas. First, it focuses attention on the rhetorical situation, providing information about the writers' purpose, audience, role, and genre. Second, it provides guidance (not shown in this figure, but available in the full article) on carrying out peer review and engaging in reflection about how the students have given and received feedback and how they might approach the revision of their draft. Finally, it provides strong cues about the type of critical thinking that should contribute to the drafting and revision of their assignment. Building on their knowledge and understanding of course content, students are asked to engage in application as they design a thalidomide analog that will be a pro-inflammatory protein mediator inhibitor (an example of creating, in Bloom's taxonomy). They are also asked to explain how they would monitor the effects of the newly designed thalidomide analog, an activity that would likely involve reflection and analysis.

The work writers carry out to complete this assignment will involve considerations of both their rhetorical situation (developing a key section in an NIH grant proposal) and the content they hope to convey to their readers. The interaction between these two considerations has been termed a process of knowledge transformation (Scardamalia and Bereiter, "A Brief History," "Knowledge Telling"), a key step in conveying complex information to a specific audience. Since the student writers are likely to have little familiarity with the NIH review process, they will almost certainly find it challenging to determine how best to present the findings from their work for inclusion in the grant proposal. In essence, even if they possess a deep understanding of the nature and characteristics of the thalidomide analog they design, they will need to think deeply about how to present that information to their readers.

This process illustrates the overlap between writing to engage and writing in the disciplines. While WID assignments more often focus on an established genre (for example, students might be asked to "write an article reporting the results of your lab experiment for the journal . . .") and clearly define audience and purpose, complex writing-to-engage activities such as the assignment from Gupte and her colleagues occupy the space between documents such as essays and reports and documents such as conference proposals and journal articles. In this case, students are writing content for a grant proposal, an activity that not only engages them in critical thinking about course content but also exposes them to specific genre conventions. As such, this assignment—like many of the others in the studies conducted by the Gere, Finkenstaedt-Quinn, Gupte, Halim, Moon, Petterson, Shultz, Thompson, and Watts research groups—falls into the overlapping space between writing to engage and writing in the disciplines.

In this way, the rhetorical and cognitive tasks required by the assignment described by Gupte and her colleagues differ in important ways from a typical writing-to-learn assignment. It requires the writers to engage in most of the cognitive skills in Bloom's taxonomy, and it requires extensive work by students in adapting their knowledge for a specific rhetorical situation. It is a high-stakes (that is, graded) activity. And, since it involves peer review and revision, it goes well beyond the requirements of a single-draft writing-to-learn activity such as developing lists, summarizing a source, or responding to a source. Finally, depending on the writer's interest in the course, it has the potential (although not a certainty) to be more meaningful to the writer than a low-stakes writing-to-learn activity such as a summary-response essay.

Figure 8.4 provides another assignment, this one reported by Finkestaedt-Quinn and her colleagues ("Capturing"), and shows a similar level of challenge and engagement for student writers.

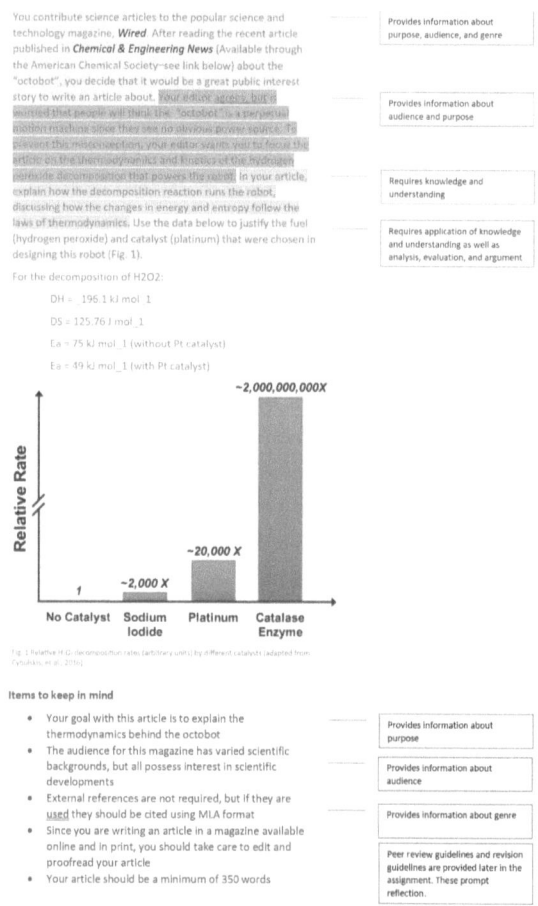

Figure 8.4. Annotated assignment for a chemistry course on thermodynamics and kinetics. Source: Finkenstaedt-Quinn et al., "Capturing" 933.

As shown by the annotations in Figure 8.4, the rhetorical considerations associated with explaining to readers of *Wired* how the octobot robot is powered are predicated on transforming the writer's knowledge of thermodynamics and kinetics into a form that is accessible to a general audience. This process will entail critical thinking activities ranging from developing their own understanding of thermodynamics and kinetics to reflecting on how to adapt that knowledge for their readers to applying that knowledge to data in the development of a justification for their decisions about using hydrogen peroxide as a fuel and platinum as a catalyst. The development of that justification will likely involve evaluating alternative fuel/catalyst combinations. Finally, the use of peer review and revision will entail additional reflection and planning, both to provide useful feedback to their peers and to improve the first draft of their article.

CONCLUSION

The straightforward distinction between viewing writing activities and assignments as either a means of supporting learning or a means of enhancing student writers' ability to communicate—that is, as either writing to learn or writing in the disciplines—is valuable. As an entry point into discussions about the role writing might play in classrooms, it serves a useful function. Once instructors have become familiar with this basic distinction, however, it no longer sufficiently conveys the complex set of roles that writing activities and assignments can play in STEM classrooms—and, for that matter, in any classroom.

Adding the concept of writing to engage to our discussions of the use of writing to support learning can clarify the wide range of uses to which we can put writing in our courses. Referring to activities as different as listing questions about a reading assignment at the start of class and contributing a section to an NIH grant proposal as writing to learn not only lacks precision but also contributes to a lack of clarity in our discussions of the potential benefits of using writing to enhance learning. The work reported by the Gere, Finkenstaedt-Quinn, Gupte, Halim, Moon, Petterson, Shultz, Thompson, and Watts research teams provides a strong example of how to use writing activities and assignments to engage students in course content in a way that goes far beyond working to remember and understand those concepts. Their work has deepened students' understanding of course concepts, supported their use of disciplinary conceptual frameworks and practices, and required them to engage in critical thinking about the information, ideas, and processes central to the course and its discipline. The assignments they have developed through their studies provide outstanding examples of writing to engage. In developing them, they have provided greater clarity about how writing-to-engage activities and assignments can benefit faculty members who seek to improve student learning, retention, and critical thinking at various points in the curriculum and how students in turn will benefit in ways that allow them to move successfully through their course sequences and into professional work.

WORKS CITED

Anderson, Loren W., and David R. Krathwohl, editors. *A Taxonomy for Learning, Teaching, and Assessing: A Revision of Bloom's Taxonomy of Educational Objectives*. Longman, 2001.

Anderson, Paul, et al. "The Contributions of Writing to Learning and Development: Results from a Large-Scale Multi-Institutional Study." *Research in the Teaching of English*, vol. 50, no. 2, 2015, pp. 199–235, https://doi.org/10.58680/rte201527602.

Balgopal, Meena M., et al. "Writing from Different Cultural Contexts: How College Students Frame an Environmental SSI through Written Arguments." *Journal of Research in Science Teaching*, vol. 54, no. 2, 2016, pp. 195–218, https://doi.org/10.1002/tea.21342.

Balgopal, Meena M., et al. "Writing Matters: Writing-to-Learn Activities Increase Undergraduate Performance in Cell Biology." *BioScience*, vol. 68, no. 6, 2018, pp. 445–54, https://doi.org/10.1093/biosci/biy042.

Balgopal, Meena M., and Lisa M. Montplaisir. "Meaning Making: What Reflective Essays Reveal about Biology Students' Ideas about Natural Selection." *Instructional Science: An International Journal of the Learning Sciences*, vol. 39, no. 2, 2011, pp. 137– 69, https://doi.org/10.1007/s11251-009-9120-y.

Balgopal, Meena M., and Alison M Wallace. "Writing-to-Learn, Writing-to-Communicate, and Scientific Literacy." *The American Biology Teacher*, vol. 75, no. 3, 2013, pp. 170–75, https://doi.org/10.1525/abt.2013.75.3.5.

Bangert-Drowns, Robert L., et al. "The Effects of School-Based Writing-to-Learn Interventions on Academic Achievement: A Meta-Analysis." *Review of Educational Research*, vol. 74, no. 1, 2004, pp. 29–58, https://doi.org/10.3102/00346543074001029.

Bloom, B. S., et al. *Taxonomy of Educational Objectives, Handbook I: The Cognitive Domain*. David McKay, 1956.

Clayton, Ewan. "Why Did Humans Start Writing?" *British Library*, www.bl.uk/history-of-writing/articles/why-did-humans-start-writing. Accessed September 9, 2023.

Elbow, Peter. "High Stakes and Low Stakes in Assigning and Responding to Writing." *New Directions for Teaching and Learning*, vol. 69, 1997, pp. 5–13, https://doi.org/10.1002/tl.6901.

Eodice, Michelle, et al. *The Meaningful Writing Project: Learning, Teaching, and Writing in Higher Education*. Utah State UP, 2017.

———. "The Power of Personal Connection for Undergraduate Student Writers." *Research in the Teaching of English*, vol. 53, no. 4, 2019, pp. 320–39. *St. John's Scholar*, scholar.stjohns.edu/english_facpubs/2/.

———. "What Meaningful Writing Means for Students." *Peer Review*, vol. 19, no. 1, 2017. *St. John's Scholar*, scholar.stjohns.edu/english_facpubs/3/.

Finkenstaedt-Quinn, Solaire A., et al. "Capturing Student Conceptions of

Thermodynamics and Kinetics Using Writing." *Chemistry Education Research and Practice*, vol. 21, no. 3, 2020, pp. 922–39, https://doi.org/10.1039/c9rp00292h.

Finkenstaedt-Quinn, Solaire A., et al. "Characterizing Peer Review Comments and Revision from a Writing-to-Learn Assignment Focused on Lewis Structures." *Journal of Chemical Education*, vol. 96, no. 2, 2019, pp. 227–37, https://doi.org/10.1021/acs.jchemed.8b00711.

Finkenstaedt-Quinn, Solaire A., et al. "Investigation of the Influence of a Writing-to-Learn Assignment on Student Understanding of Polymer Properties." *Journal of Chemical Education*, vol. 94, no. 11, 2017, pp. 1610–17, https://doi.org/10.1021/acs.jchemed.7b00363.

Finkenstaedt-Quinn, Solaire A., et al. "Praxis of Writing-to-Learn: A Model for the Design and Propagation of Writing-to-Learn in STEM." *Journal of Chemical Education*, vol. 98, no. 5, 2021, pp. 1548–55, https://doi.org/10.1021/acs.jchemed.0c01482.

Finkenstaedt-Quinn, Solaire A., et al. "Utilizing Peer Review and Revision in STEM to Support the Development of Conceptual Knowledge through Writing." *Written Communication*, vol. 38, no. 3, 2021, pp. 351–79, https://doi.org/10.1177/07410883211006038.

Flower, Linda. "Writer-Based Prose: A Cognitive Basis for Problems in Writing." *College English*, vol. 41, no. 1, 1979, pp. 19–37, https://doi.org/10.58680/ce197916016.

Gere, Anne Ruggles, et al. "Rewriting Disciplines: STEM Students' Longitudinal Approaches to Writing in (and across) the Disciplines." *Across the Disciplines*, vol. 15, no. 3, 2018, pp. 63–75, https://doi.org/10.37514/ATD-J.2018.15.3.12.

Gere, Anne Ruggles, et al. "A Tale of Two Prompts: New Perspectives on Writing-to-Learn Assignments." *WAC Journal*, vol. 29, 2018, pp. 147–88, https://doi.org/10.37514/WAC-J.2018.29.1.07.

Gere, Anne Ruggles, et al. "Writing and Conceptual Learning in Science: An Analysis of Assignments." *Written Communication*, vol. 36, no. 1, 2018, pp. 99–135, https://doi.org/10.1177/0741088318804820.

Graham, Steve, et al. "The Effects of Writing on Learning in Science, Social Studies, and Mathematics: A Meta-Analysis." *Review of Educational Research*, vol. 90, no. 2, 2020, pp. 179–226, https://doi.org/10.3102/0034654320914744.

Gupte, Trisha, et al. "Students' Meaningful Learning Experiences from Participating in Organic Chemistry Writing-to-Learn Activities." *Chemistry Education Research and Practice*, vol. 22, no. 2, 2021, pp. 396–414, https://doi.org/10.1039/d0rp00266f.

Halim, Audrey S., et al. "Identifying and Remediating Student Misconceptions in Introductory Biology via Writing-to-Learn Assignments and Peer Review." *CBE—Life Sciences Education*, vol. 17, no. 2, 2018, https://doi.org/10.1187/cbe.17-10-0212.

Kuh, George D. *High-Impact Educational Practices: What They Are, Who Has Access to Them, and Why They Matter*. Association of American Colleges and Universities, 2008.

Lewis, Gilbert N. "The Atom and the Molecule." *Journal of the American Chemical Society*, vol. 38, no. 4, 1916, pp. 762–85, https://doi.org/10.1021/ja02261a002.

McLeod, Susan H., and Elaine Maimon. "Clearing the Air: WAC Myths and Realities." *College English*, vol. 62, no. 5, 2000, pp. 573–83, https://doi.org/10.58680/ce20001182.

Moon, Alena, et al. "Application and Testing of a Framework for Characterizing the Quality of Scientific Reasoning in Chemistry Students' Writing on Ocean Acidification." *Chemistry Education Research and Practice*, vol. 20, no. 3, 2019, pp. 484–94, https://doi.org/10.1039/c9rp00005d.

Moon, Alena, et al. "Investigation of the Role of Writing-to-Learn in Promoting Student Understanding of Light–Matter Interactions." *Chemistry Education Research and Practice*, vol. 19, no. 3, 2018, pp. 807–18, https://doi.org/10.1039/c8rp00090e.

Moon, Alena, et al. "Writing in the STEM Classroom: Faculty Conceptions of Writing and Its Role in the Undergraduate Classroom." *Science Education*, vol. 102, no. 5, 2018, pp 1007–28, https://doi.org/10.1002/sce.21454.

Palmquist, Mike. "A Middle Way for WAC: Writing to Engage." *The WAC Journal*, vol. 31, 2020, pp. 7–22, https://doi.org/10.37514/WAC-J.2020.31.1.01.

———. "WAC and Critical Thinking: Exploring Productive Relationships." *English Across the Curriculum: Voices from Around the World*, edited by Bruce Morrison et al., The WAC Clearinghouse / UP of Colorado, 2021, pp. 207–22, https://doi.org/10.37514/INT-B.2021.1220.2.11.

Petterson, Michael N., et al. "The Role of Authentic Contexts and Social Elements in Supporting Organic Chemistry Students' Interactions with Writing-to-Learn Assignments." *Chemistry Education Research and Practice*, vol. 23, no. 1, 2022, pp. 189–205, https://doi.org/10.1039/d1rp00181g.

Scardamalia, Marlene, and Carl Bereiter. "A Brief History of Knowledge Building." *Canadian Journal of Learning and Technology*, vol. 36, no. 1, 2010, pp. 1–16. *ERIC*, eric.ed.gov/?id=EJ910451.

———. "Knowledge Telling and Knowledge Transforming in Written Composition." *Advances in Applied Psycholinguistics, Vol. 1. Disorders of First-Language Development; Vol. 2. Reading, Writing, and Language Learning*, edited by Sheldon Rosenberg, Cambridge University Press, 1987, pp. 142–75.

Shultz, Ginger V., and Anne Ruggles Gere. "Writing-to-Learn the Nature of Science in the Context of the Lewis Dot Structure Model." *Journal of Chemical Education*, vol. 92, no. 8, 2015, pp. 1325–29, https://doi.org/10.1021/acs.jchemed.5b00064.

Thompson, Robert J., Jr., et al. "How Faculty Discipline and Beliefs Influence Instructional Uses of Writing in STEM Undergraduate Courses at Research-Intensive Universities." *Journal of Writing Research*, vol. 12, no. 3, 2021, pp. 625–56, https://doi.org/10.17239/jowr-2021.12.03.04.

Watts, Field M., et al. "What Students Write about When Students Write about Mechanisms: Analysis of Features Present in Students' Written Descriptions of an Organic Reaction Mechanism." *Chemistry Education Research and Practice*, vol. 21, no. 4, 2020, pp. 1148–72, https://doi.org/10.1039/c9rp00185a.

CHAPTER 9.

STEM COURSES AS SITES OF WRITING: STUDENTS' DISCIPLINARY EXPERIENCES WITH WRITING-TO-LEARN ASSIGNMENTS

Ginger Shultz
University of Michigan

Amber J. Dood
University of Michigan

Solaire A. Finkenstaedt-Quinn
University of Michigan

As described by Mike Palmquist (Chapter 8, this collection), the practices of writing and writing to learn (WTL) broadly have been utilized to support conceptual learning and critical thinking across disciplines. In alignment with this broad use, many studies have characterized outcomes related to participation in WTL broadly and in STEM courses specifically. Prior syntheses indicate that the effectiveness of WTL can be tied to certain features of the assignments. Namely, assignments should include meaning-making tasks, incorporate interactive writing processes, support metacognition, and provide clear writing expectations (Anderson et al.; Gere et al.; Klein). For a discussion of these aspects of writing assignments, see in this collection Chapter 15 by Jathan Day, Naitnaphit Limlamai, and Emily Wilson. The efficacy of WTL is well established; reviews of the literature have shown that WTL fosters conceptual learning, supports development of scientific reasoning, and encourages argumentation from data, among other benefits (Bangert-Drowns et al.; Reynolds et al.; Rivard). However, despite the known benefits of WTL and characteristics that support its effective use, the implementation of writing, let alone WTL, in STEM courses can be challenging for instructors due to systematic barriers such as class size, which restrict their ability to provide detailed feedback to students and established

DOI: https://doi.org/10.37514/PER-B.2025.2456.2.09

norms in STEM fields (Finkenstaedt-Quinn et al., "Postsecondary"; Moon et al.). Consideration of both the benefits of WTL, and research thereof, and the barriers to implementing writing led to the development of MWrite at the University of Michigan.

THE MWRITE PROGRAM: PROPAGATION OF WTL AT THE UNIVERSITY OF MICHIGAN

Anne Ruggles Gere and Ginger Shultz, a faculty member in the chemistry department at the University of Michigan, were first introduced to each other by a colleague who knew that Anne was interested in increasing the use of writing in STEM disciplines on campus. They found a common goal: addressing disparities in the teaching practices traditionally used in STEM courses that might exclude certain students while also supporting rote learning—e.g., an overreliance on problem sets that allow students to utilize memorization rather than requiring problem-solving skills (Dood and Watts). Together Gere and Shultz developed the idea of the MWrite program—a program that would work with instructors to develop and implement scaffolded WTL assignments in their classrooms. As they considered what the program should look like, they decided on a target of large, introductory courses with an emphasis on STEM disciplines. The program and assignment design are described in detail in Finkenstaedt-Quinn et al.'s "Praxis of Writing-to-Learn: A Model for the Design and Propagation of Writing-to-Learn in STEM."

In their design, Gere and Shultz considered the barriers that might inhibit instructors' ability to implement writing into their courses. Through MWrite they aimed to provide instructors with a faculty learning community and to better facilitate feedback on student writing by engaging writing fellows (i.e., undergraduate students who were previously successful in the course returning to guide current students) and students' own peers via a tool facilitating anonymous, scaffolded peer review. Before instructors participating in MWrite implement WTL for the first time, they take part in the MWrite faculty seminar where they work closely with a lecturer from the Sweetland Center for Writing and one another to develop their goals for using WTL and to develop their assignments. The Sweetland Center for Writing also trains the undergraduate writing fellows. In alignment with the role of writing fellows described in the literature (Cairns and Anderson; Gladstein), these students serve as near-peers who can work with students enrolled in WTL courses as they respond to the writing assignments as well as grade and provide feedback on students' responses to the assignments. However, the MWrite writing fellows are distinguished by their focus on content as opposed to writing mechanics when working with students and during the grading process.

Additionally, drawing on Gere's expertise with the writing research literature, Gere and Shultz developed a specific form of WTL. The MWrite WTL assignments were designed considering the features of effective WTL practices (Anderson et al.; Gere et al.; Klein). As Figure 9.1 illustrates, students write a response to a prompt, go through the process of peer review, and then revise their response. The prompt presents students with a context and rhetorical features that they must critically consider and to which they apply their content knowledge, creating a meaning-making task. The processes of peer review and revision incorporate interactive writing processes into the assignment and support metacognition. Lastly, at each step the MWrite model aims to present students with clear writing expectations (e.g., by providing criteria for review and revision).

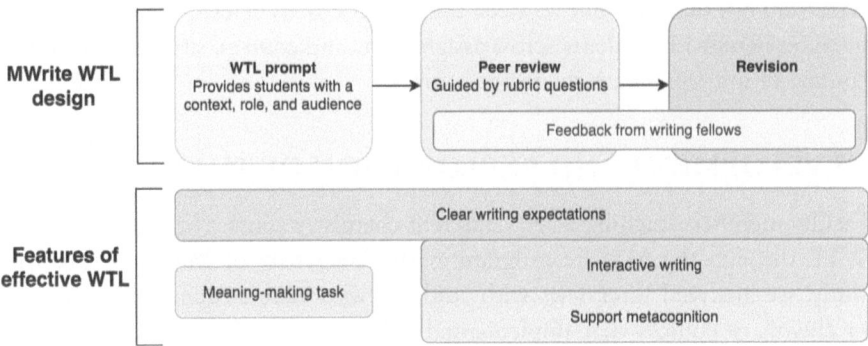

Figure 9.1. Alignment between the MWrite WTL assignment design and features of effective WTL.

Overview of MWrite Research

Beyond the practical considerations, Gere and Shultz wanted to ensure that the evidence-based design of the assignments actually translated into positive outcomes for students. Thus, they developed a research component to the MWrite program. Members of the MWrite research team, including two of this essay's co-authors, recently reviewed the existing research on student learning from and experiences with the MWrite WTL assignments using an engagement framework (Finkenstaedt-Quinn et al., "Portrait"). Briefly, the research team identified that 1) the assignments supported students to describe and learn disciplinary content, 2) the assignments engaged students in critical and disciplinary thinking, 3) the design of the assignments supported the learning process and influenced students' affective experiences, and 4) peer review and revision supported students' engagement with the assignments. While MWrite research is still ongoing, most pertinent for this chapter is students' perceptions of the WTL assignments. Students have primarily expressed how the context and rhetorical features provided in the WTL prompts and the processes of peer review and revision are tied to positive learning experiences with the WTL assignments as a whole (Gupte et al.; Marks et al.; Petterson et al.). Further research on how students perceive these features and their influence on students' affective experiences is ongoing, with some findings about students' experiences reported herein.

In the spirit of engaging in dialogue and considering what writing means to students outside of English courses, we felt that writing this chapter presented a prime opportunity to further explore the themes of how students experience writing and WTL in STEM courses. Furthermore, in this chapter, we provide an initial exploration of a few areas of interest that have emerged from past data collection but that have not yet been the primary focus of a study, and we examine interviews with students across assignments and courses, situated within the context of undergraduate chemistry courses.

DEVELOPMENT AND EXPLORATION OF THEMES

Faculty members teaching several different chemistry courses have implemented WTL through the MWrite program at the University of Michigan. For this study, we analyzed interviews with students who were currently participating in chemistry courses that implemented MWrite. Interviews took place from the Winter 2019 semester through the Winter 2023 semester in two chemistry courses: organic chemistry (18 students) and introductory biochemistry (21 students). The interviews were conducted with varying research purposes, but across these contexts students discussed their writing experiences, how they perceived writing and WTL, and their affectivity when writing. Students were not always directly asked about these experiences, but across several course contexts, students' affective experiences with WTL in STEM courses surfaced.

The co-authors engaged in an iterative process of discussing themes we noticed across interviews and returning to interviews to further explore those themes. Through this process, we refined the themes to two: students' perceptions of writing in STEM courses and affective experiences related to engaging with scientific practices through WTL.

FINDINGS

While not directly related to the questions of interest in our previous studies, the recurring themes of how students perceive writing and their affectivity about MWrite assignments led us to think about the difference between how we conceptualize writing and WTL and how students perceive and value them. We thought to use this Festschrift's celebration of the career of Anne Ruggles Gere as an opportunity to explore how students experience writing and WTL in the context of a STEM classroom.

Student Perceptions of Writing in STEM Courses

As part of two sets of interviews targeting students' experiences with WTL in chemistry, we asked students about their past experiences with writing in academic contexts and what disciplines they associated with writing. While primarily intended as questions to contextualize students' experiences, we found the responses intriguing. In both sets of interviews, students initially or exclusively described experiences with writing in non-STEM courses, despite the fact that they were mostly STEM or pre-health majors and ranged from first-year students to seniors. Of the 32 students, only about half of them mentioned without prompting a STEM course or engaging in scientific writing. After prompting, about a third of the remaining students identified writing in their STEM courses. Given the various ways writing can be and is used in STEM courses (e.g., lab reports, short answer questions), the prevalence of students connecting writing experiences to their academic experiences in STEM courses was lower than we expected. Cheri,[1] a second-year student enrolled in the organic chemistry course, captured the dissonance between their experiences with writing as an undergraduate and the disciplines they associate with writing, saying,

> For me [disciplines with writing are] more English, History. Even language. I had to write a lot of essays in Spanish in high school for AP Spanish. But it's funny because the last thing I kind of think of would be science, but I guess now, because to me the word writing kind of means a formal essay, not really a lab report, but lab reports is all the writing I've done in college basically, probably 80 percent of it. So I guess I should start counting science. But, my first thought is humanities.

Additionally, when asked about writing in courses, most students first described their English courses, and the first-year writing requirement course at the University of Michigan in particular. This is of note as it shows another way outside of MWrite that Gere has influenced these students' academic careers: it is due to Gere's efforts while director of the Sweetland Center for Writing that more STEM students do writing in both upper- and lower-level classes.

Of the students who without prompting identified writing in STEM courses,

---

1 Pseudonyms have been used for all student participants.

many were either in or had taken a writing requirement course for their discipline or had done writing as part of their research experiences. For example, Fern, a first-year student enrolled in the organic chemistry course, recognized writing as a scientific practice, but their primary association with writing in STEM disciplines was due to their research experience, rather than writing in their STEM courses:

> Yeah. In high school, I had a lot of writing experience, because that's something that they do a lot in English and reading classes. Scientific writing especially, I didn't really do anything with that until I got to college, especially in my research group. We do a lot of literature review, so I've had a lot of experience at least my freshman year with scientific writing. But yeah, I never really had too much experience.

As a first-year student, Fern might have had less exposure with writing in their STEM courses, a limitation which may have skewed how they thought about writing in STEM disciplines. In contrast, Laurel, a second-year student also enrolled in the organic chemistry course, discussed experiences with both the classic genre of laboratory reports in STEM courses and writing affiliated with their research position:

> Okay. I think starting in high school, it was just with a lot of English stuff. We didn't do a lot of writing in my other classes. Then coming to college, definitely took a first-year writing class, and that's where most of that happened. But then after that, after my first semester of freshman year, I've definitely done most of my writing actually in science classes and lab classes, doing lab report type stuff or . . . I work in a research lab, so I've helped with some of the papers and analysis we've done there. It's definitely been more academic writing and analysis, so it's weird when I have to write something that's not for a science lab . . . but yeah, since I have had a bit more experience with lab reports and stuff like that, now that's kind of what comes to mind in terms of writing for the sciences.

The greater recognition of writing in STEM courses Laurel expressed may be related to the breadth of their academic experiences. Similarly Rose, a second-year student enrolled in the organic chemistry course, said, "[My association of disciplines with writing has] expanded since coming to college."

Fern, Laurel, and Rose all described how their academic experiences with writing expanded as they moved from high school to college. This transition translates when comparing students in the organic chemistry course and the biochemistry course (where students take the organic chemistry course prior to the biochemistry course). About half of the students interviewed from the biochemistry course discussed writing in STEM courses compared to only a third from the organic chemistry course.

With the weaker association between students mentioning writing and STEM courses than we expected, we considered that students may have a narrower conception of "writing" than we do. For example, Piper, a third-year student enrolled in the biochemistry course, said, "So I don't have a ton of prior experience in writing. Like, especially not scientific, I've done a lot of scientific writing in like biology classes, and for labs and things like that. But just in general, not a ton." There appears to be a disconnect for Piper between their experiences with writing broadly and the scientific writing they did in their STEM courses. This is seen more explicitly in a statement by Heron, a second-year student in the biochemistry course, who, after prompting about their experiences with writing in STEM courses, said, "I've had to do like post-labs, but those are not, I would not call those writing. I would say, just saying what happened and why."

The potential disconnect between the writing students do in their STEM courses and how they conceptualize "writing" is interesting, as laboratory reports, pre/post-lab writing exercises, and short answer response questions are often used in STEM courses. Comparatively, Aderyn, a second-year student enrolled in the biochemistry course, recognized the traditional forms of writing in their STEM courses and discussed the difference between the MWrite WTL biochemistry course and what they normally associated with chemistry courses:

> I was a little bit confused in the beginning, just because I think it's not often in a chemistry class that like you write papers, a lot of it is like, diagram based, or a lot of it is like answering short and like short answer questions and drawing out mechanisms. But none of it is just like paragraph on paragraph on paragraph writing.

While Aderyn did recognize the writing they experienced in their chemistry courses as writing, they described how they were not used to longer writing in the context of their chemistry courses. Furthermore, as seen with Fern and Laurel, whose primary association with writing in STEM courses was the writing they had done as part of their research positions, scientific writing may not be a practice students recognize experiencing at the undergraduate level. From our interviews, even when students recognized writing as something they did in STEM courses, they did not necessarily describe experiences with writing practices that aligned with scientific writing. This may mean that students are not developing scientific practices related to writing or just do not recognize how the writing incorporated into their STEM courses serves to do so. As most of the students in our study planned to pursue STEM or STEM-adjacent careers, it is important not only to ensure students have opportunities to write in their STEM courses, but also to ensure they recognize that what they are doing is scientific writing, as this can support their affectivity towards the assignments.

Affectivity

A major theme that arose from students' interviews was the affectivity surrounding participation in MWrite assignments and the venue the assignments provided to better engage with scientific practices as compared to traditional assignments. For example, one assignment in the organic chemistry course asked students to take on the role of a scientist writing a grant proposal. This scientist was working on a newly discovered reaction (which we refer to as the "base-free Wittig reaction") and wanted to acquire funding to further study this reaction. The reaction itself was taken from the primary scientific literature and was a direct derivative of one of the reactions the students completed as part of their laboratory course (which we refer to as the "Wittig reaction"). This new reaction was presented in the context of two different real-world applications: use as an anti-cancer agent and use as an insecticide. We noted students expressing positive affectivity toward completing this MWrite assignment in the context of engaging with several scientific practices. Particularly, students engaged with the scientific practices of constructing explanations and communicating information in a more authentic scientific context (National Research Council). The MWrite assignments created a scientific context relevant to students' lives that they found to be interesting, meaningful, and engaging. Students also found that constructing explanations in the provided format (i.e., a grant proposal) allowed them a venue to better learn chemistry concepts by explaining them.

Students perceived the Wittig scenario as more enjoyable than an assignment without context and felt the genre was instrumental in bridging what they were learning in organic chemistry to how it applies to our understanding of the world scientifically. One student, Winter, a second-year student enrolled in the organic chemistry course, said,

> I would say definitely what I do like the most is, like you said, this is from actual research, and so it's nice to have something in the real world to connect like what we're learning to, because a lot of times it does feel a bit disconnected just like organic chemistry in general . . . it kind of feels like you're doing something that pertains exactly to what you want to do

> later in life. And so I feel like it's a little bit more motivating of an assignment to do when you have like a real world application in something that you're actually interested in.

Winter perceived the assignment as more interesting due to the real-world application provided in the prompt and therefore was more motivated to complete the assignment. They were able to connect what they were doing in class to the authentic practices of scientists. Another student, Autumn, a second-year student in the organic chemistry course, explained that the assignment context reinforced that organic chemistry is relevant to their life:

> I like the actual, like, prompt or like the discussing, like, the significance of it. I felt like, you know, I thought it was pretty cool. It's nice to have some context for like what it is that we're doing . . . so this is like a treatment, like a drug for a treatment. And I guess it kind of like reinforces that, like, organic chemistry is being used in a context that matters to me and that, like, I can't avoid it, it's gonna come back.

Like Winter, Autumn perceived the assignment as more enjoyable due to the context. Another student, Night, a first-year student in the organic chemistry course, noted that in addition to increased enjoyment in completing the assignment, the provided context for why the reaction was important made the assignment easier to complete and encouraged them to think deeply about their explanation of the reaction because they understood why it is important to learn these concepts:

> Giving it a context versus, you know, just saying explain the differences between the Wittig reaction and a base-free Wittig reaction, giving it that context kind of, you know, makes it a little bit easier to explain why we're focused on the differences instead of just like what the differences are. So it kind of like makes you think a little bit more about why we care about what the changes are.

Night reported more easily engaging in the scientific practice of constructing explanations because of the context provided by the MWrite assignment. Similarly, Spring, a third-year student in the organic chemistry course, felt the features of the MWrite assignment allowed them to better explain the chemistry topics: "I think that environment like created more like—and helped me to—like, explain better about certain topics because like the topic itself is very formal, and, yeah very academic. So I think it was helpful."

While Night and Spring felt constructing explanations was easier in the MWrite context, Summer, a second-year student in the organic chemistry course, praised the assignment for making them think about things differently and noted that being asked to engage in constructing an explanation was not normal for laboratory writing: "And so this made you think about things differently. Because in the lab write-up, I believe it's just claim, evidence, reasoning, or you think not in lab, and here, you're actually trying to, you know, explain a concept and prove a point." Summer felt the MWrite assignment allowed them to *explain* concepts rather than just report their results as they would in a lab report and that this was helpful for their mastery of the topic. Similarly, Day, another second-year student in the organic chemistry course, connected their engagement with the scientific practice of constructing explanations to their understanding of the course material:

> I definitely didn't quite understand the reaction as much like before I did [the MWrite] assignment. That being said, like in lab, I feel like you just kind of mix things and go with it. And I mean, we do write the mechanism in our lab books and everything like that, but this definitely was a better understanding of like, oh, like the reason why I mixed this with this is because of like this is a good leaving group and stuff.

Day, along with Night and Summer, noted they were given an outlet to engage in the scientific practice of constructing explanations and to engage with the material in a way that was different from standard chemistry assignments.

Despite not liking the WTL assignments, Bruce, a fourth-year student in the organic chemistry course, understood the importance of practicing scientific writing in STEM courses beyond just engaging in constructing explanations because students do not have many opportunities to practice writing in this context:

> Yeah, I understand why it's there, and I think I get that it is important. Not just from "explaining things helps you learn" perspective, but also from a, I think, a lot of scientists get into science and don't have a great writing background necessarily. And so it's good to get all the practice you can. So I know it's important and I know why it's in the class, but it doesn't make me like it any more.

Like Bruce, other students also found that the role they were asked to take on (e.g., a scientist requesting funding through a grant proposal) and the audience they were asked to write to (e.g., reviewers at the National Institutes of Health) were helpful for completing the task at hand. These features were designed to help students engage in the scientific practice of communicating information more authentically. Winter explained that the task of writing a grant proposal helped develop their scientific writing in a way that a standard lab report would not:

> I would say it definitely has helped my scientific writing especially . . . I think that, you know, formatting an answer in terms of like the how, what, and why is really helpful in like, kind of, just because in grant proposals, you want it to be pretty transparent, I would assume. And so like focusing on how to write in that aspect has been really helpful.

In addition to improving scientific writing, Day felt the MWrite assignment provided a more concrete way to communicate and explain science than a lab report:

> No, yeah, the lab reports definitely like, I guess, also too with the lab reports is still pretty open ended with just like the claim, the lab, [inaudible]. Whereas with this it was like let's write the mechanisms, let's like look at the properties, which I think compare very like explicit, like mechanisms where the lab reports, it's like, the data that we have from our lab, which is usually like 99 percent of the time really messed up, and so I felt like this was definitely like a more concrete way of writing scientific papers.

Finally, Summer explained that the real-world context, alongside things learned in their lecture course, provided an outlet to improve their scientific writing and pull together multiple concepts to develop an explanation. Like Day, Summer explained that this assignment was much different from other types of assignments they had been asked to do and allowed them to think in a different way than they were required to think during exams:

> Sometimes people do assignments just to do assignments, it's not for like the real world meaning . . . I was able to improve my scientific writing, you know, I was able to prove a point using evidence from stuff I've learned in class, like, you know, going to lecture you don't really know how much you know until you're forced to do something like this. And I think this is very different from like let's say an exam. Like an exam, they're meant they want you to think a specific way, but here, you have to use everything you've learned and not just, you know, specific things you've learned.

Bruce, Winter, Day, and Summer all appreciated the importance of communicating about science through writing, and the grant proposal allowed them to practice this skill.

Altogether, our findings indicate that the MWrite assignments encourage students to engage in the scientific practices of constructing explanations and communicating information in a way that students appreciate and even enjoy, for the most part. We were pleased to see evidence of most of the students viewing MWrite in a positive way; students explained to us the many perceived benefits from participating in the program. This pattern in students' views of their writing could not have occurred without Gere championing the MWrite program. We found that our chemistry MWrite assignments met the goals of the MWrite program, as students were more interested in engaging with the content specifically because of the MWrite assignments. Students also felt the assignments increased their conceptual understanding of organic chemistry through constructing explanations. They were provided with a writing outlet which allowed them to think and communicate about chemistry in a different way than traditional examinations and laboratory reports, and most had positive affectivity toward the assignments as a whole.

DISCUSSION AND FUTURE DIRECTIONS

From our results, it is clear that students have mixed experiences with writing in STEM. While most students included in this study did indeed write in their STEM courses, many did not identify the tasks they were completing as writing. Students described primary writing experiences, especially before college, as being in English courses; several students mentioned that before college they had not written in a STEM course at all. While some students did recall some writing experiences in STEM courses, the students we interviewed reported a lack of formal writing experiences in STEM courses in general, aside from MWrite. As the interviews included herein were not part of a study targeting writing in STEM courses, they may not have fully captured students' experiences. Future research should be directed specifically toward better understanding student conceptions of writing in STEM courses and how these conceptions change as they move through the STEM curriculum.

Writing is a central part of professional science communication, and future scientists should be trained in how to communicate and explain their work through writing. However, it can take some time for students to acclimate to writing in a new genre (Bazerman). Thus, it is important to provide students with opportunities to write in STEM genres and to engage students with scientific writing practices (Keys). WTL can engage students in STEM genres and scientific practices such as constructing explanations and communicating information. The specific contexts provided by our MWrite assignments in chemistry (e.g., the grant proposal) provide a more authentic venue for students to engage in these practices.

Providing students an opportunity to write in and engage in STEM genres through the MWrite assignments also encouraged positive affectivity. Furthermore, incorporating authentic contexts that encourage student engagement in scientific practices could increase not only competency with scientific practices but also meaningful learning. Additional research should explore how students engage in specifically scientific practices through MWrite and how participation in MWrite impacts students' scientific skills (e.g., research, argument, or peer review skills).

Our findings indicate that MWrite WTL can serve its main pedagogical purpose of supporting conceptual learning and disciplinary thinking while also affording students opportunities to write in STEM courses and supporting their engagement in scientific practices. Considered in context with past MWrite WTL research, the findings described herein demonstrate the diverse ways in which the MWrite program, and through it Anne Ruggles Gere, have positively impacted students in STEM at the University of Michigan.

ACKNOWLEDGMENTS

We would like to thank all of the students who have participated in MWrite courses over the years, with a special thanks to those who have volunteered to participate in our studies. This work and MWrite as a program also could not exist without the many instructors who have participated in the MWrite program and incorporated WTL in their courses, the writing fellows who have facilitated the implementation, and Larissa Sano at the Sweetland Center for Writing for her support in working with faculty and training writing fellows. We would also like to acknowledge our fellow researchers, especially those who conducted and transcribed the interviews used herein—Ina Zaimi, Katiya Barkho, Michael Petterson, and Daisy Haas. Lastly we would like to acknowledge The University of Michigan's Office of the Provost's Transforming Learning for a Third Century Initiative, The Keck Foundation, and the National Science Foundation (IUSE awards 2121223 and 1524967) for funding.

WORKS CITED

Aderyn. Interview. 21 Feb. 2023.

Anderson, Paul, et al. "The Contributions of Writing to Learning and Development: Results from a Large-Scale Multi-Institutional Study." *Research in the Teaching of English*, vol. 50, no. 2, 2015, pp. 199–235, https://doi.org/10.58680/rte201527602.

Autumn. Interview. 1 Apr. 2022.

Bangert-Drowns, Robert L., et al. "The Effects of School-Based Writing-to-Learn Interventions on Academic Achievement: A Meta-Analysis." *Review of Educational Research*, vol. 74, no. 1, 2004, pp. 29–58, https://doi.org/10.3102/00346543074001029.

Bazerman, Charles. "Genre and Cognitive Development: Beyond Writing to Learn." *Genre in a Changing World*, edited by Charles Bazerman et al., The WAC Clearinghouse / Parlor Press, 2009, pp. 283–98, https://doi.org/10.37514/PER-B.2009.2324.2.14.

Bruce. Interview. 16 Apr. 2020.

Cairns, Rhoda, and Paul V. Anderson. "The Protean Shape of the Writing Associate's Role: An Empirical Study and Conceptual Model." *Across the Disciplines*, vol. 5, no. 2, 2008, https://doi.org/10.37514/ATD-J.2008.5.2.07.

Cheri. Interview. 20 Apr. 2020.

Day. Interview. 31 Mar. 2022.

Dood, Amber J., and Field M. Watts. "Students' Strategies, Struggles, and Successes with Mechanism Problem Solving in Organic Chemistry: A Scoping Review of the Research Literature." *Journal of Chemical Education*, vol. 100, no. 1, 2023, pp. 53–68, https://doi.org/10.1021/acs.jchemed.2c00572.

Fern. Interview. 21 Apr. 2020.

Finkenstaedt-Quinn, Solaire A., et al. "A Portrait of MWrite as a Research Program: A Review of Research on Writing-to-Learn in STEM through the MWrite Program." *International Journal for the Scholarship of Teaching and Learning*, vol. 17, no. 1, 2023, https://doi.org/10.20429/ijsotl.2023.17118.

Finkenstaedt-Quinn, Solaire A., et al. "Postsecondary Faculty Attitudes and Beliefs About Writing-Based Pedagogies in the STEM Classroom." *CBE - Life Sciences Education*, vol. 21, no. 3, 2022, https://doi.org/10.1187/cbe.21-09-0285.

Finkenstaedt-Quinn, Solaire A., et al. "Praxis of Writing-to-Learn: A Model for the Design and Propagation of Writing-to-Learn in STEM." *Journal of Chemical Education*, vol. 98, no. 5, 2021, pp. 1548–55, https://doi.org/10.1021/acs.jchemed.0c01482.

Gere, Anne Ruggles, et al. "Writing and Conceptual Learning in Science: An Analysis of Assignments." *Written Communication*, vol. 36, no. 1, 2019, pp. 99–135, https://doi.org/10.1177/0741088318804820.

Gladstein, Jill M. "Conducting Research in the Gray Space: How Writing Associates Negotiate between WAC and WID in an Introductory Biology Course." *Across the Disciplines*, vol. 5, no. 2, 2008, https://doi.org/10.37514/ATD-J.2008.5.2.02.

Gupte, Trisha, et al. "Students' Meaningful Learning Experiences from Participating in Organic Chemistry Writing-to-Learn Activities." *Chemistry Education Research and Practice*, vol. 22, 2021, pp. 396–414, https://doi.org/10.1039/d0rp00266f.

Heron. Interview. 07 Mar. 2023.

Keys, Carolyn W. "Revitalizing Instruction in Scientific Genres: Connecting Knowledge Production with Writing to Learn in Science." *Science Education*, vol. 83, no. 2, 1999, pp. 115–30, https://tinyurl.com/zjr9b5b9.

Klein, Perry D. "Mediators and Moderators in Individual and Collaborative Writing to Learn." *Journal of Writing Research*, vol. 7, no. 1, 2015, pp. 201–14, https://doi.org/10.17239/jowr-2015.07.01.08.

Laurel. Interview. 27 Apr. 2020.

Marks, L, et al. "Writing-to-Learn in Introductory Materials Science and Engineering." *MRS Communications*, vol. 12, 2022, pp. 1–11, https://doi.org/10.1557/s43579-021-00114-z.

Moon, Alena, et al. "Writing in the STEM Classroom: Faculty Conceptions of Writing and Its Role in the Undergraduate Classroom." *Science Education*, vol. 102, no. 5, 2018, pp. 1007–28, https://doi.org/10.1002/sce.21454.

National Research Council. *A Framework for K–12 Science Education: Practices, Crosscutting Concepts, and Core Ideas.* The National Academies P, 2012, https://doi.org/10.17226/13165.

Night. Interview. 20 Mar. 2022.

Petterson, Michael N., et al. "The Role of Authentic Contexts and Social Elements in Supporting Organic Chemistry Students' Interactions with Writing-to-Learn Assignments." *Chemistry Education Research and Practice*, vol. 23, no. 1, 2022, pp. 189–205, https://doi.org/10.1039/D1RP00181G.

Piper. Interview. 20 Feb. 2023.

Reynolds, Julie A., et al. "Writing-to-Learn in Undergraduate Science Education: A Community-Based, Conceptually Driven Approach." *CBE Life Sciences Education*, vol. 11, no. 1, 2012, pp. 17–25, https://doi.org/10.1187/cbe.11-08-0064.

Rivard, Lé Onard P. "A Review of Writing to Learn in Science: Implications for Practice and Research." *Journal of Research in Science Teaching*, vol. 31, no. 9, 1994, pp. 969–83, https://doi.org/10.1002/tea.3660310910.

Rose. Interview. 30 Apr. 2020.

Spring. Interview. 29 Mar. 2022.

Summer. Interview. 23 Mar. 2022.

Winter. Interview. 31 Mar. 2022.

CHAPTER 10.

SITES OF DIGITAL WRITING AND COMMUNITY: ANNE GERE AND THE SWEETLAND DIGITAL RHETORIC COLLABORATIVE

Naomi Silver
University of Michigan

Founded in 2012, the Sweetland Digital Rhetoric Collaborative (DRC) comprises a community webspace for teachers, researchers, and students of digital rhetoric and an open access book series and book prize with the University of Michigan Press.[1] As of late 2023, the DRC has published almost a dozen books and supported more than fifty graduate student fellows chosen from across the country to collaborate on DRC projects. An eight-member advisory board provides guidance across all aspects of this work. As DRC co-directors, Anne Gere, Simone Sessolo, and I know of many professional and scholarly collaborations that began in the fellows program and continue to flourish, and we have seen DRC books win major awards in our field.[2] But the activities and impact of the collaborative itself have been neither officially researched nor documented.

This chapter begins to address this oversight by offering a narrative of the DRC's history drawn from my own records and experiences as co-founder with Anne and augmented by initial interviews with three long-term DRC collaborators, Jason Tham (Texas Tech University), Laura Gonzales (University of Florida), and Douglas Eyman (George Mason University). As a way into the many strands that comprise the Sweetland Digital Rhetoric Collaborative, I'll explore here the *digital*, the *rhetorical*, and the *collaborative* as braided, interweaving themes central both to the history and the present of the DRC—and to the work and influence of Anne Ruggles Gere.

---

1   Visit the Sweetland Digital Rhetoric Collaborative website at https://www.digitalrhetoric collaborative.org/ and the DRC book series at the University of Michigan Press at https://press.umich.edu/Series/S/Sweetland-Digital-Rhetoric-Collaborative.
2   *Digital Samaritans* by Jim Ridolfo won the 2017 CCCC Research Impact Award, *Rhizcomics* by Jason Helms won the 2018 *Kairos* Best Webtext Award, and *Sites of Translation* by Laura Gonzales won the 2020 CCCC Advancement of Knowledge Award.

DOI: https://doi.org/10.37514/PER-B.2025.2456.2.10

SWEETLAND

Anne Gere was the director of the Gayle Morris Sweetland Center for Writing at the University of Michigan (UM) from 2008–2019. During that time, she ushered in the broadest expansion of the center's curriculum and activities since its founding as the English Composition Board in 1978. To name a few of these, she created the "Michigan Model" of directed self-placement (Gere et al., "Assessing"; Gere et al., "Local Assessment"); founded MWrite, a writing-fellows-facilitated writing-to-learn initiative in large-enrollment introductory courses (Finkenstaedt-Quinn et al.); developed courses and community college collaborations to support transfer students at Michigan (Gere et al., "Mutual Adjustments"); worked with departments across campus to study and update UM's upper-level writing requirement (Gere et al., "Interrogating"); instituted a minor in writing with a focus in multimodal composition and electronic portfolios and conducted a major longitudinal study of it (Gere); and prompted the development of Sweetland's first "new media writing" course, which has grown into a series of special topics courses focused on "writing with digital and social media" ("Writing 200"; "Writing 201"). All of these initiatives bear Anne's signature but were undertaken in collaboration with Sweetland's faculty and staff and with stakeholders around the university; further, the lengthy author lists that appear on the publications reporting the institutional research behind these initiatives stand as a testament to Anne's mentorship of graduate students and her collaborative approach to writing.

It is the last-named of these initiatives—"new media writing" courses—I wish to begin with here, for in accounts of Anne's scholarly and pedagogical influences, digital rhetoric is not typically on the list. Yet, as the editors observe in their introduction to this collection, "Gere's scholarship has repeatedly broken new ground, inviting us to conceptualize our fields and sub-fields more expansively and interactively" (3). Always on top of the latest developments in writing studies, one of the first proposals Anne made as new director of the Sweetland Center for Writing was that we begin to offer courses in "new media writing," beginning with "The Rhetoric of Blogging" in 2009. Since then, as co-founder and co-editor of the Sweetland Digital Rhetoric Collaborative, Anne has helped to provide a venue for shared inquiry into digital rhetoric and digital media as well as an important publication outlet for innovative born-digital long-form projects.

So, Anne Gere as digital rhetoric innovator is one of the stories this chapter will tell.

DIGITAL

A related story is the role of the DRC—and Anne, as co-director—in the history of academic digital publishing. Once Anne decided that Sweetland ought to get on board with "new media" writing,³ she started looking around for opportunities to make connections in the digital rhetoric community and to find Sweetland a place in this field. These efforts eventually led to Sweetland's hosting of the 2011 Computers and Writing conference (C&W) at the University of Michigan on the theme of "Writing in Motion: Traversing Public/Private Spaces." The conference brought Sweetland to the attention of the University of Michigan Press, which had begun the process of venturing into digital publishing in 2009 under the direction of Phil Pochoda (Jaschik; Pochoda, "University Press 2.0" and "Editor's Note"). Soon after, the press proposed the idea of a digital publishing collaboration. To say the least, we were intrigued.

RHETORIC

It quickly became clear that existing academic publication frameworks were not sufficient to the needs of the digital rhetoric community, which brings us to *rhetoric*. DRC board member, book prize winner, and former fellow Laura Gonzales told me how she describes writing for the DRC website to her students as "fostering these different conversations [in the field] in a more low stakes way . . . without being necessarily a formal journal, but having a forum where people can write their thoughts on whatever the latest issue is around." Former DRC fellow Jason Tham echoed that the DRC helped them in "thinking outside of the traditional, just coursework . . . and even just writing traditional publications. . . . I think [the DRC] is sort of like a third space that is different, but I'm still considering it scholarship and research."

I'll return to the idea of a rhetorical "third space" later, but first, I turn to the *collaborative* dimensions of the DRC to begin to sketch its history.

COLLABORATIVE

As one of the central "commitments . . . highlight[ed] throughout this collection," James Beitler and Sarah Ruffing Robbins acknowledge in their introduction that *collaboration* and attention to community represent vital elements in Anne Gere's work (7). These qualities characterized her approach to the UM Press invitation, as well. In fact, her first impulse was to consult with members of the computers and writing community to learn about their needs, so that this new digital book series could best serve them. That impulse led us to WIDE-EMU, a new, one-day "unconference" held on the Eastern Michigan University

---

3   The shifting terminology to name this field of writing is an important area of research in its own right (Lauer).

(EMU) campus in October of 2011 and co-sponsored by EMU's written communication program and Michigan State University's writing in digital environments (WIDE) program. Anne and I proposed a session on "Envisioning a new digital writing/rhetoric community web space," inviting participants to help us imagine and shape it.

We were joined by a small group of digital rhetoricians with various connections to the field. Key ideas that came out of that conversation named the need for "ebooks that are more than just a pdf," a "place to design [interactive digital projects] in a longer framework," "a medium-form backchannel that operates at a different pace [from an article] but is also relative to scholarship," and "scholarship carnivals [where] you'd have a list of maybe 30 entries that are taking up various crumbs from [an] article and trying to respond and engage" (Gere and Silver). In other words, we learned that there was a need not only for long-form, interactive digital publication venues, but also for a "third space" for short- and medium-form digital writing, a community space to share digital rhetoric research and pedagogy and to carry on conversations in and about the field in a range of genres and forms.

From this discussion begun at WIDE-EMU, things moved quickly. We had enough momentum to set a goal of launching this new book series and community website at C&W 2012, to be held the following May at North Carolina State University in Raleigh. We began the process of building our advisory board, seeking a balance of members with different areas of expertise and different connections to digital rhetoric and digital publication.[4]

Email archives show that by March 1, 2012, we had our board in place and were beginning the process of naming the series and website and collectively wordsmithing a description.[5] With the subject line "Launch!" Anne sent the first collective email to our eight-member board thanking them for serving, identifying our aimed-for May launch date at C&W, and exhorting that "Your first mission, then, is to help find a name." The email thread demonstrates collegial, collective decision-making and an interest in emphasizing both the collaborative nature of digital rhetoric production and the open-ended forms it might take. A day later, on March 2, we had a name: "Sweetland Digital Rhetoric Collaborative, it is," I wrote.

---

4   The original members of the DRC advisory board were Jonathan Alexander (University of California, Irvine), Cheryl Ball (independent scholar), Kristine L. Blair (Duquesne University), Douglas Eyman (George Mason University), Troy Hicks (Central Michigan University), Derek Mueller (Virginia Tech), Jentery Sayers (University of Victoria), and M. Remi Yergeau (Carleton University). See the current board at https://www.digitalrhetoriccollaborative.org/about/board/.

5   My thanks to Douglas Eyman both for saving these email threads and for sharing them with me following our interview in September 2023.

COLLABORATIVE 2.0

The next big leap forward for the collaborative was the launch of the DRC graduate fellows program the following year, in June 2013.[6] The fellows design the shape of the DRC website and collaborate to create and curate content for it. This program arose in part from the recognition that more minds and hands were needed to support the DRC website and extend its reach. It had launched in May 2012 with the first DRC blog carnival, "What Does Digital Rhetoric Mean to Me?"—a field-defining conversation to which each of our advisory board members contributed and which traveled across several other blogs and listservs. At that time, we also launched the DRC wiki as part of the original site, the fulfillment of an extensive collaborative effort with developers and designers from the UM Press.[7] But it wasn't until we invited our first cohort of graduate fellows in August 2013 that the community website really took off.

A further impetus for the fellows program stemmed from Anne's deep commitment to mentoring and teaching and the thought that this new project could benefit students as well as be benefited by them. The DRC graduate fellows program was in some ways a counterpart to the HASTAC (Humanities, Arts, Science, and Technology Alliance and Collaboratory) Scholars program that had begun not long before—but whereas HASTAC Scholars were (and still are) financially sponsored by their universities, the DRC opted for a fellowship model with Sweetland paying each cohort member a stipend.[8] I'll return in a moment to the creative ways the fellows have molded the website over these twelve years, but first I want to describe the collaborations the program has made possible. As noted, Anne, Simone, and I have been aware of former fellows organizing conference panels together, publishing articles and books together, and becoming colleagues in their first jobs at the same university, so we knew that the fellowship year was reaping dividends beyond the tremendous growth of the DRC website.

I learned a great deal in my discussions with Laura Gonzales and Jason Tham about the quality and shape of some of these continuing connections, namely how the DRC provides a space for graduate students from different programs and institutions to learn how to collaborate and build academic community,

---

6   Learn about DRC graduate fellows at https://www.digitalrhetoriccollaborative.org/about/fellows/.

7   Jeremy Morse (Director of Publishing Technology and Data Repository Services, Michigan Publishing) and Jonathan McGlone (Digital Product Design Engineer and Accessibility Specialist, Michigan Publishing and Publishing Technology), both of whom continue to work with Michigan Publishing and with the UM Press' digital publishing platform, Fulcrum, have been especially significant collaborators throughout the DRC's lifespan.

8   More information about the HASTAC Scholars program is available at https://hastac.hcommons.org/about/hastac-scholars/.

such that it becomes "almost second nature" (Tham). They also gained confidence by reaching out to established scholars in the field on behalf of the DRC (by inviting contributions to a blog carnival, say, or editing conference session reviews). As Laura explained, the DRC functions as a "hub that brings people interested in digital rhetoric together from across different institutions. It's so powerful. But I think the power of it is seen not just in the immediate . . . production of the actual blog carnival or the DRC wiki, but in the collaborations that come many years later" (Gonzales).

RHETORIC 2.0

Turning back to the website as a "third space" for digital and interactive writing, at the WIDE-EMU session, Anne and I had heard the need for opportunities for shorter and faster forms of publication that could engage with conversations in the field without requiring a full peer review and production process. The blog carnivals published in the website's first year began to meet that need, but the first cohort of DRC graduate fellows took on the charge to imagine other avenues and genres for this writing. Building on their own interests and leading-edge knowledge of digital writing, they engaged the digital rhetoric community in "hacking" and "yacking" about tools and trends, highlighting the developing genre of webtexts, as well as opportunities for teaching and learning around these multimodal, multimedia compositions.[9]

The second cohort of fellows began the practice of publishing an end-of-year reflection, a vivid snapshot of all they and the previous cohort had accomplished:

> The 2014–15 academic year ushered in several big changes for the Digital Rhetoric Collaborative! With a major site re-design came an increased focus on ensuring the blog was engaging with the kinds of multiliteracies it heralds. While continuing features like the Webtext-of-the-Month, Wiki Wednesdays, and semester-long Blog Carnivals, new features like DRC Chat on Air, Reflections from the Cloud, and Tool Review Tuesdays were introduced. (Gonzales et al.)

The fellows invited scholars in the field to write short series of posts engaging their current pedagogical and research interests, and they took DRC content to the Twitter-verse, hosting #DRCchats on a range of topics that intersected with current blog carnivals or other publications.

---

9   Find the Hack & Yack series at https://www.digitalrhetoriccollaborative.org/conversations/hackandyack/.

This collaborative work of visioning and re-visioning the DRC website as a space for community interaction and a repository of community knowledge transforms with each new cohort of fellows. Recent cohorts have inaugurated the *DRC Talk Series* of podcasts,[10] including interviews with early career digital rhetoric faculty and "The Sonic Renaissance as an evolving conversation of black rhetorical space" (Neal and Williams), and they've boosted the pedagogical offerings on the site with a crowd-sourced syllabus repository and teaching and learning materials collection.[11] As a "third space" of digital writing, the DRC website provides the opportunity for genuine exploration. As Laura Gonzales put it: "I think that idea of approaching big disciplinary conversations as a question and from a position of 'I want to learn about this, I'm not [yet] trying to say anything about it' . . . was a really important move that I learned through the blog carnival editing [and] that . . . I've benefited from throughout my career." The rhetorical situation of the DRC site allows new ideas to be shared rapidly and new knowledge to unfold through conversation, crowd-sourcing, and collaboration.

DIGITAL 2.0

The WIDE-EMU session also surfaced the need for a scholarly publishing venue that could support long-form, interactive, born-digital projects. With our DRC advisory board, we developed a series description that outlined the areas we hoped to address: "born-digital as well as digitally enhanced submissions—in the form of collections and monographs of varying lengths and genres—that engage with digital rhetoric's histories and futures; its border-fields and transdisciplines; its ethics and aesthetics; its materialities, networks, praxes and pedagogies" ("Mission"). Among these aims, the complexity of navigating the border between "born-digital" and "digitally enhanced"—between *how digital is digital enough*, on one hand, and *how digital is too digital*, on the other—has persisted throughout our publication history. Our experience tracks the broader history of academic digital publication as it has encountered constraints posed both by the university tenure and promotion process and by the development, cost, and labor demands of digital production.

Our first three DRC series books actively negotiated these issues. Jim Ridolfo's *Digital Samaritans: Rhetorical Delivery and Engagement in the Digital Humanities* appeared in 2015 as a physical book with digitally enhanced content

---

10 Find the podcasts at https://www.digitalrhetoriccollaborative.org/category/conversations/drc-talk-series/.

11 Find the syllabus repository at https://www.digitalrhetoriccollaborative.org/teaching-materials/syllabus_repository/ and the teaching and learning materials collection at https://www.digitalrhetoriccollaborative.org/teaching-materials/teaching-learning-materials-collection/.

that was hosted on the Michigan Digital Library eXtension Service (DLXS) and referenced with printed urls appearing both in the main text and in image captions. The hope was that readers would be curious enough about that content (including videos, maps, and an interactive Samaritan keyboard) to type the urls into their browsers to experience it.[12] This book offered a kind of proof of concept of an early aim of the UM Press to allow authors "a way of presenting research data alongside their books," as well as significant, innovative supplementary digital materials (Watkinson et al.).

In October of 2016, Michigan Publishing—home of the University of Michigan Press, Michigan Publishing Services, and the UM research repository Deep Blue—announced the "beta launch" of its next-generation digital publishing platform, Fulcrum (University of Michigan Press). At that time, two new DRC books were in production: *Making Space: Writing Instruction, Infrastructure, and Multiliteracies,* edited by James P. Purdy and Dànielle Nicole DeVoss, and *Rhizcomics: Rhetoric, Technology, and New Media Composition* by Jason Helms. These projects were both proposed as born-digital webtexts whose interactive designs are an integral part of their arguments. Addressing some of the central affordances and constraints of digital publishing, Fulcrum promises its readers, authors, and publishers "flexibility," "durability," "discoverability," and "accessibility" ("About"). But these highly important values were in tension with an equally important value of digital composition, that "form and content should be imbricated," as Helms puts it in the Rationale section of "Making *Rhizcomics*." He names this tension as it manifested during the editing of *Rhizcomics*, writing in the Technical Edits section, "there were two major criteria pulling in opposite directions: sustainability and functionality. . . . The press wanted something they could maintain in perpetuity. I wanted something that was fully functional now, even if that meant it might deteriorate over time."

Testing the press' more ambitious aim to "provide the infrastructure to enable long form presentations of digital scholarship" (Watkinson et al.), *Rhizcomics* and *Making Space* reached different outcomes. For the latter, the press and the volume's editors worked collaboratively to find a novel solution: *Making Space* was "published in two digital formats: one housed on the Sweetland Digital Rhetoric Collaborative (DRC) website in its original webtext design and the other housed as an enhanced pdf for the DRC book series with the University of Michigan Press" (Purdy and DeVoss, "Preface"). As Purdy and DeVoss explain, this outcome constitutes a "rhetorical and strategic" choice that highlights a genuine innovation of digital publication: "Rather than view the project as needing to decide between

---

12   More information about DLXS is at http://www.dlxs.org/about/aboutdlxs.html. *Digital Samaritans* is now hosted by the UM Press on the Fulcrum publishing platform where the urls are hyperlinked.

either one format or the other . . . we opted for a 'both and' approach. . . . A digital publication need not be seen as singular or bounded or exist in only one 'location.'" It can "preserve the design intended by the collection's authors . . . [and] be preserved and maintained long term in a more stable space." Ultimately, *Rhizcomics* took a different path: following detailed consultation between the author and the editors and developers at the press, it was published solely as a webtext, with its complex interactivity and design unfurling as envisioned.

A chapter devoted to Anne Gere's impact on sites of digital writing would not be complete without a mention of the digitally enhanced book she edited for the DRC series, *Developing Writers in Higher Education: A Longitudinal Study*. As with so many other moments in DRC development, this book came about through collaboration and community. In fact, it specifically came about through grant funding from UM's Humanities Collaboratory, within a project titled "The Book Unbound: Enhancing Multilayered Digital Publications through Collaboration" devoted "to collaboratively study and improve the practice of digital publication in the humanities" (Watkinson). This grant project, which ran from 2017–2019, was the brainchild of the University of Michigan Press director, Charles Watkinson, and highlights the press' partnership with the DRC not only to bring ground-breaking digital rhetoric scholarship to the public, but also to co-investigate its possibilities.

The grant brought together a large, interdisciplinary team: UM faculty members, graduate students, and undergraduate students from Sweetland; classical studies; film, television, and media; and the school of information; as well as staff from the UM library and press, with Anne Gere and Nicola Terrenato (classical studies) acting as co-PIs. The project culminated in three multilayer publications on the Fulcrum platform that, as Anne describes it, offer "an opportunity to rethink the methods and meanings of publication" (qtd. in Watkinson). Each layer "address[es] multiple audiences by providing varying digitized experiences" ("Book Unbound"). *Developing Writers* comprises a more traditional book layer (published in both paper and ebook forms) directed at researchers and teachers in writing studies, a data layer directed toward future research that provides access to all of the qualitative and quantitative materials gathered for the study, and a public-facing website layer that aims to translate the concepts behind the research for a general audience. To date, *Developing Writers* remains one of the highest grossing and most viewed publications in the DRC series.

SWEETLAND 2.0

Scanning the DRC book series list, advisory board member Douglas Eyman noted during our interview that "if you look at the . . . focus of each one of these texts . . . you can almost trace where the interests in digital rhetoric are through the books themselves." He echoed and amplified the digital metaphor Gonzales used for professional collaboration, describing the DRC as "a network hub in the field" facilitating "connections across spaces that aren't happening" elsewhere. Picking up on Doug's words, we can follow the metaphorical trail left by Anne's innovative work in Sweetland and with the Sweetland Digital Rhetoric Collaborative—work that is central to "her view of scholarship as a communal and ongoing process," as Beitler and Robbins put it in their introduction to this collection (5). *Collaborations, networks, braids*—the Sweetland Digital Rhetoric Collaborative weaves and traces strands of connection across multiple sites of digital writing and community, pulling on ideas, stretching fields of research and inquiry, coming together over time and space in nodes, hubs, and relationships. The reach of the relationships rooted in DRC collaborations and the futures of the DRC's role in the ever-growing story of digital publishing remain to be traced and gathered in further articles, chapters, and books—whether born-digital or digitally enhanced. In the meantime, the collaborative community Anne Gere began continues to feed the field of digital rhetoric—the DRC series has new books under review and in production and the DRC graduate fellows are adding new content to the website. Follow the links and join in!

WORKS CITED

"About." *Fulcrum*, 2024, www.fulcrum.org/about/.
"Book Unbound." *Humanities Collaboratory*, sites.lsa.umich.edu/collaboratory/funded-projects/book-unbound/. Accessed 3 Feb. 2024.
Eyman, Douglas. Interview. 1 Sept. 2023.
Finkenstaedt-Quinn, Solaire A., et al. "Praxis of Writing-to-Learn: A Model for the Design and Propagation of Writing-to-Learn in STEM." *Journal of Chemical Education*, vol. 98, no. 5, 2021, pp. 1548–55, https://doi.org/10.1021/acs.jchemed.0c01482.
Gere, Anne Ruggles, editor. *Developing Writers in Higher Education: A Longitudinal Study*. U of Michigan P, 2019. *University of Michigan Press Ebook Collection*, https://doi.org/10.3998/mpub.10079890.
Gere, Anne Ruggles, et al. "Assessing the Validity of Directed Self-Placement at a Large University." *Assessing Writing*, vol. 15, no. 3, 2010, pp. 154–76, https://doi.org/10.1016/j.asw.2010.08.003.
Gere, Anne Ruggles, et al. "Interrogating Disciplines/Disciplinarity in WAC/WID: An Institutional Study." *College Composition and Communication*, vol. 67, no. 2, 2015, pp. 243–66, https://doi.org/10.58680/ccc201527644.
Gere, Anne Ruggles, et al. "Local Assessment: Using Genre Studies to Validate Directed Self-Placement." *College Composition and Communication*, vol. 64, no. 4, 2013, pp. 605–33, https://doi.org/10.58680/ccc201323661.

Gere, Anne Ruggles, et al. "Mutual Adjustments: Learning from and Responding to Transfer Student Writers." *College English*, vol. 79, no. 4, 2017, pp. 333–57, https://doi.org/10.58680/ce201728970.

Gere, Anne, and Naomi Silver. "Envisioning a New Digital Writing/Rhetoric Community Web Space." WIDE-EMU Unconference, 13 October 2011, Eastern Michigan University, Ypsilanti, MI. Session recording transcript.

Gonzales, Laura. Interview. 1 Sept. 2023.

Gonzales, Laura, et al. "Year-End Reflection from the 2014–15 DRC Graduate Fellows." *DRC Fellows*, Gayle Morris Sweetland Digital Rhetoric Collaborative, 14 Aug. 2015, https://tinyurl.com/5n7yhne5.

Helms, Jason. "Making *Rhizcomics*." *Kairos*, vol. 23, no. 1, 2018, kairos.technorhetoric.net/23.1/inventio/helms/index.html.

———. *Rhizcomics: Rhetoric, Technology, and New Media Composition*. U of Michigan P, 2017, https://doi.org/10.3998/mpub.7626373.

Jaschik, Scott. "Farewell to the Printed Monograph." *Inside Higher Ed*, 22 March 2009, www.insidehighered.com/news/2009/03/23/farewell-printed-monograph.

Lauer, Claire. "What's in a Name? The Anatomy of Defining New/Multi/Modal/Digital/Media Texts." *Blog Carnival #1*, Gayle Morris Sweetland Digital Rhetoric Collaborative, 15 Aug. 2012, https://tinyurl.com/bcjxcb4u.

"Mission." *Gayle Morris Sweetland Digital Rhetoric Collaborative*, https://tinyurl.com/5zj63ae2.

Neal, D'Arcee, and Kimberly Williams. "Introducing a DRC Podcast: The Sonic Renaissance." *DRC Talk Series*, Gayle Morris Sweetland Digital Rhetoric Collaborative, 1 Feb. 2021, https://tinyurl.com/my6tft4d.

Pochoda, Phil. "Editor's Note for Reimagining the University Press." *Journal of Electronic Publishing*, vol. 13, no. 2, 2010, https://doi.org/10.3998/3336451.0013.201.

———. "University Press 2.0." *University of Michigan Press Blog*, 27 May 2009, umichpress.typepad.com/university_of_michigan_pr/2009/05/university-press-20-by-phil-pochoda.html.

Purdy, James P., and Dànielle Nicole DeVoss. *Making Space: Writing Instruction, Infrastructure, and Multiliteracies*, U of Michigan P, 2017, https://doi.org/10.3998/mpub.7820727.

———. "Preface to *Making Space: Writing Instruction, Infrastructure, and Multiliteracies*." *Gayle Morris Sweetland Digital Rhetoric Collaborative*, https://tinyurl.com/y67maez2. Accessed 31 Jan. 2024.

Ridolfo, Jim. *Digital Samaritans: Rhetorical Delivery and Engagement in the Digital Humanities*. U of Michigan P, 2015, https://doi.org/10.3998/drc.13406713.0001.001.

Tham, Jason. Interview. 24 Aug. 2023.

University of Michigan Press. "University of Michigan Announces Beta Launch of New Publishing Platform, *Fulcrum*." *Fulcrum*, 24 Oct. 2016, www.fulcrum.org/blog/2016/10/24/fulcrum-beta-launch/.

Watkinson, Charles. "U-M Humanities Collaboratory Funds 'Book Unbound' Project to Improve the Practice of Digital Publication in the Humanities." *University of Michigan Press*, 29 Aug. 2017, https://tinyurl.com/ujy8ryb6.

Watkinson, Charles, et al. "Building a Hosted Platform for Managing Monographic Source Materials: Report on the First Year of the Mellon Grant to University of Michigan." *Fulcrum*, 30 June 2016, www.fulcrum.org/blog/2016/06/30/year-one-report/.

"Writing 200: Writing with Digital and Social Media." *Gayle Morris Sweetland Center for Writing*, 2024, lsa.umich.edu/sweetland/undergraduates/courses/writing-200.html.

"Writing 201: Writing with Digital and Social Media Mini-Courses." *Gayle Morris Sweetland Center for Writing*, 2024, lsa.umich.edu/sweetland/undergraduates/courses/writing-201.html.

PART 4. ENGAGING THE EXTRACURRICULUM

CHAPTER 11.
PHENOMENAL WOMEN GETTIN' IT RIGHT IN THE EXTRACURRICULUM

Beverly J. Moss
The Ohio State University

> The extracurriculum I examine is constructed by desire, by the aspirations and imaginations of its participants. It posits writing as an action undertaken by motivated individuals.
>
> – Anne Ruggles Gere, "Kitchen Tables and Rented Rooms: The Extracurriculum of Composition"

My scholarly identity is built around examining literacies in the extracurriculum, particularly in African American community spaces. Anne Ruggles Gere lays out for composition studies the value and necessity of scholarly inquiry on composition instruction outside the classroom in such spaces. Gere suggests that "in concentrating upon establishing our position within the academy, we have neglected to recount the history of composition in other contexts; we have neglected composition's extracurriculum" (79). She suggests that these community sites of writing instruction create a space where community participants see that "writing can make a difference in individual and community life" (78). While "Kitchen Tables and Rented Rooms" lays the groundwork for examining composition instruction in community spaces, I argue that one of its greatest values is providing a pathway for examining and documenting literacy practices more broadly—reading, speaking, and writing—in community spaces that have been characterized by narratives of literacy deficiencies.

In this essay, I address how Phenomenal Women Incorporated (PWInc), a contemporary Black women's club, demonstrates club-based practices of literacy instruction. I am reminded not only of Gere's work on 19th-century clubwomen's roles in literacy in the extracurriculum but also of Gere's call to "consider the various sites in which the extracurriculum has been enacted, the local circumstances that supported its development, the material artifacts employed by its practitioners, and the cultural work it accomplished" (90). I focus on the informal literacy instruction that operates in this extracurricular site as well as the role of desire and motivation that inspires PWInc members to engage in unfamiliar literacy practices that become part of their literacy identities.

THE SITE

PWInc, a nonprofit organization located in Columbus, Ohio, has been in existence since 1997. During my fieldwork, its membership has hovered between 15–20 adult Black women who range in age from their mid–20s to early 80s. Their socioeconomic classes range from working to middle class. The club came into existence because one member, Mawarine,[1] wanted to be in a club with other Black women who serve their community and with whom she could socialize. Mawarine also saw the forming of the club as continuing a legacy of civic engagement and activism passed down by the women in her family. She recalls how, as a child, she and her sister (club member Charlene) were influenced by her grandmother, great aunt, and mother (an original club member) who had been active in church groups and Black women's clubs. It was from these women and her childhood experiences that Mawarine's "vision" for the club evolved.

Much extant scholarship on African American clubwomen reveals the role of African American women's clubs in the activist, intellectual, and civic movements of African Americans. Gere discusses in "Kitchen Tables and Rented Rooms" the formation of and writing activities of African American self-help groups established in the 19th century in the form of literary clubs. As Gere and others report, these clubs were more than literary clubs in their communities. Gere states, "[F]aced with the double challenge posed by their race and gender, African American clubwomen embraced writing's capacity to effect social and economic change, to enact their [National Association of Colored Women (NACW)] motto, 'lifting as we climb'" (84). In discussing the Black women's club movement, Jacqueline Jones Royster states, "the club movement actually permitted women with different matrices of identity, different perceptions of needs, and different priorities for sociopolitical mandates (cultural, social, political, economic, religious) to form a shared space—a community" (217). The shared spaces that Black women created for themselves in these clubs became important sites for literacy learning and literacy activities. I suggest that, in this first half of the 21st century, they continue to be important extracurricular sites for examining literacy.

While Gere points to how the Tenderloin Women's Writing Workshop and the Lansing, Iowa Writers Workshop have taken up their task of bringing together individuals of varying classes, genders, and races who meet to read

---

1   All PWInc members are referred to by their first names because that is their custom and preference.

and respond to one another's writing, PWInc adds another layer. That is, these clubwomen do not meet to read and respond to each other's writing. They are not a writing group or a literary club. It is in doing the work of the club—their meetings, their record-keeping, and their planning of club activities, including community outreach and club social outings, among other events—that club members provide feedback and literacy instruction. For many members, doing this work requires that they rely on other club members as literacy resources, as informal literacy instructors, and that they extend their literacy reach, meaning that they take on literacy activities and engage in literacy practices far beyond their experiences and comfort zones. In the following I offer two examples of PWInc members whose work in the club placed them in positions where they needed to reach beyond their literacy comfort zones and rely on the pedagogical activities in this extracurricular space.

DOING THE WORK

> And I had to think about what I was gonna do to help out the club and not just myself or a few people but for everyone. . . . That really broke me out of my comfort zone.
>
> – Veronica

Veronica's quotation brings to our attention the commitment members brought to their club: helping the club achieve its goals often meant stepping out of one's comfort zone. Whether it was that specific phrase—"taking me out of my comfort zone"—or a version of it, such as "brought me out" or "bringing me forward," the sentiment was named as a powerful force by PWInc members. Charlene and Veronica are representative of most members who found that to do the work of the club, they would need to challenge themselves to engage in certain practices and behaviors that they had been reluctant to do in the past. The motivation to make the club successful and to do good work on behalf of the club provided the exigency for these women to engage unfamiliar literacy practices, refine existing literacy practices, and create new literacy and rhetorical identities.

CHARLENE

In the conversation excerpts that follow, original club member Charlene (Mawarine's sister) and I discussed her roles in the club, specifically the duties in the various offices that she's held. The narrative that Charlene told about the challenges that she faced to perform her roles effectively highlight the club's role in helping Charlene create a new identity, one that depended on her willingness to take on the literacy challenge of these offices—essentially her willingness and motivation to step outside her literacy comfort zone:

> When I was the president, okay, I'm kinda quiet, and it's really hard, I don't like to be, I'm not a speaker. And it took, uh—that was really good for me because it brought me out, and I had to talk, and you know, bring the meetings together . . . And do a lot of research so that the club can continue on. You know, like we have an agenda that we have to do and stuff like that. So, you know, you gotta hunt up that research so you know what we're talking about . . . And that was new for me.

Charlene continued:

> I had to write. And so, I've never done that before, and so that was an experience for me. And I think I did pretty good cause they let me stay for awhile! . . . And then I was the secretary, but that was a horrible job, because I'm not a good speller, okay. And they were checking my spelling and stuff like that when I would come in to read the reports and stuff like that. It was, they were very nice about it. . . . But that is something that I have never been good at, you know. And that was a challenge for me. So, this club has really brought me out, cause I'm usually the type of person who just sits back and listens, you know, and every once in a while, someone will ask me something, I'll answer their questions and stuff. But basically, I just go along with everybody else. And the club has brought me out, and I've learned to like, to speak more and to put my opinions and things that I feel . . .

As important as the offices themselves is Charlene's description of her duties, the challenges they presented, and the impact on her that fulfilling her duties had. As we go back through this interview excerpt, we see that Charlene, who repeatedly described herself as "kinda quiet," noted that her duties as president "brought her out." She found herself, a person who liked to be in the background, having to lead the group as president. She had to prepare agendas, research potential projects, present information, and make her opinions known. This list points to how these activities, by necessity, engaged Charlene in activities and events that required complex literacy skills and practices (reading, writing, and speaking) and provided an opportunity to engage in literate behavior.

The difficulty that Charlene faced in reimagining her literacy identity is most clearly exemplified in her descriptions of her adjustment to being the secretary.

And it is this experience where we see most clearly how the club members' literacy expectations about properly prepared minutes and reports guided her actions. As she stated in the previous excerpt, being secretary was the most challenging office that she held, primarily because of the literacy requirements. She described her spelling challenges as problematic as well as pointed out how club members, though "they were nice about it," corrected her spelling. Not only was she facing her fears about her spelling, but she also faced the expectations of her club members to "get it right." When she, along with three other members, presented with me at a conference, Charlene provided even more detail about the literacy challenges of the secretary's position. In the following excerpt, in addition to focusing on her writing skills (or her perceived lack of writing skills), Charlene identified computer literacy as adding to her concerns about being the secretary:

> And when they gave me that role as to be the secretary at that time, that was the hardest thing I've ever done because I'm not a writer. . . . And I have to come out of my comfort zone because I had to go into the meetings and listen to what they were saying and then write it down on paper and then go home and type out all this information, what I'd learned through that meeting, that day . . . And it was hard for me because I was just learning how to use the computer. . . . And to come in and have to sit down and type all these words, paragraphs, and lines and stuff like that, you know, it was like, I went to school and I'm, I'm just not the brainy one here, of this, ok. And it was kinda hard for me, and so what I would do, I learned that the first week I would take a risk because it was so much. Then I knew that the following week I had to sit down and type all that stuff that I hadn't, you know, what we talked about, or I would forget, you know. And then, that was a hard time because I was a grown woman sitting at the computer crying because I couldn't get it all in the way that it should be, ok. And so, I had to have, ok, so what I would do is type all the information out and, bless my husband's heart, he would come and sit down and then he would help me with the grammar and the spelling and the stuff like that, you know. Because I would be typing, and I realized I had misspelled a word or did something wrong and I would go to delete, and I would delete maybe three lines and had to start all over again. And I was so frustrated 'cause I used to call her [niece and original club member Robyn who family call Niki], "Niki Niki," I can't do this, it's just too hard for me.

As she stated, in addition to turning to her husband for help, Charlene called on her niece and club member Robyn/Niki, who encouraged her and helped her learn how to be the secretary by answering questions and showing her what to include in the minutes and what to take out. The assistance that she received is significant because it points to the role of others in the club instructing and helping Charlene acquire new literacy skills including engaging with technological literacy practices and re-imagining her literacy identity. This assistance is exemplary of how club members take on literacy sponsorship roles (Brandt) as well. Robyn explained that Charlene's need for her assistance changed during her time as secretary: "over time, our post-meeting gatherings became shorter and less frequent, as Charlene became more comfortable with word processing, printing, and copying meeting minutes and agendas on her own (using her own home computer) and using templates I had introduced to her" (qtd. in Moss and Lyons-Robinson 139).

Being secretary challenged Charlene to read, write, think, and behave in ways that she had not done before. She had to "perform" the role of secretary—the official "writer" for the club—when she did not see herself as a writer. Charlene described her process of learning to take minutes as involving "going into the meetings and listening to what they were saying and then writ[ing] it down on paper." As those who have been secretaries of organizations know, taking minutes is more than transcribing spoken words. Charlene was learning how to make decisions about what was important to write down and how to write it down. She was engaging in decision-making about how to represent the club in its official documents. And as she was making these decisions, Charlene's role was being complicated by the computer.

Not yet computer literate, Charlene was faced with learning how to compose her minutes in a digital space. When she described herself as a "grown woman sitting at the computer crying," she was describing a woman trying to engage in multiple literacies simultaneously. Charlene faced the challenges of taking accurate minutes, preparing them properly, negotiating the computer hardware and software correctly, and, as signaled by her concern with proper spelling, getting the mechanics and grammar right. Her concern about "getting it right" stemmed in large part from the expectations of the club to do things properly so that the club looked good. I saw this concern for the club's image voiced by other members as well. Charlene knew that there was an expectation that anything that represented the club must be done correctly. She offered the following example:

> We would get to the part where you'd say, "Ok, are we now going to approve the minutes?" A certain person on this end [her sister] Mawarine, would always say, "Well, hold up here,

well, you didn't spell this word right. And what were you trying to say here? You missed this part here."

Charlene understood that the community for whom she was writing had certain standards that she must meet. She also implicitly understood that the minutes were not her minutes but the club's minutes, in effect a community text (Moss). Like many documents produced for organizations by employers and/or members, ownership of the documents belonged to the larger group, not the individual who produced them. It is here where PWInc diverges from the writers Gere highlights in "Kitchen Tables and Rented Rooms" who were getting feedback on their individual texts, not community texts. Charlene, like other PWInc members, understood the importance and public nature of her literacy practices and the work these practices do for PWInc and their community, much like Black clubwomen in the 19th century, as noted by Gere and her co-author Sarah Robbins. What's important to note is that Charlene, though nervous and initially unsure, did what she needed to do, including heeding the warnings about any errors, and set about meeting the literacy standards as laid out by the club. She made use of a network of resources available to her, like her niece and husband, to meet the literacy challenges that being an active member of the club, especially one holding an office, required her to meet.

The final challenge for Charlene was reading her minutes to the group—the public presentation. For a woman who, at one time, considered herself a poor reader, Charlene was willing to meet another literacy challenge. This challenge, like all the others, was, whether Charlene knew it or not, creating a new identity for her. Note the physical and emotional discomfort that Charlene endured to meet the expectation of the club:

> And then after I would type it and make the copies and then the Friday [meeting] appeared . . . and there was all these ladies that I knew, friends and stuff, and I had to sit and read what I wrote to them. Now, I would read to myself, my books and stuff like that, but to read out loud, that was very hard for me. My stomach would get real tight. . . .

Reading the minutes in public, I argue, established Charlene's identity as a reader every bit as much as reading novels did. Reading in public provided her an opportunity to "perform" as a reader before and for an audience for whom what she read was important but also from whom she received a great deal of support. I suggest that the club expectations and role as audience signaled to Charlene that they were rejecting whatever negative opinions she had of her literacy abilities. In fact, they were providing support and teaching moments to help her. The club's presence was a necessary foundation for the re-imagining of her literacy identity.

Through the Charlene example, we see how, within this extracurricular site, the club members set expectations for written documents that dictated how Charlene performed as a writer, a reader, and a speaker. The literacy instruction Charlene received ranged from lower-order to higher-order issues, including correcting spelling, providing the right content, learning how to use a template for writing minutes (prepared by a club member), and learning how to read the minutes orally to the group. She received immediate feedback that helped her prepare for the next time, the next set of minutes. As Gere would probably attest, this "version of the extracurriculum extends beyond the academy to encompass the multiple contexts in which persons seek to improve their own writing," and it "avoids, as much as possible, reenactment of professionalization," which Gere critiques in those who "position the extracurriculum as a waystation on the route toward a fully professionalized academic department" (80). For Charlene, PWInc as the extracurriculum was the site that persuaded her to face her own insecurities about her literacies and to engage in literacy practices in front of a group of Black women who expected her to "get it [writing, speaking, and reading] right."

Veronica

Veronica, like Charlene, held many offices. While not as nervous about her literacy skills as Charlene, in our conversation, Veronica also pointed to her duties within PWInc as engaging in literacy practices and behaviors that "brought her forward." A self-described "social butterfly" who is outgoing and comfortable "speaking up," Veronica faced challenges that had an impact on her literacy identity. Her description of being taken out of her comfort zone as president is particularly interesting because Veronica points to a change in her thinking habits:

> Being vice-president, you're kind of behind the scenes 'cause you're helping out the president and you're, you know, you're gathering up information for the president, doin' what the president can't do, she just kinda passes it over to you. And that was fine with me 'cause I was behind the scenes and that was great. But when I became president, . . . I had to be structured in my thinking. And I had to think about what I was gonna do to help out the club and not just myself or a few people, but for everyone. And my goal and what the goals were. That really broke me out of my comfort zone.

Despite her discomfort, which her fellow members said they never noticed, the members of the club thought that Veronica was a "great president." What is striking about Veronica's discussion is that she clearly articulates that she was willing to change the way she thought—"be structured in my thinking"—and put the club's goals first. Again, we are reminded, as Gere notes, of "an action undertaken by motivated individuals" (80). While my fieldnotes show Veronica to be an organized person with strong leadership skills, when she became an officer she certainly seemed to think that she had to make some changes in the way that she went about her work in the club. She had been the club treasurer and historian prior to being vice-president and president. In these positions, she engaged in literacy practices that were not part of her normal routine and that, like Charlene, caused her a high level of anxiety. However, again, Veronica was motivated to do her job well and found that taking on these duties and the literacy practices and behaviors attached to them pushed her to move beyond her comfort level, to move from "behind the scenes" to the front—"out there"— where her words (spoken and written) and actions represented the club. In the following excerpt, she describes her challenges and triumphs as club treasurer:

> I found out that being a treasurer, really, really brought me forward because I, I'd never even balanced my checkbook before that. . . . But now I had to sit down and actually think about the finances [of the club] and look at it and go into the banks and talk to the officials and make sure the money is right. I had to sit down there and write out a report. And my husband reminded me, he said, "you were so nervous about being the treasurer that all I ever heard was, 'I gotta do my report (laughter). It gotta be right. I gotta look at it." And I didn't know I was that manic about it, but apparently, I was. And it just kind of helped me and it helped in my life to understand what the finances were and understanding that writing it, and looking at it, and going over it really brought me forward in my personal life. And it helped in the, in the club, you know, look at the finances and, all the activities we had to do to raise the money and make sure the money was right and make sure I always go to the bank to have the change and keeping track of everything. That was difficult but it really brought me forward in, and I really appreciate everyone who helped out, and who helped me along the way. And being treasurer, she [Charlene] says I helped her, but I had to have help, too.

When Veronica announced that she had never balanced her own checkbook before becoming treasurer for PWInc, the other members on the panel were surprised. Charlene, who became treasurer after Veronica, talked about how much

Veronica helped her learn the treasurer's job. Yet, becoming treasurer represents one of those moments when the work of the club motivated Veronica to reshape her literacy identity. As a participant in this literacy event, Veronica had to record expenses and expenditures, read bank statements, check those bank statements against the record of expenses and expenditures that she recorded, write receipts to members, write checks to appropriate parties, discuss bank and club financial records with bank officials and club members, and prepare and read aloud her treasurer's report. She engaged in each of these literate activities monthly for two years. Like Charlene's description of being the club secretary, we see that being the PWInc treasurer was not an easy role for Veronica. However, like Charlene, she was motivated by the club's needs to engage in new literacy practices.

When Veronica says the club "brought me forward" or "broke me out of my comfort zone," we, as readers, can see that PWInc has provided Veronica a space to perform literacy practices within and beyond the club on behalf of the club. Hence, the literacy identity that Veronica began to establish through her work in PWInc was one of a club member who recognized the power of literacy's reach to multiple communities and the way that literacy could contribute to how others viewed her club. It's also important to recognize that Veronica added another layer to this discussion in that she discussed how her work in the club provided a pathway for changes in her personal life in how she dealt with her own finances. In Veronica, I argue, we see another dimension of literacy as a communal resource. When she utilized literacy to do the work of the club as treasurer, as chair of a committee, as president, or as historian, like Charlene, she was no longer an individual writing a report or doing research, she was PWInc engaging in these literacy events and practices.

CONCLUSION

While one may be tempted to look solely at these women as individuals improving or enhancing their literacy skills and/or broadening the spaces in which they engage in literate behaviors and literacy practices, I offer an alternative view: that is, the ethos is so powerful, the network of resources available to these women so far-reaching, that the club becomes a powerful force shaping the motivation of these women to step out of their literacy comfort zones and to take on these new or expanded identities. I am not suggesting that this is the only social network that these women drew on to expand their literacy identities; however, it was one of the primary networks that they drew on to take risks that they would not have done previous to joining the club. That Charlene and Veronica named their club's needs as the force that pushed them to engage particular literacy practices is evidence of how important this community-based social network was to them.

I point to the power of small, community-based social groups in the extracurriulum and the needs and concerns of those groups to intervene in literacy lives and to hold sway when larger institutions or even individual needs do not. Being part of a group of Black women committed to their community and to their club is impetus for the individual members to take on new literacy challenges and for the club and the individuals within the club to teach each other. Equally important is doing the club's work in a way that signals, as member Sharon stated, "it has to look good and be good." Looking and being good, or "getting it right," though often articulated by members in terms of correct spelling or accurate financial records, is more than just being correct. For these women, it was and is about striving to honor the club, enacting the NACW motto "lifting as we climb" (qtd. in Gere 84), which in this case includes nurturing and sustaining the literacy of its members.

WORKS CITED

Brandt, Deborah. *Literacy in American Lives.* Cambridge, 2001. *Cambridge Core*, https://doi.org/10.1017/CBO9780511810237.

Charlene. Interview. 19 June 2008.

Gere, Anne Ruggles. "Kitchen Tables and Rented Rooms: The Extracurriculum of Composition." *College Composition and Communication*, vol. 45, no. 1, 1994, pp. 75–92, https://doi.org/10.2307/358588.

Gere, Anne Ruggles, and Sarah R. Robbins. "Gendered Literacy in Black and White: Turn-of the-Century African-American and European-American Club Women's Printed Texts." *Signs: Journal of Women in Culture and Society,* vol. 21, no. 3, 1996, pp. 643–78, https://doi.org/10.1086/495101.

Moss, Beverly J. *A Community Text Arises: A Literate Text and a Literacy Tradition in African-American Churches.* The WAC Clearinghouse, 2024, wac.colostate.edu/books/landmarks/arises/. Originally published by Hampton P, 2003.

Moss, Beverly J., and Robyn Lyons-Robinson. "Making Literacy Work: A 'Phenomenal Woman' Negotiating Her Literacy Identity in and for an African American Women's Club." *Literacy, Economy, and Power: Writing and Research after Literacy in American Lives,* edited by John Duffy et al., Southern Illinois UP, 2013, pp. 136–54.

Royster, Jacqueline Jones. *Traces of a Stream: Literacy and Social Change among African American Women.* U of Pittsburgh P, 2000.

Sharon. Interview. 27 August 2008.

Veronica. Interview. 5 April 2009.

CHAPTER 12.
LAYING THE MATTER ON THE TABLE: COMPOSING KITCHEN JUDAISM

Rona Kaufman
Pacific Lutheran University

In 1986, the Sisterhood of Temple de Hirsch-Sinai in Seattle published a cookbook called *Just Like Grandma Used to Make*. The cookbook is organized by holiday with sections on "Shabbot," "Rosh Hashonah," "Chanukah," "Pesach," and "Purim and Other Festive Occasions." Most of the recipes are attached to a woman's name or a woman's familial role, and the book includes many of the recipes one might expect to find in a Jewish holiday cookbook: "Betty Jaffe's Chopped Liver," "Grandma Susan's Mandelbrat," "Phyllis's Potato Latkes," "'G-G's' Matzoh Balls." Spiral-bound with a bright yellow, dot-matrix cover, the cookbook looks very much like a product of the 1980s but is clear to acknowledge a deeper tradition—not only a broad Jewish tradition but also a local, women's culture around cookbooks. This is the fourth cookbook that the Sisterhood published after *One Thousand Favorite Recipes* in 1908, *Famous Cook Book* in 1916, and *Famous Cook Book* in 1925. All were compiled by a few individuals but authored collectively by the Ladies Auxiliary to Temple de Hirsch.[1]

The 1986 Sisterhood acknowledges their inheritances in a note at the beginning of the cookbook: "Most of the recipes have been handed down from friends and family, some are from our Temple Cookbook that was published in the early 1900's [*sic*]. Others are fairly new but will be handed down to our next generation through this book." Yet this cookbook bears no resemblance to its predecessors, neither materially nor spiritually. Despite the 1986 cookbook's title, there's little evidence that these recipes *are* what grandma used to make, at least if their grandmothers were editors and contributors to the earlier cookbooks. This is not the story the Ladies Auxiliary circulated about themselves in the first part of the 20th century. The discrepancies between the most recent cookbook and the earlier ones reveal how what it means to be Reform Jews in the Pacific Northwest varies over time. In this chapter, I focus on the early 20th-century Temple de

---

1   Temple de Hirsch merged with Temple Sinai in 1971.

Hirsch cookbooks as a particular "site of writing" that illustrates the interplay between that era and trends in Reform Judaism as well as local, regional, and national cultural forces.

The four cookbooks published by the women's groups of Temple de Hirsch fall squarely into the "extracurriculum" that Anne Ruggles Gere pivotally argues for in her ground-breaking article "Kitchen Tables and Rented Rooms: The Extracurriculum of Composition." Through their work of writing, publishing, and selling the cookbooks, the women of the Sisterhood use literacy, as Gere puts it, "adapted to their interests" (79) and "constructed by desire, by the aspirations and imaginations of its participants" (80) and with "social and economic consequences" (80) to negotiate, or re-form, what it means to be Jewish American women at that time and in that place. The genre of recipes and cookbooks allows the women to negotiate publicly their intersectional identities as individuals, members of a sisterhood and local Jewish community, and participants in ideological battles initially grounded in other places but that reach into their most intimate worlds. The women appropriate generic conventions in order to create a more elastic experience of Judaism and the Pacific Northwest, using writing in an everyday, familiar form to find their place.

HISTORY OF TEMPLE DE HIRSCH

Temple de Hirsch was founded in the Capitol Hill neighborhood of Seattle in May 1899 by seventy Ashkenazi families with a mission to create a place where, according to Raphael H. Levine, who served as the rabbi at Temple de Hirsch from 1942 to 1969, "our Jewish faith and tradition could become the dynamic for effective and worthful living by being made responsive to the needs and experiences of American Jews" (Congregation). The notion of a living, responsive tradition helps indicate that Temple de Hirsch is a Reform synagogue, which separates itself from Orthodox Judaism and, later, Conservative Judaism, by re-forming, rather than perpetuating, the institution of Judaism through modification, abrogation, or addition. As Rabbi Samuel Koch, who led the congregation for the first half of the 20th century, explains in "Temple Tidings," the synagogue's monthly newsletter, "All changes whatsoever introduced by Reform have been in the direction of *ritualistic simpleness*, of *doctrinal adequacy*, of *intellectual satisfactoriness* and of *aesthetic intensity*; and have been made on the grounds of *present needs* and *present efficiency*" (vol. 1, no. 5, 1). Koch continues, "*[E]very religion that is alive* must evolve, develop, progress." Food becomes an emblem and a material good on which the different branches of Judaism divide.

Temple de Hirsch not only is a Reform synagogue but also is a Seattle synagogue. From its beginning, the synagogue has been proud of its secular ties and connections to place. It has woven its history to that of Seattle. In a publication celebrating its 50th anniversary, the synagogue notes:

> Fifty years ago our city was a small outpost of America's western frontier. Today it is a great metropolis, the Queen City of the Pacific Northwest. The first years of our congregation's life span this tremendous expansion, and in no small measure aided it through the labors of the men and women who drew their inspiration from the spiritual fountains of the Judaism which it embodied and cherished. (Congregation)

In this same publication, the synagogue boasts that the first person to win the Seattle citizenship award was a member of its congregation, and it celebrates the work Rabbi Koch did in Seattle social services, including helping to create a children's hospital. In the synagogue's 75th Anniversary publication, it further emphasizes Koch's work outside the Jewish community, and it notes that Koch's successor, Rabbi Levine, went on to create the long-running TV show *Challenge*, bringing together Protestant, Catholic, and Jewish clergy to discuss pressing matters of the day. In its 50th Anniversary celebration material, Rabbi Levine claims, "Among the finest achievements of our congregation was the leadership it gave to the movements working for better understanding between Jews and their neighbors and for a deeper appreciation of the meaning of the American dream."

Also noted in the 50th anniversary publication, the organization of a Ladies Auxiliary was one of the first acts of the new synagogue. By September 1899, four months after the synagogue's founding, the Ladies Auxiliary had elected its first set of officers. One of three women's groups drawing on synagogue membership—the other two being the Council of Jewish Women and the Hebrew Benevolent Society—the work of the Auxiliary centered on 1) the education of children; 2) the decoration of the synagogue for the Sabbath; 3) the identification and welcoming of immigrants, who are sometimes referred to as "strangers in our midst"; 4) the building of a Jewish library and creation of a Jewish reading community; and 5) the expansion of the building space (Koch, "Tidings" vol. 2, no. 2, 1). In "Temple Tidings," Rabbi Koch claimed that the Auxiliary was second only to the synagogue itself in terms of importance to the Jewish community, writing, "To be officially identified with the Auxiliary is to be identified with the most gratifying communal effort" (vol. 2, no. 2, 4).

Repeatedly in Koch's newsletters, the Auxiliary is noted as being consistently productive, often ambitious. The women are highlighted for decorating the sanctuary, buying presents for the Sunday School teachers' weddings, encouraging better attendance at services, hosting services, and building a library. Many of their synagogue-based efforts are shown as taking them out of the synagogue and into the city: they host dance after dance, dinner after dinner, in Seattle hotels and the Knights of Columbus hall, with proceeds going largely to the library. They entertain Jewish students at the University of Washington and Jewish soldiers on leave; they send holiday packages to Jewish soldiers serving abroad; they sell Red Cross seals and volunteer for the Anti-Tuberculosis League.

FAMOUS COOK BOOK

Arguably what took the women of the Auxiliary most out into the world was their cookbooks. The cookbooks put them in a network of Seattle businesses and Jewish women's groups. The resulting network was mostly regional, but the cookbooks made their way to individuals and organizations (including the Auxiliary's parent group, the National Federation of Temple Sisterhoods) in the East, too. The cookbooks enmeshed them in local, regional, and national networks that value business and culinary acumen.

First published in 1908 as *One Thousand Favorite Recipes*, according to the minutes of the Ladies Auxiliary the cookbook had a print run of 1500 and, after years of plodding away, sold out by December 1912. The Auxiliary continued to field requests for cookbooks, including from two Seattle booksellers, and considered an additional printing of 100 copies, but ultimately referred the requestors to a new cookbook, *The Neighborhood Cookbook* (1912), from the Portland Council of Jewish Women.

Yet by May 1914, the women began to consider revising their own cookbook. At the June 7, 1915, meeting, they decided to put a new book out. The minutes offer no reason for the delay in publishing a new edition, but based on the success of the first venture, the lack of recorded conversation (let alone enthusiasm) around the suggestion of a new edition, and the work involved with the 1916 edition, the labor was likely daunting. But in 1916, the women began again. Assembling advertising, business, and compilation committees, the Ladies Auxiliary took advantage of their previous success by naming this cookbook *Famous Cook Book*.

In March 1916, the cookbook committee mailed postcards requesting recipes. By June 1916, the women secured advertising and awarded the printing contract to Lowman and Hanford (Minutes, June 5, 1916), and they got their *Famous Cook Book* out in December 1916 with a print run of 2500 and an option of more copies if the initial run was successful (Minutes, August 16, 1916). The cookbooks were initially sold for $1 in the city and $1.25 out of town (Minutes, November 6, 1916), but they increased the prices to $1.25 in the city and $1.50 out of town by July 1, 1920 (Minutes, June 7, 1920). The women decided that the proceeds of the sales would go to the Temple Annex. According to available minutes, the 1916 edition was a success. The November 29, 1920, letter to the membership that criticizes the Auxiliary for an unremarkable year nevertheless celebrates the cookbook: "The steady growth of the sum to the credit of the Cook Book Committee shows what a wonderful success this book has been and may its supply be unlimited" (letter pasted into December 6, 1920 Minutes). Clearly the venture was successful enough to merit a third cookbook (another *Famous Cook Book*) in 1925.

The three cookbooks published by the Ladies Auxiliary to Temple de Hirsch in 1908, 1916, and 1925 differ most obviously in length: 194, 349, and 446 pages respectively. All three books are hardbound with cloth covers that look like they are meant to withstand the rigors of the kitchen. *One Thousand Favorite Recipes* is green with gold lettering, and both *Famous Cook Book*s are cream with black lettering. In highlighting authorship by the Ladies Auxiliary, all three covers reinforce connections across the volumes. *One Thousand Favorite Recipes* also includes a mention of Seattle, Washington, on its cover, while the other two note its birthplace on the title page. And all three are printed locally: Merchants Printing Company for 1908, and Lowman and Hanford in 1916 and 1925. The 1916 and 1925 editions include a note of thanks to the success of the early cookbook. All three use the title page to single out the chief compilers of the cookbook: Mrs. Sigismund Aronson and Mrs. William Gottstein in 1908; Mrs. William Gottstein, Mrs. Sigismund Aronson, and Mrs. Salmon G. Spring in 1916; and Mrs. Sigismund Aronson and Mrs. Samuel Brown in 1925.

Even with a few aesthetic changes and additions and subtractions, the three cookbooks are very much alike in spirit. All three are divided into typical cookbook sections, including soups, fish, entrees, salads, vegetables, cakes, bread, and beverages, as well as having sections called "Home Remedies" (or "Household Hints" in 1925) and "For the Sick." The recipes are laid out in paragraph form, one right after another, separated only by title. Ingredients, sometimes with measurements, sometimes without, are embedded into the paragraphs, not separated out the way we see them in contemporary cookbooks. Most of the individual recipes are authored by women who use the Mrs. title and their husband's first name or initial and last name. All three have advertisements for mostly local businesses.

"Ethnic" moments are balanced out with other ethnicities or with overall genericness, recipes that are or have become generally American, like "Cream of Cauliflower Soup," "Chicken Salad," "Deviled Eggs," "Rhubarb and Strawberry Pie," and "Ice Box Cake." The later editions include a "Dictionary of Cooking Terms" full of French phrases and French cooking techniques, suggesting an aspirational class affiliation more than an ethnic tradition. The later editions also include a section called "Kuchen," a German/Yiddish word for "cake," perhaps reflecting the synagogue's German American membership, and all three editions include recipes with central and eastern European roots: "Liver Kloese for Soup," "Krepchen," "Mandel Torte." Here, too, we see the only recipes that are or may be tied to a particular Jewish holiday: a handful of matzo recipes, including one that is titled "Potato Flour Cake for Easter." At the same time, all three cookbooks include recipes for dishes such as "Italian Sauce for Tongue," "Sauce Bearnaise for Delmonico," "Genuine Mexican Tamale Loaf," "Puget Sound Clam Chowder for Ten Persons," "Olympia Pan Roast," and "Tacoma Layer Cake."

Most notably, none of the cookbooks is kosher, a choice that could be read as a mark of ongoing assimilation among community members. The lack of adherence to kashruth, or Jewish dietary law, is demonstrated in inclusions and exclusions: on the one hand, the absence of a "how to keep kosher" section, which is included in *Jewish Cookery Book*, the earliest known Jewish cookbook in America (Kirshenblatt-Gimblett 78) or even acknowledgement of what is trefa,[2] and, on the other hand, the presence of recipes that call for shellfish and ham and that mix meat and dairy. None of the cookbooks includes a separate section on ham or pork, but there is a stand-alone section on shellfish, with recipes that highlight clams, crabs, oysters, lobster, and shrimp. The 1925 edition contains no fewer than 26 recipes for oysters—including "Oysters Baked on Ham" and another one called "Little Pigs in Blanket," in which an oyster, rather than the traditional sausage, is snug in its blanket of bacon. Although overall the recipes are short on the way of instruction, the absence of notes on how to prepare meat to be kosher is also telling.

Carol Gold notes that cookbooks often don't reflect how people actually eat: the preparation of everyday foods is so well known as to be superfluous in a cookbook. Instead, she argues, cookbooks tend to be prescriptive, suggesting to readers "what they ought to be eating and how they ought to eat, if not necessarily what they do eat" (qtd. in Allen 12). Anne L. Bower makes a similar point:

> Whether the group authors of a particular fund-raising cookbook actually cooked from the recipes in their book, pursuing the depicted heritage, lifestyle, and values, we cannot actually say. All we can say is that they participated in constructing these texts, usually appending their names to their recipes, so that the recipes and names remain to us as a form of self-representation. (31)

---

2   Barbara Kirshenblatt-Gimblett writes in "Kitchen Judaism" that another early Jewish cookbook, *"Aunt Babette's" Cook Book* (1889), is not kosher but includes a note on trefa, or nonkosher food, and acknowledges kosher-keeping readers (80).

Yet we do have reason to believe that at least some of the members of the synagogue ate the food in their cookbooks. First, we have record of the menus from the many dinners that the Ladies Auxiliary hosted as fundraisers and/or as ways of welcoming or celebrating the Jews in the community. The 1919 Chanukah dinner menu, for example, includes turkey, cranberry sauce, potato salad, sausage, rolls, and coffee cake (Minutes, December 2, 1919). Notably, this very American Thanksgiving-sounding Chanukah dinner was conceived at the same time that the women supported Rabbi Koch's push for a more "Jewish" Chanukah, one that "do[es] away with the usual xmas trees and xmas gifts in the homes," includes a drive for a Community Menorah with tapers "no less radiant than the Xmas candles," and ensures that each religious school child receives a present "given at Chanucah instead of at Xmas" (Minutes, October 6, 1919). In addition, we have Mary McCarthy's memoirs, which include descriptions of two of her great aunts: Eva Aronson and Rosie Gottstein. Aunt Eva is Mrs. Sigismund Aronson, the only compiler of all three cookbooks, and Aunt Rosie is Mrs. Moses A. Gottstein, who contributed many recipes. McCarthy writes in *Memories of a Catholic Girlhood* that her aunts' contributions represented their different culinary tastes and their different degrees of wealth.[3]

Significantly, the three editions of the Temple de Hirsch cookbook didn't become more or less kosher over time. There isn't a linear narrative of a cookbook initially honoring the laws of kashruth and then becoming more lax. Likewise, we don't have a cookbook that perhaps read as secular and became "more Jewish"—a phrase I'll dismantle later—as it became more known. It's fair to say that there are more recipes containing trefa ingredients in the 1925 edition than there are in the 1908, but there is a lot more of everything in the 1925 edition: the cookbook more than doubles its size. Given its lack of explicit interest in Jewish dietary law, given its lack of explicit support of observation and celebration, it's fair to ask if this is a Jewish cookbook at all.

Undoubtedly, some would read the Seattle cookbooks as a public story of assimilation. Writing about *Our Sisters' Recipes*, a cookbook composed by Jewish women in a Pittsburgh synagogue in 1909 and that bears a resemblance to *One Thousand Favorite Recipes* and *Famous Cook Book* in some key ways, not least in its lack of adherence to kosher dietary law, Anne L. Bower argues that "the book

---

3   McCarthy writes, "Aunt Rosie was poor, compared to her sisters. . . . She was active in the temple as well as in the musical world. The cookbook of the Ladies' Auxiliary of the Temple de Hirsch, a volume got up for charity and much used in our family—I still own a copy—has many recipes contributed by Mrs. M.A. Gottstein. Her chicken stewed with noodles, hamburger in tomatoes, and rhubarb pie are quite unlike the recipes contributed by Mrs. S.A. Aronson, my other great-aunt, which begin with directions like this: 'Take a nice pair of sweetbreads, add a cup of butter, a glass of good cream, sherry, and some *foie gras*'" (206).

includes foods no religious Jew would eat, such as dishes mixing meat and milk and those using shellfish. Thus, the 'Sisters' downplay their Jewishness, recounting thereby a story of assimilation into the middle-class urban community" (38). Such a position, however, rests on a limited understanding of what it means to be a religious Jew. These *are* Jewish cookbooks. They perform life as Reform Jews at that particular moment in time.

THE TREFA AFFAIR

Food is no small matter in Judaism. Scholars identify a public argument about kashruth to be one of the main events that led to the fissure between Reform and Conservative Judaism. Known as the Trefa Affair or the Highland House Affair, the banquet was held in Cincinnati on July 11, 1883. It celebrated the first ordination class, the first ordination of rabbis on American soil, and the tenth anniversary of the Union of American Hebrew Congregations, inviting more than 100 Jewish and lay leaders from Cincinnati and elsewhere. According to Jonathan Sarna, "The broadly inclusive ceremony marked 'the high point of Jewish religious unity in America' and symbolized [Rabbi Isaac Mayer] Wise's long-standing goal: to lead a broad ideologically diverse coalition committed to strengthening American Judaism" (145). To almost everyone's surprise, the menu included four forbidden foods—clams, crabs, shrimp, and frogs' legs—and mixed meat and dairy. Some guests left in protest.

It's unclear whether the inclusion of unkosher dishes was accidental or intentional—an unastute, but Jewish, caterer? a passive-aggressive rabbi?—but its effects were divisive. Lance Sussman calls the Trefa Banquet "Reform Judaism's most widely known faux pas" (29) and dubs it "a cautionary tale and an object lesson for Judaism's most liberal religious movement" (29). Sarna writes, "Symbolically, the trefa banquet separated American Jews into two opposing camps that could no longer even break bread together. The incident both anticipated and stimulated further divisions" (145). For Sussman, that the menu was pork-free is not incidental: not only did it reflect the actual eating practices of many American Jews, but "[i]t also represented a midpoint between the general compliance with traditional kashruth at public events that characterized American Reform Judaism until the 1870s and a radical break with kashruth that increasingly characterized mainstream Reform beginning in the early 1880s" (29). Sarna writes that while Reform Jews often didn't observe kashruth, even as they continued to avoid pork,

> [t]raditionalists . . . viewed the banquet as a "public insult," particularly since [Rabbi Isaac Meyer] Wise, instead of apologizing for the gaffe, took the offensive against what he called "kitchen

Judaism" and insisted that the dietary laws had lost their validity. In so doing, he appeared to undermine the "union" which the Union of American Hebrew Congregations and Hebrew Union College had earlier pledged to uphold, and to cast his lot decisively with proponents of an exclusive strategy for Reform Judaism, concerned less with compromise for the sake of unity than with firmness for the sake of principle. (145)

On his part, Wise, then president of Hebrew Union College, would later argue that Judaism is not a "'kitchen and stomach' religion" (qtd. in Sussman 35).

Two years after the Trefa Affair, a group of rabbis would write what's known as the Pittsburgh Platform, laying out the primary principles of Reform Judaism, including the rejection of all laws that they describe as "not adapted to the view and habits of modern civilization" (Sarna 149). Michael A. Meyer explains Reform Judaism's minimization of symbol and ritual, including the consumption of nonkosher food, like this: "The prevalent view was that ceremonialism amounted to Orientalism and that casting off ceremonies better revealed the purer Judaism of faith in God and love of man that lay beneath it" (280). Disregarding kosher dietary law is something Reform Jews would have done *as* Jews, not in spite of being Jews. And those ideas would have moved west and settled into a Jewish cookbook that takes stock of the region's bounty, draws on its contributors' intersectional identities, and embraces a particular and considered understanding of what it means to be Jewish.

COMPOSING KITCHEN JUDAISM

In tracing the history of charitable cookbooks, Janice Bluestein Longone writes that charitable cookbooks are not limited to any particular region or faith or class but are almost always tied to women. Longone highlights that the "popularity and rapid spread of the community cookbook phenomenon might be considered a prime example of female bonding and collective civic virtue" (20). She posits, "At a time when American women were without full political civic rights and representation, they found the community cookbook one very effective way to participate in the public life of the nation" (20). They also found a way to tell their stories in print—"print culture serving as a vital and complex intermediary connecting the two domains" of domesticity and the public sphere, as Elizabeth Long puts it (xvi)—and tell a story they would likely not feel authorized to tell in more literary ways.

As Anne Ruggles Gere notes, "History or what we say about the past has to do with the present more than with what happened at another time. The ways we think about the cultural work of women's clubs reveal more about us than about the thousands of women who inscribed themselves" within these gendered organizations (*Intimate Practices* 269). The early 20th-century Seattle cookbooks look like a story of assimilation, of choosing the secular and regional over deeper traditions of faith. But as Gere notes, that line of thinking reflects our own contemporary views about loss and assimilation and about a linearity of history. In exploring the historical, cultural, and religious "sites of writing" of these cookbooks, we gain a much richer story of the relationship between the local, regional, and national that shows how women choose, not merely lose, ways of participating in their multiple communities through food.

In the three cookbook volumes crafted by Temple de Hirsch's Auxiliary in the early 20th century, we see women contribute recipes, sign their names, make their Jewishness public, and allow their particular kind of Jewishness to circulate. The cookbooks perform daily life of Reform Jews at a specific place and time, and they do so in a way that is not only financially successful but also leaves a material and cultural legacy.

WORKS CITED

Allen, Julie K. Review of *Danish Cookbooks: New Directions in Scandinavian Studies*, by Carol Gold. *Scandinavian Studies*, vol. 80, no. 1, 2008, 125–28. *JSTOR*, www.jstor.org/stable/40920795.

Bower, Anne. "Cooking Up Stories: Narrative Elements in Community Cookbooks." *Recipes for Reading: Community Cookbooks, Stories, Histories*, edited by Anne L. Bower, U of Massachusetts P, 1997, pp. 29–50.

Congregation Temple de Hirsch. "50th Anniversary: 1899–1949." May 1949, Temple De Hirsch Sinai Records, University of Washington Libraries, Seattle, Special Collections Pacific Northwest Stacks Oversize.

Gere, Anne Ruggles. *Intimate Practices: Literacy and Cultural Work in U.S. Women's Clubs, 1880–1920*. U of Illinois P, 1997.

———. "Kitchen Tables and Rented Rooms: The Extracurriculum of Composition." *College Composition and Communication*, vol. 45, no. 1, 1994, pp. 75–92, https://doi.org/10.2307/358588.

Kirshenblatt-Gimblett, Barbara. "Kitchen Judaism." *Getting Comfortable in New York: The American Jewish Home, 1880–1950*, edited by Susan L. Braunstein and Jenna Weissman Joselit, The Jewish Museum, 1990, pp. 75–105.

Koch, Samuel. "Temple Tidings." Monthly Newsletter of Temple de Hirsch, vol. 1, no. 5, 1910. Samuel Koch Papers, 1902–1962, University of Washington Libraries, Seattle, Special Collections Manuscripts and Archives, 2370-018, box 13.

———. "Temple Tidings." Monthly Newsletter of Temple de Hirsch, vol. 2 no. 2, 1910. Samuel Koch Papers, 1902–1962, University of Washington Libraries, Seattle, Special Collections Manuscripts and Archives, 2370-018, box 13.

Ladies Auxiliary to Temple de Hirsch. *Famous Cook Book*. Rev. ed., edited by Mrs. William Gottstein et al., The Auxiliary, 1916. Temple De Hirsch Sinai Records, University of Washington Libraries, Seattle, Special Collections Pacific Northwest Stacks.

———. *Famous Cook Book*. 3rd rev. ed., edited by Mrs. Sigismund Aronson et al., The Auxiliary, 1925. *HathiTrust*, hdl.handle.net/2027/nyp.33433079745661.

———. *One Thousand Favorite Recipes*, edited by Mrs. Sigismund Aronson et al., The Auxiliary, 1908. *HathiTrust*, hdl.handle.net/2027/loc.ark:/13960/t56d6bt29.

Long, Elizabeth. Foreword. *Women in Print: Essays on the Print Culture of American Women from the Nineteenth and Twentieth Centuries*, edited by James P. Danky and Wayne A. Wiegand, U of Wisconsin P, 2006, pp. xv–xxi.

Longone, Janice Bluestein. "'Tried Receipts': An Overview of America's Charitable Cookbooks." *Recipes for Reading: Community Cookbooks, Stories, Histories*, edited by Anne L. Bower, U of Massachusetts P, 1997, pp. 17–28.

McCarthy, Mary. *Memories of a Catholic Girlhood*. Harcourt, Brace, 1957.

Meyer, Michael A. *Response to Modernity: A History of the Reform Movement in Judaism*. Oxford UP, 1988.

Minutes of the Ladies Auxiliary. Temple De Hirsch Sinai Records, 1910–1921, University of Washington Libraries, Seattle, Special Collections Manuscripts and Archives, 2370-018, box 26, folders 2–4.

Sarna, Jonathan. *American Judaism: A History*. Yale UP, 2004. *JSTOR*, www.jstor.org/stable/j.ctt1npgmq.

Sisterhood of Temple de Hirsch-Sinai. *Just Like Grandma Used to Make*. 1986, Temple De Hirsch Sinai Records, University of Washington Libraries, Seattle, Special Collections Manuscripts and Archives, 2370-018, box 26.

Sussman, Lance J. "The Myth of the Trefa Banquet: American Culinary Culture and the Radicalization of Food Policy in American Reform Judaism." *American Jewish Archives Journal*, vol. 57, no. 1/2, 2005, pp. 29–52, https://tinyurl.com/muuk6s4y.

Temple de Hirsch Sinai, 75th Anniversary Journal. 1974. Temple de Hirsch Sinai Records, University of Washington Libraries, Seattle, Special Collections Manuscripts and Archives, 2370-018, box 1.

CHAPTER 13.

"NOW I THINK WITH MY OWN MIND": MALCOLM X, EPISTEMIC DISOBEDIENCE, AND THE EXTRACURRICULUM

Elizabeth Vander Lei
Calvin University

In her essay "Kitchen Tables and Rented Rooms: The Extracurriculum of Composition," Anne Gere examines some of the "multiple contexts in which persons seek to improve their own writing" (80), particularly acts of literacy that occur outside academic settings. Gere describes this writing as "legitimate and autonomous cultural formation that undertakes its own projects" (86). Framing her essay with Simone Weil's image of two prisoners communicating through the wall that separates them, Gere argues for the importance of self-sponsored literacy activities—the extracurriculum. She suggests that paying attention to the extracurriculum "can lead us to tap and listen to the messages through the walls, to consider how we can learn from and contribute to composition's extracurriculum in our classrooms" (86). These "messages through the walls" often originate from people who, for various reasons (poverty, poor academic preparation, racism, sexism, homophobia, other life experiences or moral commitments), are absent from our field's history, our classrooms, and our scholarship. And yet the messages they are tapping out are as important today as they were when Gere first challenged us to pay attention because, if we have the courage to listen, we can learn much about what encourages people to write as if writing matters. Writers, including those in our classrooms, root their identity in and tell the truth of people and places beyond our knowledge, understanding, or control. An analysis of Malcolm X's "Message to the Grass Roots" demonstrates the importance of continuing to pay attention to the extracurriculum.

In her essay, Gere highlights features of the extracurriculum, including these three: that the extracurriculum is sponsored by many different people and groups, that it is fueled by desire, and that it provides an alternative route to social or political power. In his autobiography, Malcolm X describes his education as including key features of the extracurriculum that Gere identifies. His speech "Message to the Grassroots" showcases another: Malcolm X's extracurriculum, especially Nation of Islam (NOI) theology and his wide reading in global politics, sanctioned and sustained his epistemic disobedience. Malcolm X wielded ways of knowing that were as familiar to the "wretched of the earth," to borrow Fanon's term, as they were unfamiliar to the powerful to indict the logic used by white American power brokers to control people of color in America. Understanding how the extracurriculum fueled Malcolm X's epistemic disobedience is particularly valuable at this moment, when those who worship differently or accept a range of sexual orientations or even acknowledge the historical facts of slavery and its aftermath face ridicule, economic reprisals, or physical harm.

Malcolm X must be one of America's most famous beneficiaries of an extracurricular education, though for Malcolm X, the extracurriculum *was* his education; it was "extra" only in the sense that most of his teachers were not academics, most of his learning occurred in non-academic settings, and much of what he learned would not be sanctioned as "academic" knowledge. Gere notes that the extracurriculum "acknowledges a wide range of teachers" (80), and Malcolm X had many. From his Garveyite parents, he learned self-respect, self-sufficiency, and the importance of his membership in a global community of people who trace their ancestry to Africa (DeCaro 42). From people on the streets of Harlem he learned to hustle (X, *Autobiography* 101). From books and correspondence courses and fellow inmates during his time in prison, he learned traditional academic subjects and how to debate (198). From Elijah Muhammad, the leader of the NOI, Malcolm X learned to bifurcate humanity into Black and white, with "white people" including Europeans and people of European descent, and "Black people" including everyone else (Muhammad 49). After his conversion to the NOI, Malcolm X taught others as he had been taught.

Gere identifies desire as an important element of the extracurricular writing groups she studied; indeed, she describes the extracurriculum as "constructed by desire, by the aspirations and imaginations of its participants" (80). Malcolm X identifies desire as an essential component of his extracurricular education, recalling, "I had come to Norfolk Prison Colony still going through only book-reading motions. Pretty soon, I would have quit even those motions, unless I had received the motivation that I did" (*Autobiography* 198). For Malcolm X, his conversion to the NOI and his budding relationship with Elijah Muhammad were instrumental to improving his writing skills: "I became increasingly frustrated at not being able to express what I wanted to convey in letters that I wrote, especially those to Mr. Elijah Muhammad" (197). And his religiously motivated pursuit of literacy awakened in Malcolm X an intrinsic desire to learn, "some long dormant craving to be mentally alive" (206). In prison, Malcolm X honed his rhetorical skills by writing letters daily to his siblings; he also wrote to Elijah

Muhammad, to those from his former hustling life, and even to Boston's mayor, Massachusetts' governor, and the president of the United States (197).

After he was paroled, Malcolm X's religious fervor propelled him into an active and varied life of words. He preached on street corners and taught in NOI temple schools. He founded and penned articles for the NOI's newsletter, *Muhammad Speaks*, which NOI adherents sold in temples and on the street (Collins and Bailey 115), and he preached in Elijah Muhammad's stead on NOI Sunday radio broadcasts (X, *Autobiography*). Malcolm X offered innumerable public lectures, participated in debates, and gave many interviews; all these opportunities, especially the college lectures, nourished his desire to learn and expanded his extracurricular education. Malcolm X recalls, "The college sessions never failed to be exhilarating. They never failed in helping me further my own education" (*Autobiography* 324). When he introduced himself to the students and faculty members in the audience, Malcolm X emphasized the extracurricular nature of his education: "Gentlemen, I finished the eighth grade in Mason, Michigan. My high school was the black ghetto of Roxbury, Massachusetts. My college was in the streets of Harlem, and my master's was taken in prison" (325). In this way, Malcolm X defines himself as the intellectual equal of those in the room and his extracurricular education as equal to their advanced academic degrees.

Despite Malcolm X's relish for intellectual debate, Benjamin Karim writes, "Malcolm seemed to me to be most comfortably himself, and most at home, in the temple. In my mind's eye I see him again standing at the blackboard with the chalk between his thumb and forefinger. I hear him teaching, I recall him ministering" (129). At the temple schools, Malcolm X introduced new converts to the NOI by challenging how they understood themselves. Karim recalls how Malcolm X opened the first NOI class Karim attended: "'And now I'll tell you why you're here,' he said. 'You are here because you are black. It doesn't matter how light or how dark your complexion is because if you're not white, you're black, and the fact that you are here proves you're black'" (55). Malcolm X began with identity because the NOI taught that "the true knowledge of the black man" would provide adherents with the motivation to learn a new way of understanding themselves and their world and to unite with others who were like them (*Autobiography* 108). According to Elijah Muhammad, "Gaining knowledge of self makes us unite into a great unity. Knowledge of self makes you take on the great virtue of learning" (39). This NOI-sponsored education provided adherents with an "alternative literacy" (Miller 213) which, along with other daily practices noted by Keith Miller, such as "economic separatism and self-sufficiency" (212), "conversational signifiers," and the publication of their own newspaper, *Muhammad Speaks* (213), promoted a self-identity that was untainted by messages of inferiority.

Even a relentless schedule of preaching, teaching, and lecturing could not douse Malcolm X's desire to learn: "Every time I catch a plane, I have with me a book that I want to read—and that's a lot of books these days. If I weren't out here every day battling the white man, I could spend the rest of my life reading, just satisfying my curiosity . . ." (*Autobiography* 207). Malcolm X's curiosity led him to read widely in literature, theology, political science, and world events. He had great aspirations for people of color in America, and he relied on his extracurricular reading and writing to help them "learn to unlearn," to use Mignolo's term, to motivate them to delink from the colonial epistemology that continued to suppress them, and to encourage them to unite with other Americans of color ("Delinking" 485).

Gere argues that in addition to engaging human desire, extracurricular literacy provides an alternative route to social or political power for people who otherwise have very little. In "Kitchen Tables and Rented Rooms," Gere traces the scholarly history of the term "extracurriculum," noting that it is first used by scholars examining the extracurricular literacy practices of white male students in privileged academic settings. As she notes, Frederick Rudolph uses the term to describe "the literary clubs, the fraternity systems, and the organized athletics instigated by undergraduate students during the nineteenth century," and Arthur Applebee uses the term to describe "eighteenth and nineteenth century literary clubs" in which undergraduate students discussed "vernacular literature that was deemed not worthy of academic study" (79). In contrast, in her research Gere pays attention to the extracurricular literacy practices and epistemologies of disenfranchised people, people like Malcolm X, who live in places where higher education does not reach, people whose lives are hobbled by the monotony of manual labor or threatened by the dangers of homelessness. Malcolm X's extracurricular education introduced him to a new and powerful epistemology: a decolonial understanding of history and his place in it. From NOI theology, Malcolm X learned to see the social and political dominance of white people as transitory: NOI taught "that the white man was fast losing his power to oppress and exploit the dark world; that the dark world was starting to rise to rule the world again, as it had before" (X, *Autobiography* 186). If the white man's power was on its way out, Malcolm X would do everything possible to hasten its demise.

In his speech "Message to the Grass Roots," Malcolm X challenges his audience to rightly understand themselves, their enemies, and the strategies that their enemies use to control them. Miller, who uses whiteness theory as a lens for examining Malcolm X's oratory, argues that Malcolm X "repeatedly and thoroughly exposed, interrogated, theorized, critiqued, and debunked whiteness as an epistemology and a rhetoric. He did so through a project that amounted to nothing less than dismantling and reconstructing African American identity" (200). To do so, Malcolm X relies on his "homemade education" (*Autobiography*

113). As outlined in his speech, this education consists of what he learned from his Garveyite parents and NOI theology as well as from his reading about world politics, specifically, the 1955 Bandung Conference in Indonesia, a conference that Walter Mignolo describes as the point of origin for decoloniality among Third World countries (Mignolo, *Darker* xi–xii). In this speech, Malcolm X introduces his audience to decolonial thinking, which Mignolo describes as "a relentless analytic effort to understand, in order to overcome, the logic of coloniality" (10). To identify and repudiate the ongoing colonization of Black people in America generally and in the civil rights movement particularly, Malcolm X uses his speech to challenge his audience to engage in a disobedient epistemology—to find the minds they left in Africa—that will empower them to overthrow the white political power brokers who continue to colonize them.

Malcolm X delivered "Message to the Grass Roots" on November 10, 1963, in Detroit to an audience of militant Black Americans who "rejected the gradualism of the NAACP and SCLC and the nonviolent activism of Rustin and Farmer and were sharply critical of the Negro bourgeoisie" (Marable 264). He delivered the speech at a pivotal moment in his life: he was a few weeks away from being silenced by Elijah Muhammad, less than four months away from his break with the NOI, and five months away from the pilgrimage to Mecca that would radically alter (again) his understanding of white people. It was also a pivotal moment in the modern civil rights movement, occurring less than three months after the March on Washington and less than two months after the bombing of Birmingham's 16th Street Baptist Church that took the lives of four children. Historian Manning Marable contends that praise for the March on Washington from President Kennedy and other political leaders overshadowed a growing rift in the civil rights movement evident in the events of that day. Marable argues that "the success of the March on Washington generated great dissension inside the Black Freedom Movement. The suppression of John Lewis' controversial speech highlighted the deeper issues that divided black activists, and as 1963 wore on, the split between the conservative old guard and the militants bubbled to the surface" (263).

One of those bubbles popped when the moderate civil rights leaders who were planning the Northern Negro Leadership Conference in Detroit denied Black nationalists a place on the program. In protest, Reverend Albert B. Cleage, Jr., organized a Grass Roots Conference also in Detroit for the same weekend and invited Malcolm X to be the conference's final speaker. Marable describes the audience's response to Malcolm X's speech as "electrifying" in no small part because "Malcolm appeared to have broken free politically" from the NOI (265). An analysis of "Message to the Grass Roots" in the context of Malcolm X's extracurricular education, however, suggests that while Malcolm X was indeed nearing a separation from the NOI, he mainly relied on his homemade education, particularly what he had learned from Elijah Muhammad, to exhort his audience to think decolonially by recognizing the strategies of management and control that white people used to oppress them and to act decolonially by rebelling against that control.

Malcolm X begins his argument in "Message to the Grass Roots" by establishing the identity of "our people" (4), using an NOI strategy of expanding the scope of the term "Black people" to include all non-Europeans. Malcolm X tells his audience, "Every time you look at yourself, be you black, brown, red or yellow, a so-called Negro, you represent a person who poses such a serious problem for America because you're not wanted. . . . So we're all black people, so-called Negroes, second class citizens, ex-slaves" (4). Again echoing Elijah Muhammad, Malcolm X argues that rightly understanding one's identity is the first necessary step to achieving a disobedient epistemology: "Once you face this as a fact, then you can start plotting a course that will make you appear intelligent instead of unintelligent" (4). And like Elijah Muhammad, Malcolm X defines Americans as the descendants of Europeans: "You didn't come here on the 'Mayflower.' You came here on a slave ship. In chains, like a horse, or a cow, or a chicken. And you were brought here by the people who came here on the 'Mayflower,' you were brought here by the so-called Pilgrims, or Founding Fathers" (5). Malcolm X then identifies "the white man" as the "common enemy" of all Black people: "We have a common oppressor, a common exploiter, and a common discriminator. But once we all realize that we have a common enemy, then we unite—on the basis of what we have in common. And what we have foremost in common is that enemy—the white man" (5). In reiterating the division of Black/Aboriginal people and white/American people that he learned from Elijah Muhammad, Malcolm X creates an opportunity to apply the disobedient epistemology of global struggle for decolonization to the American civil rights movement.

After establishing the identity of his audience and "the white man," Malcolm X introduces the Bandung Conference, a gathering in Indonesia of representatives from 29 nations. He describes the Bandung Conference as "the first unity meeting in centuries of black people. And once you study what happened at the Bandung conference, and the results of the Bandung conference, it actually serves as a model for the same procedure you and I can use to get our problems solved" (5). Malcolm X continues by describing how the participants of the Bandung Conference understood the enemy they had in common: "They realized all over the world where the dark man was being oppressed, he was being oppressed by the white man; where the dark man was being exploited, he was being exploited by the white man. So they got together on this basis—that they had a common enemy" (6). Alluding to tensions in the civil rights movement that lead to competing conferences in Detroit, Malcolm X calls contemporary Black Americans to focus less on what divides them and more on who is oppressing them:

> When you and I here in Detroit and in Michigan and in America who have been awakened today look around us, we too realize here in America we all have a common enemy, whether he's in Georgia or Michigan, whether he's in California or New York: He's the same man: blue-eyes and blond hair and pale skin—the same man. So what we have to do is what they did. They agreed to stop quarreling among themselves. . . . We need to stop airing our differences in front of the white man, put the white man out of our meetings, and then sit down and talk shop with each other. That's what we've got to do. (6)

Like the decolonizers from around the world who gathered at the Bandung conference and then fought for their freedom, Malcolm X believed that the only way to upend the colonial matrix of power was for those who were its victims to put aside their differences and separate completely from their oppressors. Although his subsequent conversion to Islam would cause Malcolm X to soften his views on accepting help from white Americans, at this point he believed that any help from white Americans reinforced the colonial matrix of power; any cooperation with white Americans undermined the unity of those who had been colonized.

Toward the end of his speech, Malcolm X offers an account of the recent March on Washington, one that contrasts moderate Black civil rights leaders who operated at the behest of white power brokers within the colonial matrix of power and "the grass roots," people of color who thought decolonially and were primed for a "black revolution" (14). Interestingly, and consistent with decolonial thinking, here Malcolm X shifts from condemning white people generally to indicting powerful white politicians. Malcolm X's decolonial history of the March on Washington cites the origin of the march in plans for disruptive protests by "the grass roots out there in the street":

> They were going to march on Washington, march on the senate, march on the White House, march on the Congress, and tie it up, bring it to a halt, not let the government proceed. They even said they were going out to the airport and lay down on the runway and not let any airplanes land. I'm telling you what they said. That was revolution. That was revolution. That was the black revolution. (14)

According to Malcolm X, the increasing power of the grassroots "scared the white power structure in Washington DC to death," so President Kennedy and other white political power brokers directed moderate Black civil rights leaders to stop these disruptive plans (14–15). Malcolm X parodies the reply of moderate civil rights leaders, emphasizing their subservient status: "'Boss, I can't stop it because I didn't start it.' I'm telling you what they said. 'I'm not even in it, much less at the head of it'" (15). Malcolm X describes President Kennedy and other white leaders advancing the colonial matrix of power by taking control of the march: "And the old shrewd fox, he said, 'Well if you all aren't in it, I'll put you in it. I'll put you at the head of it. I'll endorse it. I'll welcome it. I'll help it. I'll join it'" (15). As a result, according to Malcolm X, the March on Washington "was a sellout. It was a takeover. . . . They controlled it so tight—they told those Negroes what time to hit town, how to come, where to stop, what signs to carry, what song to sing, what speech to make, and what speech they couldn't make; and then told them to get out of town by sundown" (16–17). Malcolm X is aware that his narrative of events does not match the "crooked narrative" told by white power brokers and their collaborators in news outlets (see Mignolo, "Delinking" 461). Consequently, more than ten times in "Message to the Grass Roots" Malcolm X stresses the factual basis for his narrative, asserting, for example, "I'm telling you what they said" (15) and, later, "I can prove what I'm saying. If you think I'm telling you wrong, you bring me Martin Luther King and A. Philip Randolph and James Farmer and those other three and see if they'll deny it over a microphone" (16).

Malcolm X's description of how white American power brokers controlled the March on Washington enacts another key observation about colonial power: that deciding *who* will be included and *when* is the purview of those in power. Using an analogy, Malcolm X introduces a "new logic to tell the story" (Mignolo, "Delinking" 461). He explains:

> It's like when you've got some coffee that's too black, which means it's too strong. What do you do? You integrate it with cream; you make it weak. If you pour too much cream in, you won't even know you ever had coffee. It used to be hot, it becomes cool. It used to be strong, it becomes weak. It used to wake you up, now it'll put you to sleep. This is what they did with the March on Washington. They joined it. They didn't integrate it; they infiltrated it. They joined it, became a part of it, took it over. And as they took it over, it lost its militancy. They ceased to be angry. They ceased to be hot. They ceased to be uncompromising. Why, it even ceased to be a march. It became a picnic, a circus. Nothing but a circus, with clowns and all. ("Message to the Grass Roots" 16)

According to Malcolm X, as a result of the interference of President Kennedy and other white politicians, what had begun as a Black revolution was reduced to mere entertainment: "It was a circus, a performance that beat anything Hollywood could ever do, the performance of the year" (17).

Malcolm X delivered "Message to the Grassroots" shortly before he left the NOI and undertook a pilgrimage to Mecca that changed him once again, that opened him to a new understanding of racism in America. In his last speeches, Malcolm X scholar Robert Terrill writes, Malcolm X tried "to break his audiences free from the confines of the dominant white culture while at the same time helping them avoid becoming trapped within another set of restrictions" (110). On his pilgrimage, Malcolm X encountered devout Muslims of every race; according to Malcolm X, the experience "broadened my scope. It blessed me with a new insight" (*Autobiography* 416). Returning home, Malcolm X responded to his experience by publicly recanting his adherence to Elijah Muhammad's condemnation of all white people: "In the past, yes, I have made sweeping indictments of all white people. I will never be guilty of that again—as I know now that some white people are truly sincere, that some truly are capable of being brotherly toward a black man" (416). As a result of his on-going extracurricular education and consistent with a decolonial mindset, Malcolm X condemned the actions of specific, racist white politicians and the racist society that emboldened them. Describing a conversation he had with an American ambassador in Africa, Malcolm X recalls, "That discussion with the ambassador gave me a new insight—one which I like: that the white man is not inherently evil, but America's racist society influences him to act evilly. The society has produced and nourishes a psychology which brings out the lowest, most base part of human beings" (427). In an interview upon his return to the United States, Malcolm X summed up the revolution in his thinking: "I feel like a man who has been asleep somewhat and under someone else's control. I feel what I'm thinking and saying now is for myself. Before, it was for and by the guidance of Elijah Muhammad. Now I think with my own mind, sir" (226).

It must be noted that while Malcolm X's homemade education enabled him to think decolonially, in "Message to the Grass Roots" and throughout his life, Malcolm X expressed sexist and heteronormative ideas consistent with the colonial matrix of power and NOI theology. Furthermore, other issues, including Malcolm X's use of language and images that, while provocative in his time, would now be considered offensive, create real challenges for those who would consider including Malcolm X on a syllabus. But Malcolm X still has much to teach us about the people and ideas that shape our writing and the important role that disobedient epistemology plays in a democracy. And Malcolm X offers a way to respond to Gere's call to assign the extracurriculum a more prominent place in our classrooms. We might start where Malcolm X left off by simply asking our students to describe a time when they thought with their own mind and encouraging them to celebrate the people and communities that sponsored their disobedient epistemic.

WORKS CITED

Collins, Rodnell P., and A. Peter Bailey. *Seventh Child: A Family Memoir of Malcolm X*. Dafina Books, 2022.

DeCaro, Louis A, Jr. *On the Side of My People: A Religious Life of Malcolm X*. New York UP, 1996.

Fanon, Frantz. *The Wretched of the Earth*. Translated by Richard Philcox, Grove P, 2004.

Gere, Anne Ruggles. "Kitchen Tables and Rented Rooms: The Extracurriculum of Composition." *College Composition and Communication*, vol. 45, no. 1, 1994, pp. 75–92, https://doi.org/10.58680/ccc19948799.

Karim, Benjamin. *Remembering Malcolm*. Carroll and Graff Publishers, 1992.

Marable, Manning. *Malcolm X: A Life of Reinvention*. Viking, 2011.

Mignolo, Walter D. *The Darker Side of Western Modernity: Global Futures, Decolonial Options*. Duke UP, 2011, https://doi.org/10.1215/9780822394501.

———. "Delinking: The Rhetoric of Modernity, the Logic of Coloniality, and the Grammar of De-Coloniality." *Cultural Studies*, vol. 21, no. 2–3, 2007, pp. 449–514, https://doi.org/10.1080/09502380601162647.

Miller, Keith D. "Plymouth Rock Landed on Us: Malcolm X's Whiteness Theory as a Basis for Alternative Literacy." *College Composition and Communication*, vol. 56, no. 2, 2004, pp. 199–222, https://doi.org/10.58680/ccc20044041.

Muhammad, Elijah. *Message to the Blackman in America*. Muhammad's Temple No. 2, 1965.

Terrill, Robert E. *Malcolm X: Inventing Radical Judgment*. Michigan State UP, 2004.

X, Malcolm. *The Autobiography of Malcolm X*. Random House, 1964.

———. "Message to the Grass Roots, November 19, 1963, Detroit." Grove Press, 1965, pp. 3–17.

PART 5. ADVANCING ASSESSMENT

CHAPTER 14.

THE EXTRACURRICULUM OF WRITING ASSESSMENT

J. W. Hammond
Michigan Technological University

In her contribution to the 2011 *College English* Symposium "How I Have Changed My Mind," Anne Ruggles Gere tells a tale that's part intellectual autobiography, part love story (Anson et al.). Her narrative concerns the way she first had a falling out with writing assessment scholarship, then developed a deeper passion for the topic as conversations about it blossomed beyond its psychometric roots—with writing assessment's conceptual branches extending into increasingly fruitful exchanges with rhetoric, linguistics, and genre studies, grounded in a focus on assessment's local relevance to writing pedagogy.

I came across this brief text around a decade ago, when I first met Gere. As I now re-read her reflection, what strikes me most isn't its narrative destination but the journey it describes. She writes,

> After publishing ["Written Composition: Toward a Theory of Evaluation"], I became increasingly disenchanted with the topic of evaluating writing. The ongoing dominance of the statistically based psychometric model led to a focus on issues of reliability and validity that pushed issues of meaning aside. I could see no way to forward the questions that mattered to me, *so I turned my attention elsewhere, investigating writing in the extracurriculum*, first in writing groups and later in women's clubs. I decided that it wasn't worthwhile to focus on the evaluation of writing; I didn't want to spend any more time on it.
>
> Flash forward thirty years, and I have changed my mind: the evaluation of writing preoccupies me. . . . I'm teaching a graduate seminar titled "What Makes Writing Good?" . . . I look forward to conversations about assessment. (112–13; emphasis mine)

In this telling, Gere's work on the extracurriculum of composition—the ways "writing development occurs outside formal education" ("Kitchen Tables"

76)—occupies an interstitial space, sandwiched chronologically at the center of her assessment story. As I contend in this chapter, this narrative placement is oddly fitting, for as I have come to think of it, the extracurriculum is at the heart of Gere's field-shaping scholarship on assessment. For decades, she has challenged writing studies scholars to examine the discursive reach and disciplinary effects of evaluation beyond and outside the classroom—including in matters of everyday linguistic prescriptivism and discrimination (see, e.g., Gere, "Public Opinion"; Gere et al., "Communal Justicing"; Gere and Smith).

A growing body of scholarship now explores ways that extracurricular writing products, practices, and experiences can be enclosed by academic assessment—as when they're featured as topics for reflection in self-placement (e.g., Toth and Aull) or folded into efforts to appraise writing development (e.g., Gere, *Developing Writers*; Wardle and Roozen). Despite this attention to incorporations of the extracurriculum *in writing assessment*, the matter of writing assessment *in the extracurriculum* remains underdiscussed. Writing assessment scholarship arguably now finds itself in an epistemic predicament analogous to the one that, two decades ago, Gere warned was at work in the broader field of composition studies: "In concentrating upon establishing our position within the academy, we have neglected to recount the history of composition in other contexts; we have neglected composition's extracurriculum" ("Kitchen Tables" 79). There is, she charged, an unrealized "need to uncouple composition and schooling, to consider the situatedness of composition practices, to focus on the experiences of writers not always visible to us inside the walls of the academy" (80).

Something similar is true for writing assessment scholarship: We have neglected to recount the history of judgment and response in other contexts, focusing on the assessment experiences that are most visible to us inside the walls of our colleges and schools. We have neglected *writing assessment's extracurriculum*.

We can begin to work our way out of this epistemic predicament by braiding two strands of Gere's scholarship: her studies of assessment and its manifold consequences and her work on the "myriad" spaces where students and others "write their worlds" outside and beyond formal writing classrooms ("Kitchen Tables" 91). Doing so, we find in Gere's insights a series of reminders that writing assessment isn't always coupled with schooling; it extends also to the myriad extracurricular ways that we assess our worlds—and that our worlds assess us.

The social justice significance of "extending greater focus to how writing is assessed outside of formal education spaces" (Banks et al. 388) has recently been underscored by the Conference on College Composition and Communication (CCCC) Statement on White Language Supremacy, which stresses that white language supremacy and its violent systems for "defining and evaluating" aren't confined to college writing curricula, and can be found at work "in schools, academic disciplines, professions, media, and society at large" (Richardson et al.). Dismantling white language supremacy thus requires reckoning with the reality that academic assessment is only one site among many where responses to writing and writers can participate in social (in)justice. To this end, I begin in the next section by defining the extracurriculum of writing assessment, then offer four brief sketches of assessment's extracurriculum, selected to illustrate some of its dimensions and complexities.

Ultimately, what this chapter offers is a kind of sequel to Gere's reflection in "How I Have Changed My Mind," continuing and complicating the narrative arc she sets in motion. For while Gere's narrative positions the extracurriculum as an "elsewhere" for assessment, my years of learning from and working with her have taught me that it is possible to view the extracurriculum and writing assessment as overlapping terrains, each of which can be discussed in ways that reinforce, rearticulate, and revitalize the other.

DEFINING ASSESSMENT'S EXTRACURRICULUM

The *extracurriculum of writing assessment,* as I use the term, names the myriad manifestations of writing assessment—public, private, popular, or professional—that are ubiquitous (and potentially iniquitous) outside schools and colleges. Assessment's extracurriculum is composed of the countless judgments of and responses to writing that are neither conducted in academic institutions nor compelled by them. Such assessments are enacted around the kitchen table, enmeshed in office culture, enlisted to provision public services and police public participation, encoded into algorithmic tools and platforms, self-sponsored and spread via social media, and mobilized to make "expert" determinations of various kinds—among them, judgments about mental "fitness."

Assessment may be endemic to the classroom, but it is far from exclusive to it. In Brian Huot's words, "in literate activity, assessment is everywhere. No matter what purpose we have for the reading and writing we do, we evaluate what we read and write on a fairly continuous basis" (61). Building on Huot's insight, Joseph A. Cirio has helpfully called for writing assessment scholarship to devote greater critical focus to "everyday writing assessment"—that is, "the interpretation and judgment of everyday written texts that lead to decisions, actions, or changes in everyday writing" (1). Writing assessment, viewed this way, saturates and shapes our everyday literate lifeworlds within the academy and without it.

We can gain a better (if still partial) understanding of assessment's extracurriculum when we consider the following four sketches, which speak variously to the ways that:

1. the extracurriculum of composition discussed by Gere and others is always already subtended by writing assessment;
2. public life is policed by extracurricular testing regimes;
3. everyday linguistic judgments are encoded into and enforced through digital programs and platforms; and
4. the specter of extracurricular assessment haunts and possesses academic assessment, conditioning curricular practices and priorities.

In the following sections, I turn to these cases, each of which invites challenging questions about assessment (in)justice.

ASSESSMENT AT KITCHEN TABLES, IN RENTED ROOMS

In the form of peer response and formative criticism, writing assessment functions as the lifeblood coursing through the writing groups, clubs, and literary societies discussed by Gere in her germinal work on the extracurriculum. A culture of self-sponsored evaluation sustains and structures these communities of correction and improvement. Detailing the work of groups such as the Lansing, Iowa Writers' Workshop and the Tenderloin Women's Writing Workshop, Gere notes how participants "offer one another encouragement as well as criticism and suggest revisions," and devote hours to "reading and responding to one another's writing" ("Kitchen Tables" 75). She notes, too, how writing groups not only "increas[e] positive feelings" but "discipline participants" (76), creating spaces for "'positive criticism'" (qtd. in 77).

Recovering scenes from the antebellum 19th-century extracurriculum, Gere describes how Margaret Fuller provided a subscription service whereby white women submitted compositions to be "read . . . aloud and canvassed [for] their adequacy" (qtd. in "Kitchen Tables" 84). Gere also recounts how members of the Black women's Female and Literary Society of Philadelphia "placed their anonymous weekly compositions in a box from which they were later retrieved and criticized" (84). This example speaks to a broader history of *rhetorical education through elective assessment* in 19th-century Black literary societies, described by Shirley Wilson Logan as spaces where members "performed and judged their own works and the works of others in order to perfect their skills and build their confidence" (94).

Directly responding to Gere's call for greater attention to the extracurriculum, Susan Miller stresses that the "evaluative urges" and "pejorative discriminations" associated with the composition classroom weren't originated by it, and are in evidence in a variety of sites and artifacts far removed from institutionally mandated assignments and assessments ("Things" 106). She cites, as one illustration, a 1786 letter from Charles Mortimer to his son Jack, responding to—and critiquing—the latter's writing "at a level of particularity that applies the same evaluative paradigm that mass schooling applied a century later to discursive (and cursive) practices," equating matters of capitalization, legibility, and fluency in *written characters* with the *inner character* of the author ("Assuming" 246; see also Miller, "Things"). This letter testifies to the fact that we misunderstand the shape and scope of assessment's extracurriculum if we focus only on the ways writers seek out judgment from others. In the extracurriculum, writers may solicit criticism and feedback, but self-sponsored assessment also flows in the other direction: Unsolicited judgment can be *voluntarily supplied*, as when parents privately "rage at error with . . . loving frustration" (Miller, "Things" 106).

Speaking to a related form of error-fixation in the extracurriculum, Gere points us to a popular 19th-century tradition of officiating assessment in writing groups and clubs through selecting a formal *critic*: "Usually elected on the basis of skill in identifying errors, this critic assumed special responsibility for noting faults of syntax and diction in papers read before the group" ("Kitchen Tables" 83). The corrective responsibilities of the critic included the "evaluation of the effectiveness of an argument" by means of "identifying . . . rhetorical issues such as persuasiveness and appeal" (Gere, "Public Opinion" 266). Proponents of this assessment-centric office imagined that it provided a powerful, *positive* machinery for improving writing and writers: "In rhetorical terms, the critic's observations enhance writers' audience awareness, helping them to see their work from the perspective of others. At the same time intellectual growth results from enhanced self-critical abilities fostered by recognizing one's own 'defects and errors'" (Gere, *Writing Groups* 13). This framing of improvement through criticism hints at an ever-present danger: Assessment in the extracurriculum can rehearse the kinds of prescriptivist error-fixation—the hunt for *defects* and *errors*—characteristic of the punishingly "reductive forms of assessment" too often found in the academy (Gere, "Kitchen Tables" 88).

Assessment's extracurriculum is thus a domain that may promise meaningful alternatives to the academy's cultures of correction and professionalization. Yet within that domain lurks the potential that even at kitchen tables and in rented rooms, judgments of composition can recompose discriminatory social hierarchies.

EXTRACURRICULAR TESTING REGIMES

Gere rightly observes that classroom instruction in "composition frequently serves a gatekeeping function" that doubles as "an initiation rite" ("Kitchen Tables" 89), cleaving writers *from* their communities and cleaving them *to* "the language and perspectives of others" (90). Yet when we consider the prevalence of extracurricular testing regimes, we find that the extracurriculum offers only a partial escape from exclusionary gatekeeping and assimilationist initiation. Indeed, the discriminatory power of such regimes can complexly shape, even sponsor the kinds of extracurricular writing practices, programs, and organizations discussed by Gere and others.

For one historical example, we can look to the Citizenship School Program, in operation from 1957–1970. Susan Kates explains that the Citizenship Schools, a literacy campaign by and for Black adults in the Southern US, emerged explicitly as a community response to an extracurricular exigence: state-mandated literacy tests that regulated access to the ballot box. These racist "technologies of disenfranchisement," as Natasha N. Jones and Miriam F. Williams term them, weaponized judgments about reading and writing ability as pretexts for anti-Black voter suppression. These tests did so as part of a broader tradition of white supremacist extracurricular assessment, complementary to the inculcation of white language supremacy via schooling (Inoue; Kates; Prendergast).

Speaking to this history of extracurricular testing regimes, Catherine Prendergast notes that government-enforced efforts to police literacy as "White property" (and as a defining property of whiteness) also targeted immigrants and putative foreigners:

> Beginning in the nineteenth century, literacy abilities were frequently imagined as parsed to different races, and literacy tests for immigration and naturalization were advocated under a potent racial rubric. These literacy tests were offered as the most efficient means to identify those who were of the most pure specimens of the White race. (8)

Fueled by nativist fears and eugenic fantasies of racial engineering, early 20th-century extracurricular examinations such as the New York State Literacy Tests were mandated as part of a legal machinery for regulating citizenship and restricting the flow of immigration (Serviss). Such technologies of disenfranchisement reveal the violent forms that "entrance" and "qualifying" examinations can take in the extracurriculum. They offer painful reminders that writing assessment outside academic institutions isn't always voluntary from the vantage of those assessed—and can be both high-stakes and life-altering in its cruelty.

AUTOMATING EVERYDAY PRESCRIPTIVISM

In recent years, Gere has charged that to dismantle unjust academic assessments at scale, we must intervene in the disciplinary infrastructure that enables and encourages them—that is, the assemblage of publications, policies, platforms, pedagogies, and imagined pasts that shape disciplinary assessment practices and imperatives (Gere et al., "Communal Justicing" and "Response"). A corresponding attention to extracurricular assessment infrastructure may lead us to investigate the ways that assessment imperatives are covertly encoded into or enacted by the very platforms and tools we rely on in everyday writing.

As one case, consider the ubiquitous scrutiny of writing—curricular and extracurricular—conducted by Microsoft Word's grammar checker, an "ever-present corrective force" (McGee and Ericsson 454) that "combines the functions of software as tool for correction and evaluation and software as a medium for communication in a single software package" (Whithaus 171; see also Cirio 37). The "Editor" found in the Microsoft 365 version of Word automatically evaluates and assigns writers a percentage-based "Editor Score," accompanied by recommended corrections and refinements (and the option to scan "for similarity to online sources"). More generally, past iterations of Microsoft Word have, for decades, marked writerly errors and infelicities with a squiggly underlining of text, an aesthetic invocation of the iconography of classroom assessment. "Even in its screen appearance," Tim McGee and Patricia Ericsson observe, "it harkens back to the red pencil of the obsessive English teacher who bled over 'mistakes' and paid little or no attention to the quality of thinking" (464).

Microsoft's error-fixated checking systems merit our scrutiny because their infrastructural embeddedness in extracurricular (and curricular) writing ecologies renders them, in Anne Curzan's words, "arguably the most powerful prescriptive language force in the world at this point" (64). What's more, this evaluative force "serves to reify attitudes about nonstandard grammar being 'error,'" marking expressions of African American English and other "nonstandard" language varieties as impurities in need of correction or refinement (79). Critical investigation into everyday algorithmic prescriptivism may thus have special importance for those of us committed to the promotion of linguistic justice and the dismantlement of white language supremacy (Inoue; Richardson et al.)—aims that may be in tension with the proliferation of commercial products for algorithmically generating writing (Byrd; Owusu-Ansah) and formatively evaluating it (Hazelton et al.). To the extent that these algorithmic innovations encode Standardized (white) English as correct, normative, and universally intelligible, they rehearse a tired and ignoble prescriptivist tradition: devaluing "nonstandard" language as *sub-standard*.

EXTRACURRICULAR HAUNTING

Academic assessment always exists in dialogue with public opinion and is no stranger to popular deficit discourses about (il)literacy "crises" and "Why

Johnny Can't Write" (Gere "Public Opinion"; Gere et al., "Communal Justicing"). Haunted by these discourses, some writing educators go so far as to self-consciously position academic assessment as a violent "hidden curriculum" (Jackson) of sorts, subjecting students to linguistic bigotry in the classroom in a paternalistic effort to prepare them for violent assessment in the extracurriculum.

Consider David Johnson and Lewis VanBrackle's study, "Linguistic Discrimination in Writing Assessment," in which they found that raters of a state-mandated writing examination not only identified features of African American English (AAE) as "errors" but penalized them more harshly than other (actual) errors. When discussing possible reasons for the anti-Black linguistic racism documented by their work, Johnson and VanBrackle write,

> raters may be simply trying to prepare students for the "real-world" where AAE errors will be less tolerated by potential employers, so raters fail them now in the hopes that the students will address these errors. This brings into question the pedagogical wisdom of giving students a "right" to their dialect. . . . The "real-world" of standardized writing tests and job applications will most likely continue to penalize AAE features more harshly. (46)

Herein can be found the logic of *extracurricular haunting* that too often possesses curricular assessment: Anticipating that students will be judged harshly—perhaps even unfairly—in assessment's extracurriculum, writing educators resolve to discipline and punish them in and through the curriculum. These educators submit to and surrogate racist violences they might otherwise profess to oppose.

Speaking to this haunting brand of vicarious discrimination, Vershawn Ashanti Young describes the contradictions at work when writing educators present themselves as antiracist allies, helplessly marionetted into linguistic racism by an unseen extracurricular hand:

> teachers say that they recognize the importance of language diversity for students but they tell their students that they have to get ready for . . . the employer who will not hire them—if they don't speak or write a certain way.
>
> The feat here is that the teachers want to present themselves as antiracists, while at the same time they are the ones enacting the very prejudice on the student they say the student will experience outside.
>
> In other words, the teacher is saying, I'm not racist, but I'm going to teach you in a way (how to switch off yo black) and

grade in a way (that is down if you black in yo writin) that will prepare you to be acceptable to the folks who are really racist. The teacher then becomes the stand-in, the proxy, for the would-be racist. (x–xi)

Notably, examples like this one invert and subvert a core promise of the extracurriculum, as discussed by Gere: that it represents a break from writing instruction that is *disciplinary* in multiple senses of that term ("Kitchen Tables" 87). For the kind of instructor Young describes, the extracurriculum offers not a material departure from the disciplinary violences of schooling but instead an imaginative point of departure for authorizing and enacting them.

CONCLUSION

In ways big and small, assessment saturates and subtends composition's extracurriculum. It participates in sponsoring our everyday relationships to and through writing. It partly structures whether (and how) we navigate contexts and communities that operate outside the academy. It accompanies us when we privately compose via digital programs or platforms—its trace, legible in squiggly lines underneath the words we type or the aggregated "liking" (cf. Elbow) that accretes to our social media posts. Its shadow can even follow us into the classroom, haunting responses to student writing.

Though they represent only a brief turn of talk within what must be a broader conversation, the cases I have presented productively complement and complicate existing discussions about the extracurriculum, raising questions about (in)justice and extending lines of inquiry initiated by Gere.

Assessment at Kitchen Tables, in Rented Rooms

"The extracurriculum," as Gere frames it, "is constructed by desire, by the aspirations and imaginations of its participants" ("Kitchen Tables" 80). Whose desires construct assessment's extracurriculum? Those seeking assessment, those sponsoring it, or those supplying it—parties whose aspirations and imaginations may clash? If composition's extracurriculum depends on and deepens affective attachments to criticism, habituating us to the exercise of our evaluative urges, what role does writing assessment at kitchen tables and in rented rooms play in promoting social (in)justice?

Extracurricular Testing Regimes

If the extracurriculum is a domain partly defined by the voluntary pursuit and provision of assessment, it's also a domain where writers compose their way through a maze of compulsory "gatekeeping" examinations. What role does extracurricular testing play in sponsoring and shaping not only large-scale social disparities, but also ostensibly "voluntary" extracurricular writing activities—such as soliciting peer feedback in writing groups or imparting "positive criticism" to others? Put differently, in what ways has composition's extracurriculum emerged as a response to the threat posed by extracurricular testing?

Automating Everyday Prescriptivism

If understanding composition's extracurriculum requires examining its infrastructure—including the "local circumstances" and "material artifacts" essential to its "cultural work" (Gere, "Kitchen Tables" 90)—we must ask the following questions: Does this infrastructure introduce backdoors for linguistic prescriptivism? As the algorithmic generation and judgment of writing becomes more commonplace, in what ways is automated assessment sedimented into the infrastructure of everyday writing? Indeed, in what ways is everyday writing assessment suffused and preoccupied with appraisals of algorithmically assembled texts?

Extracurricular Haunting

It may be true, as Gere suggests, that "schooling in general and composition in particular . . . inscribes itself on students' bodies" ("Kitchen Tables" 87). Yet there's also a sense in which extracurricular imaginaries can be implicated in curricular efforts to discipline writers' bodies and bodies of writing—notably, when academic assessments are patterned on discriminatory preoccupations that we fear (or fantasize) predominate in the great extracurricular beyond. To what extent do we treat our curricular writing assessments as conduits for the extracurriculum to inscribe itself on students' bodies?

EPILOGUE: "WHAT MAKES WRITING GOOD?"

It's only fitting to close by offering an epilogue to Gere's account of "How I Have Changed My Mind," the *College English* reflection that opened this chapter (Anson et al.), because her narrative is, in its way, the story of how she changed my mind as well.

As it happens, my very first course as a doctoral student was a section of "What Makes Writing Good?"—the very seminar on assessment Gere references in her reflection as an outgrowth of her renewed interest in the evaluation of writing. My earliest idea for a term paper was to craft something not unlike this chapter, a piece calling for greater disciplinary focus on writing assessment's extracurriculum. This topic was one that I ultimately jettisoned, fearing that because I had more questions than answers, I couldn't do it justice.

Flash forward a decade, and I have changed my mind about assessment's extracurriculum—though not about the ethical importance of greater attention to it. What's changed is this: The extracurriculum of writing assessment once again preoccupies me not in spite of the questions it raises, but because of them. Following Gere's example, I've come to think of justice in assessment less as a noun than as a verb—that is, as *justicing*, "an iterative and collective process" that demands that we continuously investigate (and where necessary, revise) disciplinary assumptions and aims concerning assessment (Gere et al., "Communal Justicing" 384).

Where once I was fixated on doing justice *to* a topic, Gere has helped me to recognize the deeper importance of doing justice *through* a topic. In "rethinking the narratives we construct about composition studies" (Gere, "Kitchen Tables" 90) and the ways we "share and respond to one another's writing" (91), we're prompted to rethink the scope, significance, and social justice stakes we associate with writing assessment. The importance of this work becomes clearer when we consider that to ignore assessment's extracurriculum is arguably to ignore the majority of the appraisals that our once-and-future students encounter and engage in as they read, write, and yes, assess their worlds.

"What makes writing good?" has never been, and never will be, a question that the academy alone can own or answer.

WORKS CITED

Anson, Chris, et al. "How I Have Changed My Mind." *College English*, vol. 74, no. 2, 2011, pp. 106–30, https://doi.org/10.58680/ce201118157.

Banks, William P., et al. "The Braid of Writing Assessment, Social Justice, and the Advancement of Opportunity: Eighteen Assertions on Writing Assessment with Commentary." *Writing Assessment, Social Justice, and the Advancement of Opportunity*, edited by Mya Poe et al., The WAC Clearinghouse / UP of Colorado, 2018, pp. 379–425, https://doi.org/10.37514/PER-B.2018.0155.2.12.

Byrd, Antonio. "Truth-Telling: Critical Inquiries on LLMs and the Corpus Texts That Train Them." *Composition Studies*, vol. 51, no. 1, 2023, pp. 135–42, compstudies journal.com/wp-content/uploads/2023/06/byrd.pdf.

Cirio, Joseph A. *Everyday Writing Assessment: An Alternative Approach to Writing Assessment Theory*. 2018. Florida State U, PhD dissertation.

Curzan, Anne. *Fixing English: Prescriptivism and Language History*. Cambridge UP, 2014. *Cambridge Core*, https://doi.org/10.1017/CBO9781139107327.

Elbow, Peter. "Ranking, Evaluating, and Liking: Sorting out Three Forms of Judgment." *College English*, vol. 55, no. 2, 1993, pp. 187–206, https://doi.org/10.58680/ce19939323.

Gere, Anne Ruggles, editor. *Developing Writers in Higher Education: A Longitudinal Study.* U of Michigan P, 2019. *University of Michigan Press Ebook Collection*, https://doi.org/10.3998/mpub.10079890.

———. "Kitchen Tables and Rented Rooms: The Extracurriculum of Composition." *College Composition and Communication*, vol. 45, no. 1, 1994, pp. 75–92, https://doi.org/10.58680/ccc19948799.

———. "Public Opinion and Teaching Writing." *The Politics of Writing Instruction: Postsecondary*, edited by Richard H. Bullock and John Trimbur, general editor Charles Schuster, Boynton/Cook, 1991, pp. 263–75.

———. *Writing Groups: History, Theory, and Implications.* Southern Illinois UP, 1987.

Gere, Anne Ruggles, et al. "Communal Justicing: Writing Assessment, Disciplinary Infrastructure, and the Case for Critical Language Awareness." *College Composition and Communication*, vol. 72, no. 3, 2021, pp. 384–412, https://doi.org/10.58680/ccc202131160.

———. "Response to Shawna Shapiro." *College Composition and Communication*, vol. 74, no. 2, 2022, pp. 379–87, https://doi.org/10.58680/ccc202232281.

Gere, Anne Ruggles, and Eugene Smith. *Attitudes, Language, and Change.* National Council of Teachers of English, 1979. *ERIC*, eric.ed.gov/?id=ED176309.

Hazelton, Lynette, et al. "Formative Automated Writing Evaluation: A Standpoint Theory of Action." *Journal of Response to Writing*, vol. 7, no. 1, 2021, pp. 37–91. *BYUScholarsArchive*, scholarsarchive.byu.edu/journalrw/vol7/iss1/3/.

Huot, Brian. *(Re)Articulating Writing Assessment for Teaching and Learning.* Utah State UP, 2002. The WAC Clearinghouse, wac.colostate.edu/books/usu/re-articulating/.

Inoue, Asao B. *Above the Well: An Antiracist Literacy Argument from a Boy of Color.* The WAC Clearinghouse / UP of Colorado, 2021, https://doi.org/10.37514/PER-B.2021.1244.

Jackson, Philip W. *Life in Classrooms.* Holt, Rinehart and Winston, 1968.

Johnson, David, and Lewis VanBrackle. "Linguistic Discrimination in Writing Assessment: How Raters React to African American 'Errors,' ESL Errors, and Standard English Errors on a State-Mandated Writing Exam." *Assessing Writing*, vol. 17, no. 1, 2012, pp. 35–54, https://doi.org/10.1016/j.asw.2011.10.001.

Jones, Natasha N., and Miriam F. Williams. "Technologies of Disenfranchisement: Literacy Tests and Black Voters in the US from 1890 to 1965." *Technical Communication*, vol. 65, no. 4, 2018, pp. 371–86. *JSTOR*, www.jstor.org/stable/27301555.

Kates, Susan. "Literacy, Voting Rights, and the Citizenship Schools in the South, 1957–70." *College Composition and Communication*, vol. 57, no. 3, pp. 479–502, https://doi.org/10.58680/ccc20065050.

Logan, Shirley Wilson. *Liberating Language: Sites of Rhetorical Education in Nineteenth-Century Black America.* Southern Illinois UP, 2008.

McGee, Tim, and Patricia Ericsson. "The Politics of the Program: MS WORD as the Invisible Grammarian." *Computers and Composition*, vol. 19, no. 4, 2002, pp. 453–70, https://doi.org/10.1016/S8755-4615(02)00142-1.

Miller, Susan. *Assuming the Positions: Cultural Pedagogy and the Politics of Commonplace Writing.* U of Pittsburgh P, 1998.

———. "Things Inanimate May Move: A Different History of Writing and Class." *College Composition and Communication*, vol. 45, no. 1, 1994, pp. 102–07. *JSTOR*, https://doi.org/10.2307/358591.

Owusu-Ansah, Alfred L. "Defining Moments, Definitive Programs, and the Continued Erasure of Missing People." *Composition Studies*, vol. 51, no. 1, 2023, pp. 143–48, compstudiesjournal.com/wp-content/uploads/2023/06/owusu-ansah.pdf.

Prendergast, Catherine. *Literacy and Racial Justice: The Politics of Learning after* Brown v. Board of Education. Southern Illinois UP, 2003.

Richardson, Elaine, et al. "CCCC Statement on White Language Supremacy." *Conference on College Composition and Communication*, National Council of Teachers of English, June 2021, cccc.ncte.org/cccc/white-language-supremacy.

Serviss, Tricia. "A History of New York State Literacy Test Assessment: Historicizing Calls to Localism in Writing Assessment." *Assessing Writing*, vol. 17, no. 4, 2012, pp. 208–27, https://doi.org/10.1016/j.asw.2012.05.001.

Toth, Christie, and Laura Aull. "Directed Self-Placement Questionnaire Design: Practices, Problems, Possibilities." *Assessing Writing*, vol. 20, 2014, pp. 1–18, https://doi.org/10.1016/j.asw.2013.11.006.

Wardle, Elizabeth, and Kevin Roozen. "Addressing the Complexity of Writing Development: Toward an Ecological Model of Assessment." *Assessing Writing*, vol. 17, no. 2, 2012, pp. 106–19, https://doi.org/10.1016/j.asw.2012.01.001.

Whithaus, Carl. "Always Already: Automated Essay Scoring and Grammar-Checkers in College Writing Courses." *Machine Scoring of Student Essays: Truth and Consequences*, edited by Patricia Freitag Ericsson and Richard H. Haswell, Utah State UP, 2006, pp. 166–76. *The WAC Clearinghouse*, https://wac.colostate.edu/books/usu/machine/.

Young, Vershawn Ashanti. "Foreword: A Forenote from an Angry Black Man: Blackness Should Always Be Center." *Black Perspectives in Writing Program Administration: From the Margins to the Center*, edited by Staci M. Perryman-Clark and Collin Lamont Craig, National Council of Teachers of English, 2019, pp. vii–xiv.

CHAPTER 15.
TOWARD A MORE HUMAN APPROACH TO ASSESSMENT

Jathan Day
University of Alaska Anchorage

Naitnaphit Limlamai
Colorado State University

Emily Wilson
Alfaisal University

As scholars who study students' writing and design assessments to develop their writing skills and support their conceptual learning, we often take for granted how writing facilitates that learning. And while Robert Bangert-Drowns and colleagues found that "writing can be expected to enhance learning in academic settings, . . . it is not a potent magic" (53). Paul Anderson and colleagues' study of the effects of writing-to-learn activities on student learning explored how to make writing more potent as a learning tool. The authors identified that "writing assignments that involve the three constructs of Interactive Writing Processes, Meaning-Making Writing Tasks, and Clear Writing Expectations enhance undergraduate students' participation in Deep Approaches to Learning . . ." (231).

Building on Anderson et al.'s study, Anne Ruggles Gere and collaborators added a fourth feature, metacognition, to help explicate *what* about writing leads to learning gains ("Writing"). Table 15.1 defines and offers examples of each feature of effective writing assessment design.

Gere et al.'s study echoes Bangert-Drowns et al.'s findings that writing, on its own, doesn't necessarily lead to gains in learning and that other elements of the task matter: "measurement of learning matters, implementation matters, the richness of each of the four components matters, and the meaning assigned to writing matters" (Gere et al., "Writing" 123). It is not merely the presence of the four features that matters for writing assessment but also the quality of each feature's inclusion that determines their effectiveness in helping students learn by writing. The meanings we assign to writing when we incorporate the four features of effective assessment design maintain writing as a cognitive and sociocultural process.

Table 15.1. Characteristics of Four Features of Effective Writing Assessment Design

Interactive Writing Processes	• Definition: having "student writers communicate orally or in writing with one or more persons . . . between receiving an assignment and submitting the final draft" (Anderson et al. 206). • Examples: working with fellow students while planning and writing drafts, peer review, and conferences with the instructor • Of note: Of all the features of effective writing assessment, Gere et al. found that interactive processes were the least included feature ("Writing").
Meaning-Making Writing Tasks	• Definition: "requir[ing] students to engage in some form of integrative, critical, or original thinking" (Anderson et al. 207) • Examples: making connections between the work of the current class and past experiences or other classes, "support[ing] a contestable claim with evidence, or evaluat[ing] a policy, practice, or position" (207)
Clear Expectations	• Definition: instructors offering students a way to "understand . . . what they are asking . . . students to show that they can do in an assignment" and making evident "the criteria by which . . . instructors will evaluate" student work (Anderson et al. 207) • Examples: instructors providing students with an assignment sheet and rubric, or instructors and students creating a rubric together
Metacognition	• Definition: "thinking about thinking"; "promot[ing] planning, monitoring, evaluating, and adapting cognitive strategies during the process of learning" (Bangert-Drowns et al. 32). This kind of thinking helps learners "deploy cognitive strategies flexibly and in novel contexts" (32). Metacognition also "includes planning, monitoring, evaluating, and adapting cognitive strategies" as learners develop new ideas (Gere et al., "Writing" 105). • Examples: reflecting on decision-making processes entailed in a writing assignment; examining classmates' work to see their understanding of the assignment and concepts evaluated via the assignment

While Gere et al.'s study on analysis of assignments focused on writing-to-learn pedagogies in the sciences, this chapter extends the four features of effective assessment design to facilitate student learning in the writing and education classes we teach. We draw on our work studying with Gere the four features while we were in the Joint Program in English and Education (JPEE) at the University of Michigan, which she directed during our time in graduate school there. In this chapter we are applying what we learned with Gere across platforms (from in-person to online), across cultures (from the United States to the

Kingdom of Saudi Arabia), and across disciplines (from writing studies to education). We explore what happens when we take features of assessment design and put them to work in contexts that make a variety of demands on our assessments as we seek to further humanize approaches to writing assessment. True to the ethos of JPEE, we approach this work as interdisciplinary scholars reaching across and attending to multiple fields, contexts, and student needs to build on the foundations Gere has helped construct.

Within this chapter, Jathan Day argues for a more intentional approach to interactive writing processes via online peer review that underscores the human and professional needs of students. His section presses scholars in writing studies to expand upon our understanding of interactivity, as Gere et al. suggest ("Writing"), by examining peer review and other points of human contact in the writing process.

Emily Wilson extends our understanding of what it means for a writing task to make meaning. First, she examines how a writing prompt can leverage students' aspirations. Then, she conveys how those aspirations are culturally specific, comparing how aspiration might be defined in a U.S. versus an Arab context. This knowledge helped her and her team redesign writing prompts for first-year composition students in Saudi Arabia that were more meaningful than previously because the meaning making was culturally specific.

Naitnaphit Limlamai joins metacognitive practices from writing studies and education to explore how reflection can facilitate preservice teachers' learning of how to disrupt the reproduction of white supremacy in secondary English language arts classrooms. Explicitly justice-oriented and racially conscious metacognition can support preservice teachers' learning about making teaching decisions that allow all students to thrive and that facilitate instructors' design of student learning.

JATHAN DAY: A MORE INTENTIONAL APPROACH TO INTERACTIVE WRITING PROCESSES

During the COVID-19 pandemic, while my colleagues were in the throes of learning to teach online and navigating the ever-shifting terrain of health and safety, I thought a lot about student interaction. As a writing instructor with a background in online pedagogy, one site of interaction that continues to elude me is peer review. The pandemic seems to have triggered a paradigm shift in how students and instructors interact with one another online; it feels so much harder these days to share written work with others, let alone ask questions and offer feedback. Perhaps it is harder to trust in the process of online peer review because many students who suddenly shifted to virtual formats during the pandemic perceived the quality of online instruction as inferior to that of a face-to-face (F2F) classroom (Nelson and Vee). Perhaps socioeconomic and psychological stressors (Pasquini and Keeter) have intensified the pressure of interacting with one another—even online.

I teach for an institution that has offered online courses since before the pandemic began, and while many students are eager to interact, a significant number experience challenges connecting during peer review—not posting drafts, not knowing what to write or say in response to another draft, or not being present in the process at all—making this critical component of writing assessment appear like a checklist of hurdles rather than a shared writing experience. Another challenge is when students *do* participate but do not hear or receive anything from their group members. Thus, the problem remains clear: how can writing instructors make online peer review assessments more inviting, human experiences when disconnection has become so prevalent, or even preferable?

Interaction is an important yet understudied part of the writing process (Gere et al., "Writing"), and while many scholars have addressed students' online interactions (e.g., King; Phan et al.), online peer review requires further examination. Some scholars, such as Anderson et al., suggest that interaction in writing comprises the exposure that students' drafts receive before submission, yet, despite the learning opportunities this exposure brings, many students remain resistant to the idea of peer review (Kaufman and Schunn), so how can we help our online students recognize the value of peer review when interaction itself is the challenge? How can we help students recognize the work that peer review does in building rapport and establishing human connection? And, perhaps most importantly, how might we enhance online peer review to counteract the ongoing social and educational effects of the recent global pandemic? Arguably the most pressing charge we face is helping online writing students develop confidence in their ability to offer feedback to their peers and evaluate the feedback they receive. While putting students into groups may go some distance in facilitating this process, students also require opportunities to *practice* peer review.

Students' resistance to online peer review, regardless of format, is not a new phenomenon—and students have good reasons for resisting it. In a study comparing peer review in F2F and online contexts, Ruie Jane Pritchard and Donna Morrow found that students perceive F2F peer review as a more generative space for exchanging feedback (98) and noted that students tended not to engage with their peers' questions when posted in an online format (97). Other scholars, such as Michael John Wilson and colleagues, suggest that issues of fairness, labor, and time may impact the success of online peer review, especially when writing instructors introduce a specific tool for peer review. In their study of the Moodle Workshop tool, Wilson et al. also indicate that student confusion about technology can hamper productive peer review sessions (25). Such studies raise questions, understandably, about the rules and procedures around online peer review. Although writing studies scholars appear to affirm that building rules into online peer review can increase its chances of success, the often procedural nature of rules may be taxing for students (and writing instructors) and leave little space for the kinds of human interaction present in F2F peer review. In considering a more human approach to online peer review, I turn to Gere's work.

Much of Gere's most recent research has been situated in the study of STEM writing (see Gere et al., "Writing"), but Gere's work in this area has inspired me to think about how intradisciplinarity might foster more productive communication during online peer review. In a reflection on how writing courses are now conventionally structured in higher education, Gere explains that "students' writerly growth [is] directly linked to their developing mastery of a discipline's content, methods, genres, and epistemologies" ("Ways" 140), but she found that about half of the students at her institution sought to develop their writing skills in courses *outside* of the writing program. Perhaps, then, creating opportunities for students to review the work of others in their fields might reinforce content knowledge and help them develop confidence in their interactions with others around related topics.

I find Gere's approach to writing assessment important to online peer review for two reasons. First, students who enter into online peer review for the first time often struggle to find common ground and language because they are removed from the close contact that they would otherwise experience in F2F classes. As a result, students may focus more on figuring out how peer review is supposed to operate rather than what they can learn from the experiences of their peers (or what discipline-specific writing skills they might glean). Second, we ask students to invest time and energy in their peers' work when they review it, so asking students to engage in this process with some context for the writing they might do in their own fields could give this investment a bit more purpose and direction. In addition to putting students into field-specific groups, it seems equally important to teach students about how they might network and build collegiality by learning about similar content knowledge and genre features *together*. Even if students do not claim a particular field, they can still learn about writing moves and genre conventions from students who do. After all, this is one of many activities that writing groups do.

Gere's work also teaches us that how we frame peer review matters. In her book *Writing Groups: History, Theory, and Implications*, Gere argues for a more comprehensive approach that considers both the solitary and social dimensions of writing. While Gere's book addresses these dimensions in face-to-face contexts, I draw from her work here to emphasize the social dimension in framing peer review for online students: how to ask good questions of peers' writing, how to engage with feedback, and how to develop rapport with others through the sharing of writing. And, in the spirit of gathering at the table, writing instructors in online courses might frame this assessment by sharing more of their own peer writing experiences with students. I have been part of many in-person and online writing groups, so perhaps I could do more to share the human elements of that experience (e.g., the vulnerability of sharing and talking about others' work; considering others' feedback in isolation). Sharing these experiences may better situate peer review within the writing process and show, particularly to online students, how this social dimension can help them strengthen their writing and their communication *about* it.

Ultimately, online writing instructors are uniquely positioned to support students' interactions during peer review by making connections to personal interests (building rapport with their peers) and professional interests (networking and building repertoires of shared language and genres). And although peer review will likely remain a contested activity among students, the research of scholars such as Gere illuminates two important takeaways: (1) students require more context for the professional and intradisciplinary value of sharing writing with others, and (2) students in online courses might benefit from more framing—and, indeed, more *argument*—of how peer review can help them compose the writing that matters to them. Moving forward, we should more closely examine interaction in writing groups and how conversations about writing can take place productively in the absence of physical (or temporal) presence.

EMILY WILSON: MAKING MEANING ACROSS CULTURES BY WORKING ASPIRATION INTO FIRST-YEAR WRITING

The English department curriculum committee of which I am a member was overhauling first-year writing at Alfaisal University in Riyadh, Saudi Arabia. We surveyed copies of writing assignments spread across a long table. The first prompt asked students to "[w]rite an essay comparing and contrasting your parents' attitude toward punctuality with your own attitude toward punctuality." Students were struggling to respond to these prompts, shoehorning tortured language into formulaic essays. How could we rewrite these assignments in ways that would better develop our students' writing skills? What factors, beyond a grade, could help motivate students to produce more meaningful writing?

I recalled another day at another long table in Anne Gere's office. There were writing prompts spread across that table too, as well as student responses. We were researching MWrite, the University of Michigan's writing-to-learn (WTL) program. Students had written assignments for a chemistry course, and Gere led our research team in analyzing why students had scored higher on one assignment than another. The prompt with lower-scoring responses asked students to explain a chemistry concept to their grandparents in an email. The prompt with the higher-scoring responses had the students act as a consultant for a Tour de France cycling team and offer a chemistry-informed decision about the team's diet.

Gere had us apply Anderson et al.'s characteristics of good writing assignments, and meaning-making activities seemed especially salient. The cycling-team prompt invited students to envision themselves in an aspirational role; the email to grandparents, while specific in its audience, lacked aspirational qualities. Anderson et al. "found that students need opportunities to make meaning with their writing and to engage in critical thinking" (207). In the article we wrote about those students' responses, we found that "[h]ow easily students can make meaning within the constraints of a WTL assignment depends on several factors, among them . . . aspiration. To what extent does the imagined rhetorical situation of the writing prompt tap into students' aspirations?" (Gere et al., "Tale" 163). Our findings intersected with those of Michele Eodice and her colleagues, who also connected student aspirations and meaningful writing. We discovered that "the more aspirational qualities that were present in a prompt, the easier it was for students' uptake to demonstrate effective meaning making" (Gere et al., "Tale" 163).

Back at the table in Riyadh, I thought about what I had learned about writing prompts with Gere in 2018. Although this was not a WTL situation, I considered rewriting our prompts to include more aspirational elements. But as our committee pondered the question, we realized that, as Western faculty members, tapping into our Arab students' aspirations would also necessitate us learning more about their cultures.

Aspiration involves culturally rooted conceptions of success, desire, and ambition. At Michigan, we were conceptualizing aspiration in culturally specific ways. We assumed that students were primarily motivated by individual success, focused "outward" on a future job rather than "inward" on their roots and communities. Conversations with my Arab students taught me that they construct "aspiration" more communally than I do. It meant more than envisioning themselves in prestigious future roles; it also meant connecting themselves to familial, local, or even national interests. If we were to revise these prompts to account for our students' understandings of aspiration, we needed to adopt a culturally relevant pedagogy (Ladson-Billings; Capper) that drew on students' funds of knowledge (Gonzalez et al.). We needed to craft assignments that "connected meaningfully to [students'] lifeworld locales: in effect, putting students to work as 'researchers' of their own lifeworlds" (Zipin 320). Our goal was to challenge students to "creat[e] innovations—new funds of knowledge—to stimulate a rethinking of the present and considerations of future possibilities" (Moll 133). With these ideas in mind, we rewrote the first prompt:

> You have been hired as a youth consultant for the Ministry of Tourism. Write a memo to the Chair of the Saudi Commission for Tourism and National Heritage explaining 2–3 activities here in Riyadh that would appeal to tourists in the 18–25 demographic.

This prompt invited students to connect their cultural heritage to their country's ambitions and centered their expertise in the target demographic. It envisioned students contributing toward national goals of increasing tourism and changing perceptions of Saudi Arabia.

While future studies will measure improvements more systematically, our faculty witnessed more engaged student writing in passages like these:

> Saudi traditions are rooted in Islamic teachings and Arab customs. Notably, the highlights of the year are . . . Ramadan and the Hajj season, and the national holidays that follow them. During these holidays Saudis serve Arabic coffee in small cups along with dates and sweets as a hospitality gesture. This could be a meaningful learning experience for college-aged tourists, in addition to trying to fast during Ramadan. Because I am a college-aged student, I know how interesting it is for people in the same age demographic as me to experience new cultures! (Aljohara[1])

Aljohara is using her cultural knowledge (González et al.) to highlight experiences that tourists might enjoy and to educate a foreign audience about the "Islamic teachings and Arab customs" in which those cultural experiences are rooted. She is writing to change people's perceptions of her country. And she is connecting her audience's interests to her own as a member of the same demographic.

Similarly, Felwa works to "make and extend personal connections to [her] experiences" (Eodice et al. 320):

> [C]ollege students would be fond of Saudi Arabia's annual National Heritage Festival, where cultural heritage is celebrated. I met one of my favorite poets, Rashed AlNufaie, at this festival. . . . In view of the fact that students spend most of their time studying, it's absolutely delightful to listen to a few verses of a poem to loosen up a little.

---

1   Pseudonyms are used for all student names in this chapter.

Felwa uses her knowledge of student life (i.e., "students spend most of their time studying") to write from a place of authority (Whitney). Saudi students have often told me of their frustration that the "single story" (Adichie) of their country is so negative, while the beautiful aspects of their culture are overlooked. This prompt invited them to challenge the single story; it "embraced an orientation to student writing . . . that truly capitalize[d] on the experiences, beliefs, and aspirations students bring to their learning" (Eodice et al. 320).

Before we, as Western faculty members, could create more meaningful writing assignments, we had to learn from students what kinds of cultural knowledge they were bringing to the table. From Gere, I learned the importance of aspiration in helping create meaning-making activities in writing. From my Saudi students, I learned to interrogate my own cultural assumptions about what is aspirational.

NAITNAPHIT LIMLAMAI: RACIALLY CONSCIOUS, JUSTICE-ORIENTED METACOGNITION

"I feel like I've learned what not to do. I'm hoping this class teaches me what to do." I receive lots of notes with this sentiment on preservice teachers' (PSTs) precourse surveys before our Methods for Teaching Language Arts class. Despite their desire to learn, PSTs in the United States are often "dysconscious" (Sleeter 559) of how racism works and how it is reproduced in schools (Chapman; Sleeter), specifically through decisions teachers make, such as text selection, pedagogical strategies, or assessments of student learning. Routinized teaching decisions that allow institutions like schools to function efficiently reproduce anti-Blackness and white supremacy, solidifying a racial structure (Bonilla-Silva; Diamond and Gomez).

To combat this pernicious reproduction of racism and white supremacy, educational scholars have suggested an array of self-reflective heuristics and activities for teachers that can help them recognize how their racialized identities function in the classroom. These strategies include conducting an archeology of self (Mentor and Sealey-Ruiz; Sealey-Ruiz, "Archaeology"), becoming interrupters (Perry et al.), and examining self and classroom practice via the five culturally and historically responsive pursuits: identity, skills, intellect, criticality, and joy (Muhammad). What these self-reflective activities have in common is the process—via metacognitive reflection—of excavating, questioning, letting go, and replacing dysfunctional racialized beliefs about students.

The process of self-reflection engages learners in metacognition: monitoring their learning as they work through ideas presented to them, recording their (affective) reactions, and tracking the development of new ideas. Metacognitive practices in writing-to-learn pedagogies and metacognitive practices to develop racial literacy (Sealey-Ruiz, "Learning") conceptualize writing as a sociocultural practice where knowledge is socially constructed and mediated by the contexts in which the writer writes (Gere et al., "Writing"; Rodriguez), rather than holding writing as an activity that simply promotes recall or algorithmic thinking.

In studying the efficacy of WTL pedagogies, researchers have found that metacognition is a key feature of effective assessment design. Meta-analyses of WTL assignments conducted by Bangert-Drowns et al. and Gere et al. ("Writing") show that assignments that ask learners to "evaluate their current understandings, confusions, and feelings in relation to the subject matter yielded more positive effects than instruction that did not include such metacognitive stimulation" (Bangert-Drowns et al. 47). Writing about content alone does not necessarily yield learning gains. Asking learners to engage in metacognitive practices that allow them to reflect on their learning and learning processes—including moments of understanding and confusion—is an integral component of learning.

As a researcher and teacher who moves between the fields of English and education, I consider how ideas about metacognition drawn from writing studies can join ideas drawn from education to disrupt the reproduction of white supremacy in secondary English language arts classrooms. In our methods class, we first surface and interrogate ideas about English class and what goes on there, as well as how those ideas have been shaped by our intersectional socialized identities (Crenshaw). Then, we draw on culturally relevant (Ladson-Billings), culturally responsive (Gay), and culturally sustaining (Paris and Alim) pedagogies to co-construct definitions and enactments of justice-oriented teaching (Gorski; Limlamai), creating a working rubric to guide the building of teaching artifacts (i.e., lesson plans, unit plans, classroom activities) and practice teaching sessions. Throughout our class, PSTs use their writing to spur metacognitive reflection on their previous ideas about teaching and their development of new ideas in pursuing justice-oriented teaching practices.

While Bangert-Drowns and Gere et al. ("Writing") specifically examine metacognition within writing-to-learn pedagogies, I argue that drawing on ideas of metacognition and extending them to explicitly justice-oriented and racially conscious metacognition can support preservice teachers' learning about their teaching decisions, specifically by offering opportunities for PSTs to ask questions and clarify confusions and unpack their feelings about new ideas.

Ask Questions and Clarify Confusions

Right after we developed our justice-oriented teaching rubric, students offered reflections on how their identities and experiences in English class affected how they might imagine their own English classrooms. Examining our rubric, Faegan specifically noted how she "want[ed] to improve on disruption in our discipline." To disrupt, she first recognized how her own experiences "in high school and, until recent semesters, college[,] focused on the canon of English works and the typical teaching of them." Then, she brainstormed how in her teaching her own English class could be different: despite the possibility of assigning the same novels she read, she "want[ed] to be able to take those novels that never stretch or challenge students' thinking and do the opposite of what I had so many times." In her reflections, Faegan identified the ways things have been done and wanted to change them. The question was how.

One way Faegan wanted to try entailed expanding the narrative. She wanted to use her "knowledge of the typical traumatic narratives of the oppressed and the power dynamic of history," but to also build units and lessons that helped students to know "joy . . . and complexity in power." This tension actualized as we developed the unit for our partner eighth-grade class and discussed what background information to share with the eighth graders about Jewish people before reading Elie Wiesel's *Night*. In her reflection as we built the unit, Faegan wondered, "I'm not sure how much connection to make for the students with the [H]olocaust and what I should include and what just perpetuates the trauma narrative." Faegan's justice-oriented reflections reveal how she was grappling with building students' knowledge of the Holocaust and also not allowing the story of Jewish people to only be trauma-centered.

Faegan's justice-oriented reflections helped her surface questions and conveyed to me her developing understandings about her identities and how her previous learning had narrowed her view of the world. I then used her reflections as a formative assessment and helped her build knowledge about where to start in building our unit for the eighth graders.

UNPACK FEELINGS ABOUT NEW IDEAS

Another PST's new learning entailed developing insights into his own whiteness, how this intersected with his existing ideas, and how new ideas might shape his teaching. After Brigg told me that his whiteness was inconsequential to him and that he did not see himself as white, I had him learn more about white supremacy and reflect on that learning. After listening to the first couple of episodes of the podcast *Seeing White* and developing the unit for our eighth-grade partner class, he wrote, "I think that tradition, and personal issues are the biggest factors in preventing me from engaging in justice[-]oriented practice. Not having [them] be a part of many classes which use justice[-]oriented practice leads to me having a lack of experience to draw on, and I fall back on the habits of the teachers I have examples from." He identified systemic reasons for his difficulty and was vague in identifying "personal issues" that were blocking his learning. After more listening and doing his own research, however, he recognized the obstruction: "I'd lived my whole life without actually looking at anything I was seeing, never facing down the hard truths of reality; that I was surrounded by injustice." Brigg's reflections revealed that he was developing a recognition of how his whiteness allowed him to look without seeing.

Like his classmates, Brigg's racially conscious and justice-oriented reflections surfaced knowledge that had been hidden from him—by design—throughout their schooling. In Brigg's case, he was transformed when he learned about and confronted the origins and reproduction of white supremacy and his implicit role in that reproduction. Brigg, like Faegan, wrote that he didn't have models of justice-oriented teaching in his classrooms, and thus drew from limited models to shape his teaching. Brigg loved school and found solace in English class, particularly as a student who faced poverty and experienced housing insecurity as a secondary student. Brigg's new learning about white supremacy could have backfired—he could have become fragile (DiAngelo) because I was asking him to interrogate ways he defined himself; he could have shut down. I thus used his reflections to learn how he was feeling and taking up ideas of white supremacy. I also then planned questions I might ask to further his learning and recommend additional resources. For example, I asked how his new understandings of his own whiteness might shape his teaching, particularly in his decisions about which texts to center in the classroom.

CONCLUSION

Preservice teachers' justice-oriented metacognition facilitated their transformative thinking about teaching and revealed to me, their instructor, how to plan for their continued learning. James Baldwin wrote, "Not everything that is faced can be changed; but nothing can be changed until it is faced" (148). In order to make changes so that schooling is transformed from being a racist institution, we must face and assess our current understandings of schooling and what goes on there (Diamond and Gomez), specifically as it interacts with our intersectional socialized identities (Mentor and Sealey-Ruiz; Perry et al.; Sealey-Ruiz, "Archaeology"). Justice-oriented metacognitive reflections offer a way for PSTs to face their understandings of schooling, themselves, the world, and how that knowledge shapes their teaching. As PSTs build their capacity for reflection, research has shown that they will get better at it and internalize a "self-reflective posture" (Bangert-Drowns et al. 52).

CLOSING THOUGHTS

As Hammond offers in his chapter in this collection, how we position assessment in institutional contexts matters. In line with that cue, our chapter has positioned three features of effective writing design—interactive writing processes, meaning-making writing tasks, and metacognition—in our specific contexts with specific student needs, continuing Gere et al.'s work of extension ("Writing"). Taken together, surfacing, learning about, addressing, and engaging in students' needs are at the heart of our work as instructors. By learning about students' needs and perspectives, we can humanize assessment, making it a tool that better prepares students "for the actual lives that await them" (Gere, "Presidential Address" 457).

WORKS CITED

Adichie, Chimamanda Ngozi. "The Danger of a Single Story." *TED: Ideas Change Everything*, July 2009, https://tinyurl.com/mrve4tx9.

Anderson, Paul, et al. "The Contributions of Writing to Learning and Development: Results from a Large-Scale Multi-Institutional Study." *Research in the Teaching of English*, vol. 50, 2015, pp. 199–235, https://doi.org/10.58680/rte201527602.

Baldwin, James. "As Much Truth as One Can Bear." *The New York Times*, 14 Jan. 1962, pp. 120, 148, https://tinyurl.com/5xrrdukv.

Bangert-Drowns, Robert L., et al. "The Effects of School-Based Writing-to-Learn Interventions on Academic Achievement: A Meta-Analysis." *Review of Educational Research*, vol. 74, no. 1, 2004, pp. 29–58, https://doi.org/10.3102/00346543074001029.

Bonilla-Silva, Eduardo. "The Structure of Racism in Color-Blind, 'Post-Racial' America." *American Behavioral Scientist*, vol. 59, no. 11, 2015, pp. 1358–76, https://doi.org/10.1177/0002764215586826.

Capper, Kelley. "Culturally Relevant Pedagogy in the English Curriculum." *Journal of Education*, vol. 202, no. 4, 2022, pp. 397–405, https://doi.org/10.1177/0022057421991856.

Chapman, Thandeka K. "You Can't Erase Race! Using CRT to Explain the Presence of Race and Racism in Majority White Suburban Schools." *Discourse: Studies in the Cultural Politics of Education*, vol. 34, no. 4, 2013, pp. 611–27, https://doi.org/10.1080/01596306.2013.822619.

Crenshaw, Kimberle. "Mapping the Margins: Intersectionality, Identity Politics, and Violence against Women of Color." *Stanford Law Review*, vol. 43, no. 6, 1991, pp. 1241–99. *JSTOR*, https://doi.org/10.2307/1229039.

Diamond, John B., and Louis M. Gomez. "Disrupting White Supremacy and Anti-Black Racism in Educational Organizations." *Educational Researcher*, Online First, 2023, https://doi.org/10.3102/0013189X231161054.

DiAngelo, Robin. *White Fragility: Why It's So Hard for White People to Talk about Racism*. Beacon P, 2018.

Eodice, Michele, et al. "The Power of Personal Connection for Undergraduate Student Writers." *Research in the Teaching of English*, vol. 53, no. 4, 2019, pp. 320–39. St. John's Scholar, https://scholar.stjohns.edu/english_facpubs/2/.

Gay, Geneva. "Preparing for Culturally Responsive Teaching." *Journal of Teacher Education*, vol. 53, no. 2, 2002, pp. 106–16, https://doi.org/10.1177/0022487102053002003.

Gere, Anne Ruggles, editor. *Developing Writers in Higher Education*. U of Michigan P, 2019. *University of Michigan Press Ebook Collection*, https://doi.org/10.3998/mpub.10079890.

Gere, Anne Ruggles. "Presidential Address—Re-visioning Language, Texts, and Theories." *PMLA*, vol. 134, no. 3, 2019, pp. 450–58. *Cambridge Core*, https://doi.org/10.1632/pmla.2019.134.3.450.

———. "The Ways Our Students Write Now." *PMLA*, vol. 133, no. 1, 2018, pp. 139–45. *Cambridge Core*, https://doi.org/10.1632/pmla.2018.133.1.139.

———. *Writing Groups: History, Theory, and Implications*. Southern Illinois UP, 1987.

Gere, Anne Ruggles, et al. "A Tale of Two Prompts: New Perspectives on Writing-to-Learn Assignments." *The WAC Journal*, vol. 29, 2018, pp. 147–88, https://doi.org/10.37514/WAC-J.2018.29.1.07/.

Gere, Anne Ruggles, et al. "Writing and Conceptual Learning in Science: An Analysis of Assignments." *Written Communication*, vol. 36, no. 1, 2019, pp. 99–135 https://doi.org/10.1177/0741088318804820.

González, Norma, et al. *Funds of Knowledge: Theorizing Practices in Households, Communities, and Classrooms*. Lawrence Erlbaum Associates Publishers, 2005. *Taylor and Francis eBooks*, https://doi.org/10.4324/9781410613462.

Gorski, Paul C. "What We're Teaching Teachers: An Analysis of Multicultural Teacher Education Coursework Syllabi." *Teaching and Teacher Education*, vol. 25, no. 2, 2009, pp. 309–18, https://doi.org/10.1016/j.tate.2008.07.008.

Kaufman, Julia H., and Christian D. Schunn. "Students' Perceptions about Peer Assessment for Writing: Their Origin and Impact on Revision Work." *Instructional Science*, vol. 39, no. 3, 2011, pp. 387–406, https://doi.org/10.1007/s11251-010-9133-6.

King, Stephanie B. "Graduate Student Perceptions of the Use of Online Course Tools to Support Engagement." *International Journal for the Scholarship of Teaching and Learning*, vol. 8, no. 1, 2014, digitalcommons.georgiasouthern.edu/ij-sotl/vol8/iss1/5/.

Ladson-Billings, Gloria. "But That's Just Good Teaching! The Case for Culturally Relevant Pedagogy." *Theory into Practice*, vol. 34, no. 3, 1995, pp. 159–65, https://doi.org/10.1080/00405849509543675.

Limlamai, Naitnaphit. "Complexities of Justice-Oriented Teaching." *English Journal*, vol. 112, no. 5, 2023, pp. 22–28, https://doi.org/10.58680/ej202332417.

Mentor, Marcelle, and Yolanda Sealey-Ruiz. "Doing the Deep Work of Antiracist Pedagogy: Toward Self-Excavation for Equitable Classroom Teaching." *Language Arts*, vol. 99, no. 1, 2021, pp. 19–24, https://doi.org/10.58680/la202131410.

Moll, Luis C. "Elaborating Funds of Knowledge: Community-Oriented Practices in International Contexts." *Literacy Research: Theory, Method, and Practice*, vol. 68, no. 1, 2019, pp. 130–38, https://doi.org/10.1177/2381336919870805.

Muhammad, Gholdy. *Unearthing Joy: A Guide to Culturally and Historically Responsive Teaching and Learning*. Scholastic, 2023.

Nelson, S. L., and Annette Vee. "The View from 'Zoom University': Surveillance and Control in Higher Ed's Pandemic Pedagogy Pivot." *enculturation*, vol. 34, 2022, enculturation.net/zoom_university.

Paris, Django, and H. Samy Alim. "What Are We Seeking to Sustain through Culturally Sustaining Pedagogy? A Loving Critique Forward." *Harvard Educational Review*, vol. 84, no. 1, 2014, pp. 85–100, https://doi.org/10.17763/haer.84.1.982l873k2ht16m77.

Pasquini, Giancarlo, and Scott Keeter. "At Least Four-in-Ten U.S. Adults Have Faced High Levels of Psychological Distress During COVID-19 Pandemic." *Pew Research Center*, 12 Dec. 2022, https://tinyurl.com/3jxvsdty.

Perry, Tonya B., et al. *Teaching for Racial Equity: Becoming Interrupters*. Stenhouse Publishers, 2022. *Taylor and Francis eBooks*, https://doi.org/10.4324/9781032682679.

Phan, Trang, et al. "Students' Patterns of Engagement and Course Performance in a Massive Open Online Course." *Computers and Education*, vol. 95, 2016, pp. 36–44, https://doi.org/10.1016/j.compedu.2015.11.015.

Pritchard, Ruie Jane, and Donna Morrow. "Comparison of Online and Face-to-Face Peer Review of Writing." *Computers and Composition*, vol. 46, 2017, pp. 87–103, https://doi.org/10.1016/j.compcom.2017.09.006.

Rodriguez, Alberto J. "Strategies for Counterresistance: Toward Sociotransformative Constructivism and Learning to Teach Science for Diversity and for Understanding." *Journal of Research in Science Teaching*, vol. 35, no. 6, 1998, pp. 589–622, https://doi.org/10.1002/(SICI)1098-2736(199808)35:6%3C589::AID-TEA2%3E3.0.CO;2-I.

Sealey-Ruiz, Yolanda. "An Archaeology of Self for Our Times: Another Talk to Teachers." *English Journal*, vol. 111, no. 5, 2022, pp. 21–26, https://doi.org/10.58680/ej202231819.

———. "Learning to Talk and Write about Race: Developing Racial Literacy in a College English Classroom." *English Quarterly*, vol. 42, no. 1, 2011, pp. 24–42.

Seeing White. Scene on Radio, 2024, sceneonradio.org/seeing-white/.

Sleeter, Christine E. "Preparing White Teachers for Diverse Students." *Handbook of Research on Teacher Education: Enduring Questions in Changing Contexts*, 3rd ed., edited by Marilyn Cochran-Smith et al., Routledge, Taylor and Francis Group / Association of Teacher Educators, 2008.

Whitney, Anne Elrod. "'I Just Turned in What *I* Thought': Authority and Voice in Student Writing." *Teaching English in the Two-Year College*, vol. 39, no. 2, 2011, pp. 184–93, https://doi.org/10.58680/tetyc201118384.

Wiesel, Elie. *Night*. Hill and Wang, 2006.

Wilson, Michael John, et al. "'I'm not here to mark someone else's stuff': An Investigation of an Online Peer-to-Peer Review Workshop Tool." *Assessment and Evaluation in Higher Education*, vol. 40, no. 1, 2015, pp. 15–32, https://doi.org/10.1080/02602938.2014.881980.

Zipin, Lew "Dark Funds of Knowledge, Deep Funds of Pedagogy: Exploring Boundaries between Lifeworlds and Schools." *Discourse: Studies in the Cultural Politics of Education*, vol. 30, no. 3, 2009, pp. 317–31, https://doi.org/10.1080/01596300903037044.

CHAPTER 16.

THE INTELLECTUAL WORK OF WRITING PROGRAM REVIEW

Shirley K Rose
Arizona State University

Deborah H. Holdstein
Columbia College Chicago

Chris Anson
North Carolina State University

Chris Thaiss
University of California, Davis

Kathleen Blake Yancey
Florida State University

In this chapter we honor Anne Ruggles Gere's contributions to the field of rhetoric and writing studies through her work as a member of the Council of Writing Program Administrators' (CWPA) WPA Consultant-Evaluator Service since 1985—nearly forty years. We offer a set of reflections on the intellectual work of writing program review as colleagues of Anne's who know her contributions to this work and understand its significance through our participation in it with her. Anne has been a member of the Service since very nearly its beginning, shaping the Service through each of the visits she has made and through years of participation in the panel members' annual workshops and policy discussions.

Since its establishment in 1980,[1] the WPA Consultant-Evaluator Service[2] has offered colleges and universities the opportunity to assess and improve their writing programs using processes similar to those of accrediting agencies and

---

[1] For a history of the Consultant-Evaluator Service, see Shirley K Rose's "Creating a Context: The Institutional Logic of the Council of Writing Program Administrators' Development of the Consultant-Evaluator Service."

[2] Additional information about the WPA Consultant-Evaluator Service is available on the Council of Writing Program Administrators website: https://wpacouncil.org/aws/CWPA/pt/sp/consulting-services.

academic program review, including self-studies conducted by the programs under review, brief on-site visits to the programs, written reports of findings and recommendations, and suggested steps for follow-up.

Much of the work of the Consultant-Evaluator (C-E) Service is difficult to identify, because it is conducted confidentially.[3] Despite this relative invisibility, however, it has contributed to the development of the field in important ways. In each of our contributions that follow we provide some insights into the work of the Service by sharing some of the lessons we've individually and collectively learned from working with Anne. Deborah Holdstein begins with a discussion of the process and criteria for selecting consultants for a particular visit; Chris Anson tells a story about what he learned from Anne's style of taking notes in meetings during a visit; Chris Thaiss shares an anecdote about what he learned from Anne about drafting a report and recommendations; Shirley Rose offers a vignette from a visit schedule that illustrates the multiple rhetorical situations that constitute a C-E visit; and Kathleen Blake Yancey reflects on the impact WPA C-E visits have on individual writing programs and on writing studies as a field. We hope that this chapter will be useful to stakeholders in writing programs that are preparing for reviews, to scholars who are interested in engaging in this intellectual work, and to scholars of institutional culture and field history.

DEBORAH H. HOLDSTEIN

To say that Anne Gere is a go-to, a supreme C-E among other expert C-Es, is an understatement. But first, something of an explanation. For over a decade, I had the privilege of co-directing or directing the C-E Service. One of the many responsibilities of the director—organizing and leading the annual workshop for C-Es, working with and reporting to the CWPA Executive Board, reviewing with colleagues the criteria for the self-study process that proceeds a campus visit, communicating with and facilitating the nuts-and-bolts of the visit as organizational point person, consulting with the campus representative to delineate the schedule for the visit, and the like—involves the director's all-important decision of who will be most appropriate as part of the two-person team that will visit the campus and generate the final report with recommendations.

That said, I was always aware that the initial purpose of the visit as stated by the campus writing program administrator (WPA), or whoever organizes and/or commissions the visit, might only be the tip of the proverbial iceberg. For instance, a WPA might write to me in the initial request for a visit, indicating

---

3   A copy of the WPA Consultant-Evaluator Service's "Ethics Guidelines for CWPA Consultant-Evaluators" is available as a PDF file on its website: https://wpacouncil.org/aws/CWPA/asset_manager/get_file/377903?ver=13.

that the campus would like an evaluation of the writing center. The ensuing self-study from the campus might focus on issues related to that campus writing center, again, the ostensible purpose of the visit. However, after reading the self-study and arriving on campus, the team members might find related issues that make the visit about much more than the writing center, whether related to staffing, part-time faculty members, tenure-track lines, writing center practice that interfaces (or not) with first-year writing, or writing across disciplines. It is essential to best serve the campus as a student-centered institution and to best represent the CWPA and the profession that the director and WPA C-E Service leaders keep in mind the importance of including on the panel of consultants, and sending to a campus, those who are ethical, well-versed in the field regarding administration and its constraints, and nimble in intellect and in practice. C-Es must be willing and unafraid to address issues of importance that for whatever reason the visited campus itself might not "see."

The invitation to become part of the C-E panel is not given lightly. That is, it is a capstone type of experience for those in the profession; for its credibility and in service to the profession, the organization sends to campuses not only those who are experienced teacher-scholars in their own, respective areas of rhetoric and composition, but also those who have held leadership positions in or who fully understand departments and administrative roles writ large. I have always liked to say that the best C-Es are "educated generalists," colleagues who are prepared to work and address constructively whatever they might find during a campus visit and, accordingly, to decide what (and what not) to delineate and recommend to the campus in the final report. As one might expect, it is also helpful for the C-E to bear a type of gravitas (a quality unrelated to age) in case, as often happens, one is scheduled to meet with, say, a president or provost.

Anne Gere's attributes as a scholar and teacher reflect and enhance her excellence as a C-E: Anne is intellectually nimble, analytical, highly informed, ethical, practical, result-oriented, and tirelessly accountable. I would say, in fact, that the qualities that have made Anne the outstanding scholar that she is also contribute to her standing as C-E *par excellence*. Having worked with Anne on her contribution called "A Rhetoric of Pen and Brush" for my recent volume *Lost Texts in Rhetoric and Composition*, I saw yet again how Anne's scholarly reach in an essay about the little-known work of Angel DeCora makes visible the otherwise invisible, a quality of importance as one sifts through myriad forms of evidence while visiting a campus. As Anne writes, "Given [DeCora's] audience" her work "required both courage and skill" (33). Work as a C-E requires informed skill and, often, appropriate forms of courage; Anne's work on literacy, giving voice to those without, readily extends to her analytical work as a consultant.

CHRIS ANSON

A scene: Anne and I are sitting in a meeting with some higher-level administrators while conducting a review of a writing program. The discussion is animated. Attendees respond to our questions quickly, sometimes almost interrupting each other with eager thoughts, bits of program history, and reflections entangling the issues we've raised. It's interesting, dynamic, and complicated, requiring us to sort through rapid-fire information to reach something approaching a considered, fact-based analysis.

I have found a seat near an electric outlet so I can plug in my battery-compromised laptop. Handwriting notes is out of the question because inevitably I'll hastily scratch material that later I can't decipher. Decades of typing have left me with a second-grader's scrawl, and besides, it's just too slow. I'm a fast typist, and I've developed the ability to look at people in a meeting while almost silently keystroking comments and thoughts, glancing at the screen only very occasionally. I've perfected this process to the point where attendees are unaware that I'm actively taking notes; I want them to know that I'm listening carefully and being present in the meeting, not giving all my attention to a keyboard. I can always fix the small typos later if I want, and usually I don't need to because I know exactly what I was writing. Once in a while, during a pause in the discussion, I'll add some thoughts in brackets about what I'm hearing. But essentially I'm playing the role of a court reporter, creating a raw transcript of the proceedings. Analysis, synthesis, and assessment will come later. During a full-scale C-E visit, I usually generate 30 or more single-spaced pages of typed notes, which serve as both the general and detailed support for what I contribute to the report.

At this meeting, I become aware for the first time in our years of shared contexts that Anne, sitting a few seats away, is listening attentively to the attendees, adding questions or asking for clarifications . . . and *writing almost nothing*. Every few minutes she jots down some notes on a pad for later consultation. It occurs to me that we're using entirely different processes to reach similar conclusions about the complex administrative, instructional, institutional, and employment-related issues surrounding and infusing the workings of a busy writing program.

And the differences in those processes point to something remarkable about Anne. Whereas I'm unable to recall some details of our meetings without a textual record of them, Anne is *already* analyzing, synthesizing, and assessing aspects of the program we're visiting. Whereas I can't process all the back-and-forth, all the quick comments and occasional non sequiturs that characterize the way faculty and administrators often interact, Anne is sorting through it all at lightning speed and reaching significant points to include in our report, much of it from memory. Whereas I am *deferring* some of our thinking, Anne is already thinking it.

Later, during the time set aside for us to initially compare our thoughts and impressions, I'm glued to my laptop, scrolling through hundreds of lines of text. Anne flips through a page or two of her handwritten notes, using them to jog her memory of specific details and information. We compare impressions, formulate judgments. Although I have conducted dozens of program reviews over the years, I'm in awe of Anne's calm way of unraveling everything we've seen and heard and reaching highly insightful conclusions about what the program we're visiting is doing well and where it might improve.

Then, when the visit is over and we've returned to our homes, it's time for the two of us to collaboratively draft our report. I create a Google Doc for us and write some introductory boilerplate, customizing it with the specific details of our visit. The next part is hard. We've divided up components of the program for initial drafting, and I'm working between my extensive notes and my analysis and recommendations. It's a slow composing process, requiring some of the highest-level thinking that C-Es do in their professional work. Returning to the Google Doc later, I see that Anne has added sections, elegantly written, brilliantly insightful, highly diplomatic. And I can almost see that process at work as she consults her concisely handwritten material and goes back to the ideas she had already formulated in situ.

Scholars argue that writers employ different cognitive processes when producing text. It used to be thought that there were "better" writing behaviors that generate writing of higher quality with greater efficiency. Further research has shown much greater variation in those processes without a loss of quality. About efficiency, I'm less sure.

Anne and I produced a terrific report from that visit, but there wasn't much question that Anne brought to that process a finely tuned, highly significant way of working that is clearly tied to her immense success as a scholar, administrator, and teacher.

I'm trying to learn from Anne. So I came up with an idea, jotted down a couple of sentences of notes, and a month later knew exactly what I would write about her. Now if I can only make it work this way during a program review.

CHRIS THAISS

Writing for this Festschrift for Anne Gere is a true pleasure for me, as Anne has been an exemplar of public service in literacy and writing for so many years. In particular, I'd like to focus this brief reflection on her help to me after I became a newly elected member of the WPA C-E Service in the spring of 2011. During my 35 prior years as a writing teacher and as an administrator of writing programs, writing centers, WAC/WID programs, and National Writing Project sites, I had always admired the C-E Service for the conscientiousness, thoroughness, and fairness of its members' work in responding to calls by colleges and universities for advice and assistance in resolving difficulties and aiding writing program development.

In preparing for my new role, I studied the extensive documentation of the Service's principles, rules, and procedures, and I took part in the workshop for all new members. A key part of this readiness for the actual work of program consultation is being paired with a veteran C-E on the first campus visit to which one is assigned. Now, it is a rule of the C-E Service that all consultations are done in pairs; there is constant participation by both team members in all events of a visit and ongoing communication between the two team members toward the writing of reports and the giving of oral advice to the stakeholders of the institution which has contracted with the Service. In the case of newly elected members, such as I was in 2011, this pairing facilitates having the new member observe, ask questions of, and learn helpful practices from the veteran member.

I was most fortunate to be paired with Anne Gere on my first campus visit in fall 2011. Anne had already been a C-E Service member for a number of years, so I studied carefully her interactions with the administrators who were our primary contacts with the university as well as how we created a schedule of meetings for our visit and then conducted those meetings in order to hear from as many people as possible. I could go into detail on all these facets of a C-E visit, but what stood out most sharply to me in our precious two and a half days (the C-E Service standard) on the campus was Anne's determination to have us *craft a full first draft* of what would become our final report on the evening of our second and only full day on the campus. Achieving this goal would require us to spend hours of evening and late evening time on this task—after a full day of intense meetings that had begun with a breakfast meeting just after 7:00 a.m.

Here I'd been assuming that our intensive discussions and note-taking on that Monday with many groups of faculty, students, and campus administrators—plus a campus tour—would have earned us a bit of evening down time to begin our sorting of the many inputs from the day's meetings—mostly with concerned people we were just meeting for the first time. Since we still had ahead of us a half day of more meetings, with fresh inputs, I figured that putting together all this complex information into a coherent presentation could wait until the scheduled "consultation team discussion time" on Tuesday, leading up to our formal presentation of our *preliminary* findings to our hosts on that afternoon. Then we would have a week or two of time back on our own campuses to revise the presentation into a solid multi-page report that we would send to the campus.

But Anne's justification of this seemingly draconian schedule for Monday night was convincing, so much so that I've mostly adhered to it since in all my visits, including those in which I have been the mentor to newer C-Es. She argued, first, that by the time we finished that only full day of meetings we not only had (1) our notes from those meetings on which to build a draft of our report, but we also had (2) our study of the program documents that the client institution had provided us well in advance, as well as (3) the long self-study report that the school had provided in response to our lengthy questionnaire, which detailed many program elements and which gave background on the issue that had led them to request a consultation. So all that remained of new information we'd yet to receive would come in the meetings the following Tuesday morning—and that new information we could use to revise our draft in preparation for the exit meeting with our hosts that afternoon.

Second, she counseled, our putting in the time to write on that Monday evening would allow us to begin to consolidate our thinking after all that study and actually help give us a framework for the questions we might ask the following morning. Third, we would no doubt find that whatever time, say two hours, we had after the morning meetings the next day and before the final exit meeting would be too brief to bring together the mass of information from the weeks during which we'd been preparing. So we had better put in the evening hours Monday, no matter the length of that day, to set us up for a more productive Tuesday.

While that part of my introduction from Anne Gere to the intense work of a campus visit by the C-E Service was dramatic for me, my really enduring debt to her example has been her absolute professionalism, her concern to listen to and respect everyone on a campus with whom we come into contact, and her always mutually respectful collaboration with her fellow consultant to do the best job possible for the people who have hired the C-E Service.

SHIRLEY K ROSE

Scene: It's around 10:00 on the second morning of our visit to the writing program of a large public university. Yesterday, we had meetings with the department chair and graduate program chair, administrators for the first-year composition and upper-division professional writing programs that are the focus of the visit, the college dean, the writing programs' teachers, and the administrator of the campus writing center.

But our schedule for today has been revised overnight because a snowstorm has prompted the airlines to change both Anne's and my reservations and put us on earlier flights. Over a long dinner in the hotel restaurant the evening before, Anne and I developed and outlined our six main recommendations for the program that we had planned to present in the exit interview that had been scheduled for the close of the visit. Our recommendations are based on what we've learned from the institution's website, our review of news items about recent higher-education-related legislation in the state where this campus is located, our careful reading of the self-study prepared by the WPAs of the writing programs that are the focus of our visit, and what we've heard in yesterday's meetings.

We assigned three recommendations to Anne and three to me, and after dinner, in our respective hotel rooms, we worked on drafting several paragraphs of support for each of these six recommendations for inclusion in our written report and prepared a few notes to guide our discussion in the exit interview that would close the campus visit.

However, the schedule the WPAs have carefully put together no longer works. Instead of the planned exit interview with program WPAs and department chair, we're having coffee with the WPAs, then we will go to lunch with the chair before the short trip to the airport to catch our flights. At coffee in the morning, Anne glances at her notes, then gives a quick summary of five of our six recommendations, to which the WPAs nod in response. When she comes to the sixth recommendation—that the department hire a third tenure-track faculty person with a specialization in rhetoric and writing studies—she pauses before saying, "This last recommendation is the most important one . . . ," then goes on to caution the WPAs that, without another tenure-track faculty person to share leadership responsibilities for the multiple aspects of their first-year composition program, upper-division professional writing program, undergraduate writing minor, and graduate program in rhetoric and writing, they should scale back expectations for implementing any of our other recommendations. "Take care of yourselves" is the gist of her advice.

In a few minutes, we head over to the cafeteria in the student union for lunch with the department chair. Once again, we begin with a quick summary of our six recommendations, and the chair nods at each, acknowledging that none comes as a surprise. Then Anne zeroes in on the sixth and asks what might be some strategies for getting funding for a third tenured rhetoric and writing faculty position. We spend the next few minutes brainstorming with him about some arguments he might be able to make to the college dean about re-assigning a newly opened position in the college to the English department.

When the meeting is over, Anne and I are rushed to the airport to catch our respective flights to Detroit and Phoenix, and each of us spends the time waiting for our repeatedly delayed flights at our respective gates revising our written report on our shared Google Doc to reflect the morning's conversations. The specifics of the arguments for our recommendations will align with what we've heard and said in the two meetings, though they will be phrased in more tentative language than we used in the morning's conversations.

As this vignette illustrates, C-Es encounter multiple rhetorical situations in the course of a visit; some follow a conventional format and are highly predictable while others are less so. Listening to Anne as she has nimbly shifted from the planned presentation and discussion of our six recommendations in a formal exit interview to the more spontaneous mentoring session with the WPAs and brainstorming session with the chair has reminded me that, while the purpose of our C-E visit—to help writing programs serve their students as effectively as possible—is a constant, our rhetorical strategies vary in response to audiences and always-unpredictable events. C-E work is rhetorical work.

KATHLEEN BLAKE YANCEY

The C-E Service provides two kinds of assistance, both signaled in its name. The first is a formal program evaluation, which, drawing on multiple contexts—and more about this, shortly—describes issues and makes recommendations. The second, and as important, is consultation, a kind of guidance and advice shared sometimes in the report itself and sometimes informally with program stakeholders during the visit. Critical in providing both kinds of assistance is the set of contexts that C-Es engage with; briefly outlining those gives some idea as to why and how Anne has exemplified the best of the C-E Service.

As suggested in the previous narratives, the review process itself is multi-contextual by design. Program stakeholders—sometimes the WPA requesting the visit acting as a single author but more often different stakeholders playing different roles (e.g., the director of first-year composition, the writing center director, a library services liaison)—complete a detailed self-study keyed to the heuristic for reports provided by the C-E Service. This report, thoughtfully describing, analyzing, and interpreting the institutional context, is, of course, based on local expertise, a collective knowledge about the institution and its programs that is often tacit but which writing the report helps makes explicit. The visit itself, which involves interviews and discussions with students, faculty, staff, administrators, and occasionally even alumni, is an opportunity to bring the context to life, enriching it through multiple voices while also allowing the C-Es to trace differences and tensions across and within them. In this process, the local context becomes pluralized.

Each of the C-Es brings another kind of expertise to the C-E review process, not the deep local institutional knowledge developed by the program stakeholders but rather a deep and wide knowledge about writing programs generally, about how writers develop, and about structures that support both. The C-Es' task, then, is to work together in two ways, bringing the context of local knowledge into the larger context of C-E knowledge and then, as this chapter's co-authors explain, bringing together their different individual knowledge sets into a kind of synthesis. Engaging in multiple contexts so as to understand both past and present of the writing program, the C-Es then plot a possible future for the program, one sensitive to and compatible with the institution. Plotting that possible future is a somewhat kaleidoscopic process of identifying other programs with model features, structures, or practices that, if adopted or adapted, would be of use and value to the program in question. Not least, the process itself contributes more generally to what we might call the C-E funds of knowledge. Having reviewed this program, for example, the C-Es themselves have another program to think with. Similarly, after removing identifying information and under the guidance of the C-E director, they may share aspects of the program and/or its review at a C-E workshop with other C-Es, thus contributing to their knowledge. Likewise, if a provocative, troubling, or laudable aspect of the program resembles one that has appeared in other program reviews—for instance, the proliferation of online writing programs or the development of career ladders for non-tenure-track faculty—the C-E Service may investigate that aspect more formally, for instance by inviting experts on the topic to share their knowledge on it, thus assuring that all C-Es bring knowledge on that topic to future visits. In addition, should a topic be understood as critical for all program reviews, it is added to the heuristic that guides self-study reports.

As suggested, each C-E brings multiple contexts to the review process, including their knowledge about writing programs. Much of this knowledge is based on research, of course, while some of it has been developed through C-E professional development, as noted previously, and some results from their own writing program activities. In this regard, Anne's experience is unique. At one time a high school teacher, Anne well understands the transition into college composition that many college students make in the fall following high school graduation. As a long-time director of the University of Michigan's Sweetland Center for Writing, Anne saw firsthand a full range of writing programs as she provided leadership for first-year composition, advanced writing, the writing center, and writing across the curriculum. In addition, under her leadership, the Sweetland Center created an ePortfolio-based writing minor, which also provided a foundation for the University of Michigan longitudinal writing study she coordinated, *Developing Writers in Higher Education*, with chapters authored primarily with several of her then-current or former graduate students and published in a digital format. And collaborating locally and nationally with colleagues in writing and in STEM fields, Anne has led an NSF-funded project focused on supporting student writers, especially in large lecture classes (Schultz), an especially challenging environment given the numbers of students enrolled in them. Put generally, based on these experiences, the depth and breadth of knowledge that Anne brings to C-E visits, and the C-E Service itself, is extraordinary.

CLOSING

As each of us has shown, our experiences working with Anne have been opportunities to learn in the process of making significant contributions to the college writing programs we have visited as members of the WPA C-E Service. We are grateful to Anne for the many lessons we've learned with her along the way as we've undertaken the work of the C-E Service together and for all she has contributed not only to the CWPA but also to colleges, universities, and writing programs around the country. We encourage our readers to seek out opportunities to engage with the work of writing program evaluation—both as WPAs of programs inviting evaluation and as potential program reviewers.

WORKS CITED

Gere, Anne Ruggles, editor. *Developing Writers in Higher Education: A Longitudinal Study.* U of Michigan P, 2019. *University of Michigan Press Ebook Collection,* https://doi.org/10.3998/mpub.10079890.

Gere, Anne Ruggles. "A Rhetoric of Pen and Brush." *Lost Texts in Rhetoric and Composition,* edited by Deborah H. Holdstein, Modern Language Association of America, 2023, pp. 33–42.

Rose, Shirley K. "Creating a Context: The Institutional Logic of the Council of Writing Program Administrators' Development of the Consultant-Evaluator Service." *The Promise and Perils of Writing Program Administration,* edited by Theresa Enos and Shane Borrowman, Parlor Press, 2008, pp. 21–46.

Schultz, Ginger. "Collaborative Research: Accelerating the Pace of Research and Implementation of Writing-to-Learn Pedagogies across STEM Disciplines." *National Science Foundation,* 30 Nov. 2021, www.nsf.gov/awardsearch/showAward?AWD_ID =1524967.

PART 6. ENRICHING ENGLISH EDUCATION

CHAPTER 17.

THE READINESS IS *NOT* ALL: STRENGTHENING THE BRIDGE FROM HIGH SCHOOL TO COLLEGE READING AND WRITING

Christine Farris
Indiana University

Anne Gere's distinguished career, devoted to cross-disciplinary and K–16 initiatives, is rooted in a sanguine view of "literacy as a capacious space where reading and writing could support and nurture each other" ("Presidential Address" 451). In this chapter I will situate that relationship in the space between high school and college, where teachers of reading and writing can also "support and nurture each other" through collaborations across the secondary/postsecondary divide.

Looking back, I realize my work connecting reading and writing began early. In the early 1970s, before I knew there was a field we now call writing studies, I ran an alternative school and taught children to read by writing down words that mattered to them. I learned about Sylvia Ashton-Warner's "organic literacy" method from a description of her book *Teacher* in the *Whole Earth Catalog*.

Before I knew there was a field, I had a job in the late 1970s measuring syntactic complexity in children's written narratives. I assisted two psychologists studying the impact of a creative writers-in-the-schools program on the literacy of New York City schoolchildren. Scores on the Metropolitan Reading Achievement Test were one correlational measure. The psychologists recommended a book they had just read: Mina Shaughnessy's *Errors and Expectations*. At the time, Shaughnessy was unique in shifting focus from deficiency to possibility in the work of "basic writers" and those who teach them. Others would shift further from deficiency to differences contingent on history and identity. In the same year Geneva Smitherman published *Talkin' and Testifyin': The Language of Black America*.

In 1980, I took my first graduate course with Anne Gere in the English department at the University of Washington (UW). Could I connect my disparate teaching and research experiences, I asked, and study writing development in a department devoted primarily to literary studies? Although Gere directed the Puget Sound branch of the National Writing Project, the focus in the UW English department was on college-level, not K–12, literacy. From Anne Gere I learned there was indeed a field, rhetoric and composition, with a history of theories and practices. Shaughnessy was one voice in an expanding conversation about writing development. Anne demonstrated how one might, methodologically and respectfully, enter that conversation.

Early in Gere's career, the field was building a disciplinary identity in part through research codifying the strategies of successful writers, such that novices might adopt them in courses considered preparation for writing yet to come. That ambitious aim has been modified, and rebranded, as many of us justify writing courses to administrators and policymakers focused on workforce preparation and streamlined general education requirements.

Over the decades, Anne Gere has encouraged a healthy skepticism regarding claims for any universal theory of composing, fixed definition of "good writing," or guaranteed transfer of skills. Specialists, in her view, always have more to learn about how individual writers—in and out of school—develop what she terms "rhetorical flexibility" ("Writing" 284).

The University of Michigan Sweetland Center for Writing, long under her direction, exemplifies how ongoing research informs curriculum and faculty development, with the understanding that first-year writing is not a simple correction to or an extension of writing that comes before or an all-purpose inoculation for writing that follows.

Building on prior longitudinal research (Sternglass; Beaufort; Sommers and Saltz), the Center's Writing Development Study (WDS), led by Gere, was a multi-methodological investigation of students' experiences before, during, and after four years of college. The study examined the impact on writing development of practices students encountered in various disciplines, including secondary and post-secondary English. Edited by Gere with chapters by other members of the research team, the study was published as *Developing Writers in Higher Education.*

Taking up Anne Gere's call in her MLA presidential address to "re-vision the reading-writing dichotomy" (452), I will outline ways to revise that dichotomy in professional collaborations between high school and college teachers. In doing so I will highlight several issues that came to light in the WDS regarding the transfer of writing skills, with a focus on students' perceptions of their high school preparation.

THE MICHIGAN WRITING DEVELOPMENT STUDY

As Gere indicates in *Developing Writers in Higher Education*, the WDS findings show that high school teachers influence expectations about writing that students bring to college. Those expectations are often shaped by the demands of state standards and testing as well as by Advanced Placement (AP) courses. Teachers are often pressured to introduce accessible formats for writing-on-demand as part of the assessment of student progress and school performance. High test scores are a major feature of "college and career readiness." AP testing and preparation courses, in particular, form expectations of what college writing will be like and can foster the notion that mastery of writing has been achieved—over and done.

Initial interviews with students who participated in the WDS revealed beliefs rooted in high school experiences with test-driven genres and teacher feedback. Later interviews indicated willingness and ability to pivot, or not, when faced with new writing tasks. Marie, one of the study's interviewees, was content with high school mastery of "grammar and formatting," which, though useful, may have obscured the need to develop ideas (Swofford 263). Another student, Natalie, had acquired writerly confidence in her high school and community and was able to find similar supportive networks in college (268).

A number of students initially viewed writing in "bifurcated terms, divided into two domains": "academic," often viewed as received ideas, as opposed to "creative," original ideas distinct from those of instructors (Gere, "Writing" 282). Swofford notes Marie's uncertainty about whether "analysis" falls under "creative" (277–278). Over time, some students, especially those minoring in writing, were able to integrate the two domains.

Instructor feedback on written work was one point of difference between high school and college. Particularly troubling to one student, Adrienne, was the absence of assignment "checklists" she felt had permitted high school teachers to be more "objective" than college instructors, whose evaluations she felt restricted writing and lowered her confidence (Wilson and Post 46). Other students, like Natalie, had an easier transition and came to appreciate instructors' in-depth content-specific feedback (Swofford 267). Grace, who had trouble reconciling the academic with the creative, changed her major from English to German and then was able to engage critically with feedback in a new language and discipline (Knutson 213–214). Kris, a microbiologist, was able to meld her ideas with disciplinary conventions and envision ways of writing about science for nonacademic audiences (Gere, "Writing" 297). Some students constructed their own categories for kinds of writing and met their goals by making connections across concepts and practices in more than one area of study (Gere, "Conclusion" 313).

While not always a smooth transfer of skills from high school and first-year writing, in various and complex ways, a fair number of students in the study seemed able to adapt to college discourse—repurposing and expanding their writing repertoire, achieving greater flexibility and control of genres and conventions as they tied them to content knowledge, purposes, and audiences that were now apparent in their chosen fields.

DEVELOPING RHETORICAL FLEXIBILITY IN HIGH SCHOOL

The WDS findings published by Gere in *Developing Writers in Higher Education* raise the question whether it is possible to expand students' writing repertoire sooner and accelerate the development of rhetorical flexibility in the regular high school curriculum. Can we ease the transition to college by making more visible to high school teachers and students the discursive moves academics and professionals make? To that end, Gerald Graff and Cathy Birkenstein, in their textbook *They Say / I Say*, introduce "templates," guiding structures for writing that "demystify" the moves of academia (xv; xiii). In his textbook, *Rewriting*, Joseph Harris breaks down in a series of steps the ways in which writers don't just argue but rather draw from, comment on, and add to the work of others. His aim, he assures students, is "to help you make interesting use of the texts you read in the essays you write" (1).

Not many students in the WDS directly mentioned the role of the texts they read for the college essays they wrote or the role of reading in their high school preparation for college writing. However, some appeared to struggle locating their ideas in relation to those of others, labeling what might have required analysis as "creative" or one's "own idea," seemingly in contrast to "what the teacher thinks" or wants (see Gere, "Writing"; Swofford). After high school, with fewer textbooks that synthesize the results of scholarship, undergraduates are often thrown in the deep end of inquiry in their courses, asked to write as if they know the stakes of an argument or even what would be interesting in the texts they encounter (Bartholomae 4).

Of late, more scholars (Sullivan, et al.; Carillo; Jolliffe and Harl; Horning and Kraemer) are joining those who have long argued for the interconnectedness of reading and writing (Bartholomae and Petrosky; Hutton, this volume; Scholes; Salvatori), claiming that how closely and critically students read is key to their readiness and success with college writing tasks.

INFLUENCE OF THE COMMON CORE STATE STANDARDS ON READING AND WRITING

In the last fifteen years, the assessment of "college and career readiness," particularly by way of the Common Core State Standards (CCSS) for English Language Arts, has contributed to a reshaping of the K–12 curriculum. The standards for reading comprehension place new emphasis on "informational" texts, considered more conducive than literature to the development of cross-disciplinary and workforce skills ("English Language Arts"). The CCSS for writing emphasize the conventional features of narrative, argument, and explanatory essays, with little attention to analysis or cross references to the CCSS for reading.

Originally adopted by 46 states in 2010, a number of states subsequently withdrew from the CCSS, due variously to the complexity and cost of implementation and resistance to federal overreach. Though modified, English Language Arts standards, like those in my state, Indiana, may still resemble the CCSS, retaining many of the test preparation recommendations. Students may practice evidence-based "cold readings" of suggested "exemplar" texts, answering text-dependent questions and identifying the main claim and sentences that support it. Personal connections and context background are often de-emphasized—the scaffolding one would think necessary for working with documents such as the Gettysburg Address.

In an age of misinformation, we might agree with policymakers that success in college and venues beyond should include the ability to extract and communicate facts from texts. However, as Gere's WDS findings show, success is also a matter of how well students become accustomed to writing in terms of ideas within cultural and disciplinary contexts (*Developing Writing*), which test-driven pedagogy barely permits. College instructors expect students to engage critically with not one but multiple print and visual texts in conversation, hopefully becoming comfortable with a more complex worldview.

ALTERNATIVES TO TEST-DRIVEN CURRICULA

I am not the only one to lament the bifurcation of reading and writing and of literature and informational texts in the CCSS English Language Arts standards (Applebee 28). My lamentations are the result of my having represented my state at a series of national meetings on the implementation of the already fixed standards (Farris, "Reclaiming"). When Indiana withdrew from the CCSS and streamlined its standards, I suggested alternatives to test-driven curricula that might incorporate informational texts in the teaching of literature and writing, both of which are the responsibility of secondary teachers. At that point, I had been both the Indiana University (IU) director of composition and the dual enrollment (DE) faculty liaison for over two decades, preparing qualified high school instructors to teach a college-level writing course featuring analysis of multi-disciplinary readings (Farris, "Minding the Gap").

The number of DE partnerships has grown by leaps and bounds in the last decade, tied increasingly to college readiness initiatives along with shortcuts in time-to-degree. With that growth has come attention from the field of writing studies, focused primarily on rigor but also on access and equity (Denecker and Moreland; Taylor, et al.). Not all states or institutions, secondary and postsecondary, buy in. Not all students have access to DE courses, but they still must develop reading and writing skills that keep them on track for college admission, retention, and success. Distinct from DE, AP, and test preparation, I sought to work on deeper connections across the high school/college English divide and the 9th–12th grade curriculum, aimed at sustaining students for the long game. Over several years, I developed clusters of summer courses, connecting graduate seminars for returning high school teachers to on-campus sections of first-year composition, advanced composition for preservice teachers, and the tutorial center, making possible group meetings to discuss use of readings, assignment design, and student papers.

WRITING AND READING ALIGNMENT PROJECT

In another model, with funding from the IU Center for P–16 Research and Collaboration, my colleague Ray Smith and I designed the Writing and Reading Alignment Project (WRAP), seminars in collaboration with librarians and 9th–12th grade English and history teachers from schools with low college enrollment numbers (Farris and Smith). Keeping in mind the English Language Arts CCSS for reading and writing, in tandem with the Indiana postsecondary outcomes for written communication, we developed new strategies for critical reading and evidence-based writing. Week-long seminars included the construction of text sets (fiction, non-fiction, photographs, films, government documents) as the basis for short, low-stakes writing assignments that could stand alone or progress to longer essays (Bean). While a sequence of assignments might begin with a "says/does" outline and summary, tasks can build in complexity toward the explication of a puzzling passage and the use of one text as a lens to understand or question another text—moves that can get at something more interesting than a formulaic compare/contrast of two authors' claims or themes. Graded or not, low-stakes writing can be used to jump-start class discussions. Particularly useful in designing low-stakes assignments are strategies outlined in David Rosenwasser and Jill Stephen's *Writing Analytically*. They suggest identifying binaries, repetitions, and anomalies in print and visual texts, asking not just "what?" but "*so what?*" and the extent to which something might be about X, but also (or really) about Y (16–23; 82–84).

College teachers typically create text sets in their courses, often centered on a key reading that introduces a concept that can be applied to (or challenged by) another text, situation, or subsequent research. In an English or political science course, Rousseau's concept of a "social contract" can shed light on (but not fully account for) the attempt at self-government depicted in William Golding's *Lord of the Flies*. Psychologist Stanley Milgram's findings on obedience to authority factor into psychologist Phillip Zimbardo's report on his Stanford prison experiment, but both texts can also be lenses for analyzing something else, a "test object," such as the Hollywood film about extrajudicial punishment at Guantanamo, *A Few Good Men*.

In the seminar we modeled sample text-sets centered on works the teachers had assigned in the past. For instance, the juxtaposition of Harper Lee's *To Kill a Mockingbird* (1960) with excerpts from her prior draft, published as *Go Set a Watchman* (2015), and accounts of Emmett Till's 1955 lynching can provide background and lenses that invite new questions, e.g., Why was six-year-old Scout's perspective on injustice more acceptable to publishers and some readers in 1960 than that of grown-up Scout, who, in the first draft, *Watchman*, sees the contradictions in Atticus Finch's racial politics? Similarly, pairing Kathryn Stockett's novel *The Help* with the 1964 Civil Rights Act, coverage of Medgar Evers' murder, or civil rights activist Anne Moody's autobiography *Coming of Age in Mississippi*, can provide context that raises new questions, e.g., *if* and *why* a white ally is necessary to tell the domestic workers' stories.

In constructing their own portfolios of multi-genre text sets and sequences of writing tasks (later shared in an online forum), teachers came up with units that featured more questions than answers. And not just what is the theme, but how is a text related to its historical situation? Is it factual? Why tell the story *this* way, at this time?

CURRENT SITES OF CONFLICT AS SPACES FOR COLLABORATIVE RESPONSE

Alas, our WRAP seminars were some years ago. Could we still hold such seminars today? Schools are increasingly under attack by some lawmakers as sites of "indoctrination." The book most often on my syllabi for 30 years, Toni Morrison's *The Bluest Eye*, was removed and then, after pushback, reviewed and returned to libraries in the Florida county where I graduated from high school and college and where I taught reading and writing for the first time. Other states have also enacted legislation that undermines academic freedom, restricting what students can read and what they can do in their writing with what they read. The ability to question, analyze, and synthesize ideas is *not* indoctrination. *Prohibiting* students to question, analyze, and synthesize ideas *is* indoctrination. Jumpstarting rhetorical flexibility in high school depends on not restricting engagement with new concepts, diverse perspectives, and complex issues.

Both K–12 and higher education continue to face new challenges, not just political censorship but also artificial intelligence (AI) with the potential to enhance or restrict students' capacity for original and critical thought. Textbook publishers are both partnering and competing with us as arbiters of curricula as they morph into digital providers of assessment and courses for both students and teachers. Ultimately, we do not know what future we are "getting students ready" for, but more local, face-to-face communication in the real world among educators is important if we are to share the thinking, reading, and writing habits we believe constitute a successful transition to college, career, and civic life. It is my hope that more funding for "readiness" and "success" initiatives from state governments, private foundations, and our professional organizations can be directed toward high school/college curricular partnerships and not just toward on-campus programs for college students after admission. Not everyone can hold the kind of institution-bridging roles Anne Gere has taken on through her longstanding active leadership in CCCC, NCTE, and MLA, but we can still play an active role in strengthening the connection between secondary and post-secondary literacy for all students in regular English Language Arts courses, not just AP and DE. It is crucial that college faculty not only demonstrate solidarity with teachers under siege but also learn more about the restrictions and the best practices that have shaped the writing of our undergraduate students. Even in the current moment such collaborations can make possible a more capacious understanding of our discipline and its responsibility to students as they engage with texts and ideas in order to communicate in an increasingly complex and contentious world.

WORKS CITED

Applebee, Arthur N. "Common Core State Standards: The Promise and the Peril in a Natural Palimpsest." *English Journal*, vol. 103, no. 1, 2013, pp. 25–33, https://doi.org/10.58680/ej201324241.

Ashton-Warner, Sylvia. *Teacher*. Simon and Schuster, 1963.

Bartholomae, David. "Inventing the University." *When a Writer Can't Write: Studies in Writer's Block and Other Composing Process Problems*, edited by Mike Rose, Guilford P, 1985, pp. 134–65.

Bartholomae, David, and Anthony Petrosky. *Ways of Reading: An Anthology for Writers*. 8th ed., Bedford/St. Martin's, 2008.

Bean, John C. *Engaging Ideas: The Professor's Guide to Integrating Writing, Critical Thinking, and Active Learning in the Classroom*. 2nd ed., Jossey-Bass, 2011.

Beaufort, Anne. *College Writing and Beyond: A New Framework for University Writing Instruction*. Utah State UP, 2007.

Carillo, Ellen C. *Securing a Place for Reading in Composition: The Importance of Teaching for Transfer*. Utah State UP, 2014.

Denecker, Christine, and Casie Moreland, editors. *The Dual Enrollment Kaleidoscope: Reconfiguring Conceptions of First-Year Writing and Composition Studies.* Utah State UP, 2022.

"English Language Arts Standards." Informational Website about the Common Core State Standards, National Governors Association Center for Best Practices and Council of Chief State School Officers, 2010, www.thecorestandards.org/ELA-Literacy/.

Farris, Christine R. "Minding the Gap and Learning the Game: Differences that Matter between High School and College Writing." *College Credit for Writing in High School: The "Taking Care of" Business,* edited by Kristine Hansen and Christine R. Farris, National Council of Teachers of English, 2010, pp. 272–82.

———. "Reclaiming English's Disciplinary Responsibility in the Transition from High School to College." *Improving Outcomes: Disciplinary Writing, Local Assessment, and the Aim of Fairness,* edited by Diane Kelly-Riley and Norbert Elliot, Modern Language Association, 2020, pp. 121–32.

Farris, Christine, and Raymond Smith. *Writing and Reading Alignment Project (WRAP): Final Report.* Indiana University Center for P–16 Research and Collaboration/ Indiana Commission for Higher Education, 2015.

Gere, Anne Ruggles. "Conclusion." Gere, *Developing Writers,* pp. 313–28. *University of Michigan Press Ebook Collection,* https://tinyurl.com/2s3yezpa.

———, editor. *Developing Writers in Higher Education: A Longitudinal Study.* U of Michigan P, 2019. *University of Michigan Press Ebook Collection,* https://doi.org/10.3998/mpub.10079890.

———. "Presidential Address 2019–Re-visioning Language, Texts, and Theories." *PMLA,* vol. 134, no. 3, 2019, pp. 450–58. *Cambridge Core,* https://doi.org/10.1632/pmla.2019.134.3.450.

———. "Writing Beyond the University." Gere, *Developing Writers,* pp. 281–311. *University of Michigan Press Ebook Collection,* https://tinyurl.com/f28e9ezp.

Golding, William. *Lord of the Flies.* Putnam, 1954.

Graff, Gerald, and Cathy Birkenstein. *They Say / I Say: The Moves that Matter in Academic Writing.* 4th ed., W. W. Norton and Company, 2018.

Harris, Joseph. *Rewriting: How to Do Things with Texts.* Utah State UP, 2006.

Horning, Alice S., and Elizabeth W. Kraemer, editors. *Reconnecting Reading and Writing.* Parlor Press / The WAC Clearinghouse, 2013, wac.colostate.edu/books/referenceguides/reconnecting/.

Jolliffe, David A., and Allison Harl. "Texts of Our Institutional Lives: Studying the 'Reading Transition' from High School to College: What Are Our Students Reading and Why?" *College English,* vol. 70, no. 6, 2008, pp. 599–617, https://doi.org/10.58680/ce20086370.

Knutson, Anna V. "Grace: A Case Study of Resourcefulness and Resilience." Gere, *Developing Writers,* pp. 193–216. *University of Michigan Press Ebook Collection,* https://tinyurl.com/y5fmwjhy.

Lee, Harper. *Go Set a Watchman.* Harper Collins, 2015.

———. *To Kill a Mockingbird.* Lippincott, 1960.

Milgram, Stanley. *Obedience to Authority: An Experimental View.* Harper & Row, 1974.

Moody, Anne. *Coming of Age in Mississippi*. Dell, 1968.
Rosenwasser, David, and Jill Stephen. *Writing Analytically*. 9th ed., Cengage, 2024.
Rousseau, Jean-Jacques. *The Social Contract and Discourses*. Dent, 1983.
Salvatori, Mariolina. "Conversations with Texts: Reading in the Teaching of Composition." *College English*, vol. 58, no. 4, 1996, pp. 440–54, https://doi.org/10.58680/ce19969048.
Scholes, Robert. "The Transition to College Reading." *Pedagogy*, vol. 2, no. 2, 2002, pp. 165–72, https://doi.org/10.1215/15314200-2-2-165.
Shaughnessy, Mina P. *Errors and Expectations: A Guide for the Teacher of Basic Writing*. Oxford UP, 1977.
Smitherman, Geneva. *Talkin' and Testifyin': The Language of Black America*. Houghton Mifflin, 1977.
Sommers, Nancy, and Laura Saltz. "The Novice as Expert: Writing the Freshman Year." *College Composition and Communication*. Vol. 56, no. 1, 2004, pp. 124–49, https://doi.org/10.58680/ccc20043993.
Sternglass, Marilyn S. *Time to Know Them: A Longitudinal Study of Writing and Learning at the College Level*. Routledge, 1997. *Taylor and Francis eBooks*, https://doi.org/10.4324/9780203810835.
Stockett, Kathryn. *The Help*. Penguin, 2009.
Sullivan, Patrick, et al., editors. *Deep Reading: Teaching Reading in the Writing Classroom*. National Council of Teachers of English, 2017.
Swofford, Sarah. "Reaching Back to Move beyond the 'Typical' Student Profile: The Influence of High School in Undergraduate Writing Development." Gere, *Developing Writers*, pp. 255–80. *University of Michigan Press Ebook Collection*, https://tinyurl.com/mr2y5dxw.
Taylor, Jason L., et al. "Research Priorities for Advancing Equitable Dual Enrollment Policy and Practice." *Collaborative for Higher Education Research and Policy*, University of Utah, July, 2022, https://tinyurl.com/33xan4eu.
Wilson, Emily and Justine Post. "Toward Critical Engagement: Affect and Action in Student Interactions with Instructor Feedback." Gere, *Developing Writers*, pp. 29–55. *University of Michigan Press Ebook Collection*, https://tinyurl.com/bpas9vjv.
Zimbardo, Phillip G. "The Mind is a Formidable Jailer" [The Stanford Prison Experiment]. *Writing and Reading for ACP Composition*, edited Thomas E. Leahey and Christine R. Farris, Pearson, 2009, pp. 240–52. Originally published in *The New York Times*, 8 Apr. 1973, p. 38, *https://tinyurl.com/3jtstavb*.

CHAPTER 18.

WRITING THROUGH THE COMPLEXITIES OF CULTURALLY RESPONSIVE TEACHER EDUCATION

Jennifer Buehler
Saint Louis University

I first met Anne Ruggles Gere on the pages of *English Journal* (*EJ*).

I was a high school English teacher working in a suburban district just down the road from the University of Michigan. At the start of my fourth year of teaching, I was struggling for direction in my career. I was also lonely. Yearning for opportunities to grow professionally, I read and annotated my copies of *EJ* in the bathtub.

Imagine my surprise when I came upon an essay co-authored by a professor in Ann Arbor, the town where I'd been living for the past two years. The essay was a conversation piece written for an *EJ* themed issue on veteran teachers. Titled "Teachers Yesterday, Today, and Tomorrow: Learners Forever," it was co-authored by Laura Schiller, a teacher at Birney Middle School in Southfield, MI; Cheryl L. Rosaen, a professor at Michigan State University; and Anne. Together the three veteran educators discussed events and decisions that led them to their current positions while reflecting on their lives and the teaching profession.

I got my first sense of Anne through their conversation on the page. Aspects of the stance she would later take through all my experiences writing and learning with her were evident in that first textual encounter. She spoke of being a young teacher and having questions and uncertainties about the work that led her to graduate school. She recalled the community she found in the National Writing Project after she became a professor at the University of Washington. She testified to the importance of looking carefully at one's classroom practice in the company of other teachers—and the transformations, both personal and professional, that occur when one commits to continued reflection, professional collaboration, lifelong learning, and a willingness to change.

That essay was everything I needed at that moment. It paid tribute to the complexities of teaching at a time when I was grappling with the demands of the job. It validated my hunger to learn. It planted a seed.

Ten years later, after my own transformational experience in the National Writing Project followed by two summers in Making American Literatures, a workshop for teachers co-led by Anne, Don McQuade, and Sarah Robbins and funded by the National Endowment for the Humanities, I had become a graduate student in the Joint Program in English and Education (JPEE) at the University of Michigan, and I was working on Anne's research team.

Anne had offered me a position as a graduate student research assistant with Teachers for Tomorrow (TFT), a School of Education program she created for prospective secondary school teachers committed to careers in urban and under-resourced schools. I joined Vicki Haviland, a postdoctoral researcher and JPEE program alum who co-directed TFT with Anne, and Christian Dallavis, a fellow graduate student, on the team. A Teacher Quality Grant from the U.S. Department of Education funded the program and our positions.

The focus of our research was teaching—specifically, the ways preservice teachers learn about culturally relevant pedagogy (CRP) and take up culturally responsive teaching stances. Under Anne's leadership, we published three articles focused on the challenges and complexities of CRP. Anne was lead author on our most ambitious piece, "A Visibility Project: Learning to See How Preservice Teachers Take Up Culturally Relevant Pedagogy," written for the *American Educational Research Journal* (*AERJ*), a flagship publication for education scholars. I became lead author on "Normalizing the Fraughtness: How Emotion, Race, and School Context Complicate Cultural Competence," published by the *Journal of Teacher Education* (*JTE*), a signature venue for the teacher education community. Vicki took the lead on "Making the Journey Toward Cultural Competence with Poetry," accepted by *Multicultural Perspectives*, a journal for practitioners committed to social justice and multicultural education. Each publication did its own distinct work for the field of education while also doing formative work for us as young academics writing and learning with Anne.

This chapter tells the story of those publications and the collaborative writing process that produced them. At the center of the story is Anne: research team leader, scholarly role model, and writing teacher. The same qualities that characterized her stance in the *EJ* essay—questioning, looking carefully at classroom practice in the company of fellow teachers, staying committed to continued learning, and being willing to change—resonated in the work of our team and paid dividends for our research. What the *EJ* essay does not reveal—and what this chapter seeks to highlight—is Anne's tenacity as an academic writer and her ability to foster the writing capacities of others.

Following, I provide background on TFT and our program of research. I give an overview of our three collaborative articles and the contributions we made to the literature on culturally relevant pedagogy. I take a deep dive into the most ambitious of the three, "A Visibility Project," recounting the rounds of revision required and how Anne led us through them. Looking across the publications, I trace themes in Anne's leadership and lessons she imparted—about how writing gets done and also about what kinds of writing are worth doing in the academy. Our story has value for graduate students formulating research agendas, professors guiding research teams, and teacher educators with an interest in the complexities of CRP. At its core, the story is an offering to fellow writers—naming and sharing Anne's teachings so they might guide others, as they continue to guide me.

THE TEACHERS FOR TOMORROW PROGRAM

Teachers for Tomorrow was as much a community as a credentialing space. Students applied to TFT after they were admitted to Michigan's regular undergraduate education program. A shared interest in urban teaching drew students to the program; most also shared an explicit commitment to social justice. Joining TFT was a way to both receive special training and, implicitly, to signal a set of socially progressive values. Students planned to teach the core high school disciplines of English, social studies, math, and science. Most, like us, were white.

Students added TFT requirements to their standard certification courses. The program began with a one-semester course called Study Group, focused on critical identity work and the challenges and opportunities afforded by under-resourced schools. The next semester, students took Schooling and Society, dedicated to multicultural literature, culturally relevant pedagogy, and guided experiences in our partner school and the surrounding community. Vicki and Anne co-taught both courses. As liaison to our partner school—a Title I high school serving a racially diverse, small, blue-collar town—my job was to foster relationships, recruit guest speakers, and attend TFT class sessions to share the knowledge I was gaining through ethnographic fieldwork. Students culminated their learning with a student teaching placement at our partner school, complemented by a student teaching seminar led by Christian.

We collected extensive data during the four years of TFT with the intent to analyze how students learned the tenets of CRP in coursework and then enacted culturally responsive teaching practices at our partner school. The three articles that resulted from our research traced the challenges of developing and enacting cultural competence, one of three tenets of CRP as defined by Gloria Ladson-Billings.

Perhaps because we were acutely aware of our own whiteness, we prioritized cultural competence over academic achievement and sociopolitical consciousness, Ladson-Billings' other two tenets of CRP. We saw our work as a response to the challenges posed by the "demographic imperative" of an increasingly diverse school population still being served by a largely white teaching force (Banks 24). Ladson-Billings' critique of traditional teacher education, where notions of whiteness are rarely interrogated, also resonated with us (96). Cultural competence, Ladson-Billings maintains, requires teachers to be aware of their own culture and its role in their lives, to take responsibility for learning about students' cultures and communities, and to use students' cultures as a basis for their learning (97–98). We placed these principles at the center of TFT.

We believed we could make a contribution to the research literature, where portraits of culturally competent teachers glossed over the challenges of centering culture in the classroom. Nowhere could we find accounts of the *process* by which beginning teachers developed cultural competence, so we made that our focus.

We were living the struggle with our students. Questions about their learning invariably raised questions about our teaching. We came to understand that in order to explain what we were seeing, both in students' coursework and in their interactions at our partner school, we had to turn the lens back on ourselves. Students' missteps and blind spots were connected to our own. The interconnected story was about the complexity of the work—what we came to call its "fraughtness."

THREE ARTICLES

A Visibility Project

Our research began in earnest the summer after the first year of TFT. Anne was particularly interested in students' work with multicultural literature, a signature element of the Schooling and Society course—and, we believed, one of the innovations of our approach to culturally responsive teacher education. We rooted our pedagogy in ideas from Michael Smith and Dorothy Strickland, who argue that reading multicultural literature can lead students to "adopt the perspectives of literary characters who are very different from them" and "begin to appreciate and perhaps even to apply those perspectives" (138). Smith and Strickland add that writing from someone else's perspective encourages students to focus less on their own experiences and feelings and more on the complex political and social issues raised in multicultural texts.

Working from Smith and Strickland's premise, Anne and Vicki devised an assignment series rooted in position-taking responses to literary texts including film, comics, memoir, poetry, and fiction that represented aspects of schooling for persons from marginalized U.S. populations. Presented with a menu of choices, students were asked to write from the position of a character, a parent or student from our partner school, an investigative news reporter, or a teacher, and in the form of a nontraditionally academic genre such as a poem, letter, journal entry, news article, memo, or visual response. They were also asked to write a short explanation of the choices they made.

When our first round of qualitative coding revealed a significant amount of stereotyping—more than we had recognized at the time students shared their responses in class—the project and our research questions became more complicated. Racial identity work had been a central focus of both the Study Group and the Schooling and Society course. With this form of critical preparation, how could students go on to produce position-taking writing that was, at times, riddled with racial stereotypes? We had not accounted for the complexity of the CRP learning process and the role race played in our individual and collective work.

The research questions that ultimately drove our analysis focused on a concept we called "raced consciousness," which we defined as a way of seeing the world through race even when one is not consciously aware of race. Raced consciousness, we argued, refers to the pervasive lens that race establishes, even when persons are consciously trying to be antiracist—as were we, and as were our students. Our *AERJ* article, which began as an analysis of student writing about multicultural literature, turned into an exploration of how raced consciousness inflected the developing understandings of cultural competence of all TFT participants—preservice teachers as well as us, their white teacher educators.

Through longitudinal case studies of two students, and a data set that expanded to include admissions essays, journal entries, moments from class sessions, encounters in our partner school and the surrounding community, final poems, and exit interviews, we produced a lengthy and nuanced account of the race-based tensions that accompany attempts to engage in culturally responsive teaching and learning. Raced consciousness surfaced in the ways students positioned themselves in classroom interactions and interviews; it created in students a heightened awareness of how they were being read racially by others; it shaped students' responses to position-taking assignments and our interpretations of their work; and it shaped students' processing of cultural responsiveness. Our discussion section includes an account of how our own racialized views as white instructors and researchers shaped both TFT and our analysis in the study.

Normalizing the Fraughtness

We continued to collect data as new students entered TFT and earlier cohorts progressed through the program. We knew that in order to understand how students enacted their understandings of CRP, it was essential to follow them into the field. When students from the second cohort moved on to student teaching, we identified a subset of focal students and made plans to follow their development by videotaping them teaching once a week. We paired teaching observations with weekly audio-recorded interviews where we asked them to reflect on their learning.

Dynamics at the school were complicated. Race was a frequent topic of conversation—in particular, racial division within the teaching staff. Some staff members described the school's culture as toxic. While some teachers described the experience of teaching in an under-resourced community as a privilege and a calling, others took a cultural deficit perspective towards students and the community. TFT students found themselves navigating a range of dispositions and belief systems along with conflicting advice from the school's teachers on how to manage issues of cultural difference. For TFT students who were white, their racial self-awareness created additional challenges and complexities: they wondered how they could be white and culturally competent at the same time. In a teacher education program where students framed their desire to teach as a matter of social justice, student teaching was inflected by a heightened degree of emotion. Being seen as successful with culturally competent teaching was tied to the identities they were constructing as social justice educators. Anxiety, insecurity, and fear threaded through the work.

We dug deep into the case of Kelly, which we found to be especially rich and compelling. Of the handful of student teachers we followed, Kelly stood out for her honesty and vulnerability. A preservice social studies teacher, she was placed with a mentor teacher who we believed to be among the best in the building. Kelly was smart, creative, deeply committed—and white. Drawing on my ethnographic knowledge of the school, Vicki's expertise with whiteness, and Christian's insights from the student teaching seminar, our coding led us to identify three factors—emotion, race, and school context—that frustrated Kelly's attempts to teach in culturally competent ways.

When we presented preliminary findings at the American Educational Research Association (AERA) conference, drawing from a data set that included videotapes, interviews, and Kelly's journal entries during student teaching, the response from attendees was strong. During our debriefing conversation in the conference corridor, we agreed that we had the makings of an article. We decided to target *JTE*, where Vicki had recently published an article based on her dissertation. Focusing on a single teaching moment from Kelly's classroom, we asked, what does negotiation with cultural competence look like for a white beginning teacher committed to working in urban and under-resourced schools? How do emotions, racial identity, and school context influence a white beginning teacher's negotiations with cultural competence?

Our close reading of that teaching moment and our discourse analysis of the ways Kelly made sense of it in the weeks that followed led us to an argument about the fraughtness of enacting cultural competence. Instead of a smooth arc of development, we wrote, the process of becoming culturally competent "is an arduous journey filled with forward movement followed by missteps and backsliding, followed by forward movement again" (Buehler et al. 416). Teacher educators, we maintained, "would be wise to focus not on the achievement of cultural competence, but rather on the struggle involved in enacting it" (416).

Making the Journey

As we continued our collective work on the *AERJ* piece and as Christian and I took responsibility for the *JTE* piece, Vicki envisioned an article for *Multicultural Perspectives*, a journal she knew from her work as a high school teacher. In the third year of the program, we developed a new final assignment for the Schooling and Society course—a poem in two voices that students performed on the last night of class. What would a thematic analysis of student writing in those poems add to our understanding of students' development of culturally responsive dispositions? Vicki wrote the article almost entirely on her own, but the framing and discussion sections reflected our pooled efforts and insights—one final instantiation of our collaboration.

The idea for the poem in two voices assignment was to provide a space for students to culminate their learning in the Schooling and Society course by focusing on the practicum component at our partner school. Each TFT student was assigned to a cooperating teacher in their discipline and paired with a student in that teacher's classroom. We charged them with getting to know their focal student in the classroom, the school, and the community. Writing in two voices, alternating between their own and their focal student's perspective, would both build on their experience with position-taking responses to multicultural literature and take them to a new place. Presenting their poems slam poetry-style at the end of the course, we believed, would heighten the stakes and provide a meaningful shared learning experience.

Anne recruited Jeff Kass, local teacher and award-winning slam poet, to come to class to lead a poetry writing workshop. We shared a sample poem in two voices that Vicki found through the magazine *Rethinking Schools*. Students had time in class over several sessions—drawing on their observations and conversations with their focal students—to draft their poems. When they presented on the last night of class, we provided them with affirming feedback and connected this culminating experience to their emergent identities as culturally responsive beginning teachers.

Once again, though, our analysis as a research team revealed a more complex story that belied our classroom celebration. Vicki's close readings reminded us that there are almost always nuances in student work that are not visible at first glance. While the poems included moments of critical self-awareness, we also saw continued stereotyping and occasional white saviorism. Students revealed detailed knowledge of their focal students, attention to social class differences, and an ability to see themselves through the eyes of others, but they also relied on heroic teacher narratives and were mostly silent on issues of race.

While our analysis focused on poems produced in just one semester, our interpretation reflected a research team conversation that now spanned four years. We had become steeped in shared language about the fraughtness of developing cultural competence through our work on the other two articles. With this piece, we were more prepared to center our claims about fraughtness. Given the nature of the journal and its audience, this article was shorter than the previous two—it stands out as the most accessible presentation of our research, focused on the power and the limitations that coexisted in a single assignment. We placed the lens on our students as well as on ourselves as their teachers. Analysis of students' work showed us, once again, the complexities of developing cultural competence.

WRITING AND PERSEVERING THROUGH THE CHALLENGES—WITH ANNE AS OUR GUIDE

The conference room in the JPEE suite in the University of Michigan School of Education was both the site of our writing and the site of Anne's teachings. Through leadership and example, Anne taught us how to collaborate as members of a research team and how to write for publication in academia. Threaded through these twin teachings were deeper lessons about effort and persistence, our individual and collective worth, ambition and humility, and who and what has value.

Our team met weekly and wasted little time on small talk. To work with Anne was to reckon with the expectation of focused, continuous, business-like effort. But talk was the essential ingredient in our success as a writing team. From our first summer meeting, when we discussed students' position-taking assignments and Christian shared a research memo that identified stereotypes in their writing, the bulk of our time together went to talk. How could we account for the gaps and shortcomings we were seeing in students' work? And, once we were aware, how should we respond—as writers developing articles for publication, but also as teachers?

Vicki had finished the program the same year I started, and Christian had started the year after me, so in my eyes, Vicki was the voice of authority, and

Anne was in charge—or so I thought. As the ethnographer in the room, I took notes on everything, which gave me plenty of space to listen while others talked. Over time I developed a heightened awareness of Vicki's willingness to challenge Anne. Vicki insisted that we weren't thinking enough about whiteness. She expressed skepticism when Anne said we should target our multicultural literature article to *AERJ* instead of *Research in the Teaching of English* as we'd first planned. Vicki thought ahead to next steps like applying to the University of Michigan's Institutional Review Board for human subjects research permission and what we should do for our next conference proposal. She set the terms for our research agenda.

Anne always listened and took up the thread from Vicki. As Christian and I gained experience, Anne listened to us as well. I knew our partner school better than anyone, and Christian became the expert on CRP. Vicki kept the university courses moving while Christian handled the fieldwork side. I fostered relationships and created handwritten transcripts of our research conversations as they played out in real time—often getting down the gist of the argument we would later make in writing as we spoke it into being during a meeting. We talked our way to clarity. On our team, the playing field was level. Each of us brought a crucial lens and, in time, an individual area of expertise. Anne cultivated our skills and our roles by valuing what we each had to contribute. She invested in us, imbuing us individually and collectively with a degree of authority that surprised me at the time, but that was crucial for our growth. We were novice scholars, relative to her, yet she expected us to have something to say.

The articles we published reflected our individual commitments and our collective capacity. No one else could have produced the work that our team did. It was emergent as we learned from TFT students, our school partners, and each other. It was a product of ongoing, frank, honest talk. Had we not developed so much experience and ease in our talk, we would have never coined the phrase about needing to "normalize the fraughtness" inherent in the development of cultural competence. And had we not figured out how to talk through hard things, we would have never gotten published in *AERJ*. The story of that publication is a final story worth telling.

A manuscript decision of revise and resubmit is normal in academia, so it was unsurprising when we were charged with revision after we submitted the first version, which we had worked on for a year and already revised once based on feedback from faculty colleagues in the English department and the School of Education. The revision the *AERJ* editor asked for, however, was overwhelming. The reviewers were brutal—pointing out gaps in our literature review, problems with our methodology, concerns about validity, lack of clarity in our terms, and the absence of member checking. One reviewer suggested we pivot from an analysis of a set of assignments to case studies of individual students, which the editor encouraged. Another reviewer voted to reject the manuscript entirely. I read ambivalence in the editor's message that she had "decided" to give us the opportunity to do a major revision. But she went on to share a message about the value of our research, affirming that we had conducted "a study on a critical issue that could be of strong interest to the journal readership" supported by "an important and compelling line of inquiry that we hope to strengthen with this feedback" (Valli, 16 Oct. 2007).

For me, the magnitude of reviewer critiques made our work seem illegitimate. But Anne was undaunted. We pivoted to case studies. We drew from a broader swath of the data, extending the analysis and discussion beyond our initial focus on students' writing about literature. We submitted our revision six months later. This time the editor responded with praise for the changes but with another long list of weaknesses that included structural and conceptual incoherence, multiple large and ambiguous concepts at play, misleading claims, and a suggestion to delete the entire section on stereotypes and rewrite our research questions. What, exactly, were we studying, she wondered—CRP, responses to literature, or something else? She reiterated her message about the importance of our work: "Although I cannot make promises about publication at this time, the reviewers and I would not be spending this much time providing feedback on a manuscript that we did not believe had publishing potential" (Valli, 5 May 2008).

I can't speak for Vicki and Christian, but I was crushed. Again, the flaws in our manuscript, as described by the reviewers—who did not agree on what we should do next—seemed insurmountable. But I will never forget Anne's response. She was optimistic. And determined. "We're still in the game," she said. Her confidence and her fortitude were a wonder to me.

We submitted our third revision—which was actually our fourth draft—fully two years after our first research team meeting where Christian brought his research memo about stereotypes. Two months later we received a conditional acceptance pending one last round of revision that the editor herself would oversee. Even then, she presented a laundry list of problems, culminating with questions about the discussion and implications sections and telling us that the manuscript ended on a dismal note. What was the point, she wondered, of learning to see raced consciousness in ourselves and our students? What were the implications for teacher education?

In that fourth and final round of revision, which yielded our fifth draft, we all helped out, as was customary for our team. But in this final round, Anne did the heavy lifting. I remember being impressed—deeply impressed—by the moves she made as she rewrote the discussion and implications sections. At the end of this arduous journey, it was Anne who maintained a sense of the big picture, a grasp of the field, and a degree of authority that exceeded what we could summon as younger scholars. She modeled not just perseverance, but intellectual daring. When the final acceptance arrived, midway through my final year in graduate school, we were jubilant. To celebrate, Anne had us over for dinner at her house. She even cooked the meal. I'll never forget her pride in our shared accomplishment.

As a writer, and as a writing teacher by example, Anne modeled the belief that clarity in the work would eventually come and that the best way to achieve it was through the hard work of returning to the writing desk. For me, it meant taking the transcript of our team conversation, preserved in my handwritten notes, and turning bullet points into a series of paragraphs at a coffee shop or my kitchen table with a preschooler watching videotapes of *Mister Rogers' Neighborhood* in the other room. After all, if Anne could go home after a full day of meetings on campus and draft a new section between midnight and 2 a.m., then I should be able to get something written when it was my turn.

Anne was the engine that kept our train moving. Her sense of fairness meant that all four of our names went on every publication, and the lead author was the one who had done the most work.

I remember all of these characteristics because they helped to form me. The legacy of our work can be seen in the citation record for our articles—which have indeed been taken up by other scholars, providing evidence that our research was good for the field. Talking to scholars on the pages of a flagship journal mattered, but talking to practitioners about pedagogy did, too. The richness is in the body of work as a collective, which parallels the richness in our team.

The professor whose words I first read in the bathtub became the mentor who taught me to believe in the value of collaboration and the transformations that are possible when you keep showing up—to write, to teach, and to learn from the process. The four of us were learners together—embracing the complexities of teaching, engaging in self-critique, remaining open to what was emergent in the research, and finding value in our individual and collective abilities. We were teachers, writers, and learners—transformed in the learning, shaped in the work.

WORKS CITED

Banks, James A. "Multicultural Education: Development, Dimensions, and Challenges." *The Phi Delta Kappan*, vol. 75, no. 1, 1993, pp. 22–28. JSTOR, http://www.jstor.org/stable/20405019.

Buehler, Jennifer, et al. "Normalizing the Fraughtness: How Emotion, Race, and School Context Complicate Cultural Competence." *Journal of Teacher Education*, vol. 60, no. 4, 2009, pp. 408–18, https://doi.org/10.1177/0022487109339905.

Gere, Anne Ruggles, et al. "A Visibility Project: Learning to See How Preservice Teachers Take Up Culturally Relevant Pedagogy." *American Educational Research Journal*, vol. 46, no. 3, 2009, pp. 816–52, https://doi.org/10.3102/0002831209333182.

Haviland, Victoria Shaw, et al. "Making the Journey Toward Cultural Competence with Poetry." *Multicultural Perspectives*, vol. 11, no. 1, 2009, pp. 19–26, https://doi.org/10.1080/15210960902743870.

Ladson-Billings, Gloria. *Crossing Over to Canaan: The Journey of New Teachers in Diverse Classrooms*. Jossey-Bass, 2001.

Schiller, Laura, et al. "Teachers Yesterday, Today, and Tomorrow: Learners Forever." *English Journal*, vol. 85, no. 5, 1996, pp. 40–44, https://doi.org/10.58680/ej199 65290.

Smith, Michael W., and Dorothy S. Strickland. "Complements or Conflicts: Conceptions of Discussion and Multicultural Literature in a Teachers-As-Readers Discussion Group." With John Carman et al., *Journal of Literacy Research*, vol. 33, no. 1, 2001, pp. 137–67, https://doi.org/10.1080/10862960109548105.

Valli, Linda. Email to Anne Ruggles Gere. 16 Oct. 2007.

———. Email to Anne Ruggles Gere. 5 May 2008.

CHAPTER 19.

"CHANGING WITH THE TIMES": EBONY ELIZABETH THOMAS AND ANNE RUGGLES GERE IN CONVERSATION

Ebony Elizabeth Thomas
University of Michigan

Anne Ruggles Gere
University of Michigan

One of the most important sites of Anne Ruggles Gere's influence in the field of writing studies—and more—has been the Joint Program of English and Education (JPEE) at the University of Michigan. The program began in the 1960s, under the direction of Stephen Dunning. As its name suggests, JPEE receives support from both the English department and the School of Education, including having faculty members from both those units serve on the committee that manages admissions, distributes program fellowships, and sets policy (Gere, "Establishing" 160).

As noted in one UM profile of JPEE, this doctoral pathway offers students "wide latitude" to shape their degree program, while providing them "the opportunity to pursue research projects collaboratively with faculty, including social justice- and activist-oriented research" ("Joint Program"). Consistent with Gere's own wide-ranging interdisciplinary professional profile and her leadership as chair of JPEE from 1989 to 2023, program graduates have pursued a broad range of interests, including "rhetorical theory, literacy studies, feminist theory, new media composition, disability studies, queer theory, applied linguistics, English language studies, ethnic studies, creative writing studies, and writing assessment" ("Joint Program"). Tailored for students who have already earned a master's degree in either English or education and who have prior teaching experience, JPEE cultivates a "supportive and engaging community of scholars" to enable students' individualized learning ("Doctoral English").

One of those program alumni, Dr. Ebony Thomas, succeeded Anne as chair in 2023. In the interview that follows, Ebony and Anne reflect together on connections between the field of writing studies and JPEE work, on the impact of Anne's research on the program, and on JPEE as a visionary model for graduate education.[1] Following their conversation is a list of dissertations by JPEE alumni who have contributed chapters to *Sites of Writing*. These projects, which are often scholars' first "sites of writing" in academe, speak to the interdisciplinary reach of JPEE and Anne's capacious vision for the fields of writing studies and English education.

EBONY AND ANNE IN CONVERSATION

The Field of Writing Studies

Ebony: Anne, it's such a pleasure to talk with you and celebrate your work. What have been some important or vital developments in the field of writing studies over the course of your career?

Anne: Well, I could laugh and say that actually the whole field of writing studies has developed over the course of my career! When I started graduate school, Janet Emig's book *The Composing Processes of Twelfth Graders* hadn't yet been published. Ed Corbett's book, *Classical Rhetoric for the Modern Student,* had just come out in 1968.

When I began graduate school in 1970, there wasn't yet a field of writing studies. The reason I returned to graduate school was because I didn't feel adequately prepared from my previous training as a high school English teacher to teach my students how to write. I could talk about literature all day, but I couldn't figure out how to help people write. I was one of those kids who skipped first-year writing and couldn't tell you how I first learned to write. So everything that has happened in the field has happened over the course of my career.

Ebony: Wow, that's neat! What did you learn (about the field, administrative work, writing, etc.) from your leadership roles with MLA, CCCC, and NCTE?

Anne: Starting with CCCC (Conference on College Composition and Communication), that really became my school away from home. I got to know people. We shared work. We became colleagues. That was really the incubator. And CCCC developed as the field of writing studies developed.

Again, in the 1970s, CCCC was a very tiny group, and even by the time I started at the University of Washington as an assistant professor, it was still a very small part of our academic world. Of course, over the years, it became quite central.

---

1   The interview has been lightly edited for publication.

The other organization that you didn't mention was the National Writing Project (NWP). My best self-education was through becoming the founding director of the Puget Sound Writing Project at the University of Washington, because I was working with teachers. And, as you know, in that model, teachers are bringing their practice to the program, we're all exploring the research in the field, and at the same time, we're all developing our capacities as writers. And that sort of tripartite—three-part—approach really has been how I have operated ever since. You know, constantly keeping up with the research, always being in a writing group, always sharing writing, to continually *be* a writer, and at the same time, working on my teaching practice. So that, in many ways, was enormously influential.

With MLA (Modern Language Association), I was able to figure out how to make writing studies more a part of MLA. In the very early days, there wasn't much about writing. I can't quite remember the details, but very early on, I was on a committee with Lynn (Quitman) Troyka. This was back when Phyllis Franklin was executive director. She was the first woman to ever head MLA, and she was someone who knew that MLA had to have something to do with writing. A group of us met with her, and one result was that MLA published a series on writing, and I was on the board for that. That gave me another perspective on the wider field of English studies and the role that writing could play.

Within NCTE (National Council of Teachers of English), it was really CCCC where I learned the most. So for me, it was CCCC, NWP, and MLA.

Ebony: Thank you so much! It's so wonderful to learn this history. Next, I have a question about your presidential addresses: As you look back on your own major addresses for these major organizations, what reflections might you want to share about them in their own moment? As markers of where the field has gone since then and where you hope it will go?

Anne: That's a hard question! I haven't looked at these in years, so you're going to have to bear with me. I remember that in my NCTE address, I was really trying to talk about the way that we think about teaching. Teaching was at the center. It's not just something that we do mechanically, but a robust and interesting area of study.[2]

With CCCC, it was related to my book on women's clubs. What I was interested in is what goes on outside of school—there's so much writing that people are doing that's pretty much invisible. I wanted people in writing studies to be thinking about writing outside the academy, and the relationship between that

---

2   See Gere, "Gladly Learn and Gladly Teach."

writing and what goes on *in* the academy.[3] And so I had a political agenda in that case . . . I guess they're all political!

And then with MLA, my whole agenda was to try to make writing and writing studies as visible as possible. The approach I took there was to try to talk about the relationship between reading and writing.[4] That seemed to be the obvious place to do so in that organization. So in every case, there was that political agenda.

Reflecting on Research

Ebony: As this book [*Sites of Writing*] illustrates, your research extends in many different directions. What aspects of your work have been most meaningful to you and why?

Anne: I love them all! It's like asking me which is my favorite child. I think that in some cases, I'm very self-centered when it comes to my research. All of my work comes out of something that deeply matters to me. For example, I think I've told you that my book about women's clubs[5] was written during a time that I was dealing with my mother's dementia, and trying to find a way to stay in touch with somebody who was no longer there. That book was a way to do that. Having two daughters who are Native American obviously has led to my work in Indigenous studies.

And in a different way, I've always cared about writing. I mean, I was the kind of kid who was keeping journals and diaries. And you know, that reading-writing connection was always very powerful for me.

The kind of research I've done has always done that kind of work. From MWrite to the Beyond College project to the kind of work that I'm doing now to better understand how student writers make arguments, I'm a teacher. I care about how we can do a better job in helping students to learn. So I guess I am driven by my own personal interests and concerns, and that comes into my scholarship.

Ebony: That's beautiful—beautiful! We want you to think about the influence of your own scholarship and what you might view as "unfinished business." What would you like to share about either or both of these interrelated points?

Anne: Well for sure, my next book is in Indigenous studies, and it's in the publishers' hands! I really think there's more to be said about Native American women who were teachers. My book really scratches the surface, but part of

---

3   See Gere, "Kitchen Tables."
4   See Gere, "Presidential Address."
5   See Gere, *Intimate Practices.*

what I did was try to find at least some of the names of so many other women I didn't have time to write about. And so, I really see that as an ongoing project.

And certainly the work that I'm doing with this NSF (National Science Foundation) grant, trying to figure out in a world with artificial intelligence (AI), which is the world we're all in now, how do we do a better job of teaching writing?[6] Using the strengths of AI without destroying the whole enterprise? Which is just really scary. That we don't know the possibilities of what could happen. Karthik Duraisamy was the chair of University of Michigan's GAIA (Generative AI Advisory) committee that I was on last spring, which came out with this big report that led to the decision that Michigan would develop its own AI.[7] He was just at Davos being interviewed by Bloomberg to talk about AI at Michigan. We were the first university in the United States to come up with our own AI. Now Harvard and Princeton, and I've just heard Texas, are joining the ranks. But they are following *us*.

We were the first, and that's a good thing. But also, with opportunity comes responsibility. Really thinking hard about how we can do this well is something that I care about and plan to keep working on.

THE JOINT PROGRAM IN ENGLISH AND EDUCATION

Ebony: Interdisciplinarity is central to JPEE, the program you've directed or co-directed at the University of Michigan. What do you see as some of the main benefits of this approach to graduate education that you've done so much to develop over the years?

Anne: Well, first of all, I didn't develop it. It was in place. There was always this interdisciplinarity, and I simply carried it on.

But the advantages of it, I think, are evident in our students who are able to take on varieties of different kinds of positions. Ranging from school superintendent, to headmaster of a school, to traditional academic professors on the tenure track, to people working for educational institutions, and people who simply become very good writers. And you know, I'm thinking of a student who worked for years in Washington, DC, writing policy.

Our students come out as very well educated and highly flexible people.

Ebony: That's true! I would totally agree that JPEE opens many doors. What are some of your hopes for the future of JPEE as you pass the torch on?

---

6   NSF grant details are available at https://www.nsf.gov/awardsearch/simpleSearchResult?queryText=2302564&ActiveAwards=true.

7   The report is available at https://genai.umich.edu/committee-report.

Anne: I hope that JPEE keeps changing with the times! To keep our basic model of interdisciplinary education that captures the broad range of things that people do. And for our people to keep reaching into new areas—AI being an obvious one—where education is going in the future.

Ebony: What advice would you give to new mentors or advisors of graduate students?

Anne: I just had this conversation recently. We talked about all the ways that graduate students in many departments are still being treated as students—"take this test to prove how smart you are." Of course, they're smart enough, or they wouldn't be here! My advice is to make graduate education resemble the work that people are going to do, particularly in the area of assessment. I think there should not be these comprehensive exams as they have traditionally been construed. Testing in that narrow sense is a waste of everybody's time.

Ebony: Thank you! Is there anything else you'd like to add?

Anne: That's it!

EXAMPLES OF DISSERTATIONS BY JPEE ALUMNI

To underscore this interview's points about the interdisciplinarity of the JPEE and its graduates' broad interests, we list in chronological order dissertation titles of program alumni who contributed chapters to *Sites of Writing*. For a more complete list of JPEE alumni dissertation titles, see https://sites.lsa.umich.edu/jpee/our-people/alumni/.

> Gere, Anne Ruggles. *West African Oratory and the Fiction of Chinua Achebe and* T. M. *Aluko*. 1974. University of Michigan, PhD dissertation. *Deep Blue Documents*, https://doi.org/10.7302/21103.
>
> Robbins, Sarah Ruffing. *Domestic Didactics: Nineteenth-Century American Literary Pedagogy by Barbauld, Stowe and Addams*. 1993. University of Michigan, PhD dissertation. *Deep Blue Documents*, hdl.handle.net/2027.42/129148.
>
> Minter, Deborah Williams. *Writing (To) Work: Metaphors of Fitness in Contemporary Arguments about Literacy and Work*. 1996. University of Michigan, PhD dissertation. *Deep Blue Documents*, hdl.handle.net/2027.42/105124.

Young, Morris S. H.. *Literacy, Legitimacy, and the Composing of Asian American Citizenship.* 1997. University of Michigan, PhD dissertation. *Deep Blue Documents,* hdl.handle.net/2027.42/130617.

Willard, Margaret Katharine. *Interanimating Voices: Theorizing the Turn Toward Reflective Writing in the Academy.* 1998. University of Michigan, PhD dissertation. *Deep Blue Documents,* hdl.handle.net/2027.42/131353.

Sinor, Jennifer Ann. *Making Ordinary Writing: One Woman's Diary.* 2000. University of Michigan, PhD dissertation. *Deep Blue Documents,* hdl.handle.net/2027.42/132684.

Kaufman, Rona Diane. *Reading Materials: Composing Literacy Practices in and out of School.* 2002. University of Michigan, PhD dissertation. *Deep Blue Documents,* hdl.handle.net/2027.42/132255.

Sassi, Kelly Jean. *Rhetorics of Authority, Space, Friendship, and Race: A Qualitative Study of the Culturally Responsive Teaching of Native American Literatures.* 2008. University of Michigan, PhD dissertation. Deep Blue Documents, hdl.handle.net/2027.42/60712.

Beitler, James Edward, III. *Rhetorics of Interdependence: Composing the Ethos of the Greensboro Truth and Reconciliation Commission.* 2009. University of Michigan, PhD dissertation. *Deep Blue Documents,* hdl.handle.net/2027.42/62437.

Buehler, Jennifer Lyn. *Words Matter: The Role of Discourse in Creating, Sustaining, and Changing School Culture.* 2009. University of Michigan, PhD dissertation. *Deep Blue Documents,* hdl.handle.net/2027.42/63815.

Thomson, Heather E. *When God's Word Isn't Good Enough: Exploring Christian Discourses in the College Composition Classroom.* 2009. University of Michigan, PhD dissertation. *Deep Blue Documents,* hdl.handle.net/2027.42/64759.

Thomas, Ebony Elizabeth. *"We're Saying the Same Thing": How English Teachers Negotiated Solidarity Identity and Ethics Through Talk and Interaction.* 2010. University of Michigan, PhD dissertation. Deep Blue Documents, hdl.handle.net/2027.42/77791.

Aull, Laura Louise. *Forgotten Genres: The Editorial Apparatus of American Anthologies and Composition Textbooks.* 2011. University of Michigan, PhD dissertation. *Deep Blue Documents,* hdl.handle.net/2027.42/84469.

Hutton, Elizabeth Bachrach. *Textual Transactions: Recontextualizing Louise Rosenblatt's Transactional Theory for the College Writing Classroom*. 2018. University of Michigan, PhD dissertation. Deep Blue Documents, hdl.handle.net/2027.42/143921.

Hammond, James Watson. *Composing Progress in the United States: Race Science, Social Justice, and the Rhetorics of Writing Assessment, 1845–1859*. 2019. University of Michigan, PhD dissertation. Deep Blue Documents, hdl.handle.net/2027.42/151715.

Wilson, Emily M. *Restorying in the Discourses and Literacies of Military-Connected Students*. 2019. University of Michigan, PhD dissertation. *Deep Blue Documents*, hdl.handle.net/2027.42/149930.

Day, Jathan. *Extension, Engagement, and Agency: Canvas as a Network for the Writing Classroom*. 2022. University of Michigan, PhD dissertation. *Deep Blue Documents*, https://doi.org/10.7302/6109.

Limlamai, Naitnaphit. *Constructions and Enactments of Justice in Secondary English Methods and Student Teaching Spaces*. 2022. University of Michigan, PhD dissertation. *Deep Blue Documents*, https://doi.org/10.7302/4600.

WORKS CITED

"Doctoral English and Education: Overview and Requirements." *Marsal Family School of Education*, 2024, marsal.umich.edu/academics-admissions/degrees/doctoral/english-and-education#tab1.

Gere, Anne Ruggles. "Establishing the Field: Recognition, Interdisciplinarity, and Freedom in English Education Doctoral Studies." *The Doctoral Degree in English Education*, edited by Allen Webb, Kennesaw State P, 2009, pp. 157–65.

———. "Gladly Learn and Gladly Teach." National Council of Teachers of English Annual Convention, Nov. 2000, Milwaukee, WI. Presidential Address.

———. *Intimate Practices: Literacy and Cultural Work in U.S. Women's Clubs, 1880–1920*. U of Illinois P, 1997.

———. "Kitchen Tables and Rented Rooms: The Extracurriculum of Composition." *College Composition and Communication*, vol. 45, no. 1, 1994, pp. 75–92, https://doi.org/10.2307/358588.

———. "Presidential Address 2019–Re-visioning Language, Texts, and Theories." *PMLA*, vol. 134, no. 3, 2019, pp. 450–58. *Cambridge Core*, https://doi.org/10.1632/pmla.2019.134.3.450.

"Joint Program in English and Education: Degrees and Certifications." *Marsal Family School of Education*, 2024, marsal.umich.edu/academics-admissions/jpee.

PART 7. RHETORICS OF RENEWAL

CHAPTER 20.

MAKING THE CASE FOR READING AND WRITING AND TEACHING AND RESEARCH

Paula M. Krebs
Modern Language Association

Anne Gere became president of the Modern Language Association (MLA) in 2018, after having held the presidency of the National Council of Teachers of English in 2000–01 and having been the chair of the Conference on College Composition and Communication in 1993 (we can be a bit slow at the MLA). Gere's leadership of the MLA brought into focus for that organization the often-underacknowledged ties between reading and writing, between literary study and the study of rhetoric, and, perhaps most significantly, between the teaching of writing and every other aspect of higher education.

Gere's presidential address at the 2019 MLA Annual Convention asked us to "reorient our field's vexed approaches to the relation between reading and writing, specifically the underconceptualization of reading by colleagues in writing studies and of writing by colleagues in literary studies" (452). This chapter argues, following Gere's focus during her MLA presidency on thinking outside our separate communities' categories, that public discourse—about politics, climate, race, health, education, and so many other issues—needs to be grounded in both reading and writing, in what we in the humanities teach.

Critical thinking, cultural competence, clear and concise writing, the ability to tell legitimate information from false—these are humanities skills, and they are deeply necessary to a functioning democracy. These skills are learned in the humanities classroom as part of a larger set of skills, values, and perspectives that shape humanities students' vision of the world and themselves when they graduate. The humanities, including writing studies, philosophy, language and literature, cultural studies, and more, are foundational to a liberal education. At the heart of the humanities, since ancient Athens first articulated what the liberal arts are, is the study of rhetoric, grammar, and logic.

No study of literature or culture would be possible without an understanding of rhetoric, and no understanding of rhetoric stands on its own outside an understanding of culture. Bringing together the study of reading with the study of writing, and learning how to use the tools gained in that study, helps students become better community members, better voters, and (and this is important to Anne Gere as well) better family members (see Gere's "Kitchen Tables and Rented Rooms: The Extracurriculum of Composition"). Across too many states, higher education has come under fire for providing exactly the kind of education that equips students to be critical consumers of their own cultures, to be careful readers of the world around them. Starting with a warped perception of critical race theory, state legislatures, school boards, and college and university boards of governors have decided that teaching students to be "critical" is dangerous.

A confused understanding of the concept of critical race theory and a distrust of the expertise of professors, teachers, and librarians has resulted in book bans and course restrictions all over the US. History courses have received extra scrutiny when faculty members ask students to consider histories of oppression, including legacies of slavery in the US, the treatment of the country's Indigenous populations, and the Holocaust. Such scrutiny is not confined to history courses, however. Any teaching that centers on race or sexuality can be fair game in some states, and faculty members have been required to have syllabi vetted and, in some cases, to submit email histories for scrutiny. We at the MLA have recently had a member resign from a leadership position in an internal forum on race because the member worried that doing such MLA service work, focused on race and ethnicity, would put their job, in Texas, at risk.

The desire to keep universities from acknowledging race, gender, and sexuality has prompted states to pass laws forbidding public higher education institutions from having offices of diversity, equity, and inclusion and even from teaching courses that acknowledge the existence of systems of oppression in the US. Much of the hostility has been directed at history courses, but courses in literature and cultural studies and, indeed, any course that educates students about theoretical frameworks for examining their own culture have been in for the same treatment.

Attacks on teaching the humanities in the US have contained quite a few internal contradictions. The humanities have been portrayed as misleading and dangerous, causing students to question traditional values and sowing social discord. Yet at the same time, the humanities have been described as frivolous and useless, as distracting wastes of students' time. So, the humanities are dangerous and must be eliminated while at the same time are fluffy and silly time-wasters no one could take seriously.

This contradiction must be considered in relation to the center of the argument against the humanities put forward by every campus that wants to eliminate humanities departments and faculty members: humanities courses and majors are unnecessary because they prevent students from focusing on what really matters—getting a job. The focus, in these narrow approaches, is on vocational curricula, designed to prepare students for a first job after graduation rather than for a lifetime of adapting to various jobs and careers. We in the humanities have failed to make the case that while students do want to be confident that they will be employed as soon as they graduate, they also want to understand the world around them, to study things they know they can't learn on their own, and to have skills, values, and perspectives that will help them in the third or fourth job down the line, the managerial or executive position, not just the entry-level job. Making the case for the value of humanities study is making the case for reading and writing and analysis and interpretation.

That set of skills is established first, in U.S. higher education, in the general education or core curriculum. The idea of the core curriculum is under threat these days, with attacks against the notion of liberal arts education. The model of a full liberal arts education, a general education, that wraps around a major in a specialized field has set the U.S. bachelor's degree apart from models in other countries, which, as in England, feature three years of specialized coursework in a single field. Students in U.S. universities are encouraged to experiment, required to take courses outside the major to gain a fuller understanding of the methods and matter of a range of fields. This general education, done right, supplements the specialized knowledge of the major with a broader perspective. It introduces students to fields they would have been unlikely to have encountered in secondary school (anthropology, art history, sociology, communications, less-commonly-taught languages) and allows students a freedom to switch majors that does not exist in other higher education systems.

Because of general education, students who enter college convinced they need to choose a major that correlates directly with a particular job (accounting, computer science) nevertheless are required to take courses in humanities, social sciences, physical sciences, and languages. That broad general education curriculum, shaped differently at each university, is the object of attention in many statehouses today. Legislators who see higher education as simply job preparation reject majors in the humanities, to be sure, but they also reject the assertion that coursework outside of majors in STEM (science, technology, engineering, and mathematics) and business fields is important at all, whether that coursework be in literature, history, art, philosophy, or writing. Anne Gere's work with writing across the curriculum and, especially, with STEM disciplines (e.g., Gere et al.), reinforces the importance of writing as essential to learning in other fields and strengthens support for general education across the board (see chapters by Ginger Shultz and colleagues as well as Mike Palmquist, this collection). Just as science students learn better by writing, so do business students learn better by reading literature and watching films and studying how systems and structures shape both economics and culture.

In this new vocationally focused approach to higher education, epitomized recently by West Virginia University's attempt to eliminate all language instruction, its creative writing MFA program, and much more, college administrators have often failed to support liberal arts education on their campuses in the mistaken belief that abandoning the humanities, social sciences, and even basic science will enable them to give students greater odds for securing good jobs after graduation. But talking with employers would give them a different perspective on the question. The American Academy of Arts and Sciences Humanities Indicators Project (Bradburn et al.), the American Association of Colleges and Universities' employer surveys (e.g., Finley), the MLA's own research (Arteaga et al.), and many more studies indicate that employers value the skills, values, and perspectives that humanities students bring to their work. They value facility in language—English and other languages—and the ability to thrive in conditions of ambiguity. They want employees who can construct arguments and know how to communicate. They need people who can do research and evaluate and synthesize sources. Employers say they want humanities skills. Yet when they construct the algorithms that sort through the resumes on application sites, those algorithms are more likely to toss out the resumes of humanities majors than to pull them to the top of the stack. The knee-jerk privileging of majors that seem to indicate career preparation means that we in the humanities more often than not are forced to encourage our students to seed their resumes with internships and other business-coded activities so they can land that first job. Getting internships is not the problem. Failure to contextualize those internships in relation to the skills, values, and perspectives gained in humanities courses and majors is the problem. We need to be producing humanities students who understand and can articulate the value of the study of reading and writing and critical analysis for the work they will do outside of the classroom.

So the work of higher education in an anti-liberal-arts climate is to assert the use value of what the liberal arts teach at the same time as asserting its intrinsic value. Reading, writing, and critical thinking are what enable students, and voters, to see beyond the surface of propaganda, advertisements, ideology-based and emotion-based incitement. It takes work to defend the notion that the humanities teaches students to understand how to tolerate ambiguity while at the same time challenging the notion that one should teach "both sides" of the history of slavery or the Holocaust. The complex analytical tools of philosophy, literature, and rhetoric allow students to move beyond the entry-level jobs that are too often the focus of shortsighted college recruitment pitches. Humanities Indicators data show an over-representation of humanities graduates in managerial positions (Bradburn et al. 19), but that information somehow never makes it into admissions tours.

Why do we not interrogate that over-representation? What is it about humanities education that produces great executives? It reminds me of when I was a dean and visited a network engineering firm whose recruiter told me how great humanities majors were at network engineering, once they'd had the required training course, because they knew how to ask questions, ask follow-up questions, and try different solutions until they found one that worked. Humanities grads were great network engineers, he told me, yet he never thought to actually tell university careers officers that or to ask specifically for humanities graduates when he visited campuses. We have to work harder to surface the value of the habits of mind, and not just the content, that we teach in our courses.

The study of reading and writing gives students skills and perspectives that serve them well on the job market and as participants in a democracy, and we indeed must champion the inclusion of literature, writing, and language study in general education curricula. But first- and second-year courses are not enough. Studying reading and writing and analysis and communication can't stop at the introductory and intermediate level. Just as first- and second-year language courses alone do not result in proficiency, general-education level reading and writing cannot be all that is available for students, especially students at state universities.

The threats to humanities departments and curricula since the economic meltdown of 2008–09 often take as the starting point of their arguments that the job of public colleges and universities is simply to prepare workforces for their states. If reading and writing have a place in that preparation, the argument goes, it is certainly not at an advanced coursework or graduate level—reading and writing is important only as far as necessary for getting and keeping that entry-level job. And, in states whose legislators see critical analysis as threatening, where language and literature study is portrayed as frivolous or distracting, budget-cutting takes the form of a slash-and-burn of any advanced courses (and the faculty members who teach them) that are not understood to feed directly into low-level employment in tech and business in the state. Students whose sole option for higher education is a public college or university are the ones whose access to advanced thinking, writing, and communication courses is restricted. The effect of these cuts is to restrict access to a full liberal arts education; any state resident who cannot afford a private university education must be content with a vocational track.

Attacks on the humanities as frivolous, on English degrees producing baristas, for example, have not been limited to the political right. Politicians on both sides of the aisle have called for less focus on art history or English or philosophy or gender studies and more focus on computer science or even, in Florida's case a few years ago, on welding (Jaschik; Condon). At state universities, these calls, along with recent cuts to the humanities and even to advanced degrees in such fields as mathematics, carry with them an implied belief that public university students do not need, or are not entitled to, education that does anything but shape them into entry-level wage workers. This contempt for working-class students would deny an education that was not directly vocational (think of majors that carry a particular job in their title: accounting, engineering) to any student who could not afford to attend a private university. The refusal of access to critical and analytical education not only bends the knee of the state university to narrow economic (and often political) interests, but it also betrays a lack of understanding of the post-graduation value of education in humanities fields.

Institutions of higher education are not simply preparers of future workers. They are also sites for specialized expertise in both teaching and knowledge creation. The generation of new knowledge goes hand in hand with teaching, and the creation of tenure was designed to protect faculty members as both researchers and teachers. In the "1940 Statement of Principles on Academic Freedom and Tenure" by the American Association of University Professors (AAUP), we see the following:

> The purpose of this statement is to promote public understanding and support of academic freedom and tenure and agreement upon procedures to ensure them in colleges and universities. Institutions of higher education are conducted for the common good and not to further the interest of either the individual teacher or the institution as a whole. The common good depends upon the free search for truth and its free exposition.
>
> Academic freedom is essential to these purposes and applies to both teaching and research. Freedom in research is fundamental to the advancement of truth. Academic freedom in its teaching aspect is fundamental for the protection of the rights of the teacher in teaching and of the student to freedom in learning.

Similarly, the work of Anne Gere has always combined research and teaching just as it has combined reading and writing. And that is the way forward in advancing the case for liberal arts education in the US today. The championing of teaching the humanities, social sciences, basic sciences, and mathematics—anything that is not directly vocational in approach—has to be a championing of the importance of knowledge creation side by side with teaching. Humanities expertise is specialized expertise as much as expertise in epidemiology or theoretical physics. It is deeply rooted in years of study, with shared references and a critical conversation that can be as specialized as the shared references and conversation of the physical sciences and that is essential to moving forward our knowledge about how the world, and culture, works.

In conjunction with that work of experts talking to other experts, however, is a new focus in the humanities. What many humanists are developing now, and not a moment too soon, is the ability to bridge the gap between specialist humanities expertise and the public need for humanities expertise that make it possible to be an informed member of a shared community. Writing for each other is one thing—advancing scholarship shifts the way disciplines do their work and changes the ways we understand texts, writing habits, reading practices, language acquisition, and more. But writing for everybody else, what we now call the public humanities, is another thing entirely. It calls on us to draw on our deep expertise and use it to shift the way people think about the culture in which they live. We translate our new knowledge, we share our traditions, we invite the public in, we create new knowledge with community partners and learn from them. This, of course, is exactly the kind of translation of expertise we do in our classrooms every day. But when we do that translation in print, or at a public library, or in a book group, for readers and listeners outside the campus, we raise the stakes. We make the case for the value, for the centrality, of reading and writing in and across our communities.

From my position at the MLA, I have seen a shift in recent years in the sense of who is the audience for humanities scholarship. More and more language and literature scholars are moving toward sharing their research with wider audiences, connecting with communities outside higher education, and working with science and technology researchers on their own campuses and beyond. The MLA encourages and facilitates these kinds of expansion of what counts as humanities work, and we're really glad to see it. Writing studies, however, has been way ahead of literary studies here. Writing studies' focus on the process and product of student writing is an inherently generous approach to scholarship, one aimed at generating research results that have a large public impact. And Anne Ruggles Gere's leadership in the MLA, bringing writing studies to the forefront in the organization, has been key in helping push language and literature scholars to think about the value of our scholarship making an impact beyond our subfields.

Writing studies, in the person of Anne Gere, has brought to the MLA a focus on links to secondary school teaching; the impetus to expand the MLA International Bibliography's coverage of rhetoric, composition, and writing studies research; a new understanding of the value of writing-to-learn instruction in majors and fields; and so much more. Our expanded focus on the skills, values, and perspectives learned in language, literature, writing studies, and cultural studies allows us to assert our value in a hostile anti-humanities climate. And our shift toward emphasis on public humanities work enables us to better make a national case for the importance of knowledge creation in reading and writing and language and culture.

Reading and writing have never been more important in our culture. We understand them together, understand that studying or researching one cannot stand without the other. The future of humanities study needs both; it needs the work so ably championed by Anne Gere, and it needs the advocacy of the organizations to which she has so generously given her service. The focus has to be a dual one—on reading and writing, but always as well on research and on teaching. That's the model Anne Gere, in her research, her teaching, and her professional leadership, has set for us. Let's live up to it.

WORKS CITED

Arteaga, Rachel, et al. *Report on English Majors' Career Preparation and Outcomes.* Modern Language Association of America, 2024, https://tinyurl.com/yc5a45yx.

Bradburn, Norman N., et al. *State of the Humanities 2021: Workforce and Beyond.* Humanities Indicators Project / American Academy of Arts and Sciences, 2021, https://tinyurl.com/4r7sj2wj.

Condon, Stephanie. "GOP Debate Fact Check: Was Marco Rubio Right about Welders vs. Philosophers?" *CBS News*, 10 Nov. 2015, https://tinyurl.com/25a8nxxk.

Finley, Ashley P. *The Career-Ready Graduate: What Employers Say about the Difference College Makes.* American Association of Colleges and Universities / Morning Consult, https://tinyurl.com/3z4czec9.

Gere, Anne Ruggles. "Kitchen Tables and Rented Rooms: The Extracurriculum of Composition." *College Composition and Communication*, vol. 45, no. 1, 1994, pp. 75–92, https://doi.org/10.58680/ccc19948799.

———. "Presidential Address 2019–Re-visioning Language, Texts, and Theories." *PMLA*, vol. 134, no. 3, 2019, pp. 450–58. *Cambridge Core*, https://doi.org/10.1632/pmla.2019.134.3.450.

Gere, Anne Ruggles, et al. "Writing and Conceptual Learning in Science: An Analysis of Assignments." *Written Communication*, vol. 36, no. 1, 2019, pp. 99–135, https://doi.org/10.1177/0741088318804820.

Jaschik, Scott. "Obama vs. Art History." *Inside Higher Ed*, 30 January 2014, https://tinyurl.com/4jcpwp3y.

"1940 Statement of Principles on Academic Freedom and Tenure." *American Association of University Professors*, www.aaup.org/report/1940-statement-principles-academic-freedom-and-tenure. Accessed 27 Dec. 2024.

CHAPTER 21.
LISTENING, WHEN THE LISTENING IS HARD

Cheryl Glenn
Penn State University

Heather Brook Adams
University of North Carolina Greensboro

Over the course of her luminous career, Anne Gere has offered the field of rhetoric and writing studies numerous landmark studies, ranging from the history of women's clubs and the evolution of writing groups to ethical hiring (and retention) practices and productive writing pedagogies. Our chapter builds on just one site of Gere's much-heralded scholarship: her groundbreaking explorations of silence and listening as rhetorical strategies. In "Revealing Silence: Rethinking Personal Writing," Gere rues the diminishment if not dismissal of silence in writing studies despite its "productive and empowering" qualities (209). Gere's foray into silence was extended by Cheryl Glenn's development in her book *Unspoken* of a rhetoric of silence as a historically persistent phenomenon (the counterpart of speech), a source of power when deployed across rhetorical situations, and, thus, a means of communication.

The practice of rhetorical silence, however, remains a challenge for those of us who are steeped in Western traditions and belief systems. After all, our spoken language has long been considered a gift from the gods, with Wilhelm von Humboldt assuring us that language is the distinguishing blessing immediately conferred on humans (Isham and Frei 485); Max Picard declaring that it is "language and not silence that makes [us] truly human" (xix); and Thomas Mann arguing that "speech is civilization itself" (518).

If silence has been marked as suspect, listening has been marked as a position of weakness, passivity, even stupidity. Yet Gere has interrogated both rhetorical positions, offering rhetoric and writing studies scholars good reasons to consider them. In her landmark *Writing Groups*, Gere extols listening as an effective method for cultivating responsive writerly practices, one that supports writers as they develop the intellectual capacity of listening to one another and "learn to extract meaning from one another's language" rather than "relying on the teacher [or group leader] to make connections between statements and answer all questions" (105). Such listeners "create meaning through dialogue" among themselves, which enables them to "re-vision their work, improving it substantially" (93). They give their peers' comments "careful attention," "become more willing to take risks with their own language," and ultimately use their deepening listening skills to "engage in productive problem solving" (105).

THE PROMISE OF SILENCE AND LISTENING

Across these works, Gere underscores the fundamental capacities of silence and listening: trusting that others just might have good ideas that may transform one's own thinking and action, quieting one's own anxiety or confidence; opening oneself to communicative discomfort (even confusion); attending to the ideas of others; and collaborating in both shared problem-solving and democratic meaning-making. In short, Gere helps her readers appreciate how listening can serve as the basis for surprisingly successful collaborations and rhetorical engagements.

WHY LISTENING?

To be sure, Gere's early emphases on the significance of productive silence and attentive listening remain relevant, given the ongoing urgency for better communication practices in our classrooms, in our homes, in the workplace, and in our public—and political—lives. The quotidian violence in our schools (from bullying to physical and sexual violence), in our homes (domestic violence of all kinds), and in our civic lives (seemingly unbreachable political polarization, widespread institutional distrust, and merited racial unrest) call for the palliative practice of listening, a rhetorical position animated by the feminist rhetorical theories of the last two decades. For instance, Jacqueline Jones Royster and Gesa E. Kirsch affirm that the ever-developing project of feminist rhetorical studies includes "sharpening rhetorical listening and responding skills" (126), which aligns with the open-ended initiative led by Krista Ratcliffe on the power and potential of rhetorical listening. Developing the ability to remain silent while listening productively might be one of the most necessary and challenging features of a rhetorical education today—one that implicates not only our classroom practices but the rhetorics in which we engage in all parts of our lives.

A commitment to a stance of productive silence or deep listening is, of course, rarely an easy matter, even when people come together in goodwill with an agreement to engage, exchange, collaborate, and problem-solve. Remaining silent when the listening is easy—when we're among like-minded people (listening to Rachel Maddow or Tucker Carlson, for instance)—can affirm our sense of self-righteousness, bolster our feelings of identification with others (and separateness from Others), offer succor to the aggrieved, spark productive emotions that foster collective identity and action, and otherwise bring pleasure. Easy silence and listening might be neither good nor effective listening at all—but experiencing it may encourage us to think of ourselves as good or effective listeners (after all, we have remained silent) rather than alert us to the presence of our confirmation bias or the likelihood that our interlocutors are (helpfully or not, depending on our rhetorical purposes) already like us in important ways.

Easy listening is, well, easy. But hard listening is, well, something else.

Hard Listening

Listening to everyday complaints, worries, pain, anxiety is demanding enough, but "hard listening," when the messages are unsettling, is even more difficult. When we are confronted with bad news, seemingly unreasonable demands, painful or offensive words, we want to talk—not listen or remain silent. Instead of silently considering our lack of patience and stamina, our emotional rigidity, our own (often unacknowledged) feelings of guilt, defensiveness, and anger, our impulses to fix the situation, we want to talk. We want to defend ourselves, critique the other, advise, explain, express our frustrations, compare our own experiences. And little wonder.

After all, our words (not our silence) are our gifts. For most humans, maybe especially for folks like us (scholar-teachers of rhetoric and writing), speaking has always been the cynosure of our efforts, not only our endowment, but our calling. Most of us have been trained to speak up and out, to proclaim our advice (and our innocence), and to explain *our* own emotions, response, rationale, arguments. We struggle to listen. Speaking is our work, even as Mary Oliver reminds us, "To pay attention, this is our endless / and proper work" (264).

This chapter focuses on the rhetorical activity of listening when it's hard. Despite explicit calls by Gere, Glenn, Royster and Kirsch, and, of course, Ratcliffe, research on listening remains fairly new. Few of us in rhetoric and writing studies have concentrated on developing our own listening power, let alone theorized it toward conceptual or pragmatic ends. Ratcliffe demonstrates how listening facilitates identification between self and other. Alli Tharp and Emily Johnston, warning that "not everyone listens the same, or listens at all," scale the work of rhetorical listening to account for possibilities in first-year composition programs, which they offer as an approach to teaching "actionable empathy" (734). And Cristina Ramirez, Ellen Cushman, Phillip Marzluf, Julie Jung, and

Brian Gogan advocate for listening that goes *beyond* the Rogerian rhetoric of "I hear what you're saying" to reach the level of self-reflective meditation of "Why am I so threatened by this speaker's argument?" All of these scholars recognize what Ratcliffe and Kyle Jensen refer to as the "systemic constraints and . . . possibilities of the rhetorical worlds in which they listen and speak" (7).

Deepening our listening skills—especially when the listening is hard—can enrich our strategies for resourceful problem-solving across varying rhetorical situations. It can also, in the process, illustrate the good reasons for taking up such demanding rhetorical work, work that often entails, according to Ratcliffe and Jensen, (1) realizing that one often stops listening when engaging like-minded speakers, (2) clarifying one's own beliefs while listening in disagreement, (3) recognizing that some people act in bad faith, (4) and attending to weariness in body and mind (7–9). In this chapter, then, we explain the dimensions of hard listening, offer strategies for becoming good listeners when the listening is hard, and conclude with the potential rhetorical power of hard listening.

Indeed, hard listening is, well, *hard*.

WHAT HARD LISTENING CAN FEEL LIKE

In preparing for this chapter, Cheryl and Heather kept records of instances of hard listening they found themselves (imperfectly) practicing in their everyday lives. We share the following stories and strategies as a way to reconsider contexts of hard listening and to reconceptualize them not as "destructive collisions" but rather as "entanglements," rich sites of unexpected possibility (Gere, "Presidential" 134).

In the following section, Cheryl recounts a complaint that nearly every WPA (writing program administrator) has heard a version of at least once. Heather follows by recounting her experiences with listening to and through shame in unfamiliar and uncomfortable work in a community-partner-led writing collaboration.

Cheryl's Experience

The most demanding listening I've done of late was in response to a complaint that I tried *very hard* not to take personally. After stepping into my office on campus and before I'd gotten off my coat, hat, gloves, scarf, and down vest, I was visited by a new adjunct instructor, whom I'd been wanting to see. He told me he'd recently seen our department head because he was so ticked about having to take our year-long teaching practicum and having to follow the protocols of the Program in Writing and Rhetoric (PWR), a nearly 20,000-student writing program that I direct. Requiring him to do so was disrespectful, he said, and "I do not condone nor deserve this kind of disrespect."

The previous semester, he had walked out of our practicum (admittedly, the graduate-student presentation was not very good), and he hadn't returned this semester, refusing my several email invitations to meet for coffee so that I could listen to his concerns and maybe try to address them. You see, I was trying to relieve his pain, resolve his complaint—all the while thinking about me, me, me in trying to relieve my own discomfort. Yes, I wanted to hear more of what he had to say when we met, yet somehow, I wanted to find the space to talk about *my* confusion and anger and to offer *my* intentions and rationale—to defend myself! But I listened, remembering Deborah Tannen's dictum that people who come into a conversation with the most real-world power tend to display the signs of that power within the conversation by asserting their own position rather than deferring to the position of the other, by speaking rather than listening (231). But listening, according to *my* own dictum, does not guarantee any shift in those power dynamics.

This man went on to tell me that he felt denigrated by the graduate students involved in the practicum, that his previous teaching experience had been invalidated, that he had much experience teaching the modes, and that the entire PWR lacked direction, purpose, and logic. Ouch! So much of what he said just isn't true to me. But that doesn't matter, does it? He needed to complain. I needed to listen, just listen. I needed the practice. Heck, I still need the practice because I need to tell you that we don't teach "the modes"; we focus on genres. The PWR has direction, purpose, logic. I want to defend and explain. But more important was listening, paying attention.

After all, as Simone Weil reminds us, "L'Attention est la forme la plus rare et la plus pure de la générosité" ("Attention is the rarest and purest form of generosity"; Weil and Bousquet 18; my trans.). We all need that attention.

Was his speaking an instance of "invitational rhetoric" that leads to mutual participation and understanding, as Karen Foss, Sonja Foss, and Cindy Griffin have taught us? Nope. Was this an instance of Diana Mutz's "hearing the other side" that develops greater self-understanding, understanding of others, and tolerance? Nope. Was this an opportunity to relinquish persuasion and control and to coalesce, to come together in a moment of inherent worth, equality, and empowered action? Yes—but not for him. Did he want any explanations about the PWR, its philosophies, practices, rhetorical foundation, logic? Nope. Did he want to unpack any of his assertions (which felt like accusations to me) to see if together we could translate his complaints into actionable change? Nope. He wanted me—as Mikki Kendall succinctly puts it—to "STFU and listen." And I did, all the while struggling with my instincts to say "Yes, but. . . ."

Surely, I'm not the only person who, instead of remaining silent and purposefully listening, too often listens to detect openings for talking in these situations, for trying to fix a situation. Isn't doing so considered to be a "natural" response to someone else's pain—as though *our* words can relieve *their* pain? As though our words can make *it* stop? Make *them* stop?

Heather's Experience

I have been challenged to rethink how I listen as I participate as an academic partner with a group of harm reduction activists—people whose grassroots efforts aim to reduce the negative consequences of (in this case) drug use in ways that do not demand abstinence and that do affirm others' inherent worth. Among other activities, this group develops and delivers trainings to help professionals (including care providers) identify how their implicit (or explicit) biases toward people who use drugs contribute to stigmatizing attitudes and behaviors. Biases have consequences; they can, for instance, result in situations where people who use drugs are discouraged from seeking care or situations where a parent loses custody of a child, even if they are making reasonable—and objectively good—parenting choices. The group shares personal stories about the struggles of surviving and parenting—stories of near-death overdose scares and stories that depict the taboo, if not largely unconceivable, daily realities of being a good parent who uses drugs. Given my research on shame, stigma, and pregnancy, I was invited to collaborate on a grant sponsoring this participant-led research.

Although I tried to listen carefully during our early web meetings, my mind was full of nervous chatter. *Did the others in the meeting know why I was there? Would they see me as an uninformed and troublesome interloper? What would my contributions to this important work be, given that I had not participated in harm reduction activism? How might I be of use to this group when their expertise is so unlike my own?* Although I was not searching for gaps in conversation to fill with my own voice, I was letting my insecurities usurp my ability to be present and listen. I wanted to respond with understanding and care, but as a newcomer to this group, I lacked the language to do so. Instead of settling into active and open listening, I worried about how I could be a useful ally.

In some ways, this anxious non-listening was noise that distracted me from the deeper listening challenge at hand. Unsurprisingly, given the aims of this group, I grappled with my own biases as I experienced the discomfort (in my thoughts, in my body) of hearing stories that dug into the realities of pregnant and parenting people who use drugs. I had to—and to be honest, still have to—wrestle with the incompatibility of the narrative of (bad, immoral, irresponsible) "drug user" that is lodged in my mind and the stories of parental joy, care, and love that some of the stories convey. One such story depicts a mother and her sister being high and safely playing a tabletop game with the woman's gleeful daughter, who was thrilled to have so much uninterrupted time with the adults. The story leaves no room for the ubiquitous characterization of drug users—zombie-like, not present—especially because it depicts a deep and loving connection between a mother and her daughter. It is a hard story to listen to because hearing it without objection feels like an act of condoning what can feel like—what many of us tell ourselves is—unassailably bad behavior. Hearing one team member's story of anger at a friend's overdose—ire that comes from this not being the first time that the friend nearly died—is hard because I struggle to even imagine what such a situation would look like apart from some dramatized depiction on Netflix.

In so many of the group's stories, the "good" person/"bad" person tropes that characterize drug war and moral panic messaging fall away as listeners get glimpses of what bias and struggle look like from within this harm reduction community. I ask myself, *How can this horror be someone's reality? Who should have my empathy here?* My reactions range from surprise and disbelief to confusion. Intellectually, I am pushing myself not to judge, but the story's compelling narrative is meant to force listeners to grapple with these very challenges of bias. The story is doing its job. Listening is very hard.

How ironic. In my effort to support this group—a group whose primary goal is to explore with others the value of listening through hard stories and putting that listening to work—I have shown up as a bad listener.

It has been relatively easy to share a sense of frustration within the group as we agree that *other* listeners, those outside our team, are resistant to what the story-share method offers. One hospital resident participating in a training session disrupted the workshop by suggesting that a person who uses drugs could in no way be a good mother. This vocal resistance to listening made me mad. How could the resident encounter these brave, heart-breaking stories (read aloud by presenters of our group) and then vocally and publicly reject a story and its teller? My anger lingers, but it also forces me to do the harder work of confronting my own (undisruptive) resistance when listening to these stories. Through hard listening, I gain a deeper understanding, a fuller sense of how stigma propagates, lingers, harms. Such insights are part of the ongoing labor of being a listening ally, offering opportunities to extend our group's shared work and aims.

Together, we—Cheryl and Heather—contemplate these experiences in an effort to recognize and render more legible these various experiences of hard listening. Moving from recognition to responsive rhetorical action, we offer three considerations emerging from this collaborative reflection.

THREE STRATEGIES FOR LISTENING WHEN LISTENING IS HARD

Listening in Neutral

As we have learned in sharing these representative experiences, hard listening comes in many forms and varieties. Our own attention to the challenges of listening enables us to appreciate even more situations and contexts in which listening is hard. Our attunement, then, leads us to explore the range of *ways* in which these situations are thorny "entanglements," each with their own dynamics and (frequently) power differentials that prompt us to reflect on *how* we listen. Cheryl could have written about the teaching faculty member who came to her office to talk about her long-depressed adult child who had recently died by suicide or about the phone call from a dear friend whose middle-school niece was cut down by a speeding car when walking in a crosswalk at dusk and who is now facing a long recovery from severe brain trauma. Or she could have written about her good colleague, whose tumor was recently debulked, who called to talk about being suddenly moved out of her clinical trial at Johns Hopkins and into brain-stem surgery because her cancer has spread. Perhaps the only reliable gauge of hard listening is our own discomfort.

Listening can be hard, as Heather's example illustrates, when we listeners don't feel qualified or worthy of listening to such measures of pain, suffering, and shame. Instead of quieting ourselves, sitting silent with our discomfort, we listen only to the nattering of our insecure selves. Our negative self-talk is unproductive. More, it can take up the listening space that could be held for others' voices. Heather could have shared stories of other compromised listening situations: A family member's political aside about the harm educated "elites" are inflicting "on" the US feels like a personal barb directed at her. The literature colleague's invocation of a dystopian future where everyone has to teach writing stings because it suggests hierarchy—until Heather realizes that it probably reflects that person's (justified) fears. In these cases, a defensive mental script, a (troublesome) sense of having already reached an impasse, fills the space of listening. In other cases, we worry about what on earth we can say instead of sitting and listening to stories of grief and struggle. Each of those examples of opportunities to practice listening-when-it's-hard was in response to people's biases, to their sharing of problems, to their unloading of their pain, sorrow, fear, and shame. Maybe if we think of this genre as neutral, we can listen. After all, it asks only that we bear witness to another's pain and injustice and to acknowledge the other's knowledge of their own reality.

In some instances, though, listening seems loaded, not neutral at all, as in Cheryl's example of the disgruntled new teacher who was leveling a complaint or Heather's example of a colleague whose frustration seemingly reifies divisions and hierarchies within our academic field. Whether fair or not, a complaint often calls on us to listen to ideas that we consider to be wrongheaded, an accusation, a poor use of our time, or our problem to solve. Maybe we should work to consider the complaint a neutral genre, to consider the complainant nothing more than a conduit of information rather than doing what we too often do: nullifying the complaint while rendering the *complainant* the actual, negative problem. How we listen to a complaint, a complainant, matters. If we do not listen, we might save time, but we waste rhetorical possibility and opportunity. After all, the richest and most complex of questions, Adrienne Rich reminds us, is "what do we know when we know your story?" (*Arts* 155).

Appreciating (and Practicing) Silence

If we cannot actively listen rhetorically, then we can choose to occupy an expectant, intentional, and open listening-silence. When we stop talking, stop defending, stop letting our internal chatter occupy all the rhetorical airspace, perhaps we create an aperture for more gentleness, more possibility-rich outcomes. Our silent listening with kindness, maybe even compassion, lowers our defenses, helps us see things differently, even to hear the previously unheard. What is at stake in any silent listening is understanding, coming to accept what has been up until now unheard, maybe even unthinkable or unbearable. Such silence means, "I am here for you." Or as Rich suggests, "The earth [is] already crazed / *Let me take your hand*" ("Terza Rima" 877).

To appreciate the value of silence, however, we must also actively *practice* holding silence. For those of us trained in Western traditions, such practice is an effortful activity that can disabuse us of our learned desire to respond, to disrupt (uncomfortable) silence, and to talk over others' voices and ideas. Perhaps we can bring this attention to silence into our personal conversations, the discussions around our tables be they kitchen or conference room, and the interactions in our classrooms. We can also seek out opportunities to scale our practices of active listening with attention to silence. For instance, activist-teacher Loretta J. Ross has leveraged decades of organizing experience and wisdom to articulate the value—and needed dispositions and skills—of "calling in" culture, which provides an alternative to blame-focused "call-out" or "cancel" culture ("Loretta"). Part of Ross' work has been to create and offer a low-cost "calling in" course that includes "learning labs" ("Calling In Course"). Devoted to "explor[ing] challenging questions" and moving "from theory to action," these labs ask participants to actively listen and to avoid participating in any sort of cross talk, or the talkative habit of verbalizing one's own connection to or take on another person's comment.[1] The course privileges the collective experience of remaining quiet, of holding space for others to share, and of listening openly as an expected disposition.

Engaging in these activities in community experientially demonstrates the sway many of us feel toward talk and away from intentional listening silence. When people choose to be silent together, they may not be choosing to (individually) meditate in the presence of others. Instead, practices of collective listening silence can encourage us to listen for knowledge with *and* beyond our talkative minds—and in "holistic and kinesthetic" (or embodied) ways (Searl). Adopting some regularity in the practice of occupying silence holds great promise for developing the skills of hard listening. We might consider how such practice is similar to the many other habits of mind and rhetorical dispositions (such as contributing to discussion, inventing arguments, developing main ideas, and responding to our own and others' writing) that we center in our pedagogy.

ANTICIPATING IMPERFECT LISTENING

Indeed, listening is critical to establishing identification, invitation, mutual understanding, maybe even mutual respect and trust. And listening is foremost an act of compassion, especially when it's hard, when we find ourselves bearing witness to someone's suffering, shame, or complaint, someone who might be taking a risk by speaking. Still, the need is for us to be fully present to the measure of their pain without trying to point out the silver lining, their misperception, our own fragility. The loving action that constitutes such listening establishes a mutual relationship, if only temporarily. We can recognize another's insights as well as their wrong perceptions, as we come to realize our own wrong perceptions, too—about the issue, the other person, ourselves.

Listening that is hard demands that we release hold of our desire for perfection (in ourselves and in others) and embrace our human fallibility and propensity for imperfection in our rhetorical encounters. Truly listening requires that we approach others *and* ourselves with a sense of humility and a willingness to "think again" (Grant). Or as adrienne maree brown advises, truly listening means that we take time *after* we have (imperfectly) listened to formulate reflective and self-directed questions, questions that help us better formulate listening as a practice in and of community (54–55). After all, what other option do we have, save hunkering down in our staid positions and reveling in our echo chambers?

Listening is hard because our gift of speech is also our limitation. As Kenneth Burke reminds us, we are "symbol-using, symbol-making, and symbol-misusing"

---

1   Heather participated in a Calling in Course in August 2023. See https://www.lorettajross.com/callingin-descriptions for more information on the course and learning labs.

beings (60) who, though "goaded by the spirit of hierarchy," are "rotten" in our pursuit for order and ideal (70). To be sure, it does not feel good, right, or useful to admit that to show up for the hard work of listening means doing so inelegantly. We know that in embracing this work, we will trip up and make mistakes along the way. By foregrounding our human imperfection, we set the stage for listening work that is effortful if not impeccable and that leaves space for development, growth, and (necessary) introspective reflection.

These strategies are not exhaustive (as feminists, we resist closure and certitude) but they are sites of possibility. We offer them in the spirit of Gere, whose careful contemplation of writers and contexts in which their writing develops encourages her readers to assess and reassess practices and dispositions from the classroom and from everyday life. So, too, have we considered the all-too-familiar experience of listening-when-it's-hard (in the light of contemporary scholarship) in order to recommend possibilities, practices, and dispositions for attention-giving.

CONCLUSION

Yes, it can be an honor to be entrusted with someone's pain, their confidences, their frustrations—their complaints. But that does not make it easy, especially when we cannot fix things, when we may be part and parcel of the complaint, when we are being asked to listen *only*. Not to explain, not to advise, not to solve, not to brainstorm. Just listen. As Native American Earl Ortiz says, "Be quiet. Listen. And you will learn" (qtd. in Glenn 142).

From Cheryl's reflection on a disgruntled instructor leveling complaints to Heather's reflection on the stories shared by harm reduction activists, the examples in this chapter remind the two of us of the difficult and vulnerable work of speaking up in ways that call for hard listening. The messages of shame and sadness that we encounter are, after all, a part of and not apart from the speaker, the person who wants us to listen. Hard messages might reveal a person's anxiety or fear—at least if we are patient and attentive enough to consider this possibility. That speaker may also be reexperiencing the injustices, harms, wrongs, and other negative emotions that constitute the problem or complaint itself. They might find themselves sharing their pain with a listener who is not just a listening ear but is—directly or indirectly—a source of that very same distress. In speaking up, a speaker may court risks—dangers that could jeopardize their status or reputation or that may exert an emotional toll on those to whom they speak. And such speakers can pay a heavy price for choosing to voice their troubles, especially if they end up losing—status, a job, a home, a life—because they did not remain silent. They can be judged unworthy of a listen, incredible, illogical, uninformed, ill-fitting—they are whiners and complainers. And they can be undone by a judgment—our judgment.

After all, there is an immense difference between having permission, a platform, to speak and enjoying the hope that someone might actually listen to you.

So how we listen matters.

When we listen with kindness, maybe even compassion, when we lower our defenses, we can begin to see things differently, to notice the previously unseen. This is listening-silence that constitutes bearing witness, which means simply taking the person's hand, walking them home, giving them the psychic companionship they know they need, that they are asking for specifically. Such silent listening does not mean taking on their emotions but rather standing silently with them, seeing them, hearing them, respecting their story. What is at stake in any listening is understanding. Such silence is hard, as is the listening. But when we can stop talking and listen, something of the other person's stance seeps into us; we can begin to understand.

When we practice such compassionate listening, we are creating an imaginative space that opens up possibilities between two people or within a group, possibilities of invitation into the future, transformations of understanding and an expanded sense of self. Anne Lamott reminds us that most of us are stripped down to the bone, living along a thin sliver of what we think we can bear and control. But bearing witness to some one or some thing—when the listening is hard—can nudge us into baby steps of expansion, to an expanded sense of self, of understanding.

Let's face it, it's ridiculous how hard life can be. Because it's one of the most powerful statements ever, we end with Ram Dass's brilliant meditation: "When all is said and done, we are just walking each other home" (qtd. in Lamott, 109).

WORKS CITED

brown, adrienne maree. *We Will Not Cancel Us: And Other Dreams of Transformative Justice.* AK Press, 2020.

Burke, Kenneth. *On Symbols and Society.* Edited by Joseph R. Gusfield, U of Chicago P, 1989.

Cushman, Ellen. "Toward a Rhetoric of Self-Representation: Identity Politics in Indian Country and Rhetoric and Composition." *College Composition and Communication,* vol. 60, no. 2, 2008, pp. 321–65, https://doi.org/10.58680/ccc20086869.

Foss, Sonja K., and Cindy L. Griffin. "Beyond Persuasion: A Proposal for an Invitational Rhetoric." *Communication Monographs,* vol. 62, no. 1, 1995, pp. 2–18, https://doi.org/10.1080/03637759509376345.

Gere, Anne Ruggles. "Presidential Address 2019–Re-visioning Language, Texts, and Theories." *PMLA,* vol. 134, no. 3, 2019, pp. 450–58. *Cambridge Core,* https://doi.org/10.1632/pmla.2019.134.3.450.

———. "Revealing Silence: Rethinking Personal Writing." *College Composition and Communication,* vol. 53, no. 2, 2001, pp. 203–23, https://doi.org/10.58680/ccc20011448.

———. *Writing Groups: History Theory, and Implications.* Southern Illinois UP, 1987.

Glenn, Cheryl. *Unspoken: A Rhetoric of Silence.* Southern Illinois UP, 2004.

Gogan, Brian. "Laughing Whiteness: Pixies, Parody, and Perspectives." *The Comedy of Dave Chappelle: Critical Essays,* edited by K. A. Wisniewski, McFarland, 2009, pp. 72–85.

Grant, Adam. *Think Again: The Power of Knowing What You Don't Know.* Viking, 2021.

Isham, Howard, and Tamra Frei. "von Humboldt, Wilhelm." *Encyclopedia of Philosophy.* 2nd ed., vol. 4, edited by Donald M. Borchert, Macmillan Reference, 2006, pp. 484–86. *Internet Archive,* https://tinyurl.com/ydt9pta4.

Jung, Julie. *Revisionary Rhetoric, Feminist Pedagogy, and Multigenre Texts.* Southern Illinois UP, 2005.

Kendall, Mikki. *Hood Feminism: Notes from the Women That a Movement Forgot.* Penguin, 2020.

Lamott, Anne. *Almost Everything: Notes on Hope.* Riverhead Books, 2018.

Mann, Thomas. *The Magic Mountain.* Translated by H. T. Lowe-Porter, Modern Library, 1927. *Internet Archive,* https://tinyurl.com/yn2fz5m3.

Marzluf, Phillip P. "Originating Difference in Rhetorical Theory: Lord Monboddo's Obsession with Language Origins Theory." *Rhetoric Society Quarterly,* vol. 38, no. 4, 2008, pp. 385–407, https://doi.org/10.1080/02773940802167591.

Mutz, Diana C. *Hearing the Other Side: Deliberative versus Participatory Democracy.* Cambridge University P, 2006. *Cambridge Core,* https://doi.org/10.1017/CBO9780511617201.

Oliver, Mary. "Yes! No!" *Devotions: The Selected Poems of Mary Oliver.* Penguin, 2017, p. 264.

Picard, Max. *The World of Silence.* Translated by Stanley Godwin, Gateway, 1988.

Ramirez, Cristina D. "Forging a Mestiza Rhetoric: Mexican Women Journalists' Role in the Construction of a National Identity." *College English,* vol. 71, no. 6, 2009, pp. 606–29, https://doi.org/10.58680/ce20097171.

Ratcliffe, Krista. *Rhetorical Listening: Identification, Gender, Whiteness.* Southern Illinois UP, 2005.

Ratcliffe, Krista, and Kyle Jensen. *Rhetorical Listening in Action: A Concept-Tactic Approach.* Parlor Press, 2022.

Rich, Adrienne. *Arts of the Possible: Essays and Conversations.* Revised ed., W.W. Norton and Company, 2002.

———. "Terza Rima." *Collected Poems: 1950–2012.* W. W. Norton and Company, 2016, pp. 877–84.

Ross, Loretta J. "Calling In Course." *Lorossta Consulting,* 2024, lorettajross.com/calling-in-descriptions.

———. "Loretta J. Ross." *Lorossta Consulting,* 2024, lorettajross.com/.

Royster, Jacqueline Jones, and Gesa E. Kirsch. "Ethics and Action: Feminist Perspectives on Facing the Grand Challenges of Our Times." *After Plato: Rhetoric, Ethics, and the Teaching of Writing,* edited by John Duffy and Lois Agnew, Utah State UP, 2020, pp.117–40. *JSTOR,* www.jstor.org/stable/j.ctv13qfw0s.10.

Searl, Stanford J. "Words, Silence, and the Body in Quaker Worship." *Friends Journal,* 1 March 2011, friendsjournal.org/3011029/.

Tannen, Deborah. *Talking from 9 to 5: Women and Men in the Workplace: Language, Sex and Power.* Avon Books, 1994.

Tharp, Alli, and Emily Johnston. "Actionable Empathy through Rhetorical Listening: A Possible Future for First-Year Composition." *College Composition and Communication,* vol. 74, no. 4, 2023, pp. 731–57, https://doi.org/10.58680/ccc202332524.

Weil, Simone, and Joë Bousquet. *Correspondance 1942.* Editions l'Age d'Homme, 1982.

CHAPTER 22.

INTIMATE PRACTICES FOR NEOLIBERAL AND PANDEMIC TIMES

Margaret K. Willard-Traub
University of Michigan-Dearborn

Deborah Minter
University of Nebraska-Lincoln

Recent scholarship in writing studies has documented the impact of neoliberalism on the academic community (Stenberg; Welch and Scott). Neoliberalism, as we're defining it here, is "an order of normative reason that, when it becomes ascendant, takes shape as a governing rationality extending a specific formulation of economic values, practices, and metrics to every dimension of human life" (Brown 30). Neoliberalism, thus functioning as an ideology with profound consequences for human communities, calls for an understanding of its impact and potential responses.

We encounter neoliberalism in all aspects of our lives: from our work to our private lives, from the informational media we consume to entertainment media, and increasingly in the public sphere, within educational institutions, and at all levels of government. Within university administrative contexts this mode of reasoning often is accompanied by dwindling budgets, retrenchment, and top-down decision-making. Questions accompanying the retrenchment and redistribution of resources within academic contexts include: What kinds of courses are most "valuable"? What is the value-added worth of one major over another? What is the return-on-investment of a particular major, or of a college degree itself? What areas of professional, academic endeavor merit serious investment by the institution? What are the political risks and costs (in terms of public support) of reaffirming faculty governance vs. top-down administrative decision-making? What is, in dollar terms, the value attached to universities and public institutions broadly? All of these questions pre-date, but have been re-emphasized since, the beginning of the COVID-19 pandemic, which put additional stressors—logistical, health-related, and especially financial—on institutions of higher education nationally.

Given this economic framing, in our own experiences we have observed that the academic, neoliberal context is characterized on multiple levels by four kinds of dynamics: 1) competition as a defining element of professional relationships; 2) the pressure for efficiency; 3) an emphasis on individual (and often private) decision-making or achievement, suppressing collective or collaborative actions which are often cast in terms of "redundancies"; and 4) an impulse toward "standardizing" decision-making processes, such as decision-making focused on the distribution—or redistribution—of limited resources. All of these dynamics discourage the kind of reflection (and supporting organizational structures for reflection) that leads to the cultural work of challenging institutional inequities and forging new practices.

As we search for new ways to engage with the neoliberal pressures on agency that confound our work, we believe that looking back on U.S. clubwomen's work may help us imagine strategies for productive leadership in these neoliberal times. In this chapter we examine two moments of administrative challenge during which neoliberal assumptions come to the fore and suggest how faculty's and administrators' responses to these challenges might be informed by the insights of Anne Ruggles Gere's scholarship on U.S. women's clubs at the turn of the 20th century. We draw on scenarios from our home institutions in order to explore the dynamics of neoliberalism on our campuses and the efforts at collective agency to address those dynamics. Ultimately, we focus especially on the promise of critical reflection, reimagined as a collaborative and public strategy for leadership in the increasingly corporatized and neoliberal higher educational context in which we find ourselves.

Within neoliberal contexts authoritarian perspectives "exploit [challenges or crises] in order to consolidate power" (Snyder 103). Even in the absence of such exploitation, however, real or perceived crises actually increase our reliance on others for sharing responsibilities and resources. Yet the pressures of efficiency and competition, made manifest especially through eroding resources and streamlined reporting structures, promote an understanding of neoliberal expertise as solitary, even unitary—just the kind of dynamic that succeeds in propagating a cycle of competition and individualism. Within such a context, deans, for example, may frown on the distribution of course releases or other support to multiple faculty, seeing such distribution as promoting "redundancy" rather than supporting distributed leadership. Such a framing makes even more difficult the pursuit of collaborative, reflective work, as individuals are increasingly siloed into narrowly defined roles and job descriptions. At the same time, any decision-making that might benefit from collective, faculty-administration reflection—reflection that mobilizes affect and results in shifts in the institutional culture—is moved to strictly administrative (or staff) oversight.

Specifically, it is the cultural and affective or emotional work that 19th- and 20th-century women's clubs achieved over time, and which Gere explores at length, that is most significant for thinking through many of the challenges inherent in a 21st-century academy profoundly shaped by neoliberalism as well as by lingering effects of the pandemic. Furthermore, these women's clubs illustrate the reflective and collaborative strategies that faculty and administrators might adopt to address neoliberal challenges. Gere writes:

> Women's clubs were part of public life, but as intermediate institutions located between the family and the state, they also fostered intimacy among members. That is, clubs had political as well as personal dimensions, and literacy figured prominently in both. Although clubs occupied a subordinate political position, they offered strong and creative resistance to that subordination through literacy practices that cultivated the making of meaning in the company of others. At the same time that clubwomen used literacy to resist the limitations, distortions, and denigrations imposed on them, they used it to develop strong affective ties. Literacy is, as Roger Chartier has observed, at once a private, hidden practice and manifestation of power, "power more effective than that of public office," and clubwomen used this power in their cultural work on behalf of the nation and themselves. (13)

We propose that the leadership needed to interrogate the status quo of power and control in the neoliberal university must attend to both the cultural (political) and affective (personal) dimensions of academic life. Such leadership draws on Gere's "ideas and analytical perspectives which are capable of deconstructing [institutional] interests and political processes" (Reynolds and Vince 4)—at times directly challenging long-standing assumptions about what's "best" for the university while simultaneously having the potential to build personal bonds between individuals (both faculty and administrators alike).

Effective leadership in the 21st-century neoliberal university includes personal as well as political dimensions. In this chapter we use personal experience and observation culled from our respective institutional contexts as sources of knowledge-making and analysis, an approach affirmed in much of Anne Gere's scholarship. Such experience and observation very frequently (though not always) mobilize literate acts which challenge prevailing ideologies and help to form affective bonds within a community. These literate acts may take a range of forms and formats, from targeted email communications to faculty handbooks to policy statements and even mission statements (or the critique of mission statements). Due to workplace climates (including in higher education) "which are increasingly governed by risk aversion, fear of blame and economic stringency" (Fook et al. 2), however, such literate acts of leadership as those we describe in the following are increasingly rare. But they are necessary for maintaining the integrity of, among other principles, academic freedom and for pushing forward the internal, cultural progress of universities, which is required to maintain the integrity of the research and teaching enterprises. These literate acts of leadership are also necessary for communicating to the larger public the goals and value of higher education more broadly.

PROTEST AND AFTERMATH AT THE UNIVERSITY OF NEBRASKA-LINCOLN

The first scenario we consider took place at the University of Nebraska-Lincoln (UNL), the state's flagship campus. In late August 2017, a small group of protesters assembled outside the student union where an undergraduate student was recruiting students to form a campus chapter of Turning Point USA (TPUSA). The undergraduate began to film the protest, and one of the protesters, a graduate student who was also employed as a lecturer, began a verbal exchange with the undergraduate that grew heated. According to an American Association of University Professors (AAUP) investigative report, the protest ended shortly thereafter when the undergraduate, who was upset by the confrontation, packed up her table and left (Monnier et al. sec. 2). As the report notes, the undergraduate sent the video she had taken to a TPUSA colleague shortly after the protest ended, and "Within a few hours, Campus Reform, a conservative student news outlet, and similar websites posted the video taken by Ms. Mullen," the undergraduate student (sec. 2). The follow-up to this event lays bare the challenges of post-secondary leadership in neoliberal times in which practices of shared governance are challenged by a tendency toward privatizing and streamlining decision-making and by a privileging of efficiency. In this particular case, as well, we'll explore the important place of affect and collective reflection in this work of standing ground and rebounding from a violation of trust—intimate practices for neoliberal times.

Perhaps not surprisingly, representations of this conflict (and comments about it) began circulating on social media within 48 hours. Numerous published accounts of this incident and its aftermath provide details, but—in broad strokes—the graduate student/lecturer was removed from her classroom teaching duties, initially for her own and her students' safety (Kolowich; Glass; Schleck). According to the AAUP report on the incident, there was considerable media coverage, including an opinion piece published in a local newspaper by three

Nebraska state legislators alleging that the university was hostile toward conservative students and insinuating that the investigation of this incident was dishonest, and an open records request from the Nebraska Republican Party which surfaced a set of email messages between a current and former university administrator in which they worried about the climate on campus for conservative students (Mennier et al. sec. 2). In the midst of this swirl of publicity, the university was also facing the possibility of severe budget cuts as the state government was facing a very large tax revenue shortfall. Eventually, the graduate student/lecturer was informed that she would retain her stipend and benefits but she would not be permitted to resume teaching in the spring semester because the university anticipated further threats to her safety (Erdman, qtd. in Mennier et al. sec. 2). In essence, her removal from the classroom would extend to the end of her contract.

By the time the AAUP imposed censure on the administration at UNL in 2018, faculty had repeatedly and collectively signaled its disagreement with the administration's handling of this case. As early as a September 5, 2017, meeting of the Faculty Senate, one senator took the floor during the open mic time and drew the faculty senate's attention to the incident which had begun to garner local news coverage ("UNL" [September] sec. 7.4). On October 3, 2017, UNL Chancellor Ronnie Green made a routine appearance at the faculty senate meeting, but it was his first address to the senate on this topic since the incident ("UNL" [October] sec. 3.0).

A look at the October 3 minutes provides an interesting representation of the dynamics of collective reflection as a feature of shared governance. As the minutes state, Chancellor Green "reminded the Senate to not believe everything that people have heard or read about the way things have been handled in regards to the incident that occurred on August 25. He noted that the university has dealt with the issue in an appropriate and private manner although others have tried to make it a public issue" ("UNL" [October] sec. 3.0). One faculty member asked "if at some point the true facts of what happened at the August 25 incident will be made [public] to some subset of the faculty" to which Chancellor Green responded that "some of the information is confidential because it is a personnel issue" ("UNL" [October] sec. 3.0). In these earliest public exchanges, we see calls from faculty for a less neoliberal and more collective approach to due process—one that involves faculty review. In addition, we see a warning about the dangers of "trusting" circulating news stories. Ironically, rebuilding trust among faculty and administrators is exactly the cultural work that the campus will have to undertake in the aftermath of the lecturer's eventual dismissal following her political activity on campus.

Before turning to an account of the collective work that has seemed crucial to rebuilding trust, it is important to note neoliberal dynamics at play in this controversy. Most pronounced is the chancellor's relegation of this decision to a private, legal matter rather than a collective concern of the faculty. It is this tension (between privatization and a more collective deliberation at the heart of shared governance) that vexes public colleges and universities as they pursue shared governance in an increasingly neoliberal environment. The political stakes, of course, complicated this moment even further: State legislators were weighing in; state-aided budgets were at risk. Intimate practices for these neoliberal times require that we recognize the affective experiences that are inevitably tied to such high stakes—the sense of threat, perhaps unexpected, as a student embarks on their first effort at political work involving recruiting other students and facing resistance; the sense of threat experienced by an individual instructor faced with an organization such as TPUSA that publishes a "professor watch list" designed to intimidate; the sense of political threat to the autonomy of the post-secondary institution as legislators publicly (mis)represent the experience of students on campus and call for reduced public support of the campus; the disappointment of a governing body denied insight into the dispensation of a case that *feels like* the disciplining of a teacher who exercised her right to free speech in a public space that happened to be on campus (despite its characterization by the institution as an issue of safety).

Among the events that played out in the wake of the graduate student/lecturer's removal from the classroom in 2017 was a meeting between university administrators and three state senators who had called for the lecturer's termination. One of the senators asked the university to consult with the Foundation for Individual Rights in Education (FIRE), assuming (presumably) that the organization would identify the lecturer's speech as intimidating or silencing by its intensity. In a letter to the university's chancellor, Adam Steinbaugh, a senior program officer with the organization, instead argued for the reinstatement of the lecturer, writing in defense of speech protected by the first amendment: "'Words,'" he wrote, quoting from the case of *Cohen v. California*, "'are often chosen as much for their emotive as their cognitive force'" (7). He went on to note, "The university can ask, but it cannot *require*, students and faculty to be polite when confronted with expression they find to be morally repugnant" (7).

Interestingly, only a few days earlier, another letter was also in circulation. Posted to the Nebraska Chapter of the AAUP's website and delivered to the University of Nebraska Board of Regents, the letter begins with the following lines:

> We are concerned that at the highest levels of the University of Nebraska system, decisions involving the future of the University are being made without transparency or proper governance and under improper exertions of influence by the

legislative and executive branches of the state government. We fear that financial hostage-taking by members of the state government will result in changes by the administration in the intellectual offerings of the University and opportunities for our students. We believe it is imperative to express our alarm now, before irrevocable damage is done to the mission of the university and the value it contributes to the state of Nebraska. (Schleck et al.)

Here, too, the tone carries an emotional charge in terms of "fear" and "alarm" that is sustained throughout the letter. This tone helps to amplify the convictions the letter writers seek to convey—that the work of a university and the free-speech rights of campus community members are settled law and norms that should not be violated. The cultural work of the letter, though, allowed the faculty from across the University of Nebraska system's four campuses (including the campus at the center of the controversy) to identify collectively with the shared principles expressed in the letter and with each other. More than three hundred signatures were collected in the three weeks between the removal of the lecturer from the classroom and the December 2017 Board of Regents meeting where the letter was read aloud.

In one way, the letter might be seen as a failure in the sense that the lecturer was not reinstated and the administration gave no ground on allowing any kind of peer review of this decision to remove a teacher from the classroom (Monnier et al. sec. 4). That said, the letter codified the commitments of the signers and, as it circulated, drew attention to the principles at stake in this decision. It also helped to clarify, for faculty on UNL's campus, needed changes to the bylaws which would make clear that reassignment to non-teaching duties through the end of one's contract amounts to a suspension from teaching and, thus, should be grounds for filing a due-process grievance on campus. (Administrators had argued that the graduate student/lecturer wasn't hurt by this employment action because she continued to be employed. She had only been reassigned to non-teaching duties.)

Ultimately the administration and a subset of faculty did work together to revise the bylaws concerning major reassignments through the end of one's contract. This change to the bylaws was significant in the AAUP's decision to remove the institution from censure in 2021. In addition, the chancellor and members of his senior leadership team participated in a professionally-moderated retreat with members of the faculty senate executive committee that was focused on clarifying shared commitments to principles of due process and shared governance—a retreat in which one of the co-authors participated.

A LITERATE ACT OF LEADERSHIP AT THE UNIVERSITY OF MICHIGAN-DEARBORN

While the prior example explores efforts at and deferments of collective reflection on a very public moment involving the University of Nebraska faculty senate and other constituents on campus, the next scenario considers a literate action taken by the faculty senate of the University of Michigan-Dearborn (UM-D) in response to a top-down (classically neoliberal) administrative decision which significantly undermined trust between the chancellor's office and the faculty while also threatening the principles of shared governance. This literate response arguably fostered "intimacy among [faculty] members," and had "political as well as personal dimensions" (Gere 13) that contributed (along with other factors) to changes in the campus culture.

In early June of 2021 the faculty senate of the UM-D campus sent a letter signed by 160 faculty members to the campus' chancellor, Domenico Grasso, protesting his sudden firing of the campus' provost, Susan Alcock (UM-Dearborn). Alcock had served less than two years on the job and was fired without cause or faculty consultation. Grasso's brief email announcement of a "Provost Transition" in May of 2021, subsequently posted online, came as a shock to most faculty. It offered no details about why the change in leadership was happening, noting simply that Alcock was "stepping down" and that the university was "grateful for her leadership" (Grasso). Nevertheless, this administrative decision was widely understood among faculty and staff as resulting from a relatively minor disagreement between the two leaders about a small campus initiative.

Some important background: a regional commuter campus of about nine thousand students in the Detroit metropolitan area, UM-D for years before the pandemic had been under significant economic strain due to dwindling overall enrollments, while at the same time it was serving an increasingly diverse (and strained itself) student body. These multiple stressors not surprisingly weighed heavily on faculty, whose teaching loads are much higher than those on the flagship campus in Ann Arbor and who often also identify teaching as not only a professional priority but a political commitment. Faculty teach many non-traditional students who themselves balance family and full-time work responsibilities along with their college coursework. Students are refugees from countries such as Iraq, Afghanistan, and Syria (the city of Dearborn having the highest proportion of Arab Americans in the US) and include others who have served as English-Arabic translators for the U.S. military or who are veterans of the U.S. military themselves. Many students are recent immigrants, the children of immigrants, or international students hailing from dozens of nations within the Middle East (especially Lebanon and Palestine), from Europe (especially eastern Europe),

Asia, Africa, and South America. And a large number of students are L2 and 1.5 Generation language learners and first-generation college students. Approximately 40% of the university's undergraduates are first-generation (Tuxbury).

Not surprisingly, such demographic, socio-political, and linguistic complexities in the student body lead to significant challenges—both professionally and pedagogically—especially for faculty who have high teaching loads. In the spring of 2020 the COVID-19 pandemic added to these existing pressures, as both students and faculty transitioned to required remote and hybrid options while also safeguarding their own and others' well-being. The personal and professional stakes for faculty during this time increased exponentially, as they did for faculty across the country.

Alcock, an archaeologist and past MacArthur fellow who was tenured at the University of Michigan in Ann Arbor and previously had served as interim provost on UM's Flint campus, was hired at Dearborn in 2019 just prior to the onset of the pandemic. Very early on Alcock's leadership style emphasized offering frequent (optional) meetings with faculty and staff, which one of the co-authors often attended. These "listening sessions" became more frequent with the pandemic: With no preset agenda and an open question-and-answer format, the sessions centered on listening to and "closing the loop" on faculty's questions and concerns, striking an unusually personal tone in word and visual effect (e.g., including in view of her camera during one Zoom session a dog she had adopted mid-pandemic).

During her time on campus she garnered rave reviews from faculty and staff for her interpersonal style, and especially for her handling of the pandemic and its impact on teaching and learning (Alcock). The faculty senate letter in reaction to her dismissal therefore expressed surprise, dismay, and—in contrast to past correspondences—a pointed challenge to the chancellor to explain his decision and address the mistrust it had engendered. The letter began:

> The abrupt departure of Provost Alcock has come as a shock to many of our faculty and raised a number of questions about why she has left after such a short tenure, and what the next steps are for the university. It is highly unusual for a provost to leave on such short notice, with so little warning and explanation. The Faculty Senate asks that Chancellor Grasso uphold his commitment to shared governance and provide an explanation for this action, as well as offer a clearer statement on its implications for our future direction.
>
> Of particular concern is the striking discrepancy between Provost Alcock's sudden departure and the support Provost Alcock has gained among the faculty in this crisis year.

> During her short tenure here, Provost Alcock has successfully built a relationship of trust with the faculty. Her distinct leadership style, pairing direct and clear statements about her own perspectives with a strong emphasis on listening and participatory involvement to gather others' perspectives, allowed for numerous initiatives (including through the strategic planning and implementation process) that many faculty perceived as promoting and developing our strengths as a campus. Provost Alcock's efforts have been even more impressive considering that they were accomplished under the unique challenges experienced by all of us during this unprecedented global pandemic. (UM-Dearborn Faculty Senate)

Words such as "striking" and "shock" convey the emotional impact of the provost's firing among faculty, a tenor which was unheard of in previous communications from the Faculty Senate. Historically such communications were assiduously devoid of pathos. The letter's pathos suggesting distrust is furthered by two important points: first, uncertainty among faculty going forward about the integrity of shared governance and, second, wider fears about "the future of our institution." The final two pages of the letter consist of a litany of pointed questions for the chancellor about the lack of transparency in the process of and follow-up to the firing, about the specifics of the provost's removal and implications for "campus initiatives and strategic direction," and about implications for shared governance. On the annual performance evaluation of administrators which shortly followed the faculty senate's letter, an overwhelming majority of faculty members reacted negatively to the chancellor's overall performance and specifically to the firing of the provost (University of Michigan Administration Evaluation). Representative comments included a sense that the "sudden and secretive move" was "confusing" and "disconcerting."[1] One long-time faculty member commented, "I also would like to know why the first Provost that actually listened to the faculty was fired."

Although the chancellor never responded publicly to any of the questions posed in the faculty senate's letter, this letter nevertheless stands out in combining an attention to the practical matter of the administration's decision and the deeper, philosophical and affective impact of these events. Like the clubwomen whose cultural work Gere so elegantly explores, senators composing the

---

1 Comments originally submitted by faculty are not available for reading at this point on the UM administration's webpage, where a note indicates that "The free-form anonymous advice and confidential remarks included in the survey have been submitted to the appropriate administrators." See https://aec.umich.edu/.

letter—and indeed the wider faculty community, who three and a half years later have organized a union (UM-Dearborn AAUP)—"'looked deeper and recognized another and profounder . . . need . . . for substantive intellectual work in an intimate social context'" (Croly qtd. in Gere 11).

CRITICAL AND INTIMATE REFLECTION IN THE NEOLIBERAL UNIVERSITY

These brief retellings of serious political conflict on campus remind us of the important cultural work that often unfolds in otherwise mundane workplace genres. In letters and meeting minutes the cultural work unfolds—documenting efforts at collaborative problem-solving, outlining competing stakes, holding leaders accountable, clarifying values, and mobilizing faculty across very different campuses. Moreover, these same texts evidence the emotional charge that surrounds institutional conflicts and the efforts to resolve them and that binds individuals to each other and to the institutions of which they are a part.

These examples also point to the power of public and collective—even intimate—reflection in post-secondary institutions in the US, shaped as they increasingly are by fast capitalism and globalization that actively detract from the valuing and visibility of slow processes such as those involved in shared governance. We propose such critical reflection, like writing itself, as a social and rhetorical activity. Our need for connection with others is heightened, not diminished, by fast capitalism and the neoliberal context. This need has only been strengthened and made more visible by the pandemic. We thus propose critical reflection as an important strategy not only for building individual, professional connections and relationships but also for building curricula, administrative processes, and other outcomes which will best serve faculty and students within increasingly neoliberal and corporatized environments.

We acknowledge the challenges to this kind of critical reflection, such as the pressures of mandates from bodies like the Higher Learning Commission to achieve accreditation; the political pressure from state legislatures; and procedural pressures emanating from (extant or threatened) lawsuits. But Stephen Brookfield posits critical reflection as being about the "uncovering of power and hegemony" that characterizes such pressures, with the "critical dimension of reflection to be drawn from critical theory's concern to demonstrate how ideological manipulation forces us to behave in ways that seem to make sense, but that actually keep us powerless" (11). The examples drawn from our professional experiences illustrate aspects of neoliberalism's ideological manipulation and the effects of that manipulation on faculty and student experiences of the educational context. Disrupting neoliberal approaches to administration, in particular in the context of economically stressed institutions such as ours, is in no way a simple or quick process. Yet a pursuit of critical reflection that is both public and collective, and that takes into account contexts both local and more global, we believe is a first step in such disruption, as it makes clear how the power of neoliberalism is made material. Such critical and intimate reflection may also lead to a more nuanced institutional ethos which takes into account and attempts to address the toll of neoliberalism on the humanistic enterprise.

WORKS CITED

Alcock, Susan. "Just checking in . . . read if you have time!" Received by Margaret Willard-Traub, 26 Mar. 2020.

Brookfield, Stephen. "So What Exactly is Critical About Critical Reflection?" *Researching Critical Reflection: Multidisciplinary Perspectives*, edited by Jan Fook et al., Routledge, 2016, pp. 11–22.

Brown, Wendy. *Undoing the Demos: Neoliberalism's Stealth Revolution*. Zone Books, 2015.

Fook, Jan, et al. "The Promise and Problem of Critical Reflection." *Researching Critical Reflection: Multidisciplinary Perspectives*, edited by Jan Fook et al., Routledge, 2016, pp. 1–7.

Gere, Anne Ruggles. *Intimate Practices: Literacy and Cultural Work in U.S. Women's Clubs, 1880–1920*. U of Illinois P, 1997.

Glass, Ira, host. "645: My Effing First Amendment." *This American Life*, WBEZ, 4 May 2018, www.thisamericanlife.org/645/my-effing-first-amendment.

Grasso, Domenico. "Provost Transition." *University of Michigan-Dearborn*, 14 May 2021, https://tinyurl.com/569hd3wk.

Kolowich, Steve. "State of Conflict: How a Tiny Protest at the U. of Nebraska Turned into a Proxy War for the Future of Campus Politics." *Chronicle of Higher Education*, 27 April 2018, www.chronicle.com/interactives/state-of-conflict.

Monnier, Nicole, et al. "Academic Freedom and Tenure: University of Nebraska-Lincoln." AAUP, May 2018, https://tinyurl.com/3ujtwrcv.

Professor Watchlist. Turning Point USA, 2025, www.professorwatchlist.org/.

Reynolds, Michael, and Russ Vince. "Organizing Reflection: An Introduction." *Organizing Reflection*, edited by Michael Reynolds and Russ Vince, Routledge, 2017, pp. 1–14.

Schleck, Julia. *Dirty Knowledge: Academic Freedom in the Age of Neoliberalism*. U of Nebraska P, 2022.

Schleck, Julia, et al. "An Open Letter from University of Nebraska Faculty on Recent Attacks on Our Institution." *Nebraska AAUP*, 27 November 2017, https://tinyurl.com/542brf6b.

Snyder, Timothy. *On Tyranny: Twenty Lessons from the Twentieth Century*. Tim Duggan Books, 2017.

Steinbaugh, Adam B. "FIRE Letter to the University of Nebraska, Lincoln, December 8, 2017." *Foundation for Individual Rights and Expression*, https://tinyurl.com/336twhyr.

Stenberg, Shari J. *Repurposing Composition: Feminist Interventions for a Neoliberal Age*. Utah State UP, 2015.
Tuxbury, Sarah. "New Org Supports Students Who Are First in Their Families to Attend College." *News University of Michigan-Dearborn*, 31 Mar. 2021, https://tinyurl.com/5xeeea39.
UM-Dearborn AAUP. https://sites.google.com/view/um-dearborn-aaup/home.
UM-Dearborn Faculty Senate. Letter to Chancellor Grasso. 3 June 2021.
University of Michigan Administration Evaluation Committee. "Chancellor, University of Michigan-Dearborn, Domenico Grasso." *University of Michigan*, aec.umich.edu/results2021/Dcha.php.
University of Nebraska System. Budget Response Initiative. https://nebraska.edu/brt.
"UNL Faculty Senate Meeting Minutes." University of Nebraska-Lincoln Faculty Senate, 3 Oct. 2017. *Internet Archive*, https://tinyurl.com/3224advj.
"UNL Faculty Senate Meeting Minutes." University of Nebraska-Lincoln Faculty Senate, 5 Sept. 2017. *Internet Archive*, https://tinyurl.com/csycr99c.
Welch, Nancy, and Tony Scott, editors. *Composition in the Age of Austerity*. Utah State UP, 2016.

CHAPTER 23.
FOR SITES BOTH SACRED AND SECULAR: COMPOSING A LANGUAGE TO BRIDGE SPIRITUAL IDENTITY AND RHETORICAL PRACTICE

Heather Thomson-Bunn
Pepperdine University

> We require an ethical vocabulary that speaks beyond the practices of skepticism and critique to address the possibilities of opening dialogues, finding affinities, acknowledging interdependencies, and talking to those strangers we most fear and distrust.
>
> – John Duffy, "The Good Writer: Virtue Ethics and the Teaching of Writing"

In 2001, Anne Gere wrote in *College English* that "[t]hose who wish to write about religion not only lack the highly complex and compelling language of, say, queer theory, but they face an implacable secularism" (Brandt et al. 47). Her essay—part of a symposium focused on exploring the politics of the personal in relation to composition and literacy studies—came at a time when little space had been made for these matters in those fields, or in higher education more broadly. Though she reflects on her experiences as a Christian professor, the text is not about her individual negotiation of religious beliefs at a public university. Rather, she highlights the consequences for an academic world that fails to engage seriously with the spiritual: it becomes a rhetorical space in which a significant dimension of human identity is excluded, and one in which it is easy to exoticize and dismiss religious and spiritual practices that "fall outside traditional norms" (Brandt et al. 46).

Gere was calling not simply for the inclusion of religious ideas but for an intentionally *academic and intellectual* engagement with them. Queerness existed long before queer theory, of course, but theory sprung from the recognition of queerness as a subject of intellectual import—and not only to those who identify as queer. Theoretical lenses and languages are applied to the complex and the critical, to that which is considered worthy of academic attention. Gere's point was not to equate the silencing she experienced to the struggles faced by queer people but to highlight the ways in which the "highly complex and compelling language" of theory can make way for the careful examination of experience—and for questioning various forms of "implacable" resistance.

In 2001, composition scholarship that engaged with religious discourses was sparse, but the two decades since have brought forth a burgeoning body of work in which we see the development and evolution of the "complex and compelling language" that Gere identified as a critical need. This chapter traces the lineage of what is becoming a robust area of study and highlights how Gere's work has been foundational to it.

HISTORY AND CONTEXT

The historical ties between religion (Protestant Christianity in particular) and universities in the US may have made Gere's call for greater academic attention to religion seem odd to some. How could we lack a complex language for something that dominated education for hundreds of years? Hasn't a stricter separation of the religious and the secular in higher education made way for the inclusion of people traditionally denied access? Given the myriad political and cultural issues that orbit religion—not to mention the ways in which religion has been weaponized against various peoples—it may seem like simple common sense to, as Gere puts it, "militate against writing about religious experience" (Brandt et al. 46–47). However, as Gere and now many others have observed, a strict no-admission policy for religion carries significant risks.

Before exploring the 21st-century surge of scholarship on religion, it is important to examine how, by the late 20th century, U.S. higher education had developed "a scholarly culture that tends to assume that religion is a dead force intellectually" (Turner 20). Though tensions between religious interests and higher education have a long and complex history, I focus here on a few key moments that historians such as George Marsden and Warren Nord point to as crucial times of change or turmoil for American universities as they struggled with and against their Protestant Christian heritage. The first is the mid to late 19th century. In the mid-century, even state universities typically "had all Protestant faculties, had clergymen as presidents, and required Protestant chapel services" (Marsden, *The Soul . . . Revisited* 4). By 1890, most state universities still had institutionalized religious practices such as required chapel services, but higher education was rapidly secularizing (Nord 84). Evangelicalism and literal biblical interpretation were beginning to come under fire as Enlightenment ideals and the work of intellectuals like John Dewey and Charles Darwin gained popularity.

By the 1920s, chapel services were no longer mandatory at most state universities, there had been a sharp decline in Christian campus ministries, and changing mores around sex and alcohol had contributed to a decrease in student involvement in Christian churches and groups (Marsden, *The Soul* 343–44). In the 1940s–1950s, however, there was a resurgence of religious fervor on college campuses and in the United States more broadly, precipitated by WWII and the emergence of totalitarian governments. In the 1950s, college students were as likely as the rest of the population to belong to a church, and mainline Protestantism "could genuinely be considered to be flourishing" (Marsden, *The Soul* 14).[1] Even during this time, however, formal institutionalization of Christianity was held at bay by questions of pluralism—particularly in terms of whether institutionalized religion meant including Jewish and Catholic faculty members and heritage—and by educational secularism, which had grown in favor beginning in the late 19th century.

The 1960s brought dramatic social change—civil rights activism, anti-establishment sentiment, the impact of the war in Vietnam—that had a significant influence on campus life. In 1963, the Supreme Court outlawed formal religious exercises in public schools with its *Abington School District v. Schempp* case (United States). Formerly Protestant institutions were dropping denominational ties and religious standards for faculty members (Marsden, *The Soul . . . Revisited* 366). Concurrent with these changes in culture and policy was the establishment of religious studies as a discipline defined via the scientific method and social science methods. This move positioned religion as an object of study and corralled it into a specific department, set apart from inquiry in other disciplines. According to Marsden, these factors led to the official disestablishment of Protestant Christianity at public universities (*The Soul* 414, 435).

It is no surprise, then, that when Gere became a professor in the mid–1970s, she "learned early in [her] career that it was better to keep some things to [her]self, especially religion" (Brandt et al. 46). This was not a concern unique to Gere, or to that decade. In the early 1990s, hiding religious identity struck some devout scholars as safer than an attempt to integrate it with one's intellectual identity. David Holmes, who published *Where the Sacred and Secular Harmonize: Birmingham Mass Meeting Rhetoric and the Prophetic Legacy of the Civil Rights Movement* in 2017, reports that during his graduate study at the University of Southern California in the 1990s and in his early years as a professor, he "kept any connection between [his] growing faith and burgeoning scholarship to [him]self" (172).

---

1 It was perhaps not considered by *all* to be flourishing; in 1951, William F. Buckley published *God and Man at Yale*, a scathing critique of what he saw as Yale's rejection of Christian principles.

In the mid to late 1990s, religion—when it was discussed at all—was most often approached in composition studies as a pedagogical dilemma, a difficulty faced by instructors when religion didn't stay where it belonged. It was also equated almost entirely with Christian beliefs, and Christian *student* beliefs in particular. Even as the emphasis on other facets of identity grew stronger, religion and spirituality were largely absent from scholarly exchanges. This was a time when Christians "were one of the only cultural groups openly and comfortably disparaged by many otherwise sensitive writing instructors" (Perkins 586) and when students' religious beliefs were typically presented as barriers to the work of composing.

INTIMATE PRACTICES, FROM A DISTANCE

Given the ways that religious belief was often either excluded or disparaged in the 1990s, it is perhaps telling that Gere's scholarly engagement with religion during that decade appeared in a historical study of U.S. women's clubs in the late 19th and early 20th centuries. In *Intimate Practices: Literacy and Cultural Work in U.S. Women's Clubs, 1880–1920*, Gere acknowledges religion as a significant factor in the rhetorical and social work of women's social clubs, highlighting the influence not only of white Protestant Christian women, but also "considering clubs formed by women from Mormon [and] Jewish" backgrounds, which had traditionally been ignored (3).

This is not to imply that Gere chose this project as a means by which to engage with religious discourses or to represent this book as being primarily about religion (it is not). I simply suggest that this historical consideration of religion—the view of religion as artifact—is indicative of what was primarily available as a respected scholarly approach to religion at the time. A historical study of religion—certainly a worthy enterprise, then and now—is quite different from examining its role(s) in contemporary classrooms and scholarship; it is another step removed from a scholar acknowledging their own orientation toward religion as a subject position relevant to their profession. *Intimate Practices* focuses on a time when Protestant Christianity was the norm, both in and out of the university, when 98.7 percent of U.S. residents were religious—and 97 percent were Christian (Johnson and Zurlo 841).[2] This is the religious nation of a former time, gone the way of the Edwardian fashion that many women in these social clubs would have worn.

The current religious terrain is more complex, with about 64 percent of Americans identifying as Christian and 30 percent identifying as nonreligious

---

2   Christians (of all types) made up 97 percent of the U.S. population, Jews made up 1.4 percent, and the "nonreligious" made up 1.3 percent.

(Kramer et al.). An even greater contrast may appear when we look specifically at faculty: a 2006 survey found that "while most professors believed in at least the possibility of God's existence, they were more than twice as likely to be skeptics or atheists as the general population" (Barlett). What those numbers mean for scholarship or the academic climate is a matter of debate. Some claim that religious beliefs are held to a much higher standard of evidence than nonreligious beliefs, if they are allowed into academic conversation at all (Edwards 147). Others assert that "religious skepticism represents a minority position, even among professors teaching at elite research universities" (Gross and Simmons 103). What does seem clear is that religion, once an assumed presence across the university, is now a contested one. It was into this more contested space that Gere spoke in 2001.

A SPARK AT THE TURN OF THE CENTURY

Gere's contribution to the article she co-authored with Deborah Brandt and their colleagues was published in September 2001, just as the horror of 9/11 thrust religion into the cultural consciousness with debates about whether the attacks were religiously or politically motivated, or both. Remarkable growth in scholarship related to religion followed, and during the first decade of the 21st century, theoretical engagement with religion and its connections to writing, rhetoric, and pedagogy flourished. Anne Gere, along with Tom Amorose, Beth Daniell, David Jolliffe, and Elizabeth Vander Lei, laid the foundation for what would become, in 2003, the CCCC Special Interest Group on Rhetoric and Christian Tradition (now called Rhetoric and Religious Traditions).[3] *College English*, *College Composition and Communication*, *WPA*, and other prominent journals published articles approaching religion with complexity and rigor. Shari J. Stenberg, in a *College English* article, called the skepticism about Christian students and what they bring to college classrooms "intellectual distrust," critiquing an academic culture in which "religious ideologies are often considered hindrances to—not vehicles for—critical thought" (271).

The 2005 book *Negotiating Religious Faith in the Composition Classroom*, edited by Elizabeth Vander Lei and bonnie lenore kyburz, took up the task of reflecting on how religious identity affects pedagogical decisions, student-instructor relationships, and institutional mission. The collected essays make a case for "acknowledging the presence of religious faith in our classrooms"

---

[3] A brief history of the Special Interest Group on Rhetoric and Christian Tradition can be found at https://rhetoricandchristiantradition.wordpress.com/about/. Information on the Rhetoric and Religious Traditions Special Interest Group is available at https://sites.google.com/view/rhetoricandreligioustraditions/home.

and for "teach[ing] students about the potential for religious faith to inspire and nurture effective rhetorical practice" (Vander Lei, "Coming to Terms" 3). This was a text that acknowledged the risks of silencing religious expression that Gere had pointed to a few years earlier. Bronwyn T. Williams, in his contribution to *Negotiating*, writes, "There are no simple solutions to cross-cultural conflicts involving faith and rhetoric. Yet it is folly to imagine that they are not already in the classroom with us. We must bring religion into open discussion . . . so that we can engage in thoughtful conversations about its influence in how we write and read" (117). He then warns, "If we don't address these issues directly, however, they will still emerge, but in ways that anger and frustrate both teacher and students" (117).

In just a few years, the strident secularism that Gere had identified was being challenged by scholars advocating not just for the toleration of religious discourses in the classroom but also for the deliberate acknowledgement and inclusion of them. There were calls for greater scholarly attention to religion as well, with concerns raised about how "rarely topicalized" religion was in comparison to other forms of difference (Wallace 518). Faculty members from various disciplines noted the "increasingly consequential" nature of religion, even at secular institutions (Diamond and Copre xv).

Religion, it seemed, had become too important to dismiss, and its intellectual, rhetorical, and pedagogical significance was coming into sharper focus (Edwards 28; Fish C1; Griffith B6). Sharon Crowley's book *Toward a Civil Discourse: Rhetoric and Fundamentalism* explored the cultural and rhetorical tensions between liberalism and Christian fundamentalism, which Crowley presented as dominating the "discursive climate" of American life (2). The book won the 2008 CCCC Outstanding Book Award—affirmation from the largest professional organization supporting research in writing studies that religion mattered to the field.

Among the many texts that added to and complicated this growing area of research was *Renovating Rhetoric in Christian Tradition* (2014), edited by Elizabeth Vander Lei, Thomas Amorose, Beth Daniell, and Anne Gere. The book grew out of "a persistent scholarly curiosity about the relationship of rhetoric and religion" and the perspective that "examining this relationship produces useful insights about complex rhetorical acts" (Vander Lei, Introduction ix). Gere's chapter, titled "Constructing Devout Feminists: A Mormon Case," dives directly into that rhetorical complexity, exploring the ways in which 19th-century Mormon women would "ally themselves rhetorically with progressive women" on issues such as education and women's suffrage, even as they remained devoted to a belief system deeply rooted in a patriarchal structure of power (7, 4). The fact that these dual allegiances strike us as an odd—perhaps impossible—pairing is precisely Gere's point. As Gere puts it, the "impoverished terms of academic discourses about religion make it difficult to perceive and explore the complexities that enable adherents of a given faith to remain completely devout while simultaneously embracing progressive secular causes" (15).

This connection to our current academic discourses is what makes Gere's study of 19th-century women in "Constructing Devout Feminists" so distinct from the one in *Intimate Practices*. Here, the reader is considering these women and their work not as distant history but as reflections of our current rhetorical (mis)understanding of the many ways that religious faith informs culture, politics, and education. As she did in 2001, Gere points to the continued need for theoretical tools to help scholars "'see' religion in a secular context" ("Constructing Devout Feminists" 15). She highlights how the "conflation of institutional with intellectual secularization has rendered the discourses surrounding religion stunted" and left us with such "limited secular academic language for religion" that the agency and complexity of religious rhetors is left unexamined (15). In "Constructing Devout Feminists" Gere invites the reader to imagine common rhetorical ground with women whose religious practices may be unfamiliar and even repugnant to them. Through this rhetorical connection, Gere expands and complicates the notion of how religious perspectives may be enacted.

Gere's essay stretches the discourses surrounding religion to supply new and more nuanced language for considering religious rhetoric. *Renovating Rhetoric in Christian Tradition* as a collection presents the possibility of "religious belief as a dynamic process of meaning-making"—a significant divergence from the common view of religion as rigid, anti-intellectual, and repressive (Vander Lei, Introduction xi). It also lays the foundation for subsequent work exploring the rhetorical possibilities of religious belief. Michael-John DePalma, for example, builds on the ways that the contributors to *Renovating Rhetoric* "challenge the binaries associated with religious discourses" in order to explore "the potential of undergraduate writing courses centered on religious rhetorics to cultivate capacities that are essential to thoughtful civic engagement" (253). My own article, which follows DePalma's in the same volume of *College English*, suggests that "[r]ather than simply *hope* that students will either leave religious discourses out of their writing or use them appropriately, instructors can direct students' attention to how these discourses might effectively be used" by engaging in thoughtful, rhetorically-grounded discussions (Thomson-Bunn 293). In their introduction to *Mapping Christian Rhetorics*, Michael-John DePalma and Jeffrey M. Ringer write that "Christian rhetorics specifically and religious rhetorics more broadly are *essential* to rhetorical studies" (2). It is difficult to see how such assertions could have been made effectively—let alone published for a wide readership—without the conversations that Gere, Amorose, Daniell, Vander Lei, and others began.

Kelly Ritter's "From the Editor" introduction to that volume of *College English* is compelling for the way it reveals the shifting disciplinary perceptions of religious belief and its relationship to writing and rhetoric. Despite being "a nonreligious person [her]self, who actively *avoids* discussions of faith in [her] own classes," Ritter observes that we are "in need of a meaningful education in rhetoric and ethics—one that is not in opposition to forces such as religious faith, for example, or other personal imperatives, but is instead in productive dialogue with it" (225, 223). This is a scholar with no personal or scholarly investment in religion, positing religious belief as culturally, ethically, and pedagogically relevant—to everyone.

DESCENDANTS

Gere's scholarship, in both breadth and depth, is staggering; it is daunting to read just a *list* of her publications and awards. What may not be as noticeable, or as widely celebrated, is the breadth and depth of her mentorship. Beyond her significant individual contributions to composition, rhetoric, literacy studies, and education, she has nurtured the scholarship of many students, encouraging their voices and lines of inquiry.

When I began my doctoral studies at the University of Michigan, I had no plans to write a dissertation exploring religious discourses and their relationship to composition. It was not until the end of my second year, when I composed my Theorization of Learning exam, that I confronted the fact that despite all of my formal education happening in public schools and universities, I could not address my intellectual development without acknowledging my religious upbringing. My earliest thinking—contemplating big questions, struggling with abstract concepts, wondering at the complexity of texts like the Bible—was ignited by my Christian parents and stoked by my church. To have faith—in my experience—was to ponder, to question, to read closely, to reckon with never knowing all. I surmised very early, however, that school was not the place for all that. For the next 20 or so years, I let my academic and spiritual selves develop in separate spheres. It never occurred to me to connect them.

And then, at the third public university I attended, where I'd gone to pursue a degree unrelated (I thought) to religion, the connections seemed obvious and inescapable. Still, I don't know that I would have pursued those connections, or even allowed them into that second-year exam, had I not worked with Anne Gere. I knew what she had written in 2001, and suddenly that text was an invitation.

Her graduate students interested in religion and spirituality not only found the door open to those interests but were equipped with methodologies, texts, and frameworks to support them. When I began my dissertation work in 2006,

I found that in five short years, Gere's call had sparked much important work and that I had walked into a small but blossoming subfield. I am not an isolated case; I witnessed graduate student colleagues like Jim Beitler, Christian Dallavis, Zandra Jordan, and Melody Pugh weave religion and spirituality into their dissertation projects and then on into their professional lives and publications. Their work, then and now, speaks to how carefully Gere made space for her students' minds *and* spirits.

In her foreword for Jim Beitler and Richard Hughes Gibson's 2020 book *Charitable Writing*, Anne Gere writes that she was "a tenured full professor before [she] could utter phrases like 'singing in my church choir' or 'the homeless shelter sponsored by my church' at the university" (xi). She then marvels at the ways the authors—one of whom (Beitler) is her former student, now a tenured professor himself—have connected writing instruction to spiritual formation and "transformed [her] thinking about what it means to write and teach writing" (xiii). The transformation has not moved in only one direction, however. Beitler and Gibson acknowledge Gere as a "guide" to their work, one who years before had "countered the myopia of the field's way of accounting for itself . . . [and] sought a more panoramic view of writing lives" (130). She helped prepare the way for scholarship that would transform her own ways of knowing, and those of so many others.

PATHS YET TO BE EXPLORED

As Gere's wide-reaching work attests, she is a scholar attuned to the unexamined. Even in 2001, Gere was resisting a narrow definition of religion and spirituality as she wrote about her own position as a religious person. In fact, the inclusion of minority traditions and thoughtful attention to underrepresented spiritual practices is central to her argument in that piece. She recognizes the risks of marginalizing that which exists outside of mainline Protestant Christianity, and describes how her own "understanding of religion broadened" as her daughter, an Athabascan person, "initiated [her] into Native American spirituality" and sacred rites (Brandt et al. 46). She does not shrug off her own faith, but she is willing to look beyond it.

That more expansive view of religion/spirituality is still relatively rare, but it is making its way into more of our professional spaces. John Duffy argues for an articulation of virtue in the writing classroom that escapes the narrow bounds of Christian morality and invites students to practice humility, honesty, and mutual respect as rhetorical virtues (238). At the Rhetoric and Religion in the 21st Century conference in 2018, Lisa King led an illuminating and well-attended seminar on Indigenous Rhetorics and Rhetorics of Religion. In 2023, the Rhetoric and Religious Traditions conference included panels on Medieval and Renaissance Kabbalah; the intersections of rhetoric, education, and Islamic traditions; the Sinhala Buddhist rhetoric of sovereignty; disability and Christian rhetorics; queer youth and Catholicism; ritual practices of the Indigenous Galos tribe of India; and Jewish identity in the composition classroom.[4] Conferences and academic journals are beginning to examine religion in ways that few would have imagined not long ago.

Of course, there is much work yet to be done. Higher education in the US is more religiously diverse than it has ever been, and students from other countries are contributing significantly to the changing landscape of religious belief on our campuses (Marsden, *The Soul . . . Revisited* 357). The intersections of religion, spirituality, rhetoric, writing, literacy, research, and teaching remain nascent areas of study, with many questions not yet asked, let alone answered. Still, in the two decades since Gere was "just beginning to untangle the politics that underlie the insistence upon secular to the exclusion of sacred" (Brandt et al. 47), scholarship and professional discourse in these areas has flourished. That is in no small part due to the rhetorical space that Gere helped to create.

WORKS CITED

Barlett, Thomas. "Some Evangelicals Find the Campus Climate Chilly—but Is That about Faith, or Politics?" *The Chronicle of Higher Education,* vol. 54, no. 5, 28 Sept. 2007, p. B6, https://tinyurl.com/y6prtnrt.

Brandt, Deborah, et al. "The Politics of the Personal: Storying Our Lives against the Grain." *College English,* vol. 64, no. 1, 2001, pp. 41–62, https://doi.org/10.58680/ce20011239.

Buckley, William F., Jr. *God and Man at Yale: The Superstitions of "Academic Freedom."* Henry Regnery Company, 1951.

Crowley, Sharon. *Toward a Civil Discourse: Rhetoric and Fundamentalism.* U of Pittsburgh P, 2006.

DePalma, Michael-John. "Reimagining Rhetorical Education: Fostering Writer's Civic Capacities through Engagement with Religious Rhetorics." *College English,* vol. 79, no. 3, 2017, pp. 251–75, https://doi.org/10.58680/ce201728893.

DePalma, Michael-John, and Jeffrey M. Ringer. "Introduction: Current Trends and Future Directions in Christian Rhetorics." *Mapping Christian Rhetorics: Connecting Conversations, Charting New Territories,* edited by Michael-John DePalma and Jeffrey M. Ringer, Routledge, 2015, pp. 1–13.

Diamond, Miriam Rosalyn, and Christina Copre. "Faith in Learning: An Overview." *Encountering Faith in the Classroom: Turning Difficult Discussions into Constructive Engagement,* edited by Miriam Rosalyn Diamond, Stylus, 2008, pp. xv–xxiii.

---

4 Among many others: https://drive.google.com/file/d/1oLfmwAum8BEMNviTrO3cMj9-a3x8cYSu/view.

Duffy, John. "The Good Writer: Virtue Ethics and the Teaching of Writing." *College English*, vol. 79, no. 3, 2017, pp. 229–50, https://doi.org/10.58680/ce201728892.

Edwards, Mark U., Jr. *Religion on Our Campuses: A Professor's Guide to Communities, Conflicts, and Promising Conversations*. Palgrave Macmillan, 2006. *Springer Nature Link*, https://doi.org/10.1057/9780230601109.

Fish, Stanley. "One University, Under God?" *The Chronicle of Higher Education*, vol. 51, no. 18, 7 Jan. 2005, p. C1, www.chronicle.com/article/one-university-under-god/.

Gere, Anne Ruggles. "Constructing Devout Feminists: A Mormon Case." Vander Lei et al., pp. 3–16.

———. Foreword. Gibson and Beitler, pp. xi–xiii.

———. *Intimate Practices: Literacy and Cultural Work in U.S. Women's Clubs, 1880–1920*. U of Illinois P, 1997.

Gibson, Richard Hughes, and James Edward Beitler III. *Charitable Writing: Cultivating Virtue Through Our Words*. IVP Academic, 2020.

Griffith, R. Marie. "The Gospel of Born-Again Bodies." *The Chronicle of Higher Education*, vol. 51, no. 20, 21 Jan 2005, p. B6, www.chronicle.com/article/the-gospel-of-born-again-bodies/.

Gross, Neil, and Solon Simmons. "The Religiosity of American College and University Professors." *Sociology of Religion*, vol. 70, no. 2, 2009, pp. 101–29, https://doi.org/10.1093/socrel/srp026.

Holmes, David G. *Where the Sacred and Secular Harmonize: Birmingham Mass Meeting Rhetoric and the Prophetic Legacy of the Civil Rights Movement*. Cascade Books, 2017.

Johnson, Todd M., and Gina A. Zurlo. *World Christian Encyclopedia*. 3rd ed., Edinburgh UP, 2019.

King, Lisa. "To Do Things in a Good Way: Putting Indigenous Rhetorics and Rhetorics of Religion in Conversation." Rhetoric and Religious Traditions Conference, 4–7 October 2018, University of Tennessee–Knoxville.

Kramer, Stephanie, et al. "Modeling the Future of Religion in America." *Pew Research Center*, 13 Sept. 2022, www.pewresearch.org/religion/2022/09/13/modeling-the-future-of-religion-in-america/.

Marsden, George. *The Soul of the American University: From Protestant Establishment to Established Nonbelief*. Oxford UP, 1994. *Oxford Academic*, https://doi.org/10.1093/oso/9780195070460.001.0001.

———. *The Soul of the American University, Revisited: From Protestant to Postsecular*. 2nd ed., Oxford UP, 2021. *Oxford Academic*, https://doi.org/10.1093/oso/9780190073312.001.0001.

Nord, Warren A. *Religion and American Education: Rethinking a National Dilemma*. U of North Carolina P, 1995.

Perkins, Priscilla. "'A Radical Conversion of the Mind': Fundamentalism, Hermeneutics, and the Metanoic Classroom." *College English*, vol. 63, no. 5, 2001, pp. 585–611.

Ritter, Kelly. "From the Editor." *College English*, vol. 79, no. 3, 2017, pp. 223–28, https://doi.org/10.58680/ce201728891.

Stenberg, Shari J. "Liberation Theology and Liberatory Pedagogies: Renewing the Dialogue." *College English,* vol. 68, no. 3, 2006, pp. 271–90, https://doi.org/10.58680/ce20065021.

Thomson-Bunn, Heather. "Mediating Discursive Worlds: When Academic Norms and Religious Beliefs Conflict." *College English,* vol. 79, no. 3, 2017, pp. 276–96, https://doi.org/10.58680/ce201728894.

"Toward a Civil Discourse." *University of Pittsburgh Press*, 2025, upittpress.org/books/9780822959236/.

Turner, James. "Does Religion Have Anything Worth Saying to Scholars?" *Religion, Scholarship, and Higher Education: Perspectives, Models, and Future Prospects,* edited by Andrea Sterk, U of Notre Dame P, 2002, pp. 16–21. *JSTOR,* https://doi.org/10.2307/j.ctvpj7cdt.6.

United States, Supreme Court. *Abington School District v. Schempp. United States Reports*, vol. 374, 17 June 1963, pp. 203–320. *Library of Congress,* www.loc.gov/item/usrep374203/.

Vander Lei, Elizabeth. "Coming to Terms with Religious Faith in the Composition Classroom: An Introduction." Vander Lei and kyburz, pp. 3–10.

———. Introduction. Elizabeth Vander Lei et al., pp. ix–xvi.

Vander Lei, Elizabeth, et al., editors. *Renovating Rhetoric in Christian Tradition*. U of Pittsburgh P, 2014.

Vander Lei, Elizabeth, and bonnie lenore kyburz, editors. *Negotiating Religious Faith in the Composition Classroom*, Heinemann, 2005.

Wallace, David L. "Transcending Normativity: Difference Issues in *College English*." *College English,* vol. 68, no. 5, 2006, pp. 502–30, https://doi.org/10.58680/ce20065033.

Williams, Bronwyn T. "The Book and the Truth: Faith, Rhetoric, and Cross-Cultural Communication." Vander Lei and kyburz, pp. 105–20.

PART 8. REFLECTIONS AND RECOLLECTIONS

CHAPTER 24.

THE SPACE BETWEEN BUTTER AND SALT

Jennifer Sinor
Utah State University

The road to Delphi is paved with flowers. Fountains of Spanish Broom spill yellow blossoms onto the asphalt; oleander in pink, purple, and white grow so close together a fence becomes unnecessary. Fields of red poppy. Stems of hollyhock. Purple bougainvillea, like a flock of florescent fish, school on the walls of houses, stores, and ruins. If we were to stop the car and step out, I imagine the air would smell like my childhood, one spent among the flowers of Oahu. I stumble upon my past often in Greece, mostly in the blossoms that scent the air. Jacaranda, a door.

We don't stop though. We left Athens at five in the morning so that we could be among the first at Delphi when the grounds open. My husband, Michael, drives the tiny white Nissan, while our son, Aidan, navigates from the phone. We pass through towns that gave birth to mythic heroes, places like Thebes, home to Hercules and Oedipus, and beneath mountains that fostered muses and demigods. Even though I have never been to Greece before, the names are familiar.

In his book *The Oracle*, William Broad describes arriving at Delphi as "a revelation" (4). I, however, am unsure we have come to the right spot.

"This can't be it, Aidan," I say, looking at the empty road, the lack of both parking lot and signage, the absence of crowd.

"Look," he says, showing me the phone. Google insists that this rift valley tucked amid the limestone peaks of Mt. Parnassus is, indeed, the home of Pythia. The only car parked on the side of the road, we get out and are met with silence. Not the lack of sound but the fullness of emptiness.

This place asks nothing.

~~~

When my youngest brother died, we had only questions. What day had he died? Had he been in pain? What was the cause? Drugs? Heart attack? A year later, most of these questions remain unanswered. I learned of Bryan's death on a Wednesday, though he could have died any time between then and the Sunday before. It appears he went to bed and never woke up. Based on the mess left by his dogs on the bedroom carpet, he most likely died Tuesday, the night of the full moon in June, the strawberry moon. He was 46.

We arrived at his house that Friday, my parents, my other brother, Scott, and my aunt. Bryan was a hoarder, so his double-wide left no surface bare, no room empty, no closet or shelf free. Some of it valuable, much of it not. We each took a black garbage bag and began clearing things away. No matter where you started—kitchen, bathroom, bedroom—you dug through layers of time, arriving, always, at childhood. In the kitchen: the silverware from when we were young, collectable glasses from Burger King, our Tupperware lunch pails. In the office: piles of bills and random receipts that gave way to the newspaper clipping of when he was named "Carrier of the Month" for *The Navy News* as well as the photo buttons my mom used to wear on her straw hat during Little League: That's My Boy. In the bookshelves that housed a pristine collection of *Cycle World* magazine: the book of poetry he wrote in the fourth grade.

Bryan was unable to determine what he could live without, so he never threw anything away. Days after his death, we faced the same dilemma. If Bryan felt all of this was worth saving, how could we determine it was not? Still, we filled bag after bag and hauled them to the roll-off dumpster we had rented, the heat of the Texas sun scalding the backs of our necks as we dragged bloated sacks across scrub grass.

It was the morning of the first day that I saved one of the only things I took from Bryan's house: a grocery list penned on the back of an envelope in handwriting cramped and contorted. I didn't want the Les Paul guitars or the framed puzzles, the Zildjian cymbals, or the collection of pre-production model cars lonely in their unopened boxes. Instead, I took a list from the kitchen counter where it sat amid scores of bills, receipts, pens, keys, matchboxes, essential oils, beer caps, business cards, hundred-dollar bills, and half-empty Coke bottles. I placed the list in my pocket and returned to clearing the shelves of a house I had entered only one other time in my life.

> Dr. Pepper
> Salt
> Butter
> Vegtables
> Potatoes
> Pills?
> Pepper?

I am unsure of what I saved.

~ ~ ~

The first written record of the Oracle of Delphi comes from Homer in the eighth century BCE, but the site as a place of spiritual power and worship can be dated to a thousand years before that. It was then that the first temple was erected to honor the goddess Gaia, the earth mother whose abode was guarded by a giant python. Only much later did Apollo arrive and make Delphi his home. So when we step from the car and enter the silence, we step onto ground that has been held sacred for thousands of years. When I look from the southern slopes of Mt. Parnassus where we stand and gaze toward the Straits of Corinth, my eyes trace the same fundamental shape of mountain and water that untold numbers sought as refuge, sanctuary, last hope. It is impossible, if you read the histories of Delphi, to overstate its importance not just to the Greeks but to the rise of humanism in the West. As William Broad writes, "Delphi was the spiritual heart." He continues, "No authority was more sought after or more influential, none" (11).

Entering the temple grounds that morning, I carry no petition. We begin below the Temple of Apollo, the main temple where seekers would hear the council of Pythia, the oracle. Walking up the slope, we follow what's called the Sacred Way, stepping on the stones that thousands of others walked, passing alongside walls that still bear the names of the slaves who worked on the temple and then, because Pythia declared it so, were emancipated for their service to her. The site sits in a cleft in the mountain, and limestone cliffs guard the temple on three sides. Olive trees, fir, and juniper grow amid the ruins. Birds sing from their branches.

Before long, we stand in front of the omphalos, an ovoid-shaped rock absent of marking or decoration, humble on the bare red dirt. Weeds grow between the stones placed around the navel of the world. Given the power of the oracle—in its thousand years of active use it foretold the Trojan War, revealed to Oedipus that he would kill his father and marry his mother, declared Alexander the Great invincible, helped establish the democratic laws of Athens and Sparta—it is no surprise that it was considered the earth's umbilicus, the point at which spirit becomes manifest. Had the sign not alerted me, I would have walked right past the stone. It looked like much of the rubble around me.

~ ~ ~

In his cultural history, *Speculation*, Gayle Rogers begins by saying, "The world gives us imperfect and incomplete information for forecasting the future. We look for signs, we read everything around us, but we can never know with certainty what tomorrow will bring" (1). And yet, whether through augury or hard evidence, we have been trying to determine the future for almost as long as we have been around as a species. Both gifted and limited by the fact that our eyes are at the front of our heads, we tend to believe what can be seen, even as we know, on a deeper level, that there must be more that we are missing. Rogers tells us that it is during times of scientific advancement that our technologies for speculation and divination become more elaborate, not less. The more we know, the more we recognize exists outside the known. Our modern understanding of the word "speculative" derives from two roots, the first Latin, *speculum*, a mirror. Rogers points to St. Augustine, in commenting on Paul's well-known passage in Corinthians, as one of the first to attend to the importance of *speculum*. In this case, Augustine translates Paul's "beholding as in a glass" (*speculum*, mirror) as instructions to see the created world as a reflection of God. This idea was central to early Christianity and in line with Greek philosophy: though imperfect the present world is a mirror of the divine. As Christianity developed and spread, the ability to see the reflection, read it, rested increasingly on the purity of your faith. To the devout, God's signature was found in the grasses, the trees, the flight of birds.

~~~

In saving this particular grocery list, I threw hundreds of other pieces of writing away, including letters half written, journal-like rants on pages creased and bent, papers from grade school and college. I don't know why I chose a piece of paper that contains more space than word. The envelope is white with two cellophane windows for address and return address. Postage has been paid. The list could be months or years old, or it could have been written the night he went to bed and never woke up. Time does not seem to mark the paper in any way. The handwriting is unruly, almost like that of a child still learning to shape their letters, but I know the hand as my brother's.

It's a strange sort of list, though maybe all grocery lists are strange to those who have not made them. Bryan wasn't one to cook, so I can't see him gathering ingredients for a meal. It's the staples that stop me: butter, salt, and pepper. Three basic and essential items. How often do you buy salt? How odd that you would need pepper at the very same time. But maybe he doesn't. Pepper ends with a question mark. Pepper? Who will answer that question and how? Or is the pepper a bell pepper instead? The list is a conversation he is having with himself, what is gone, what is needed, what remains uncertain. He is asking and will answer, and I, as the reader, remain outside.

~~~

Leaving the omphalos behind, we arrive at the Athenian Treasury where gold and jewels were kept, sent by kings from far-flung lands in gratitude for Pythia's guidance. Birds replace the metopes in the marble walls and call to us from holes made into homes. In the quiet morning, you would not know that Delphi has experienced several renovations and rebirths. For hundreds of years, it lay buried beneath a town after an earthquake razed the buildings. At one point, the complex stretched across the entire slope of the mountain; now you visit it in sections, never really experiencing the grounds united.

Continuing up the mountain, we come to Apollo's massive altar, a giant slab of bluish stone that stands at the entrance to the Temple of Apollo, the place where Pythia arrived after bathing in the enchanted Castilian springs. Originally, Pythia spoke for Apollo only once a month, on the seventh, Apollo's day. But as the oracle grew in importance, Pythia began speaking more often. A petitioner would sacrifice a goat or ram on the altar before the temple to determine if Apollo was present that day. A priest would read the behavior of the goat as well as its entrails to know whether the petitioner should proceed inside. If the goat trembled in the leg, Apollo was nearby, a decision made by the priest. Pythia, though, needed no such interpretation, for she channeled Apollo directly. At a time when women weren't allowed to petition the oracle, were, for the most part, kept at home, Pythia's voice carried across oceans and continents.

Once we move beyond the altar, we stand above Apollo's Temple, which of course is a ruin, so we stand above fallen rocks and fallen walls high on a landscape familiar with falling earth. From the adyton, an orange cat emerges: Pythia.

~~~

I was not close to my brother. I do not know how he spent his days. Years could pass before I would see him, and then only if I traveled to Texas. A year after Bryan's death, his dogs will visit my house in Utah, though he never did. Bryan never saw a single place that I have lived. I knew he slept late, so I would only call after noon. The conversations were unpleasant, even though hearing his soft voice always made me smile at first. Bryan was full of anger and would turn the discussion red with rage. I have seen him kick his dogs, punch walls, storm from houses and then shriek away on his Ducati. My two children, teenagers now, didn't like to be around him, fearing what he might say or do. Yet, the single time I knew him to fly on an airplane, it was to join our family on Christmas Day in Tucson. Bryan wore all the clothes he would need—three pairs of underwear, two shirts, three pairs of socks—so that the Lego set he brought for Aidan and Kellen would count as his single carry-on.

Sometimes I feel guilty for not grieving Bryan's death more. I think of him every day, but when I do it is the Bryan of childhood I remember, the one who would let me put barrettes in his hair like a doll. Maybe I chose to save the grocery list because of its apparent neutrality. Basic. Butter and salt. It appears just as it is, a reminder of what not to forget. It does not kick or rage or leave my mother in tears.

But even that is not true, for in the misspelling of vegetables, I read my brother's struggles in school, his undiagnosed dyslexia, the teacher who hit him with a book, the teacher who dumped the contents of his desk on the floor and screamed at him to clean it up, the moment, every day, when he was pulled from class and taken down to "LD," the learning disabled room. In the anxiety over correctness in his own grocery list on the spelling of potatoes, I read a child who was told at a very young age that he was stupid, unruly, and a failure.

~~~

A speculum allows one to read what cannot be read. Originally a mirror used by doctors to see behind, the modern-day speculum gives access to orifices in the body hidden from view. The idea of seeing behind or around, seeing what cannot be seen, is central to the word "speculative" as we use it today, but equally important is the second etymological root, the Greek root of *specula* as watchtower. According to Rogers, both the Greek and Latin roots inform our understanding of why and how we try to fill the gaps of what we cannot know. While a *speculum* encouraged one to reflect/see inward, a *specula* encouraged one to look out. These watchtowers dotted both Greece and Rome, giving soldiers views and advantage. Our desire to speculate is tied to soldiers who climbed the specula in search of a new perspective. Rogers points out how *specula* and *speculum* come together to form "a route toward the divine that escapes and surpasses the very material world that it first ponders" (20). Another way to think about that desire to see beyond what is right before us is hope. Hope, by definition, extends to the future, one we cannot access if we keep our feet on the ground, limiting knowledge to the known. We must climb the watchtower.

~~~

When Apollo arrives in Delphi to build his temple, around 1000 BCE, he first must destroy Python, who guards Gaia. The battle is fierce, but Apollo succeeds and the giant snake is cut into pieces. Pythia, whose name shares the root with the python he slayed, is born. Pyth means rot; goddess risen from ruin.

In later years, Pythia was always a woman over the age of fifty, a crone, and therefore wise with the knowledge that decades of inhabiting a body provides. Originally, researchers thought Pythia consumed mystic pneuma, a hallucinogenic vapor that rose from cracks running the fault line under Delphi, and then spoke in trancelike hysteria, while the male priests translated. More recently, researchers have suggested that Pythia spoke on her own, without translation, mediation, or men.

What Pythia offered, though, in either version, was far from clear. The oracle spoke in riddles, verses that appeared incomplete and full of holes. She left it to the petitioner to decode. If the result did not seem to align with what Pythia had said, the fault was never hers. Rather, the petitioner had misunderstood, failed to read between the lines. The most famous case of the inability to interpret correctly comes from King Croesus, who asked Pythia if he should wage war against Persia. Pythia responded that if he did, a great empire would be destroyed. Croesus assumed that meant the enemy and began the war. Of course, it was his own great empire that met its end.

That morning, I cannot enter the temple but can only call to the orange cat below. She ignores me, stretches in the sun, shows me her tail. The walls are long gone, but if they were still standing, I would read a carved notice at the entrance: "Know thyself." It is difficult from our standpoint today to understand how radical this advice would have been in the ancient world. A platitude now, then, it was revolutionary. One of the most astounding roles of Pythia was her insistence on introspection. The oracles at Delphi shaped not only the outcome of history but helped refine Western morality and the sense of an individual conscience. Until Pythia's council, blood killings were common, but Pythia, through her prophecies, taught respect for human life as well as nuance and empathy. Broad argues that her "oracular vagueness" led to the establishment of democracy as the rulers learned to bring her prophecies into conversation and to weigh various options with one another (54). It was her insistence on incomplete messages that nudged the Western world toward reflection, contemplation, and individual moral reckoning.

~~~

When Brenda Miller writes about the gaps created by writers on the page, she begins with the reader. Unlike the adyton at Delphi, the hole in the ground that no one but the oracle could enter, the hole on the written page asks the reader to step inside. While a linear essay often offers narrative completion, an essay that delights in fragmentation relies on the reader to complete the meaning. More exists, the writer implies, than what can be said on the page. In jumping the chasm of white space between sections, the reader is acknowledging their willingness to explore, in Miller's words, "what is unknown rather than the already articulated" (16). A gap in a text has an almost divinatory power. It signals that what is already known, what could be narrated, is limited, and the only way to access the unknown, to climb the watchtower or look through the mirror, is by creating a space of speculation, one that Miller says can trip the reader, cause them to stumble and sprawl. In their inaccessibility, their vagueness, their refusal to yield, the gaps become, Miller writes, "the most honest moments in the essay" (18).

～～～

Bryan's list is more hole than whole. Never meant to tell a story, the list is complete on its own, what Anne Ruggles Gere in her ongoing examination of personal writing might call an "incomplete completeness" (212). At the same time, the list points to the holes in the pantry. The question is what to do with list and ruin. The temptation, the tug, is toward narrative, toward reconstruction, yet it is the gaps themselves that make list and ruin what they are: partial. Both force me into a space of speculation where I stand in front of Apollo's Temple and try to pull columns from the ground, erect a ceiling made of timber, reforge the bronze bowl that sat upon a column of snake. In the same way I try to imagine the night my brother went to bed for the last time, the poker hands he played that night, the last thing he said to his dogs, the moment that his heart arrested, the possibility that he was scared and in pain. At some point, my brother needed butter and salt. It may have been a day that he made my mother cry or it may have been a day that he taped another picture of Aidan and Kellen to his walls. He may or may not have bought the salt. List, ruin, and essay don't simply invite speculation; they exist in the speculative. Their completion is their partiality; their perfection is their inscrutability. And imperfection is the only place from which hope can arise. The perfect, the read, the built has no need for new ways of seeing.

～～～

As busloads of tourists start arriving at Delphi, we return to the car. We would prefer not to share Delphi, especially with those who do not see Pythia as cat. Aidan and Michael make their way back down, but I look for a bench in the shade. I have long planned to read my cards at the home of oracle itself, and my Tarot deck nestles in my bag, carefully wrapped in scarves. Sifting through the cards, I gaze across the valley. I wait to feel the moment in the shuffling when I know to pause, a kind of gap that opens and a card steps forward. The question I ask is one I often ask in my own readings: what am I not seeing?

In ancient times, when Pythia was not available, petitioners could come to Delphi bearing two dried beans of different colors. Holding both in hands behind their back, they could ask the oracle a yes/no question and then see which bean was revealed. I had thought about bringing dried beans with me, but I realized there was no question I was willing to ask Pythia with such a direct response. Is Bryan okay? Did he feel pain at the end? Is he at peace? Such questions felt too weighty to be answered by a single word. I wanted the room speculation provides, the portal to a place that is both familiar and unfamiliar, known and unknown, virgin and trod. I wanted to travel the route to the unmanifest that can only be followed by contemplating what is right in front of you. I brought my cards to Pythia. In the cleft of mountains that birthed the muses, fifty feet from where Pythia encouraged seeker after seeker to look inside, I pulled the Knight of Cups.

~~~

The gaps in an essay require, Miller tells us, a more active reader. The reader is the one who charts their course across the blank space; readings become multiplied. Those readings are not externally determined but internally born. In Marjane Satrapi's graphic memoir *Persepolis*, she describes the trauma of an adolescence spent in Iran during the Islamic Revolution. The drawings are simple and stunning, and we follow young Marjane as she tries to navigate an increasingly unstable landscape. In the middle of the book, Satrapi's neighborhood is bombed. Satrapi is not home at the time but returns to her street as soon as she hears of the destruction. Her family is safe, but her friend's family is not. She learns that her childhood friend has been buried in rubble. That moment is rendered by Satrapi as an entirely black cell.

As a reader, we are felled by her grief.

The empty cell, the hole on the page, is left by Satrapi for her reader to fill. We might begin by imagining her horror, but we quickly realize that we can't. We then fill it with our own sorrow. The hole on the page acts as a mirror and throws the reader inward to contemplate, reflect, grapple. A portal opens.

~~~

I imagine other lists sat on the kitchen counter the morning I arrived at my dead brother's house. Lists for car parts. Lists of dog medicines. Lists of jobs that needed to be done around the house. I saved the list of food, a fundamental need. When we were younger, too small to remain at home alone, my brothers and I often accompanied my mother to the military commissary. Walking across the parking lot, two of us would hold a hand, while the third grabbed her macramé purse, pulled like a kite along the asphalt. Even though my mother is far from tall, her pace was furious, and we stumbled to keep up.

Almost every building in the military is built for purpose rather than beauty, and the commissary was no exception. We would leave the Hawaiian sun and be consumed by a sea of tiled flooring and metal shelves. The commissary was enormous, with fathoms of hard, cold air and strident fluorescent lighting. You did not enter; you surrendered.

My mother's lists matched the enormity of the store, often written on the back on a business envelope in black military-issue ballpoint pens. Because she hated going to the commissary and couldn't face the lines more than twice a month, she always grabbed two carts. As the baby, even when he was no longer a baby, Bryan rode in one of the carts, bracing himself against the metal sides. Scott pushed one cart, while I maneuvered the other; my mother warned us not to crash into her bare legs. Up and down every aisle: my mother, list in hand, one cart, a second cart, Bryan reaching for anything that looked like candy on the shelves. Boxes of Tide, gallons of milk, trays of hamburger meat, cereal, cereal, cereal. We never lingered. My mother knew the store like she knew our house, down to the baseboards.

All along the way, my mother might complain about the poor quality of produce, or the stale meats and cheeses, the lack of variety, but we never shopped anywhere else. The chill of the meat counter remains with me, frost cresting like waves at the edges of the horizontal freezers, raised goose bumps on sun-browned arms, blood seeping beneath the plastic wrap. But also, summer days spent with my mother and two brothers, the satisfaction found in completing the list, filling the van with crisp brown-paper bags, doubled for milk, stiff as soldiers, the promise of a box of animal crackers at the end. Part of me yearns for the days when I was led, before choices were made, paths set. I want to climb into the cart with Bryan, hold his sticky hand, tell him that he doesn't have to worry, food will be provided, meals made, the pantry always filled.

~~~

I don't know what the Knight of Cups holds in his chalice. He sits astride his horse, headed for a river, bearing a cup rather than a sword. Traditionally the cup is filled with water or wine and symbolizes love, but maybe his cup is empty and the knight quests for nothing, cares not for winning, defines reward in absence. When I draw the Knight of Cups at Delphi, I am surprised. Surrounded by so much feminine energy, I had thought I would pull the High Priestess or the Queen of Wands, but that is what I love about Tarot: you draw what you need. I will never know if my brother was happy. I will never know if his heart attack could have been prevented by medication or diet. He cannot tell me what we should have saved from his house or what we failed to see.

What fills the knight's cup will never be known to me, but that also means I can fill it again and again and again. The gaps in between are the doors to possibility. Delphi may be a ruin or it may be home for Pythia as cat to roam. Nothing needs to be rebuilt, the spaces between the rocks sing even if we mistake it for birdsong. I want to imagine that Bryan chose to die that night because he could not face the death of another one of his dogs, could not watch our aging parents fade any further. He didn't want to confront the hole that we, as his family, now gather around. I don't blame him, but I am also aware that holes are not places of absence but rather hope's only home.

WORKS CITED

Broad, William J. *The Oracle: The Lost Secrets and Hidden Message of Ancient Delphi*. Penguin, 2006.

Gere, Anne Ruggles. "Revealing Silence: Rethinking Personal Writing," *College Composition and Communication*, vol. 53, no. 2, 2001, pp. 203–23, https://doi.org/10.58680/ccc20011448.

Miller, Brenda. "A Braided Heart: Shaping the Lyric Essay." *Writing Creative Nonfiction: Instruction and Insights from the Teachers of the Associated Writing Programs*, edited by Carolyn Forché and Philip Gerard. Story P, 2001, pp. 14–24.

Rogers, Gayle. *Speculation: A Cultural History from Aristotle to AI*. Columbia UP, 2021.

Satrapi, Marjane. *The Complete Persepolis*. Pantheon Books, 2007.

CHAPTER 25.
MEMORIES

Victor Villanueva
Washington State University

Let me open with a memory, something of an aside rather than a thesis.

In April 1984, the Sunday edition of *The Seattle Times* included a half-page article with the heading "The American Family is Alive and Well." The article featured a picture of Anne, her husband (Brewster, if I remember right, though he introduced himself to me as "Budge"), and their children sitting around a dinner table, holding hands for the dinner blessing. It was clear that her world was so very different from mine. While she was in the Sunday *Times*, I was living with my mate and our three kids at the time in what was literally—quite literally—the oldest apartment house in the city of Seattle (a slum that got around Landlord-Tenant rules because the place was officially a historical landmark).

Now, I mention this not to point to race and class and the like, but to mark a memory of how I could believe at the time that, thanks to Anne, I could someday enjoy a lovely house with wife and children in a lovely neighborhood. I could believe that because whatever my abilities or their lack, I could count on Anne to be direct and truthful, not have to worry about the pity or the condescension I often felt at Big University.

And that's what this chapter is about.

For the rest of this brief chapter, I will continue to carry on about myself, but I do so as a means to describe Anne Gere the Mentor. I write this chapter less to honor the researcher and scholar that is Anne Gere than to give thanks to the person who helped launch a relatively successful career. Professor Gere's academic career as a professor is about ten years longer than mine, and our ages are even closer than that. Yet whatever successes I have enjoyed over the last 40 years or so would have never been realized if it weren't for her. This is less to honor Professor Gere than to thank her, a very long overdue thank you.

In 1979, I entered graduate school at the University of Washington in Seattle. Three years earlier, I had entered a community college with a high school GED that I earned while in Vietnam. I had entered the community college to acquire a bona fide high school diploma. I had already tried to secure a job with a GED after seven years in the military, where I had been a personnel specialist for most of my service (with a brief stint as an infantryman). I was a well-trained clerk, even a non-commissioned officer overseeing the large personnel offices of Ft. Lewis, WA. But a clerk without college, never mind a conventional high school diploma, was not going to land me a job. I transferred to the University of Washington after receiving an AA because I had gotten bitten by the learning bug but also because it was nearby, having decided to stay in the Pacific Northwest. And the nearby, beautiful campus was affordable for Vietnam veterans ($177 per quarter. Imagine *that*!). It was rough going, but I stayed past the undergraduate degree, even as I was insecure, lacking graduate writing abilities (or even an understanding of what those abilities might entail). I had simply decided to continue in college until I failed. And it was clear that I was admitted to the graduate program because of my minority status. It was written on my GRE score sheet. In those days there was a notebook where graduate students could read informal comments written by our professors. The notes about me were kind but not encouraging, and among those notes was my GRE score sheet with something like "Minority applicant" written on it. I would stay until I couldn't. Dropped out once, after trying to write a paper on Keats' "Ode on a Grecian Urn." What? I had nothing to say. I don't know why I came back the next quarter.

My GRE scores were pretty high when it came to Quantitative Reasoning and Verbal Reasoning, but the Literature Advanced test was a washout. I really knew very little—and it showed. Among the literary categories, I scored lowest in American Lit.

～～～

Then in 1981, I stumbled into Anne Gere's "Theories of Invention" graduate seminar. As a kid I saw something from Benjamin Franklin in which he signed a document as "Inventor." I needed more American Lit credits, so I thought that Professor Gere's course was an American Lit course, "Theories of [the Literature] of Invent*ors*." What I discovered, thanks to Anne, changed the rest of my life: *rhetoric*, the discipline that continues to shape how I see, hear, and read the world. I stumbled in that class, trying to grasp Kenneth Burke (as if anyone really could, but at the time, I *knew* the problem was within me). Anne assigns me to present on Ann Berthoff's *Forming/Thinking/Writing: The Composing Imagination*. The focus of my presentation was on Burke-in-Berthoff. But more important was that I discovered rhetoric *in* writing, that there were theories that could guide not just the teaching of writing but writing itself. Later I would find that Berthoff relied on Burke and on Aristotle but mainly on I. A. Richards (the one who wrote *The Philosophy of Rhetoric*, putting aside the same Richards who wrote basal readers).

That same semester in 1981, maybe, I took a class from Bill Irmscher. It'd be years before I'd discover that he had been NCTE (National Council of Teachers or English) president and 4Cs (Conference on College Composition and Communication) chair—or what that even meant. With Irmscher, there was more Burke, plenty more Burke. But as kind and gentle a man as he was at that time (there were tales of a less-gentle Irmscher), it was Anne to whom I would turn to talk about these things. Irmscher seemed always to like my writing. I hadn't the confidence to believe him. It was Anne who I trusted to be honest with me about my writing, such as it was.

Anne Gere didn't seem to treat me like the poor unfortunate (the only Latino grad student, the only grad student of color, the less-than-able writer, veteran, raising children, all those things that give rise to a sympathy that reinforces insecurities; tokenism is a sin). I never got the sense that Anne Gere saw me as anything but the student before her.

Somehow, I got through the doctoral exams (two of which I failed and would have to take over). Anne was my director. I asked if she would stay with me, blunders and all. I was advised by others against her: she was a new associate professor (as if I knew what that meant), that she had not yet directed a doctoral student, and most of all, that she was "tough." But it was that very no-nonsense toughness that attracted me to her. She opened up a new world to me, and she was direct without malice or arrogance. Just straightforward. I needed that. I knew I was in a world in which I did not belong.

1983. Anne agrees to mentor me. I bounce around ideas for a diss. Anne's face drops. I was playing the "doubting game," as Peter Elbow would call it (149). It's a game common to graduate students starting out, I've discovered over the years: find the fault. That's fail safe. There is no such thing as a bulletproof paper or a bulletproof theory. Fault is always there to be found. But seeing the contributions is so much harder. And actually providing a contribution harder still. But what the heck? Two years earlier I hadn't even known there were such things as rhetoric or composition.

After recovering from her discovery of how much I didn't know, Anne handed me articles she had copied for her own research, and she handed me *every* issue of *College English* (*CE*), *College Composition and Communication* (*CCC*), and *Research in the Teaching of English* (*RTE*). I really don't know how literal that is—every issue. I know that I had several stacks on my living room floor; each stack was about three feet high. And if I were to be analytical, every issue was possible. *CE* was 40 years old, *CCC* 35 (I was chair of the organization, 4Cs, during its 50th year and my 50th year on earth), *RTE* about 15 years old. All issues was possible. But literal or not, Anne cleared out her shelves, told me to prepare a 3x5 card for each article in each journal, then come back to her. And I did that. I thoroughly learned rhetoric-and-comp (learning rhetoric, the ancient study, would take much, much longer; or, honestly, was never as thoroughly understood by me as rhet-comp would be). Eventually, that task would provide not only for a dissertation but the foundation for *Cross-Talk in Comp Theory* (and everything else I would produce).

Still 1983, Anne adds my name to a proposal for a 1984 4Cs panel. Scary. I would be on a panel with Melanie Sperling, Ann Matsuhashi (who would, as Ann Feldman, be the local arrangements chair for the 4Cs program that I would chair 14 years after that first 4Cs), and Anne. I was to be the respondent. Anne advises me to read their work, to understand their mindset as well as their scholarship, so that I'd be prepared to respond. Reading Melanie Sperling was different. Her research and scholarship concerned education. I didn't realize that Anne's did too, apart from her work for the Puget Sound Writing Project. I think I did well in responding for that panel. At least I was told by Anne that I had done well, that I had a talent for speaking. She wasn't one to dole out empty compliments. So I wanted to believe her, but I couldn't quite, not yet. Now, 40 years later, I have delivered over a hundred talks, more than half of which have been keynotes. She was right. Am I bragging? Of course I am! But I would have never discovered that ability if it hadn't been for Anne. If I hadn't done well, she would have tactfully told me so. She gave me that first taste of confidence, of something more than, greater than, bravado.

1985, I land a tenure-track job, with my all-but-dissertation (ABD) status. I send Anne (over the mails in those days) the first draft of the dissertation. I had no idea what I was doing, but I needed to keep that job, and I needed to complete the dissertation to do so. We were a family of seven by that point (five kids), and insofar as my wife was also a high school dropout, I was the primary income source. I was desperate.

Schedule a phone call with Anne (email would come some years later, modems and command strings, and the like).

"Hi, Anne."

Anne: "What *is* this?"

End of conversation. One doesn't forget a "conversation" like that.

I would have to rethink everything but the theory chapter and the literature review. Yet I had to have a degree in hand by that June, or lose my job.

I think. I write. The study: a comparison of basic writers of color and writers of color in a conventional first-year composition class. The literature of the time had decided that students of color don't do well in college because they are stuck in an oral culture, that literacy makes for higher-order thinking (replete with "proofs" from Vygotsky and Piaget and even Plato). My father got an eighth-grade education through the GI Bill; Mom never completed high school. Yet she was a voracious reader. And so was I. Yet I failed and stumbled nevertheless. And here I was, stumbles notwithstanding, trying to get a Ph.D. I could not buy the cognitive deficit theory. Anne supports my empirical study: recording group work in both classes, looking for the connections among reading, writing, speaking, and listening. Anne provides the lavalier mics and recording equipment. Her own research at the time concerns group work (a matter I didn't put together until her book *Writing Groups: History, Theory and Implications* was published). I work it. After all, it has to be acceptable to Anne. I write. I mail the diss.

Anne and I speak on the phone, late night on a Sunday. I'm in my office (we didn't have a house phone; couldn't afford it). Over the phone, Anne goes through the three hundred or so pages with me, page by page, line by line by line, not just with revisions but with detailed copy editing. All those graduate students I have directed (nearly 100, including a couple of 4Cs chairs) had to "suffer" through that same treatment—because I learned how terribly important it is, because there would have been no dissertation without the deep guidance I received from Anne. There was no Word app, no Google Docs. She sat on the phone with me for hours! Who does that?

And at the oral defense, when folks were kind, asking questions because I still wasn't really a writer (and as far as I'm concerned, I was in this profession nearly ten years and well published, even receiving national awards for what I had written, before I truly discovered the writer in me). Then the graduate representative (which in those days was someone from another discipline, in my case someone from speech communication) pulls out a dissertation with a title very much like the title of mine. I am devastated. Anne whispers, "I read it; don't worry."

~~~

A few years later, I publish my first single-authored article (I had a co-authored piece before that). It was a reaction to a speech delivered at NCTE by Richard Rodriguez, whose political views were initially offensive to me and to those of color who had become my convention buddies (and with whom I still communicate). I write an article on the mindset of those who are immigrants (like Rodriguez) and those who are Americans of color (like me). It appears in *The English Journal*. Two people tell me there's a book there: the late and wonderful Mike Rose and Anne. But it's Anne I knew and trusted at the time (a friendship with Mike Rose would come later). That book would become *Bootstraps: From an American Academic of Color*. Anne, not exactly holding my hand, more like putting my feet to the fire, was there for me, guiding me.

Over the years, we have become colleagues, Anne and me, each of us with our own successful careers, crossing paths at this organization and that. Most, I imagine, see us as peers. But she is always my mentor in my eyes. I thanked her in my acceptance of the 2009 4Cs Exemplar Award, but I still don't know if she knows that I couldn't have had this successful career but for the care she showed me 40 years ago, this tough, respectful new associate professor who guided me, who believed in me.

So Anne: Thank you. Not just from the bottom of my heart but from deep within my soul.

WORKS CITED

"The American Family is Alive and Well." *The Seattle Times*, 22 Apr. 1984.
Elbow, Peter. *Writing Without Teachers*. Oxford UP, 1973.

CODA

Anne Ruggles Gere
University of Michigan

Reading through this book reminded me of a film where a teacher of long-standing sits on her porch as a parade of former students comes to greet her. As I turned each page, memories of classroom discussions, meetings about a piece of writing, collaborative projects, joint appearances on panels, shared meals, and ongoing conversations floated by. The faces of former students who have become colleagues and dear friends, along with precious colleagues who have been interlocutors across the years, all paraded through my mind. At the same time, though, I realized that the film got it wrong: it represented the former students and colleagues exactly as they had been years earlier—the same gestures, the same youthful faces, as if they had been frozen in time.

In contrast, one of the many pleasures of reading through this collection was—and is—being reminded of the shifting specializations, emerging interests, and new perspectives that the writing in this volume represents. Thinking back to my earliest encounter with each of the authors, at the University of Washington or the University of Michigan, at CCCC, or NCTE, or MLA or WPA, I am reminded of how the questions being asked, the specific language chosen, and the terms of arguments have shifted. We have all changed our words and been changed by the words of others as we've read new things, written in various publications, and participated in different conversations. I am deeply grateful to each contributing author for recalling moments and ideas shared, for recollecting projects initiated years ago, for recounting recent conversations, and for citing emerging concepts.

My most profound appreciation goes to Jim Beitler and Sarah Ruffing Robbins, who imagined this book and undertook all the labor of recruiting, organizing, and editing to create this capacious perspective on my work. The 25 chapters they have organized under eight different categories touch on the ways my work—and the work of so many of us in the related fields of writing studies, rhetoric, and teacher education—has evolved during more than three decades. This book is a gift.

It is a gift to me, but also a gift to other scholars and researchers because it offers new perspectives on several related areas of study. Lewis Hyde reminds us that a gift must always move, and in so doing it creates connections that bind communities together. My fondest wish is that this gift, this collection, will move across groups of readers to affirm existing bonds and create new ligatures within our several related fields as we continue to deepen understandings of teaching, learning, language, literacy, and writing.

WORK CITED

Hyde, Lewis. *The Gift: How the Creative Spirit Transforms the World*. 3rd ed., Vintage, 2019.

CONTRIBUTORS

Heather Brook Adams is Associate Professor of English and Principal Investigator/Director of Humanities at Work, a paid internship program, at UNC Greensboro. A feminist historiographer of the recent past, her scholarship investigates themes such as health and wellness through a focus on rhetorics of reproduction and emotion. She is the author of *Enduring Shame: A Recent History of Unwed Pregnancy and Righteous Reproduction* (U South Carolina P, 2022) and coeditor of *Inclusive Aims: Rhetoric's Role in Reproductive Justice* (Parlor Press, 2024).

Chris Anson is Distinguished University Professor and Senior Strategic Advisor for the Campus Writing and Speaking Program at North Carolina State University. He has published extensively in writing studies and has spoken and consulted widely across the US and in several dozen other countries. He is Past Chair of the Conference on College Composition and Communication and Past President of the Council of Writing Program Administrators and is currently Chair of the International Society for the Advancement of Writing Research. More about his work can be found at https://www.ansonica.net.

Laura Aull is Professor of English and Writing Program Director at the University of Michigan. She teaches English linguistics, is the editor of the *Assessing Writing* Tools and Tech Forum, and is the author, most recently, of *You Can't Write That: 8 Myths about Correct English* (Cambridge UP, 2024).

James Edward Beitler is Director of the Marion E. Wade Center and Professor of English at Wheaton College, where he holds the Marion E. Wade Chair of Christian Thought. He is the author of three books: *Charitable Writing: Cultivating Virtue Through Our Words* (with Richard Hughes Gibson, IVP Academic, 2020), *Seasoned Speech: Rhetoric in the Life of the Church* (IVP Academic, 2019), and *Remaking Transitional Justice in the United States: The Rhetorical Authorization of the Greensboro Truth and Reconciliation Commission* (Springer, 2013).

Jennifer Buehler is Associate Professor of Education at Saint Louis University. She is the former host of Text Messages, a monthly young adult literature podcast sponsored by ReadWriteThink.org; a past President of ALAN, the Assembly on Literature for Adolescents of the National Council of Teachers of English; and the author of *Teaching Reading with YA Literature: Complex Texts, Complex Lives* (NCTE, 2016). In addition to her work in young adult literature, Buehler is an ethnographer who received the NCTE Promising Researcher Award for her ethnographic study of "toxic" school culture in an under-resourced high school. Her current work on young adult literature book bans is anchored in a study of the Judy Blume papers at Yale University.

Contributors

Anne Curzan is Geneva Smitherman Collegiate Professor of English Language and Literature, Linguistics, and Education; Arthur F. Thurnau Professor; and former dean of the College of Literature, Science, and the Arts at the University of Michigan. Her research focuses on the history of the English language, attitudes about language change, language and gender, and pedagogy. She has published multiple books and dozens of articles and won awards for her teaching, research, and public intellectual work. She wrote for six years for the blog Lingua Franca for the *Chronicle of Higher Education* and is the featured expert on the segment "That's What They Say" on local NPR station Michigan Public.

Ellen Cushman is Dean's Professor of Civic Sustainability and Professor of English at Northeastern University and a citizen of the Cherokee Nation. Her work explores how people use literacy and language to endure and create change. Her current research takes up Cherokee philosophies of collective change and reevaluates the commitment to civic-mindedness at the heart of American literary and rhetorical studies. Her book *Cherokees Writing Resilience: Everyday Literacies of Collective Action* (working title) will be the first monograph to treat the common writings of Cherokee people as evidence of a lived ethic of individual perseverance and a people's collective resilience, and has received fellowship support from the National Endowment for the Humanities. She is the project leader of *The Digital Archive of Indigenous Languages Persistence (DAILP)* project, which has been generously supported by the National Archives: National Historical Preservation and Records Commission (NHPRC) to expand the current corpus of translated texts into a fully-fledged digital edition, titled, *Cherokees Writing the Keetoowah Way*. The archive is also supported by a National Endowment for the Humanities: Digital Humanities Advancement Grant and receives continued support from the Henry K. Luce Foundation to evaluate the impact of DAILP and expand the number of Cherokee community members who produce audio files and translations.

Jathan Day is an adjunct instructor of writing at the University of Alaska Anchorage. He has taught a wide range of courses over the years, both face-to-face and online, including first-year composition, technical writing, and writing in the sciences. His current research focuses on digital literacies, learning management systems, and collaboration. In 2022, Jathan graduated from the Joint Program in English and Education at the University of Michigan.

Amber J. Dood is a Faculty Success Manager at Catalyst Education. She was previously a postdoctoral research fellow at the University of Michigan, working with the MWrite program and jointly advised by Ginger Shultz and Anne Ruggles Gere. She completed her Ph.D. in chemistry at the University of South Florida. Her postdoctoral work specifically explored how students experience writing-to-learn assignments and peer review using a combination of qualitative methods and automated analysis with machine learning.

Contributors

Christine Farris is Professor Emerita of English at Indiana University in Bloomington where she served as director of composition and associate chair and taught writing, rhetoric, and literature. Her publications include *Subject to Change: New Composition Instructors' Theory and Practice* (Hampton, 1996) and several co-edited collections: *Under Construction: Working at the Intersection of Composition Theory, Research and Practice* (Utah State UP, 1998); *Integrating Literature and Writing Instruction* (MLA, 2007); and *College Credit for Writing in High School: The "Taking Care of" Business* (NCTE, 2010), which won the Council of Writing Program Administrators 2012 Best Book Award. Other honors include the Indiana University President's Award for Distinguished Teaching and the W. George Pinnell Award for Outstanding Service.

Solaire A. Finkenstaedt-Quinn is a research scientist and the former program manager for the MWrite Program at the University of Michigan. She completed her Ph.D. in analytical chemistry at the University of Minnesota before transitioning to chemistry education research as a postdoctoral researcher at the University of Michigan, jointly advised by Anne Ruggles Gere and Ginger Shultz. As MWrite program manager she supported both sides of the MWrite Program—coordinating with stakeholders in the implementation of writing-to-learn in large classrooms and the research and evaluation of how writing-to-learn supports student learning. Her research focuses on student engagement with writing-to-learn in STEM, with a current focus on the role of peer review and revision.

Anne Ruggles Gere is Gertrude Buck Collegiate Professor Emerita, Marsal Family School of Education; Professor Emerita of English Language and Literature, College of Literature, Science, and the Arts; and Arthur F. Thurnau Professor. In addition to her professorships, Gere chaired or co-chaired the Joint Ph.D. Program in English and Education from 1988 to 2023 and served as Director of the Sweetland Center for Writing from 2008 to 2019. She also served as president of the National Council of Teachers of English, chair of the Conference on College Composition and Communication, and president of the Modern Language Association. Gere received the Regents' Award for Distinguished Public Service, the D'Arms Award for Distinguished Graduate Student Mentoring, a Distinguished Faculty Achievement Award, a Michigan Humanities Award, a fellowship from the Institute for the Humanities at the University of Michigan, and a Distinguished Professor of the Year award from the Michigan Association of State Universities. She also received fellowships from the National Endowment for the Humanities and the Spencer Foundation. In addition, her research has been sponsored by the National Science Foundation, and she and her chemistry colleague Ginger Schultz developed the MWrite program, for which they received the Provost's Teaching Innovation Award. She is the author of a dozen books and over 100 articles.

Contributors

Cheryl Glenn is Distinguished Professor of English and Women's Studies, Emerita, at The Pennsylvania State University, where she served as Director of the Program in Writing and Rhetoric and co-founder of the Center for Democratic Deliberation. An award-winning scholar, teacher, and mentor, she has delivered lectures and workshops around the world. In 2015 she received an honorary doctorate from Orebro University (Sweden) for her rhetorical scholarship and influence; in 2019 she received the Conference on College Composition and Communication Exemplar Award; and in 2024 she was inducted as a Rhetoric Society of America Fellow.

J. W. Hammond is Assistant Professor of Rhetoric and Composition at Michigan Technological University. His research and teaching center on writing studies, social justice, and science and technology studies, paying particular attention to the cultural histories and afterlives of writing assessment. In 2020 he was awarded the Conference on College Composition and Communication's James Berlin Memorial Outstanding Dissertation Award. His recent publications can be found in *College Composition and Communication*, *Review of Research in Education*, *Assessing Writing*, and *Scientific American*, as well as in edited collections such as *Rhetorical Machines*; *(Re)Considering What We Know*; and *Writing Assessment, Social Justice, and the Advancement of Opportunity*.

Douglas Hesse is Professor of Writing at the University of Denver, where he has been named University Distinguished Scholar and was founding Executive Director of the Writing Program. He has won the Francis A. March Award from the Association of Departments of English/MLA and the Lifetime Achievement Award from the Council of Writing Program Administrators. He has been President of the National Council of Teachers of English, Chair of the Conference on College Composition and Communication, President of the Council of Writing Program Administrators, Chair of the Association for Writing Across the Curriculum, Chair of the MLA Forum on Nonfiction Prose, editor of *WPA: Writing Program Administration*, and Chair of the Executive Committee of the MLA Division on Teaching. Hesse is author of over 80 essays and book chapters and co-author of five books, including *Nonfiction, Teaching Writing and the Contributions of Richard Lloyd-Jones* (with Laura Julier, The WAC Clearinghouse, 2023), *Creating Nonfiction* (with Becky Bradway, Bedford/St. Martin's, 2009) and the *Simon and Schuster Handbook for Writers* (with Lynn Troyka, 2016).

Deborah H. Holdstein is Professor of English and past Dean of the School of Liberal Arts and Sciences at Columbia College Chicago. Holdstein has served as editor of the premier journal in writing studies, *College Composition and Communication*. She has published widely, and her most recent books are *Lost Texts in Rhetoric and Composition* (MLA, 2023) and the co-authored *The Oxford Reader* (Oxford UP, 2023). A former director of the WPA Consultant-Evaluator

Service, among other positions, including two terms on the MLA Publications Committee, Holdstein began a two-year term on the Advisory Committee of *PMLA*, the flagship journal of the Modern Language Association, in the fall of 2023. Holdstein's current research interests include the Hebraic sources of Jesuit rhetoric, and her essay on this subject is forthcoming in a volume entitled *Jesuit Rhetoric Across Space and Time*, to be published by Brill.

Lizzie Hutton is currently the Director of the Howe Writing Center and Associate Professor of English at Miami University, Ohio. Her scholarship, which lives at the intersection of reading studies, writing studies, and writing center studies, has appeared in journals including *College Composition and Communication, Journal of English Linguistics,* and *Writing Center Journal*; she is also an award-winning poet whose debut book of poems was selected as Editor's Choice by New Issues Press and whose poems have appeared in journals including the *Yale Review, Denver Quarterly* and *Antioch Review*. After teaching for 12 years as a lecturer at the University of Michigan's Sweetland Center for Writing, she returned to school as a doctoral student in the University of Michigan's JPEE program, where she worked as a GSRA with Anne Ruggles Gere and was awarded the Stanley E. and Ruth B. Dimond Best Dissertation Award for her work on the intellectual legacy of Louise Rosenblatt.

Rona Kaufman is Professor of English at Pacific Lutheran University, where she teaches writing, memoir, and the English language and directs the First-Year Experience Program and the Writing Center. Her work has appeared in *ISLE, JAC*, and other publications. She is the co-editor of *Placing the Academy: Essays on Landscape, Work, and Academic Identity* (Utah State UP, 2007). She is one of the founding members of PLU's Holocaust and Genocide Studies Program and is co-author of the *Jewish Diaspora in Uruguay*, an on-going, multidisciplinary digital project that collects, records, translates, and shares the testimonies of Jewish Uruguayans who have experienced the Holocaust, migration, and the diaspora.

Paula M. Krebs is Executive Director of the Modern Language Association, the largest scholarly organization in the humanities. She has written on higher education, diversity, languages, literature, cultural studies, and writing studies for the *Chronicle of Higher Education, Inside Higher Ed*, CNN, *The Washington Post, Slate*, and other publications. She has a doctoral degree in 19th-century British literature and culture from Indiana University and was Professor of English and Department Chair at Wheaton College and Dean of the College of Humanities and Social Sciences at Bridgewater State University. Before becoming a professor, she worked as an editor for the National Science Teachers Association and as a sportswriter for daily newspapers in New Jersey and Indiana.

Naitnaphit Limlamai is Assistant Professor of English Education at Colorado State University. She teaches and studies secondary English teacher preparation and how it manifests justice, specifically investigating how justice is defined and enacted in methods and secondary classrooms. Her additional research includes how writers develop as such, collaboration, and antiracist organizational change. Naitnaphit was a fellow in the 2022–2024 cohort of NCTE's Cultivating New Voices among Scholars of Color program. Before teaching teachers, Naitnaphit taught high school English for 13 years. She is a 2022 graduate of the Joint Program in English and Education at the University of Michigan.

Deborah Minter is Chair of the Department of English and Associate Professor of English at the University of Nebraska - Lincoln. She has served as Director of Composition, Associate Dean, and Chair of the Faculty Senate. Her research and teaching focus on composition studies and administration as well as the teaching of writing. Her work has appeared in several edited collections and journals, including *College English*, *Pedagogy*, and *CCC*.

Beverly J. Moss is Professor of English in the Writing, Rhetoric, and Literacy program at The Ohio State University. Her scholarly and pedagogical interests include examining literacy in African American community spaces, composition theory and pedagogy, and writing center theory and practice. She is the author of *A Community Text Arises: A Literate Text and A Literacy Tradition in African American Churches* (The WAC Clearinghouse, 2024), co-author of *Everyone's an Author* (W. W. Norton, 4th ed., 2023), editor of *Literacy Across Communities* (Hampton, 1994), and co-editor of *Writing Groups Inside and Outside the Classroom* (Routledge, 2004) and *The Best of the Independent Journals in Rhetoric and Composition 2012* (Parlor Press, 2014). Professor Moss also serves as Director of the Middlebury Bread Loaf School of English Bread Loaf Teacher Network (BLTN).

Mike Palmquist is Emeritus Professor of English at Colorado State University. Prior to returning to his role as a faculty member in the 2020–2021 academic year, he served for 14 years in various university leadership roles, including Founding Director of the Institute for Learning and Teaching (TILT), Director of CSU Online (CSU's Division of Continuing Education), and Associate Provost for Instructional Innovation. His scholarly interests include writing across the curriculum, the effects of computer and network technologies on writing instruction, and new approaches to scholarly publishing.

Sarah Ruffing Robbins is Lorraine Sherley Professor of Literature at TCU. She is the author, editor, or co-editor of ten academic books, beginning with the ALA/Choice-honored monograph, *Managing Literacy, Mothering America* (Pitt Series in Composition, Literacy, and Culture, 2004), the award-winning critical edition of *Nellie Arnott's Writings on Angola* (Parlor Press, 2011) with historian Ann Pullen, and, more recently, her co-edited teaching anthology, *Transatlantic Anglophone Literatures, 1776–1920* (Edinburgh UP, 2022). She was founding director of northwest Georgia's National Writing Project site, the Kennesaw Mountain Writing Project, and has directed numerous grant-funded public humanities programs placing writing at the center of shared cultural work. She regularly collaborates with students and community members in web-based writing in connection with public projects, as in the *The Genius of Phillis Wheatley Peters* initiative and the *Teaching Transatlanticism* online anthology. She co-edits Edinburgh University Press's book series, Interventions in Nineteenth-Century American Literature.

Shirley K Rose is Emeritus Professor of English at Arizona State University, where she was Director of Writing Programs from 2009–2019 and taught graduate courses in writing program administration, scholarly writing for publication, and archival theory from 2009–2024. She is a Past President of the Council of Writing Program Administrators and former Co-Director of the WPA Consultant-Evaluator Service. She has served as a Peer Reviewer for the Higher Learning Commission of the North Central Association of Schools and Colleges since 2007. She has published articles on writing pedagogy and on issues in archival research and practice. With Irwin Weiser, she edited four collections on the intellectual work of writing program administration, including *The Writing Program Administrator as Researcher* (Boynton/Cook, 1999), *The Writing Program Administrator as Theorist* (Boynton/Cook, 2002), *Going Public: What Writing Programs Learn from Engagement* (Utah State UP, 2010), and *The Internationalization of U.S. College Writing Programs* (Utah State UP, 2018).

Kel Sassi is currently Assistant Professor of English at Northern Michigan University (NMU) in Marquette, where she teaches courses in English education. Dr. Sassi also co-directs the Northern Shores Storywork Writing Project site at NMU. Previously, she was professor of English and education at North Dakota State University, where she directed the Red River Valley Writing Project. She has published three books with Anne Ruggles Gere and Leila Christenbury, including *Writing on Demand for the Common Core State Standards Assessment* (Heinemann, 2014).

Ginger Shultz is Associate Professor of Chemistry at the University of Michigan. Her science education research program focuses on understanding how writing-to-learn pedagogies contribute to learning in STEM, mapping the development of college chemistry instructors' knowledge and beliefs about teaching, and operationalizing the community-based design of culturally relevant curricula. Together with Anne Ruggles Gere she is Co-Principal Investigator for MWrite, a program that implements writing-to-learn pedagogies in large-enrollment courses at the University of Michigan.

Naomi Silver is Teaching Professor in the Sweetland Center for Writing at the University of Michigan and co-founder of the Sweetland Digital Rhetoric

Collaborative with Anne Ruggles Gere. She served as Associate Director of Sweetland during the ten years Gere was its Director. She has published on topics including reflective pedagogies, multiliteracy centers and consultant training, and electronic portfolios. Her current teaching at Michigan centers on multimodal composition and histories and rhetorics of race and ethnicity.

Jennifer Sinor is the author of several books of literary nonfiction, most recently *The Yogic Writer: Uniting Breath, Body, and Page* (Bloomsbury, 2024). Her essay collections include *Sky Songs: Meditations on Loving a Broken World* (U Nebraska P, 2020), and *Letters Like the Day: On Reading Georgia O'Keeffe* (U New Mexico P, 2017). She has also written the memoir *Ordinary Trauma* (U Utah P, 2017). The recipient of the Stipend in American Modernism, her work has appeared in *Best American Essays* and *The Norton Reader*. Jennifer teaches creative writing at Utah State University where she is Professor of English.

Chris Thaiss is Professor Emeritus of Writing and Rhetoric at the University of California, Davis, where he was Clark Kerr Presidential Chair and Director of the University Writing Program, as well as Director of the UC Davis Center for Excellence in Teaching and Learning. He went to UC Davis from George Mason University, where he chaired the English Department and co-developed writing across the curriculum and the writing center. From 2005 to 2015, he coordinated the International Network of Writing-Across-the-Curriculum Programs. The author, co-author, or editor of fourteen books, his most recent are *Writing Science in the Twenty-First Century* (Broadview P, 2019) and the 4th edition of *A Short History of Writing Instruction: From Ancient Greece to the Modern United States* (ed. with James Murphy, Routledge, 2020).

Ebony Elizabeth Thomas is Chair and Associate Professor in the Joint Program in English and Education at the University of Michigan's School of Education. Previously, she was Associate Professor in the Literacy, Culture, and International Education Division at the University of Pennsylvania Graduate School of Education. A former Detroit Public Schools teacher and National Academy of Education / Spencer Foundation Postdoctoral Fellow, she serves as co-editor of *Research in the Teaching of English*. Her most recent book is *The Dark Fantastic: Race and the Imagination from Harry Potter to the Hunger Games* (New York UP, 2019), which received the 2020 World Fantasy Award, among other honors.

Heather Thomson-Bunn is Associate Professor of English and Director of First-Year Writing at Pepperdine University, where she teaches courses in composition, rhetoric, language theory, professional writing, and creative writing. Her research is focused on religious rhetorics as they relate to academic norms, institutional values, and writing. Her work has appeared in *College English*, *Pedagogy*, and *Composition Forum*, as well as in *Mapping Christian Rhetorics* (Routledge, 2014).

Contributors

Elizabeth Vander Lei is Professor of English Emerita at Calvin University, where she also served as Academic Dean, Department Chair, and Director of Composition. She taught courses in linguistics, first-year composition, academic and professional writing, and English secondary education. She is co-editor of two scholarly collections, *Negotiating Religious Faith in the Composition Classroom* (Heinemann, 2005) and *Renovating Rhetoric in Christian Tradition* (U Pittsburgh P, 2014). With Dean Ward, she published *Real Texts: Reading and Writing Across the Disciplines* (Longman, 2012). She has published articles on academic writing, rhetoric and religious faith, and the rhetoric of the civil rights movement.

Victor Villanueva is Regents Professor Emeritus and Edward R. Meyer Distinguished Professor of Liberal Arts, retired at Washington State University. He has served as Director of Composition, English Department Chair (twice), Associate Dean, Director of American Studies, and Director of the University Writing Program. He was also Chair of the Conference on College Composition and Communication (CCCC) and editor of the CCCC *Studies in Writing and Rhetoric* monograph series. Over the years, he has received a number of honors, including the Richard A. Meade Award for Distinguished Research in English Education from the National Council of Teachers of English (NCTE), the NCTE David H. Russell Award for Distinguished Research and Scholarship in English, Rhetorician of the Year from the Young Rhetorician's Conference, the NCTE Advancement of People of Color Leadership Award, and the CCCC Exemplar Award. He was also honored with the publication of *Memoria: Essays in Honor of Victor Villanueva* (NCTE, 2024). Among honors at Washington State University, his most prized has been having his seminar recognized as the year's best by the graduate students on three occasions. Villanueva is the author, editor, or co-editor of nine books and over fifty articles or chapters in books. Among his books is the award-winning *Bootstraps: From an American Academic of Color* (NCTE, 1993) as well as *Cross-Talk in Comp Theory: A Reader*, now in its fourth edition (NCTE, 2024), the last two editions co-edited with Kristin Arola, and *The Forever Colony* (Parlor Press, 2024). All his efforts center on the connections between language and relations of power, especially racism.

Margaret K. Willard-Traub is Associate Professor Emerita of Composition and Rhetoric at the University of Michigan-Dearborn, where she taught introductory and upper-level courses in writing, rhetoric, and women's and gender studies. Prior to UM-Dearborn she was Assistant and then Associate Professor of Rhetoric at Oakland University. At UM-Dearborn she served for many years as Director of the Writing Program and Writing Center, was member of a campus-wide task force charged with revising general education, and had leadership positions in the faculty senate, among other roles. Her work has appeared in *College English*, *Assessing Writing*, *Feminist Studies*, *Rhetoric Review*, and *Pedagogy*, as well as in a number of edited collections. Her current scholarship addresses the impact of the COVID-19 pandemic on the decision-making and reflective processes of faculty and administrators at post-secondary institutions nationwide.

Emily Wilson is Chair of the English Department and Assistant Professor of English at Alfaisal University in Riyadh, Saudi Arabia, where she is also the founder of the Academic Success Center, a peer-based writing and tutoring center for undergraduate students. She teaches first-year composition, communication for leaders, and technical writing, and she led her department in launching its Strategic Communication minor in the fall of 2023. She was a high school teacher for 11 years before returning to graduate school, and she graduated from the University of Michigan's Joint Program in English and Education in 2019. Her research interests include code-switching and language ideologies in English medium of instruction (EMI) institutions as well as the dynamics of class discussion in Arab contexts. She loves life in Riyadh and studies Arabic.

Kathleen Blake Yancey, Kellogg W. Hunt Professor and Distinguished Research Professor Emerita at Florida State University, has served as president/chair of several U.S. literacy organizations, including the Council of Writing Program Administrators (CWPA), the Conference on College Composition and Communication (CCCC), and the National Council of Teachers of English (NCTE). She also participates in U.S. and global assessment efforts, most recently as a faculty member for the American Association of Colleges and Universities' Institutes on ePortfolios; board member for the Association of Authentic, Experiential, and Evidence-based Learning; and consultant for Trinity College Dublin's School of Pharmacy and Pharmaceutical Sciences Student ePortfolio Research Project. Author/co-author of 100+ refereed articles and book chapters as well as author/editor/co-editor of 16 scholarly books, she has received numerous awards, among them the FSU Graduate Teaching Award (twice); the Purdue University Distinguished Woman Scholar Award; the CWPA Best Book Award (twice); the CCCC Exemplar Award; and the NCTE Squire Award.

Morris Young is Charles Q. Anderson Professor of English at the University of Wisconsin-Madison. His work focuses on writing and identity, the intersections of literacy and rhetorical studies, and Asian American culture. His current work considers the generation and function of Asian/American rhetorical commonplaces as a response to exigencies of exclusion, marginalization, and containment. His book, *Minor Re/Visions: Asian American Literacy Narratives as a Rhetoric of Citizenship* (Southern Illinois UP, 2004) received the 2004 W. Ross Winterowd Award from the Association of Teachers of Advanced Composition and the 2006 CCCC Outstanding Book Award. His co-edited collection (with LuMing Mao), *Representations: Doing Asian American Rhetoric* (Utah State UP, 2008), received honorable mention for the 2008 MLA Mina P. Shaughnessy Award.

www.ingramcontent.com/pod-product-compliance
Ingram Content Group UK Ltd.
Pitfield, Milton Keynes, MK11 3LW, UK
UKHW041937210426

5322IPUK00016B/228